More Wiley Concise Guides to Mental Health

Need Help Jump-Starting Your Career?

Practice*Planners*®

Homework Planners feature dozens of behaviorally based, ready-to-use assignments that are designed for use between sessions, as well as a disk (Microsoft Word) containing all of the assignments—allowing you to customize them to suit your unique client needs.

❏ Brief Therapy Homework Planner ....0-471-24611-5 / $49.95
❏ Brief Couples Therapy Homework Planner ....0-471-29511-6 / $49.95
❏ Child Therapy Homework Planner, Second Edition ....0-471-78534-2 / $49.95
❏ Child Therapy Activity and Homework Planner ....0-471-25684-6 / $49.95
❏ Adolescent Therapy Homework Planner, Second Edition ....0-471-78537-7 / $49.95
❏ Addiction Treatment Homework Planner, Second Edition ....0-471-27459-3 / $49.95
❏ Brief Employee Assistance Homework Planner ....0-471-38088-1 / $49.95
❏ Brief Family Therapy Homework Planner ....0-471-38512-3 / $49.95
❏ Grief Counseling Homework Planner ....0-471-43318-7 / $49.95
❏ Divorce Counseling Homework Planner ....0-471-43319-5 / $49.95
❏ Group Therapy Homework Planner ....0-471-41822-6 / $49.95
❏ School Counseling and School Social Work Homework Planner ....0-471-09114-6 / $49.95
❏ Adolescent Psychotherapy Homework Planner II ....0-471-27493-3 / $49.95
❏ Adult Psychotherapy Homework Planner, Second Edition ....0-471-76343-8 / $49.95
❏ Parenting Skills Homework Planner ....0-471-48182-3 / $49.95

Progress Notes Planners contain complete prewritten progress notes for each presenting problem in the companion Treatment Planners.

❏ The Adult Psychotherapy Progress Notes Planner...0-471-76344-6 / $49.95
❏ The Adolescent Psychotherapy Progress Notes Planner ....0-471-78538-5 / $49.95
❏ The Severe and Persistent Mental Illness Progress Notes Planner..................0-471-21986-X / $49.95
❏ The Child Psychotherapy Progress Notes Planner...0-471-78536-9 / $49.95
❏ The Addiction Progress Notes Planner ....0-471-73253-2 / $49.95
❏ The Couples Psychotherapy Progress Notes Planner ....0-471-27460-7 / $49.95
❏ The Family Therapy Progress Notes Planner ....0-471-48443-1 / $49.95

Client Education Handout Planners contain elegantly designed handouts that can be printed out from the enclosed CD-ROM and provide information on a wide range of psychological and emotional disorders and life skills issues. Use as patient literature, handouts at presentations, and aids for promoting your mental health practice.

❏ Adult Client Education Handout Planner..0-471-20232-0 / $49.95
❏ Child and Adolescent Client Education Handout Planner ....0-471-20233-9 / $49.95
❏ Couples and Family Client Education Handout Planner....................................0-471-20234-7 / $49.95

Name _____

Affiliation_____

Address_____

City/State/Zip_____

Phone/Fax_____

E-mail_____

❏ Check enclosed ❏ Visa ❏ MasterCard ❏ American Express

Card # _____

Expiration Date_____

Signature_____

Add $5 shipping for first book, $3 for each additional book. Please add your local sales tax to all orders. Prices subject to change without notice.

■ **To order by phone in the US:**
Call toll free 1-877-762-2974

■ **Online: www.practiceplanners.wiley.com**

■ **Mail this order form to:**
John Wiley & Sons, Attn: J. Knott,
111 River Street, Hoboken, NJ 07030

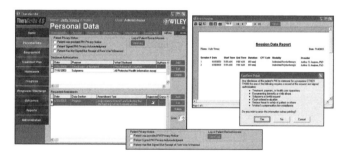

Posttraumatic Stress Disorder

The Wiley Concise Guides to Mental Health

Series Editor, Irving B. Weiner

Substance Use Disorders
Nicholas R. Lessa and Walter R. Scanlon

Posttraumatic Stress Disorder
Adam Cash

The Wiley
Concise Guides
to Mental Health

Posttraumatic
Stress Disorder

Adam Cash, PsyD

John Wiley & Sons, Inc.
WILEY

Copyright © 2006 by John Wiley & Sons, Inc. All rights reserved.
Published by John Wiley & Sons, Inc., Hoboken, New Jersey.
Published simultaneously in Canada.

Library of Congress Cataloging-in-Publication Data:

Cash, Adam.
  Posttraumatic stress disorder / by Adam Cash.
    p. cm. — (Wiley concise guides to mental health)
  ISBN-13: 978-0-471-70513-0 (pbk.)
  ISBN-10: 0-471-70513-6 (pbk.)
  1. Posttraumatic stress disorder. 2. Posttraumatic stress disorder—Treatment.
  I. Title. II. Series.
RC552.P67C374 2006
616.85'21—dc22
           2005034275

Printed in the United States of America

10 9 8 7 6 5 4 3 2 1

To

My wife— always beautiful, always brave

My daughter— my heart, my Zen teacher

My son— lionhearted, destined for love

CONTENTS

Section Three: Special Sections

Section Four: Appendixes

SERIES PREFACE

The *Wiley Concise Guides to Mental Health* are designed to provide mental health professionals with an easily accessible overview of what is currently known about the nature and treatment of psychological disorders. Each book in the series delineates the origins, manifestations, and course of a commonly occurring disorder and discusses effective procedures for its treatment. The authors of the *Concise Guides* draw on relevant research as well as their clinical expertise to ground their text both in empirical findings and in wisdom gleaned from practical experience. By achieving brevity without sacrificing comprehensive coverage, the *Concise Guides* should be useful to practitioners as an on-the-shelf source for answers to questions that arise in their daily work, and they should prove valuable as well to students and professionals as a condensed review of state-of-the-art knowledge concerning the psychopathology, diagnosis, and treatment of various psychological disorders.

Irving B. Weiner

ACKNOWLEDGMENTS

For the countless hours away, I thank my wife and children for their patience, admiration, and sacrifice. Our trauma has been my strength and source of clarity.

I would also like to thank David Bernstein for his patience and professionalism and those at John Wiley & Sons, Inc. for giving me the opportunity to learn, explore, and share through this work.

—Adam Cash, June 2006

INTRODUCTION

Trauma is a topic with which many people find themselves unfortunately familiar. Along with death and taxes, it would seem that nobody is immune from the reaches of a traumatic loss or traumatic event. A seemingly universal constant, trauma has touched many of us, challenging our basic sense of a secure world around us. Is it safe? Will I ever be safe again? Is disaster just around the corner?

As exciting as it has been to write this book, the topic itself has brought up strong emotions. The events and situations that have come up in this study of trauma and traumatic stress have been powerful *evocateurs* of my own fears and concerns for a safe world, sometimes leading me to wonder exactly how just and fair our world really is.

But as constant as the barrage of trauma has been, so, too, has been our pursuit to cope, overcome, and rise above these tragedies. One could argue that history itself is a collection of trauma stories and different cultures' and peoples' experiences as they struggle. The recent past century alone, the twentieth century, gives us countless examples of collective traumas on an incredible and horrific scale. But trauma is as personal as it is collective. Traumatic experiences reach deep into our psychological existence, straining our bodies on a level unexplainable in words and in turn giving us words and images that may stay with us or haunt us for the rest of our lives. The ancient Greeks seemed to embrace trauma in their tragedies, facing soberly the reality of trauma's centrality in our lives and our responses to it, while attempting to master this inevitable reality through an ancient form of stress-inoculation training and behavioral rehearsal.

Fear and safety lie at the heart of trauma and traumatic stress. Erik Erikson placed a basic sense of trust and safety at the root of psychological development.

Our cognitive and intellectual processes work hard to order and make predictable the world and its whizzing and whirling objects and subjects around us. The unknown is a central theme throughout literature, theatre, and film. From chaos comes fear, and safety lies in predictability and organization. When we are threatened, our fundamental sense of survival as a basic organism is activated. Traumas challenge our will to survive.

Unfortunately, as many of us again know all too well, the stress of trauma can linger on long after the strain of a specific challenge has abated. The *posttraumatic* effects of a traumatic event or situation can shape our lives and psychological functioning in powerful ways. For some, these changes and effects become absorbed into one's daily life, leaving only a trace. For others, daily existence is plagued by an event that may be as fresh in the present as it was 1 year, 5 years, or 20 years ago.

When I was in graduate school, a classmate of mine was working on a research project with veterans from the Vietnam War. Her job was to conduct prestudy interviews for subject selection. One day she was interviewing a Vietnam veteran, diagnosed with Posttraumatic Stress Disorder (PTSD). As one might expect, many of the interview questions were related to his service and experience in the war. During the interview, the phone rang in the office they were located in. At that instant, the man jumped and began to weep uncontrollably. The memories of the war were fresh. The phone startled him. This was in 1998, 30 years after he saw combat.

Both my personal and professional life have presented me with countless stories of tragedy and trauma. Sometimes mental health professionals will joke about going into the various fields of psychology, psychiatry, social work, or counseling in order to figure ourselves out. I haven't figured myself out yet, so I don't know if that is why I went into the field. But there is one particular event that stands out as, let's just say, a point of interest in my professional interest in PTSD.

While in college, I traveled to Mexico to study Spanish at a language institute. I went with a group of students, and while there each of us lived with various families affiliated with the school. There were students from all over the world. One day, a group of students took a local bus to a shopping district. While on the trip, the bus was robbed by several bandits in masks, toting machine guns. In addition to the robbery, at least two of the female students were sexually assaulted.

The buzz on campus after the robbery and assault was intense. Even those of us who weren't there felt the intense fear and a sense of violation. My own emotional reactions ranged from anger to fear: "Those bastards!" and "I'm not getting on a bus for any reason!" But it wasn't so much my own reaction that I remember being of most interest; it was the variety of reactions. Some people were shocked and overwhelmed. Some were numb. Some laughed. That's right—laughed! Still many others dismissed it as no big deal. At the risk of sounding like I'm making this up for literary purposes, I remember taking keen notice of these varied reactions and was truly intrigued in finding out how each was possible. I also remember feeling extremely sad and concerned for the victims and felt a strong urge to help, only at that time I had no idea how. My desire to help and having no knowledge of how to help beyond a compassionate and supportive response is likely playing out in my current interest in PTSD. Ah, the unconscious is a powerful thing!

I know for a fact, however, that if you had asked me at that time if I would ever write a book about PTSD, I would have looked at you with a face of dread and fear. At that time, I thought I didn't know anything about trauma and posttraumatic reactions. Little did I know that if you've been exposed to it, you know something about it. In a way, that makes all of us pros of sorts. Some of us have formal and professional training and experience. Some of us have first-hand experience. You don't have to have a PhD to have access to knowledge about trauma.

That is exactly what this book is about—access! Back in Mexico I could have used a quick guide or reference to address the issues, thoughts, and concerns at the time. Maybe I could have offered some advice or more proficient help. I had nothing at my disposal. Of course, I can't imagine I would have carried a *Concise Guide to Posttraumatic Stress Disorder* (*CGPTSD*) around with me like an item on my "bat utility belt," but I can imagine it being available in the school library. And of course there would be other books in the library about PTSD and trauma, wouldn't there? Yes, of course. But could they provide me with what I wanted to know in a quick and efficient manner? If only someone had written this book sooner.

The Purpose of the *CGPTSD*

Few clinicians or mental health professionals can say they have *never* had a patient or client who presented with Posttraumatic Stress Disorder. Whether the trauma is war, car accident, or medical event, most mental health professionals will at some point be faced with the challenge of helping a traumatized person regain his or her sense of trust and safety. Professionals and lay people alike often find themselves needing more information on a particular disorder or case. Yet the seeming paradox of this "information age" is that there is sometimes too much information out there. Wait a minute, too much information? How can there be such as thing as too much information? Well, in an absolute sense there cannot be. However, the rate at which information is generated today is unprecedented. It's extremely difficult, if not impossible, to keep up. In true modern fashion, most us need and often look for a shortcut.

I see each of us in this information-driven world as synthesizers of vast amounts of knowledge. But bringing together the totality of information one wants on a particular topic in a concise and useable form is a daunting task.

There is so much information to be condensed and so little time. That is exactly the role of a book like the *Concise Guide to Posttraumatic Stress Disorder*. The guiding principles of the *CGPTSD* are *concise* and *useful*. The *CGPTSD* strives to be brief, eliminating superfluous and excessively elaborative detail, while delivering solid information. Each section and chapter stands on its own in order to eliminate the typical necessity of having to read chapters the knowledge seeker does not have the time for nor the interest in. By being concise, this book saves the knowledge seeker valuable time and energy. One need not be thoroughly intrigued by the topic of PTSD in order to benefit from this book. Because it is a guide, it is intended to be a roadmap, essentially useful by getting you to where you want to be without unnecessary detours and sightseeing. Keep in mind, however, that you can sightsee if you wish. There is plenty of information to attract the wandering mind. But if you want something specific, all you have to do is go the section you want to know more about. If you want to know about treatment of PTSD, go to the treatment section. If you want to know what the newest research is focusing on, go to the newest research section.

I have a mechanic friend that came over to my house after I had moved. I was apologetic about how my office looked and how even though I had increased my office space seemingly exponentially, I still didn't have enough room, and I recall making some self-deprecating comment about having too many books and articles. His response was inspirational, not to mention a good excuse to keep amassing:

> Your books and articles are your tools. You can never have enough tools. Sometimes having the right tool can make all the difference in getting a job done. I'm always looking for new tools and making sure my tool selection is as diverse as possible. Don't apologize for having too many tools or knowledge at your disposal.

He was right. Along with my clinical skills, experience, and training, my books and articles are the tools of my trade. My hopes for the *CGPTSD* is that it will be the crescent wrench or hammer in your home. I hope it's the duct tape of your work with those coping with PSTD. The *CGPTSD* should be an overused tool that can always do the job and fit your needs as a clinician, student, or layperson. So don't think of the *CGPTSD* as just another book. Think of it as an instrument necessary to the operation of your vocation, a means to an end, an instrument to be manipulated to help you get your particular job done.

Why Use This Book?

There are several *common reasons* why you might use this book:

- You need a quick but reliable and comprehensive review of PTSD and related issues
- You need help with a particular patient or client

- You need help with review for a licensure exam, a paper, a thesis, or a dissertation
- You need help as a teaching resource
- You need a precise but comprehensive introduction to PTSD

How This Book Can Help You

Does the *CGPTSD* make promises, guarantees, or assurances of satisfaction? Well, sort of. It should be able to do the following:

- *Guide you toward some answers for your specific question.* If you know what you're looking for, simply find it in the Contents, the Quick Start Guide, the FAQs, or the Index.

- *Help you formulate new questions.* Sometimes when we approach a topic, we are not entirely sure what we want to know or learn. The *CGPTSD*'s short but comprehensive coverage can help you browse the topic area, stirring your interest and helping you develop leads.

- *Serve as a textbook.* This book can serve as a textbook for abnormal psychology classes, courses on Anxiety Disorders, public lectures, continuing education for professionals, emergency personnel training, and disaster response agency training.

Special Features

Here are some features you'll find in the *CGPTSD* that are intended to help you remember key points and emphasize particularly salient bits of information, depending on who the reader is and what the reader is hoping to get from this book.

Alerts. As you are reading, you might come across an *alert.* Some of these will be targeted toward professionals, clinicians, students, or lay persons. When you see an alert, you are being alerted to a particularly useful bit of information, depending on your purpose for reading this book.

Quick Review. At the end of each chapter you'll find a quick and short, bulleted summary of what the chapter just covered. It's a good way to brush up on things quickly and to scan for possible further inquiry.

Case Study. Examples always facilitate the learning process. In these sections, there will be examples of the topic being discussed in order to put a real-world face on what sometimes seem like abstract, academic concepts.

Getting Started

Here are some tips and suggestions, along with some strengths and weaknesses of each, designed to help you get started using the *CGPTSD*, save time, and save effort.

- *Straight read.* You could just dive in and start reading the book from cover to cover.

  Strength. Comprehensiveness! You won't miss anything, and your coverage of the topic will be comprehensive.

  Weakness. It is time consuming.

- *Frequently Asked Questions (FAQs).* Maybe you've got just one question. Where can you find the answer in the quickest and easiest manner? Maybe your question is a FAQ.

  Strength. If your question is there, you can go directly to an answer.

  Weakness. Your question might not be there, or you might not have a specific question in mind.

- *Quick-Start Guide.* This feature is intended for those of you who have a more vague sense of what you want to find and need a little guidance. Research has shown that guidance facilitates our thinking, learning, and creativity, so let the Quick start Guide help get you started.

  Strength. It can help you formulate a vague question.

  Weakness. It can limit what you see and may misdirect you.

- *Contents.* Scanning the contents is always a good way to get familiar with a book and see what it has to offer. It's not advised to judge a book by its cover, but the contents can oftentimes send you in the right direction.

  Strength. It can save time!

  Weakness. It helps to have a good psychological and mental health vocabulary and requires you have some idea of what you are looking for.

- *Index.* If you have a particular term or concept in mind, just look it up in the index to see if it's there and where to find it.

  Strength. It saves time!

  Weakness. This requires you know the exact concept you are interested in, and the author might not be using the same terms or words that you have in mind.

Quick Start Guide (in Alphabetical Order)

Topic	Where to Look
Assessment and diagnosis	Chapter 3 Chapter 10
Biological effects of trauma	Chapter 3 Chapter 6
Burnout in professionals	Chapter 19
Children and adolescents	Chapter 20
Comorbid disorders and complications	Chapter 8
Cultural and international issues	Chapter 9
Difficult patients and clients	Chapter 19
History of PTSD concept	Chapter 1
Medications	Chapter 14
9/11 and terrorism	Chapter 22
Patient resources	Appendix B
Psychological effects of trauma	Chapter 3
Research: Latest and cutting-edge	Chapter 18
Social effects of trauma	Chapter 3
Spiritual effects of trauma	Chapter 3
Stress and coping	Chapter 2
Stressor types	Chapter 2
Treatment	Chapters 11–17
War, combat, and the military	Chapter 21

Frequently Asked Questions (FAQs)
and Where to Look for the answers!

What causes PTSD?	Chapters 4–7
How do I know if I am suffering from PTSD?	Chapters 3, 10
Why do I keep having nightmares about what happened?	Chapters 4–7
Why do I feel keyed up, stressed-out, and on-guard all the time?	Chapters 4–7
Why can't I let go of what happened?	Chapters 4–7
Will I ever be or feel normal again?	Chapter 11, 22
Does drinking alcohol or using drugs help or make things worse?	Chapter 8
Can you become an alcoholic or drug addict because of trauma?	Chapter 8
What's the best treatment or form of help?	Chapters 11–17
Are some people more prone to developing PTSD than others?	Chapter 4

I hope that the *CGPTSD* can live up to your expectations as well as my own. These were just a few points and tips to grease the intellectual gears and help ease you into your study of a tough and oftentimes disturbing topic. Just as many of us know the power of trauma, we also know the desire and pull to help those who suffer. If you haven't noticed so far, I tend to be light at times, and I like to use humor. This should not be mistaken for a carelessness toward PTSD or a minimization of the pain that PTSD can bring. I hope that my respect for survivors, their friends and family, and the countless others who reach out to help, shows in the thoroughness of this work and the quality of its presentation.

Theoretical and Empirical Foundations for Working with Posttraumatic Stress Disorder

THE WILEY
CONCISE GUIDES
TO MENTAL HEALTH

Posttraumatic
Stress
Disorder

Introduction to Posttraumatic Stress Disorder

*Suffering breaks our world. Like a tree struck by lightening—
splintered, shaken, denuded—our world is broken by suffering, and
we will never be the same again.*

—Nathan Kollar

*A timid person is frightened before a danger, a coward during the
time, and a courageous person afterward.*

—Jean Paul Richter

Happiness is nothing more than good health and a bad memory.

—Albert Schweitzer

Nothing fixes a thing so intensely in the memory as the wish to forget it.

—Michel de Montaigne

*The superior man, when resting in safety, does not forget that danger
may come. When in a state of security he does not forget the
possibility of ruin. When all is orderly, he does not forget that
disorder may come. Thus his person is not endangered, and his States
and all their clans are preserved.*

—Confucius

The preceding quotations each address a different component of the experience of trauma or of being traumatized. The lines "like a tree struck by lightning . . ." and "we will never be the same again" in the quote from Nathan Kollar, a professor of religious studies at St. John Fisher College, invoke thoughts of suddenness and permanence. Richter's quote addresses the complexity of fear. Albert Schweitzer's and Montaigne's quotes call our attention to the diligence of memory. Finally, the quote by Confucius is perhaps the best description of the traumatic motto, "always alert and forever safe," lived as a guiding narrative in those who suffer from the profound effects of traumatic experience.

One cannot talk about *trauma* in general and *Posttraumatic Stress Disorder* (PTSD) specifically without addressing the issue of memory. Some might argue that the central component to the long-term effects of trauma is memory. Some might argue that this is the case for nearly all psychiatric disorders, for depression as an example might be characterized as the perpetual memory of loss. Posttraumatic Stress Disorder might be viewed as the perpetual memory of fear, danger, or threat.

There is something inherently powerful about the experience of trauma that somehow encourages us to separate ourselves from it, either through time, distance, or within the recesses of our unconscious. Trauma is something that happens to someone else, right? Murder and violence only happen in the bad parts of town. War happens on someone else's land, in a far-off country, or on the safe technological distance of our television screens. We want to leave it behind. We want to forget about it. This logic makes sense in our day-to-day lives. Our everyday language reflects this desire in our responses to those wounded and stunned around us: "put it behind you," "try to focus on the future," "it happened in the past, and there is nothing you can do to change that."

For some of us, however, escape seems impossible. We can't escape the intense memories of what has happened. We are haunted by the workings of our own minds and bodies. The logic of forgetting fails to provide relief as it breaks down into chaos or into a logic all its own. This book is about those of us who struggle to forget, struggle to make sense of, or struggle to heal from a traumatic experience or experiences. It is about those who have been so impacted by trauma that they have developed an illness, a syndrome of reliving or reexperiencing their particular trauma or traumas again and again. In his chapter in the *International Handbook of Human Response to Trauma*, Allan Young has described the disorder resulting from trauma as a disorder of memory par excellence, "the disorder's pathology is said to reside in the fact that certain memories will neither fade nor submit to a process of assimilation" (Young, 1999, p. 55). Some memories seem never to die. This book is about those who cannot forget.

The words, *Posttraumatic Stress Disorder* can be read from this perspective as a pathological reaction to a traumatic event or events. At the heart of PTSD is a constant remembering or reliving. Let's approach our conceptual understanding of PTSD in stepwise fashion.

Conceptualizing Trauma

Personal and Philosophical Perspectives

A person's worldview or conceptual framework for understanding the world should never be taken for granted. The branches of philosophy known as epistemology and ontology are devoted to understanding the *how* of knowledge (epistemology) and the *what* of the knowledge (ontology). How we as individuals come to know what we claim to know, our own personal epistemology is an important feature of our educational experience. What is happening when we attend class, listen to lectures, and read books and articles is a complex process of using our existing ways of knowing and current conceptual base to perceive, analyze, process, and integrate the newer incoming information. Basically, none of us is an empty vessel, showing up to the learning experience with a mind void of concepts or ways of knowing.

These points are particularly salient when it comes to the topic of trauma and posttraumatic reactions. Why? Trauma invokes powerful images, thoughts, and feelings. It is a concrete and heavy concept because it is far too real for so many people. Because of this, each of us shows up to the trauma epistemology and ontology game with a lot of conceptual baggage. The philosophy of Edmund Husserl held that each of us possesses conceptual frames or brackets by which we organize and understand the world around us. He supported exploring these brackets in order to understand where our ideas about the world come from. This process was intended to address bias and misconception. I won't be asking you to discard your baggage or explore your frames necessarily, but simply to be aware. Self-awareness in the learning process is a powerful ally. As a therapist working with PTSD patients, I have seen my own conceptual baggage interfere with the listening and empathy process. As a writer, I am aware that to best teach the concept of PTSD, I must respect the diversity of perspectives of the readers picking up this book.

Before I start indoctrinating you with the philosophical, historical, psychological, and psychiatric frames of understanding posttraumatic experience, let's do a quick exercise commonly used in psychological assessment known as the *sentence completion technique*. The instructions are simple; just fill in the blank at the end of each sentence with a word (or words) that makes sense to you.

Life is full of adversity; the best way to cope with it is to _____.

Soldiers who break down during combat are _____.

My own life has been _____ of trauma.

People who talk a lot about their traumatic experiences are _____.

An important aspect of history is remembering things such as _____.

I never knew how _____ I was until something traumatic finally happened to me.

What were your responses? I hope that these few simple sentences were good enough to get you thinking about your own personal and preconceived views of trauma and posttraumatic reactions. Maybe you view trauma as rare, maybe for the weak of spirit, maybe unavoidable, maybe psychological or neurotic, or maybe physical.

Although it may sound surprising, the recognition that people who experience trauma may suffer adverse consequences and that these people need to be listened to and their experience acknowledged has not always been the case.

Harold Kudler (1999) states that current thinking or the modern paradigm reflects an understanding that there are psychological consequences to exposure to trauma, implying that this may not have always been the case, at least on the same scale as modern thinking. A *paradigm* is a worldview that "organizes observations, theories, and facts about a given subject." (Kudler, 1999, p. 3) Hopefully, you are becoming more aware of your own paradigm. The paradigms for this book come, most broadly, from the fields of psychology, psychiatry, and the mental health field. Moreover, I am a psychologist writing about PTSD. A psychiatrist, social worker, or anthropologist writing about PTSD may have written a very different book. The language of psychology and the related disciplines is a tool for organizing observations of traumatic experience or reactions.

Certainly, however, humans are or have been able to talk about trauma before the modern language of psychology or psychiatry came along. Literature, folktales, stories, and various other forms of cultural narrative represent their own ways of organizing observations, theories, and facts about trauma. Hopefully, the psychological approach mirrors or reflects these forms as they reveal themselves to be accurate descriptions of the natural phenomenon of posttraumatic experience. A writer's account of the carnage of war can accurately reflect modern psychological understanding of posttraumatic stress, without such writer having ever studied clinical psychology. In fact, this account may have occurred hundreds of years prior to the advent of modern psychological theory or practice. What is most important to gleam from this discussion is that regardless of exactly what language one uses to describe them, posttraumatic reactions do, in fact, exist in the natural realm of human experience. They are not or were not simply invented by mental health professionals.

Again, Harold Kudler states, "prior to the 1980's it was unlikely that a clinician would inquire about a history of trauma or connect current problems to past traumatic experiences" (1999, p. 4). Does this mean that these experiences and connections didn't exist until mental health practitioners started asking about them? Of course not, just as microbes existed prior to the invention of the microscope. Perhaps the microscope that allowed us to see PTSD was an advance in human compassion for those suffering the effects of trauma. Perhaps it was the plethora of traumatic experiences so often found in the form of modern warfare, with its capacity for massive destruction and death that brought trauma closer to our collective consciousness. There is, perhaps, more evidence for the latter as historically it seems that interest in trauma is highest toward the end of or immediately following war (see the Historical Perspectives section in this chapter).

Traumatic reactions are connected to bad things, events, or situations that we typically wish to avoid, such as wars, illness, and other events that speak of death or dying. Our delicate consciousness may steer us clear of facing trauma. Yet Alexander McFarlane argues that despite our desire to avoid a face-to-face meeting with trauma, the "field of inquiry" evidences remarkable, "durability" over time (McFarlane, 1999, p. 12). Perhaps this demonstrates our own schism when dealing with trauma, a type of approach-avoidance conflict. Further, the enduring nature of traumatic symptoms in the form of PTSD holds us to never forgetting.

Historical Perspectives

The modern concept of PTSD has always been with us. It was first officially introduced into the mental health nomenclature—in the American Psychiatric Association's *Diagnostic and Statistical Manual of Mental Disorders, Third Edition* (*DSM-III*)—in 1980 after a hard-won struggle by activist-professionals.

As is the case with so much in psychology and psychiatry, the professional establishment has obviously been behind the times. Lay people, individual professionals, and, of course, survivors and sufferers have known the reality of PTSD long before it was officially recognized.

Along the way, there have been many "smaller" versions of PTSD, a set of symptoms or syndromes identified more with a specific stressor, rather than as a universal syndrome or disorder resulting from a traumatic stressor of any type, given it is of sufficient intensity.

Allan Young (1999) identifies early clinical interest in posttraumatic symptoms with John Erichsen's 1866 work on railway spine. Victims of railway collisions were experiencing shock, intense fear or fright, and physical and emotional problems. This work is identified as unique because symptoms were not exclusively connected to a physical injury, and the actual injury suspected was essentially "invisible." Experts at that time believed that victims sustained neurological injury, perhaps as a consequence of overwhelming emotions. This was referred to as the *nerve-trauma hypothesis*.

Jean-Martin Charcot, the famous neurologist that trained Freud and who popularized the clinical use of hypnosis, suspected the symptoms observable in railway spine were the consequence of nerve damage from the train collisions themselves. However, he introduced the importance of memory in such reactions, believing that in some cases a type of traumatic memory, different from normal memories in its formation and maintenance in that it was not integrated with other memories and consciousness, was involved in the maintenance of symptoms. Allan Young cites Charcot's portrayal of traumatic memory as "a coherent group of associated ideas which install themselves in the mind in the fashion of a parasite, remain isolated from all the rest, and may be explained outwardly by corresponding motor phenomena" (cited in Janet, 1901, p. 267). Young further characterizes the understanding of posttraumatic syndromes during this time period as being related to traumatic memory or amnesia in one form or another. Already, in such early work, we can see the centrality of memory in the pathogenesis of PTSD (see the Psychological and Psychiatric Perspectives section in this chapter for more on the role of memory in PTSD).

In France in 1890, Charles Sugois edited a medical sciences volume that contained a discussion of *traumatic neuroses* as a single concept for grouping the terms *railway spine* or *railway brain*. This was an early attempt at unifying the concept of posttraumatic experience. During this time, there was considerable debate among medical professionals regarding the physical versus psychical (mental) nature of the condition.

Sigmund Freud's work (Freud, 1896/1964) with neurosis contributed to the trauma field. He stated that trauma was at the center of the etiology of neurosis and stated that trauma was "a breakthrough of the brain's defense against stimuli. Such a breakthrough set up a great amount of anxiety identifiable in dreams and is followed by an event on the part of the organism to free itself of this anxiety by constant repetition" (Kardiner, 1959, p. 247). Further, Freud's and Josef Breuer's work on hysteria continued to hold that memory is a central component of traumatic syndromes. Breuer believed that traumatic memories somehow became displaced in the mind and were therefore unavailable for normal conscious processing and subsequent resolution. Freud and Breuer disagreed on exactly how such memories came to be displaced, with Freud believing that such a process was an action of the defense mechanism process employed to protect an individual. In either case, once again, memory sat center stage.

Historians identify World War I as the next time period of significance in the conceptual development of PTSD. The casualty toll of World War I was immense and, for some, unfathomable. The harsh conditions of life and death in the trenches inevitably lead to breakdown, both physical and psychological. Those who presented with psychological trauma or related symptoms were not necessarily viewed from a standpoint of compassion. In fact, the medical or health-oriented interpretation of their problems was forgone for more moral or social judgments. Medical experts sometimes would label those suffering from shell shock as morally inferior and weak, not having the wherewithal to face combat and defend their respective nations. These individuals would sometimes receive dishonorable discharges from the military or were treated by a form of disciplinary therapy and returned to the warfront. Some were treated with a form of aversion therapy in which the consequences of being traumatized were more aversive or unpleasant than of actually returning to battle. Alexander McFarlane (1999, p. 20) refers to proponents of the moral and/or social approach to trauma as ascribing to the "disciplinary school" of thought. These views were inherently tied to an emotional view of traumatic responses. Still other proponents of the physical perspective held that the result of shell shock was due to microhemorrhaging in the brain. McFarlane further claims that these theories essentially fail to comprehend that the "medical or social narrative" simply did not allow for the belief that war had the capacity to "scar the mind."

Abram Kardiner's 1941 book *The Traumatic Neuroses of War* is considered a direct source of the modern concept of PTSD (Young, 1999). Unlike the predecessors of World War I, Kardiner's work puts the focus back on the (negative) transforming power of traumatic stress and its challenge to adaptation. Working partially from a psychoanalytic perspective, sufferers are thought to experience a reorganization of the sense of self to a state of lesser ego functioning. They are believed to be "fixated on their traumas, their conceptions of the selves and the outer world are distorted, they experience characteristic dreams, they are irritable, and they exhibit a tendency to explosive aggressive reactions" (Young, 1999, p. 57).

The official guide to mental disorders developed and published by the American Psychiatric Association, the *Diagnostic and Statistical Manual of Mental Disorders* (*DSM-I*) was first published in 1952 and made no mention of Posttraumatic Stress Disorder. The veterans of World War II and the Korean War were being seen with traumatic symptoms and were described as suffering from *gross stress reactions*. (*DSM-I*, p. 40) Conceptually, the symptoms of trauma were viewed as the "aftereffects of previously healthy persons who began having symptoms related to intolerable stress" (Bloom, 1999, p. 34) In 1968, the *Diagnostic and Statistical Manual of Mental Disorders, Second Edition* (*DSM-II*) replaced "gross stress reaction" with "transient adjustment disorder of adult life."

Following this period in the late 1960s and early 1970s, deeply compassionate and dedicated professionals began to respond to the traumatized returning from the Vietnam War. Dr. Chaim Shatan and a colleague were working with Vietnam veterans in New York City who had traumatic symptoms. In 1972, Shatan wrote an article in which he referred to these symptoms as part of *Post-Vietnam Syndrome*. Shatan and Lifton were intensely involved in helping Vietnam veterans cope with their experiences while advocating for better treatment by the military medical establishment—the Veteran's Administration. Many individuals were being misdiagnosed as a consequence of the lack of an official and accurate concept of posttraumatic stress. Dr. Philip May, Shad Meshad, and William Mahedy were conducting similar work on the West Coast in California. In 1974, Sarah Haley published a paper in the *Archives of General Psychiatry* titled "When the Patient Reports Atrocities" that got the attention of the American Psychiatric Association. Shatan was asked by the APA to contribute to this developing concept and polled the members of the Vietnam Veterans Working Group for their ideas. What emerged was a classification system resembling Abram Kardiner's 1941 work (Bloom, 1999). Eventually, through the work of these dedicated people and countless others, Posttraumatic Stress Disorder was added to the *DSM-III* in 1980.

Amidst this important political and social advocacy and during this same period in 1976, Mardi Horowitz, a psychiatrist, introduced his work *Stress Response Syndromes* (see Chapter 13 for more of Horowitz's work). Horowitz contributed an elegant conception of the response to trauma. In essence, Horowitz held that traumatized individuals are chronically attempting to process their traumatic experiences and memories while engaging in alternating phases of engagement and avoidance. Horowitz's work was undeniably incorporated into the *DSM-III* conceptual framework.

Professional interest in PTSD has been growing ever since. Although the concept was intensely tied to the experiences of those suffering the ill psychological effects of war, PTSD has grown to apply to a much larger group of stimulus or causal events, including rape, natural disasters, automobile accidents, and child sexual abuse (see Chapter 17 for more on these topics).

Contemporary Psychological and Psychiatric Perspectives

Hopefully, the previous discussions have introduced some ideas central to defining and understanding what PTSD is, for example, that a reaction to trauma involved a persistent memory of that trauma. Essentially, it should be clear by now that exposure to traumatic events has the potential to bring about serious consequences. But historically the focus was on stressor- or event-specific syndromes. As was just discussed, the *DSM-III* concept of PTSD reflects the seemingly revolutionary idea that the symptoms experienced across events represented a unified pathological process. Harold Kudler states that the eventual development of the *DSM-III* concept of PTSD was the result of a recognition that different patients with different stressors "had responded in a similar manner" and "were consistent in clinical presentation and course across different populations" (1999, p. 4). That is, it is now widely believed that PTSD represents a distinct clinical entity.

Modern psychological and psychiatric nosology relies on factorial models of clinical disorders in which signs and symptoms are measured across populations and observed to cluster together in a way that form distinct clinical entities. These clinical entities cluster to form a diagnostic core. The signs and symptoms looked for across populations are based on the conceptual core of the observed clinical phenomenon. For example, therapists and mental health professionals were witnessing or observing the presence of PTSD-like symptoms without a formal label to apply to them. As professional dialogue progressed and these professionals got together to discuss their observations, the conceptual core of the PTSD construct began to emerge. Oftentimes in science, observations made by multiple independent investigators and practitioners are pulled together by an acknowledgment of their similarity. In fact, the validation of individual observations is a central tenet of the scientific method and works toward the organization of individual data points into a cohesive theory. It is a collective process of deductive reasoning.

The core signs and symptoms of PTSD first officially identified in 1980 in the *DSM-III* are currently formally identified in the fourth edition, text revision version of the *Diagnostic and Statistical Manual of Mental Disorders* (*DSM-IV-TR*). Posttraumatic Stress Disorder, as recognized in the *DSM-IV-TR*, comprises two main components:

1. An individual is exposed to a traumatic event that involves either directly experiencing or witnessing death, serious injury, or threat to physical integrity, and his or her response involves intense fear, helplessness, or horror.

2. Reactions involve symptoms of reexperiencing, avoidance and numbing, and hyperarousal.

The first component of the contemporary and formal concept of PTSD necessitates the presence of a stimulus, an event or situation. This event is viewed as "outside the range of usual experience" (*DSM-III-R*, p. 250), intensely challenging, and often catastrophic. The stressors are necessarily experienced with intense fear, terror, or helplessness.

Case Study 1—Responding to the Unexpected

A man and his 22-year-old daughter were waiting in line on a sidewalk outside a bookstore to get their favorite author's signature in his latest book. A car on the road beside them had swerved out of control, jumped the curb, and struck both of them. They both sustained serious but not life-threatening injuries and eventually gained a full physical recovery. Because of his obsessive calling and checking on his daughter's well-being for almost 2 years after the accident, the father sought psychotherapy for help. During the intake and initial interview, the man recalled the event and at times began to cry and shake, stating, "We couldn't move. It happened so fast; there was nothing I could do to keep her from getting hit."

The criterion of outside the range of usual experience can be observed here, as the statistical likelihood of being struck by a car while waiting in line on a sidewalk is relatively rare. The criterion of intense fear, terror, or helplessness can be observed in this vignette by the patient's statements, "We couldn't move. It happened so fast; there was nothing I could do to keep her from getting hit."

The required trigger or stimulus for PTSD is referred to as the *stressor criterion* or Criterion A in the *DSM-IV-TR*. An individual has to be exposed to war, for example, or a natural disaster and so on. Green (1993) proposed eight *dimensions of trauma* or examples of traumatic stressors that would qualify for Criterion A:

1. Threat to life and limb.
2. Severe physical harm or injury.
3. Receipt of intentional injury/harm.
4. Exposure to the grotesque.
5. Violent/sudden loss of a loved one.
6. Witnessing or learning of violence to a loved one.
7. Learning of exposure to noxious agents.
8. Causing death or severe trauma to another.

March (1993), another researcher, provides still another list of what he calls *characteristic PTSD stressors*:

Combat

Criminal assault

Rape

Accidental injury

Industrial accident

Automobile accident

Hostage situation

Prisoner of war (POW) situation

Natural disasters

Human disasters

Witnessing homicide

Sudden illness

Severe burns

He states further that such stressors constitute what we have generally come to believe or expect, that such events elicit "intense fear" and "helplessness" (*DSM-IV-TR*, p. 463).

With this concept of trauma, we obviously make a distinction between *every-day* or *normal* stressors and more extreme stressors. One may assume that traumatic events are not the norm, not everyday, but certainly there are people who live amidst the preceding list of stressors virtually everyday. This is where the second part of the first component of PTSD becomes important. Everyday, critical stressors or critical events may not necessarily result in extreme responses of fear, helplessness, or horror. A combat solider, for example, may witness or cause death nearly everyday without these concomitant emotions and subsequent PTSD (see Chapters 4 to 7 for more on models of PTSD and at-risk populations). Therefore, the subjective experience of the traumatic-stressor survivor is critical in his or her development of symptoms and pathological reactions. Figure 1.1 should help illustrate these concepts.

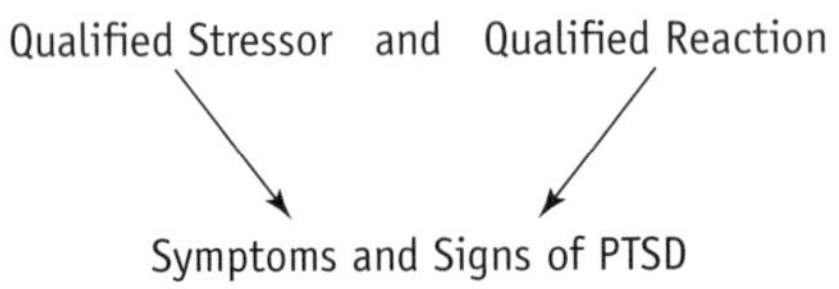

Qualified Stressor   and   Qualified Reaction

Symptoms and Signs of PTSD

FIGURE 1.1 *Pathways to PTSD.*

Professional Alert

The Criterion A issue seems like a slippery slope, perhaps leading to the inclusion of events subjectively experienced with intense fear, helplessness, or horror but perhaps not strictly meeting Criterion A-1 in the *DSM-IV-TR*. Here is where the issue of clinical judgment comes into play. A professional must use his or her best clinical judgment at times of ambiguity. After all, the purpose of diagnosis is to aid in treatment. An adopted stance of overinclusiveness or false-positive diagnosing may contribute to effective treatment. That is, sometimes it is advisable and smart, clinically and ethically, to be conservative. This is, of course, an issue of clinical philosophy, whether you seek to be overinclusive or underinclusive. (For more on this issue, see Chapter 10.) Nonetheless, a stance of best clinical judgment is advised when diagnosing a patient with PTSD based on a nontraditional Criterion A-1.

Now that the two requisite components of PTSD have been established, let's take a closer look at its core symptoms. A visual representation of PTSD is shown in Figure 1.2.

Each of these three core areas, *reexperiencing, avoidance,* and *increased arousal,* has various and numerous symptoms clustered within it. For example, reexperiencing can be determined by the presence of recurrent distressing dreams of a traumatic event (Criterion A-1). Avoidance and numbing is sometimes signaled by the presence of an individual's sense of a foreshortened future in which he or she may feel that he or she will have no career or a family. (See Chapter 3 for more detail about the symptoms of reexperiencing, avoidance, and hyperarousal.) Keep in mind that the symptoms that fall within each of these three categories do not always occur together in the same pattern or patterns and will typically vary in severity and intensity.

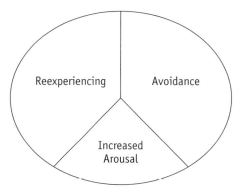

FIGURE 1.2 *Core Triad of PTSD.*

Reexperiencing a traumatic event is directly related to the historical conceptions covered earlier in the chapter and the emphasis on the role of memory in traumatic reactions. Reexperiencing is sometimes referred to as *intrusion* because of the obviously unwanted nature of the recollection.

The following vignette should help illustrate the core phenomenon of reexperiencing in PTSD:

Mr. Jones made several frantic attempts to contact me (his psychologist and therapist) after getting into a severe argument with his wife about stopping for gasoline at a local mini-mart gas station. Once we were face to face, he told me that he had pulled into the station and quickly noticed what he described as "little thugs, gangbangers" standing by the door of the mini-mart. He immediately felt a chill and began to sweat heavily. His heart raced, and he felt he needed to take off running or drive away extremely fast. He did, in fact, hit the accelerator, and took off rather recklessly from the lot. "They looked just like those bastards that shot me, Doc! My wife was yelling at me for driving crazy, asking what the hell I was doing. I yelled back at her, telling her something was gonna go down! Even though I risked running out of gas, there was no way I was sticking around that station!"

Mr. Jones was responding to the stimuli of the "thugs" with intense distress and with a sense that the event (being shot in the head and back over 10 times) or a very similar event was about to occur again. He was reexperiencing his trauma.

This case illustration, or vignette, also demonstrates well the second core phenomenon of PTSD—*avoidance*. This patient's behavior perfectly demonstrates an attempt to avoid a stimulus that arouses recollections or memories of his trauma. The experience of *numbing*, also a component of the avoidance component, involves a general reduction in responsiveness to one's environment, such as feeling socially detached and estranged and exhibiting a restricted range of emotional response. Mr. Jones constantly fought with his wife in reaction to her persistent statements that he was "cold-hearted and unloving." She would say, "The only emotion you've got is pissed off!"

This last point illustrates the final core concept of PTSD—*increased arousal*. These symptoms typically involve feeling *on edge* or *on alert* seemingly all the time. Difficulties sleeping, irritability, poor concentration, and being easily startled are common symptoms. Recall the Vietnam veteran from the Introduction who, stimulated by a simple phone call, exhibited the disproportionate response of his jumping out of his seat and crying?

Finally, we have arrived at a point where a good working definition of Posttraumatic Stress Disorder, based on a solid conceptual understanding, can be presented and used for the remainder of the book:

Posttraumatic Stress Disorder is a maladaptive reaction to a traumatic event in which a person experienced, witnessed, or was confronted with an event that involved actual or threatened death or serious injury or a threat to the physical integrity of self or others and experienced intense fear, helplessness, or horror. Afterward the person developed symptoms of reexperiencing the traumatic event in various forms, avoidance of stimuli that are associated with the event, emotional numbing, and hyperarousal to a degree that is disruptive to his or her functioning.

Hopefully this chapter served as a proper conceptual orientation and, along with the working definition at which we have arrived, you can explore PTSD more thoroughly in the chapters that follow. Here is a short summary of what you can expect:

Chapter 2. General theories of stress are covered, along with a discussion of coping in response to stressors.

Chapter 3. An empirical discussion of PTSD and its biological, psychological, and social effect are discussed. The core symptoms of PTSD will be discussed in more detail, along with the clinical course and prognosis. Patterns of recovery are discussed, and there is a discussion of resilience.

Chapter 4. Exposure and risk factors for the development of PTSD are discussed.

Chapter 5. Cognitive and behavioral models of PTSD will be covered, including memory distortions and associative learning mechanisms.

Chapter 6. This chapter addresses the biological models and underpinnings of PTSD.

Chapter 7. This chapter addresses numerous alternative models and explanations of PTSD such as psychodynamic or narrative models.

Chapter 8. This chapter addresses other potential consequences of trauma such as traumatic grief or Borderline Personality Disorder.

Chapter 9. This chapter will discuss the importance of placing PTSD in a cultural context in research and practice. Recommendations are made to help avoid the pitfalls of approaching the disorder from a culturally biased perspective.

Chapter 10. This chapter will discuss various evaluation methods. The diagnostic criteria of the *DSM-IV-TR* are presented in more detail as well as the overall approach to psychological assessment of PTSD, including a listing and discussion of specific instruments.

Chapters 11 to16. These chapters cover the various treatment techniques for PTSD, including cognitive treatments, psychodynamic treatments, pharmacological treatments, integrated approaches, and other treatments.

Chapter 17. Specific therapies for specific types of trauma such as rape, child abuse, and car accidents are discussed.

Chapter 18. Cutting-edge research and future directions are reviewed, including a discussion of the use of virtual reality technology in treatment.

Chapter 19. This chapter covers issues relevant to professionals who work with the traumatized, including discussions of compassion fatigue and various pitfalls.

Chapter 20. This chapter addresses children, adolescents, and families with PTSD as special populations.

Chapter 21. This is a special chapter on PTSD in war, combat, and the military. It is set aside as a special section because of the abundance of research and clinical work in these areas.

Chapter 22. This chapter will discuss the issues of hope, resilience, and the path to recovery from trauma.

Quick Review

- There is something inherently powerful about the experience of trauma that somehow encourages us to separate ourselves from it, either through time, distance, or within the recesses of our unconscious.

- Working with those who are traumatized evokes powerful images and emotions and therefore it is important to be aware of our worldview, personal biases, and conceptual frameworks.

- This book approaches PTSD from the paradigms and languages of psychology and psychiatry.

- At some points in history, there was little acknowledgment that persons exposed to traumatic events sometimes suffered adverse psychological consequences.

- Historically, PTSD has been viewed in various ways—as a neurological disorder, as a disorder of memory, and even as a disorder of morality.

- In 1980, PTSD was formally recognized by the mental health community and was included in the *DSM-III.*

- PTSD is currently recognized as a distinct clinical entity with three large categories of symptoms: *reexperiencing, avoidance,* and *increased arousal.*

- Examples of reexperiencing symptoms include recurrent and intrusive recollections and dreams and acting or feeling as if the event is being relived.

- Examples of avoidance symptoms include efforts to avoid activities, places, or people that arouse recollection and an inability to recall important aspects of the trauma.

- Examples of increased arousal symptoms are difficulties with sleep, irritability, and hypervigilance.

References

American Psychiatric Association. (1952). *Diagnostic and statistical manual of mental disorders* (1st ed.). Washington, DC: Author.

American Psychiatric Association. (1968). *Diagnostic and statistical manual of mental disorders* (2nd ed.). Washington, DC: Author.

American Psychiatric Association. (1980). *Diagnostic and statistical manual of mental disorders* (3rd ed.). Washington, DC: Author.

American Psychiatric Association. (1987). *Diagnostic and statistical manual of mental disorders* (3rd ed., revised). Washington, DC: Author.

American Psychiatric Association. (2000). *Diagnostic and statistical manual of mental disorders* (4th ed., text revision). Washington, DC: Author.

Bloom, S. (1999). Our hearts and our hopes are turned to peace: Origins of the International Society for Traumatic Stress Studies. In A. Y. Shalev, R. Yehuda, & A. C. McFarlane (Eds.), *International handbook of human response to trauma* (pp. 27–50). New York: Springer.

Erichsen, J. E. (1866). *On railway and other injuries of the nervous system.* London: Walton and Maberly.

Freud, S. (1964). *The standard edition of the complete psychological works of Sigmund Freud.* J. Strachey (Ed. & Trans.). Oxford, England: Macmillan. (Original work published 1896)

Green, B. (1993). Identifying survivors at risk: Trauma and stressors across events. In J. P. Wilson & B. Raphael (Eds.), *International handbook of traumatic stress responses* (pp. 135–144). New York: Plenum Press.

Haley, S. (1974). When the patient reports atrocities: Specific treatment considerations of the Vietnam veteran. *Archives of General Psychiatry, 30*(2), 191–196.

Horowitz, M. J. (1997). *Stress response syndromes: PTSD, grief and Adjustment Disorders* (3rd ed.). Lanham, MD: Jason Aronson.

Janet, P. (1901). *The mental state of hystericals: A study of mental stigmata and mental accidents.* New York: G. P. Putnam.

Kardiner, A. (1941). *The traumatic neuroses of war.* New York: National Research Council.

Kardiner, A. (1959). Traumatic neuroses of war. In S. Arieti (Ed.), *American handbook of psychiatry* (pp. 245–257). New York: Basic Books.

Kudler, H. (1999). The limiting effects of paradigms on the concept of traumatic stress. In A. Y. Shalev, R. Yehuda, & A. C. McFarlane (Eds.), *International handbook of human response to trauma* (pp. 3–10). New York: Springer.

March, J. S. (1993). What constitutes a stressor? The "criterion A" issue. In J. R. T. Davidson & E. B. Foa (Eds.). *Posttraumatic Stress Disorder: DSM-IV and beyond* (pp. 37–54). Washington, DC: American Psychiatric Press.

McFarlane, A. (1999). On the social denial of trauma and the problem of knowing the past. In A. Y. Shalev, R. Yehuda, & A. C. McFarlane (Eds.), *International handbook of human response to trauma* (pp. 11–26). New York: Springer.

Shalev, A. Y., Yehuda, R., & McFarlane, A. C. (Eds.). (1999). *International handbook of human response to trauma.* New York: Springer.

Wilson, J. P., & Raphael, B. (Eds.). (1993). *International handbook of traumatic stress responses.* New York: Plenum Press.

Young, A. (1999). An alternative history of traumatic stress. In A. Y. Shalev, R. Yehuda, & A. C. McFarlane (Eds.), *International handbook of human response to trauma* (pp. 51–66). New York: Springer.

CHAPTER 2

Theories of Stress and Coping

U nderstanding PTSD necessarily involves having an understanding of the concept of stress as a whole and its different gradations because it is a specific type of Stress Disorder. (For a discussion of other types of Stress Disorders, see Chapter 13 and the discussion of Mardi Horowitz's work.) Obviously, *traumatic stress* is only one type of stress or stressor. Researchers have engaged in heated debate on whether to consider PTSD as a phenomenon that exists independent of stress in general or whether it lies somewhere on a continuum with other reactions to stress. In other words, is PTSD just an extreme version of a typical or normal stress response, or is it something completely different? Ruscio, Ruscio, and Keane (2002) have concluded in their work that PTSD "is continuous with milder stress reactions" (p. 7). That is, PTSD is similar in kind to other, less clinical types of stress reactions.

When dealing with the stress of trauma or traumatic stress of PTSD, we are perhaps dealing with the ultimate stressor, the threat of death or injury. As defined in Chapter 1, a diagnosis of PTSD necessitates the experiencing, witnessing, or confrontation of an event or events that "involved actual or threatened death or serious injury, or a threat to the physical integrity of self or others" (APA, 1994, p. 425). There are few events or situations more stressful than possibly dying or being injured. Perhaps there are some situations that one may consider a fate worse than death itself, but the stress of potential death or injury is virtually unsurpassed.

Certainly, however, there are many other forms of stress other than death and injury. Anyone who commutes on a crowded freeway can attest to that. We all know stress in one form or another. Most of us know it in multiple forms. In fact, we all experience multiple stressors every day of our lives. Let me make a quick point about the words *stress* and *stressors*. Sometimes these words are used interchangeably. However, *stress* typically refers to a person's experience of a stressful event or stimulus. *Stressor* typically refers to the actual event or the stress-inducing stimuli or stimulus.

What Are Stressors?

Goldberger and Breznitz (1993) group stressors into two large groups, *common stressors* and *extreme stressors*.

Common stressors are stimuli that are commonly experienced by many people. Traffic jams and job stress are good examples. Common stressors can emanate from a physical environment, such as living in an urban setting or being snowed in during winter or living in a metropolis with its noise and crowds. If you're not used to being crammed into a subway car with hundreds of people, it can be pretty stressful. Our social and interpersonal lives, too, can be sources of stress. The pressures to keep up with the Joneses and stay on top of our workload at work are certainly familiar stressors to many Americans. There are also aspects inherent in our culture and social organization that can place a burden on our ability to maintain a balance and equilibrium, such as parenting or caring for an elderly or sickly relative.

Extreme stressors are stimuli that happen relatively rarely and are extremely powerful and intense, such as war or a catastrophic illness. Both human-made disasters and natural disasters can test our ability to provide even the most basic of needs, such as shelter, food, and physical safety. Human-made disasters can refer to incidents such as wild fires set by an arsonist or an airplane crash caused by pilot error. Natural disasters are commonly associated with weather and geologic phenomenon, such as floods, hurricanes, tornadoes, earthquakes, and volcanoes.

Whether a stressor is considered common or extreme in and of itself may not lead to a severe or clinical stress reaction such as PTSD. This outcome depends on numerous variables (see Chapters 4 to 7 for theories of PTSD and risk factors). Further, the level of stress experienced by an individual depends on the stress process, if you will, in which cognitive appraisal and physiological factors interact to derive the subjective experience of stress.

What Is Stress?

Let us start off with a working definition. Following this definition is a refinement of the idea.

> Stress is the physiological and psychological response and experience to a stimulus that strains one's ability to maintain his or her equilibrium, ability to adapt, or ability to adjust.

Common stressors

Environmental

Urban living

Noise

Air pollution

Traffic

Crowding

Social

Society

Rapid social change

Moral values

Pressure to succeed

Socioeconomics

Work stress

Threat of job loss

Bureaucracy

Coworkers

Bosses

Crime

Sociocultural and developmental

Parenting

Marriage

Adolescence

Caregiving

In all the years I've taught introductory psychology, "What is stress?" is the one question that probably evokes the most responses from the class. The word *stress* has become synonymous with depression and anxiety. I know a lot of men who are reluctant to say they are worried about a particular situation, but they usually won't hesitate to say they are "stressed out" about it. Here are some of the responses that I've heard over the years:

Pressure

Having too much to do and not enough time to do it

Extreme stressors

Violence

War

Migration

Illness

Natural disasters

Human-made disasters

Injury

Terrorism

Bill collectors breathing down my neck

A feeling of being wound up or on-edge all the time

Feeling overwhelmed

Thinking you can't handle it

Feeling anxious and having a racing heart

Feeling agitated

Thinking about all the problems and things you have to do all the time

Sometimes people have a hard time answering this question and instead find it easier to answer either "What is stressful in your life?" or "What stresses you out?" Here are some answers to these questions:

Being a parent is stressful.

My job is stressful.

School is stressful.

Getting sick stresses me out.

These questions in part seem to be asking different things. The question "What is stress?" seems to be getting at a person's experience of stress, and they describe it in biological terms (pounding heart), psychological or emotional terms (agitated or anxious), psychological or cognitive terms (thinking you can't handle it), and social terms (the bill collector breathing down my neck). These responses mirror the field of psychology's approach to many phenomena, the *Biopsychosocial Model*. In short, all psychological phenomena can be understood in terms of its biological components, psychological components, and social components. A complete understanding of any phenomenon necessitates an understanding of all these components.

The question "What is stressful?" is asking about the stressor. The first question is about the experience, and the second is about the stimulus. This is an important distinction because some people can experience an event (stressor) as stressful, and others might not experience that very same event as stressful. The experience of stress is an individualized phenomenon, depending on multiple factors and including a person's background and their available coping resources.

Let's now turn to a more technical discussion of stress.

Definitions of *stress* have ranged from descriptions of physiological reactions to cognitive or mental interpretations of a stressful event or events. Let's go back to the definition at the beginning of this section. The following technical and research-based definitions of *stress* address different aspects of the Biopsychosocial model. Each of them covers either one or a combination of more than one feature of the following aspects of stress. Stress necessarily involves the following features:

Biological/Physiological reactions

Emotions

Cognitions

Lavallo (1997) defined *stress* as a bodily or mental tension resulting from factors that tend to alter an existent equilibrium. The concept of equilibrium is based on the notion that living organisms must maintain a balance between their internal environment and the external environment in order to survive and function optimally. In 1929, Walter Cannon introduced his concept of stress as a physiological reaction caused by the perception of aversive or threatening stimuli. He also made reference to this concept of balance and referred to it as homeostasis.

Stress, then, can be further understood as the result of such an imbalance, originating in either the external or internal environments, and can be precipitated by any stimulus that threatens the homeostasis of an organism. Or, more succinctly, *stress is a physiological and mental reaction resulting from factors that alter our equilibrium or balance.* The resulting strain of attempting to maintain or restore this balance can also be viewed as stress. We are stressed when we are straining to maintain physiological and mental balance.

The Biology/Physiology of the Stress Reaction

Some have considered Hans Selye the father of stress research. In the early twentieth century, Selye introduced the concept of the *general adaptation syndrome* (GAS) to delineate the human response to stressful stimuli. Selye was studying the physiological reactions of pigeons to extreme cold and to extreme fluctuations in temperature. In essence, he would expose a pigeon to extreme temperatures and temperature fluctuations and monitor their bodily responses. Based on his observations, Selye (1993) identifies a three-stage model of stress responding.

The initial reaction to a stressor is characterized as the *alarm* stage. Alarm is a state of physiological arousal that involves activation of the hypothalamus in the brain and release of the adrenocorticotrophic hormone (ACTH) by the endocrine system. The adrenocorticotrophic hormone leads to the secretion of corticoids into the bloodstream, and the body is provided with energy to perform adaptive responses to the stress (avoidance, attack, etc.). In essence, the alarm stage gives us the energy to react. When confronted with a perceived stressor, our brains and bodies will react with a series of responses designed to mobilize energy. Our sympathetic nervous systems are activated, and we enter into a flight-or-fight mode of responding where we metaphorically, at least, prepare to flee a stressful situation or fight or resist the stressor we are faced by. The adrenal glands secrete epinephrine, norepinephrine, and steroid stress hormones. Epinephrine and norepinephrine spur metabolism and provide more glucose to our muscular system by increasing the output of the heart.

Following the alarm stage, an organism enters the *resistance* stage, which entails the activation of the body system most able to cope with the stressor, whether it be our legs to help us run away or our temporal lobes and frontal lobes to help us talk our way out of a sticky situation.

If the stressor continues without successful resolution, resistance, or avoidance by the organism, the organism enters the final stage of the GAS—exhaustion. The *exhaustion* stage is a condition in which after prolonged resistance the body becomes unable to resist stress any longer and becomes vulnerable to disease and breakdown.

Selye divided human responses to stressful stimuli into two basic categories, *syntoxic* and *catatoxic*. Syntoxic responses allow an organism to tolerate invasive stimuli or aggressors until destruction of them can occur. Catatoxic responses mobilize the organism to destroy the aggressor immediately. An example of each response is demonstrated in the case of a pathogen invading body tissue. An example of a syntoxic agent is cortisone, an anti-inflammatory agent allowing for toleration of foreign entities in the body. Inflammation prevents the spread of these entities by localizing them within a barricade. Syntoxic reactions are akin to tolerating a stressor. An example of a catatoxic reaction is the use of chemical messengers sent to tissue to increase the level of defensive reaction in response to the presence of foreign bodies. Catatoxic reactions are akin to destroying the stressor.

Emotions, Cognitions, and the Stress Reaction

Richard Lazarus (1966) argues that stress should be considered an emotion in and of itself, just like sadness and anger are. He believes that emotions exert a very powerful influence on the ways we think and behave. He defines an *emotion* as an organized psychophysiological reaction to information and knowledge about significance for personal well being with respect to our relationship with our environment. Our emotions tell or give us input about where we stand in relationship to the world around us and whether our needs, both simple and complex, are being met. Just as we feel hungry when we need food or nutrition, we may feel fear when we are in need of safety.

The emotions of stress typically involve what Lazarus calls *negative emotions*, such as anger, anxiety, or guilt. Positive emotions are happiness, pride, and love. When there is a discrepancy between our intended or desired goals and actual outcomes, negative emotions are typically generated. Stress can be viewed in this context as our experience of this discrepancy or disequilibrium. Thus, our emotions are a significant aspect of our internal or mental environment, and all emotions are appraised with respect to their immediate and potential significance. When we experience an emotion, we undergo a process of determining whether that emotion is telling us something meaningful. The appraisal process is an evaluation that endows a situation with meaning and consists of two processes: *primary* and *secondary appraisal*.

A situation or event is labeled as *stressful* if there is something important at stake for us, such as our reputation, our job, or our physical health. The predicted consequences of a situation determine its significance. Test-taking anxiety provides a good example of this. Some test takers get completely stressed out before a test, worrying over whether they are going to pass or get the top grade. Still others don't get to that level. Research has shown that students with high levels of test-taking anxiety spend a lot of time thinking about the short-term and long-term consequences of their performance, for example, "If I fail, I won't be able to get into college." Students who worry less don't consider such consequences. They are more in the moment. For them it is just a biology exam, not an admissions test for Harvard. This evaluation of the consequences or what is at stake is the process of *primary appraisal*. If something is not perceived as important or if nothing important is at stake, then stress levels are lower. With PTSD, what is at stake is our life or physical health. These stakes are high and typically perceived as important.

In addition to evaluations of what is at stake, evaluations related to the resources available to deal effectively with the stressor take place. This is known as *secondary appraisal*. In secondary appraisal, our evaluations of our ability to cope are based on our previous experience, our beliefs about ourselves, and the availability of resources. Different appraisals can lead to different outcomes and can lead to different behaviors. Again, in the case of PTSD, the secondary appraisal process often results in the conclusion that we are unable to successfully cope with the stressor, resulting in the experience of severe or traumatic stress.

Hamilton (1980) further delineated the role of cognitive processes in stress and stress reactions in his information processing analysis. Crisis and stress require cognitive and behavioral responses that will allow an individual to adequately cope. When these responses are lacking, an individual is considered stressed or under stress. Stress is then seen as a consequence of limited coping ability. Hamilton did not consider stress an inherent property of the stressors themselves. Hamilton viewed stress as both an agent (stressor) and a response. According to Hamilton, someone who is deficient in specific cognitive processes or processing abilities is vulnerable to stress responses when exposed to stress agents.

In addition to post hoc cognitive evaluations of the significance of the stressful situation and of available resources, preceding beliefs of personal control have been implicated in stress reactions. Martin Seligman (1975) has shown that repeated exposure to events that overtax individuals because of a lack of or a perception of a lack of personal control can have negative psychological and physical consequences. It is the perception of one's sense of control that is central and not the real lack of control per se. The positive psychological effects of believing that one has more control over a situation than he or she actually does are well founded in the literature. Having a belief of control in certain situations, even if this belief is illusory, is a positive predictor of good adjustment and coping. Research done with cancer survivors has consistently shown that even an exaggerated belief of control in the possibility of affecting a cure or of prolonging one's life in the face of extremely poor odds can have a positive psychological effect.

Mandler (1982) also discussed the role of cognitive processes and the sense of personal control in stress reactions. Mandler's cognitive definition of *stress* holds that psychological (cognitive) interpretive mechanisms and threat evaluations determine the stress value of an external event or situation. This concept is known as *mastery,* which is defined as the thought or perception that things in an individual's environment can be brought under his or her control. Mastery is similar to secondary appraisal in Lazarus's (1966) model. Mandler (1982) wrote, "Without doubt, the sense of mastery in many cases reduces the deleterious effects of stress and alleviates the subjective sense of emotional disturbance" (p. 41).

The Effects of Stress

Hans Selye's work pioneered a line of research exploring the connections between stress, psychopathology, adjustment problems, and physical conditions. He stated that the same physiological responses that help an organism cope with a stressor could cause disease. He stated that this is possible under conditions of "innate defects, understress, overstress, or psychological mismanagement" (Selye, 1992, p. 14). He went on to delineate what he called the *diseases of adaptation,* which included peptic ulcers, high blood pressure, heart accidents, and nervous disturbances. Our coping mechanisms and the stressors themselves have been connected to many pathological and deleterious effects, including psychological and physical disease. Stress can make us sick. Stress can damage our relationships. Stress can result in destructive emotions.

Within the last 20 years, medical and health professionals have consistently moved away from a disease model of health to a wellness model in which illness is viewed within its behavioral, psychological, and sociological contexts while still concentrating on the physiological and biological mechanisms involved. As part of this change, stress has come into focus as a major component of health and disease. The relationship and interaction between stress and physical illness has been explored in several common and serious conditions. These findings should not be taken to mean that stress *causes* these conditions but rather that stress has been found to be a factor in their development, maintenance, or course.

- Some patients seem to develop abdominal pain or irritable bowel syndrome in response to serious environmental stress (Brown & Harris, 1989; Craig, 1989; Craig & Brown, 1984; Creed, 1981; Creed, Craig, & Farmer, 1988).

- The onset of peptic ulcers has been associated with the frustration of an important life event by a stressor (Craig & Brown, 1984; Ellard, Beaurepaire, Jones, Piper, & Tennant, 1990).

- The occurrence of myocardial infarction has been associated with frustration of an important life event by a stressor (Neilson, Brown, & Marmot, 1989).

- Significant occurrence of stressful events has been associated with non-specific back pain compared to organic back pain (Craufurd, Creed, & Jayson, 1990).

- The onset of multiple sclerosis has been associated with reduced immune functioning secondary to severe life stressors (Cohen, Tyrell, & Smith, 1991; Grant, McDonald, Patterson, & Trimble, 1989; Irwin et al., 1990).

In addition several other health effects are possible. High blood pressure is a common consequence of someone living in a chronic state of stress. High blood pressure can lead to heart attacks and increases a person's odds of having a stroke or other cardiovascular accident. Stress is now widely considered a common cause of immunosuppression, which leaves us vulnerable to opportunistic infections. Stress has been shown to seemingly speed up the aging process.

It should be noted that the relationship between physical disease, illness, and stress should not be oversimplified. Despite the fact that research continues to come out showing the relationship between illness and stress in more and more conditions, the risk of oversimplification is high. The illness and disease process is complex and continues to challenge medical practitioners and researchers alike. The information presented here is only meant to provide a brief introduction. For a more detailed account, see *The Handbook of Stress, Medicine, and Health* edited by Cary L. Cooper (1996).

The following are some of the psychological and social effects that can result from the experience of stress:

Posttraumatic Stress Disorder

Generalized Anxiety Disorder

Alcohol Abuse

Drug Abuse

Depression

Adjustment Disorders

Interpersonal conflicts

Secondary Traumatic Stress Disorder

Rage

There is a vast literature connecting psychiatric conditions and stress, including the development and exacerbation of anxiety and clinical depression. Stress is a phenomenon that an individual experiences as overtaxing and overwhelming. Anxiety is a condition that exemplifies fear and worry, which are similar, both quantitatively and qualitatively, to the experience of stress itself. Situations that engender fear typically engender stress in the form of fear. As was explored earlier in Arnold Lazarus's work, stress itself can be viewed as a negative emotion among others such as fear and worry.

Stimuli that lead to depression are often associated with a loss of control, contingency, or self-efficacy. In the learned-helplessness model of depression, individuals are thought to develop a cognitive set that interprets situations as out of one's control. Again, the very concept of stress involves the experience of, at the very least, a challenge to one's sense of control. The various aspects of stress appraisal, coping (see the next section), and depression all overlap in ways that make the connection between depression and stress far too obvious.

Mental health practitioners and researchers have also addressed the connection between stress and substance abuse. The *self-medication hypothesis* holds that individuals abuse substances to cope with the negative emotions such as tension, worry, or sadness that are associated with stress. Relapse or a return to substance abuse is often associated with either a significant stressor or a stressor of perceived significance. Therefore, stress reduction and the learning of effective coping strategies are important aspects of substance abuse treatment.

As stress challenges our ability to effectively cope and our resources become tapped, our relationships with people may sometimes suffer. For some people, coping might require less contact with or exclusion of other people, such as sleeping or isolation. It is not unusual for couples presenting for couples therapy to complain that each partner is not receiving what he or she needs from the other in times of stress.

Finally, it is not uncommon for some individuals to react to the strain of a stressor with anger or rage. For those familiar with California highway driving, the concept of road rage is one that evokes images of car shootings and assaults. To say that stress alone can account for such extreme behaviors or acts would be ridiculous. Many more drivers experience stress on the road without lashing out. But the connection between stress and anger must be acknowledged, albeit anger is just one of the many emotional reactions to stress.

Coping

In attempting to understand stress and its impact on humans, it is essential to look at the concept of *coping*. According to Zeidner and Endler, "It is commonly recognized that it is not stress per se that determines adaptive outcomes, but rather how we cope with ongoing challenges and stressors that is critical in affecting our psychological and physical health" (Zeidner & Endler, 1996, p. xv). *Coping* is defined as the reaction of people to stressful and upsetting situations (Parker & Endler, 1996). The differential effects of different coping processes can range from increasing to attenuating the effects of stress on psychological and physical well-being.

Even a casual observer can notice that some people appear better at coping with stress than others. This observation is in line with research and theory. Some theories propose that there are inherent characteristics, such as personality traits, that some of us possess and others do not that determine whether we are good at coping with stress or bad at coping with stress. These theories are often referred to as *dispositional theories*. Think of these characteristics as personality traits or consistent and stable characteristics of thinking, feeling, or behaving. Some coping resources that can be viewed as stable personality traits or capacities are self-efficacy, optimism, hardiness, a sense of coherence, and internal locus of control.

Zeidner and Hammer (1992) performed a comprehensive review of the coping literature in which they identified several personal resources. They list several components of coping, such as optimism, perceived control, resources, and mediator variables. These authors found a significant relationship between perceived control, emotion-focused coping, state anxiety, physical symptoms, and cognitive functioning.

Identified earlier as a personal resource used in coping, self-efficacy is a specific theoretical construct that falls under the more general heading of perceived control. Self-efficacy refers to personal action control or agency and is based on evaluations of one's experience (Schwarzer, 1992). Self-efficacy is one of the strongest predictors of coping from infancy to old age (Baltes & Baltes, 1986; Bandura, 1977). Taken in conjunction with the work of Lazarus and Folkman (1984), the variables of self-efficacy beliefs and perceived control are good predictors of perceived challenge and threat and loss. High self-efficacy and perceived control lend themselves to lower levels of perceived challenge and threat or loss. Individuals that score low on self-efficacy measures tend to become more distressed in stressful situations (Jerusalem & Schwarzer, 1992). Further, high self-efficacious individuals seem less vulnerable to stress.

In addition, perceived control has been found to predict performance and stress levels in many domains (Skinner, 1992). Situations that engender feelings or experiences of noncontingency, inconsistency, unpredictability, failure, and ineffectiveness can lead to the experience of low perceived control and the experience of stress. Thus, situations that can come under contingency, predictability, and effectiveness will be experienced as less stressful.

Psychoanalysis provided a comprehensive view of coping through discussion of defense mechanisms (Freud, 1896/1955; Vaillant, 1986). Sigmund Freud was concerned with outlining the mental behavior individuals used to insulate or protect themselves from unacceptable ideas or feelings that might cause significant stress or distress. The working definition of *stress* used in this chapter resembles Freud's notion of *unacceptable*. Anna Freud refined and added to Freud's concept of defense and set the stage for most of the analytic investigators who followed her. Similar to Selye's belief that our so-called adaptive physical responses to stress can be the culprit in creating health problems, Anna Freud believed that specific psychological defense mechanisms and their habitual implementation can sometimes lead to specific psychological problems as well. The behavior of mental processes we use to cope may be the very process that produces psychological symptoms.

Folkman (1992) and Lazarus and Folkman (1984) presented a comprehensive example of a contextual theory known as the *appraisal-based model*. Coping is viewed as a response to specific stressful situations where active and conscious cognitive appraisals of potential threat are made. These appraisals mediate between the stressor and an individual's coping processes.

Hamilton's (1980) information-processing model of stress holds that adaptive coping is a function of reduction in informational load. This reduction is the operative function in any coping behavior or defensive operation. Two or more coping strategies can be viewed as similar if they reflect the same resultant simplifications of stressor characteristics. There must be suitable operations to contain the information being offered by the stressor. Effective coping results from effectively reducing the amount and form of stimulation and essentially simplifying one's contact with stressful stimuli.

Finally, Moos and Schaefer (1993) have created a useful conceptual framework that illustrates the main tenets of the integrative theories of coping. Most current researchers acknowledge the dual impact of both dispositional and contextual factors in coping. In their model, Moos and Schaefer pull from the strengths of both approaches: coping styles that cross situations (dispositional approaches) and coping behaviors that change in response to specific situations (contextual approaches). Their model stresses the importance of both in shaping coping responses. Any life event that a person encounters is duly influenced by the interaction of the person's ongoing life stressors, social coping resources, demographic characteristics, and personal coping resources. Further, the person's cognitive appraisals of the stressor contribute to his or her health and well-being. In summary, the integrative approach takes into consideration what resources an individual possesses prior to a stressor or stressful event, the event itself, and the appraisal of such event in attempting to predict health outcome. This integrative approach is the most comprehensive and perhaps most effective conceptual model for understanding the coping process.

So far we have focused on an internal or inherently psychological aspect of coping. But an individual's ability to resist stress depends upon both his or her coping responses and his or her resources. Resilience is in part a function of the interaction between personal and social resources and coping efforts. Lazarus and Folkman (1984) defined *resources* as what a person "draws on in order to cope" (p. 158).

The people around us are important features of the coping picture. Social resources can aid in coping by providing support, information, and problem-solving suggestions (Carpenter & Scott, 1992; Cohen & McKay, 1984). Examples of social resources are family, friends, and supervisors. The power of counsel from a trusted or respected confidant or the warm presence of a close friend can rarely be denied as powerful medicine in times of stress.

Summary

Understanding stress—how it develops, how it is maintained, and how we cope with it—is an important feature of understanding Posttraumatic Stress Disorder. Stress is as much a mental process and subjective experience as it is a physiological process. The consequences of stress can range from minor frustration to significant health and mental health problems. Our ability to successfully cope with stress depends upon a complex interplay between our personalities, mental processes, and environment, including the people around us.

Quick Review

- Posttraumatic Stress Disorder is similar in kind to other less clinical types of stress reactions.

- *Stressor* typically refers to the actual event or the stress-inducing stimuli or stimulus.

- Stressors can be common (e.g., work stress, marriage, or traffic) or extreme (e.g., war, disaster, or terrorism).

- Stress is the physiological and psychological response and experience to a stimulus that strains one's ability to maintain his or her equilibrium, ability to adapt, or ability to adjust.

- Hans Selye introduced the concept of the general adaptation syndrome (GAS) to delineate the human response to stressful stimuli.

- The biological/physiological response to stress involves the activation of the sympathetic nervous system and engagement of the fight-or-flight response.

- The experience of stress is the result of a cognitive appraisal process by which an individual decides if there is something important at stake and whether he or she can manage the stressor based on experience and available resources.

- Stress has been shown to be connected to a number of physical health problems, such as peptic ulcers, high blood pressure, heart attacks, immune suppression, and headaches.

- Successful coping is a consequence of the interaction between what resources an individual processes prior to a stressor or stressful event, the event itself, and the appraisal of such event in attempting to predict a positive or healthy outcome.

References

American Psychiatric Association. (1994). *Diagnostic and statistical manual of mental disorders* (4th ed.). Washington, DC: Author.

Baltes, M., & Baltes, P. (1986). *The psychology of control and aging.* Hillsdale, NJ: Erlbaum.

Bandura, A. (1977). Self-efficacy: Toward a unifying theory of behavioral change. *Psychological Review, 84,* 191–215.

Brown, G. W., & Harris, T. O. (Eds.). (1989). *Life events and illness.* New York: Guilford Press.

Cannon, W. B. (1929). *Bodily changes in pain, hunger, fear, and rage* (2nd ed.). Oxford, England: Appleton.

Carpenter, B. N., & Scott, S. M. (1992). Interpersonal aspects of coping. In B. N. Carpenter (Ed.), *Personal coping: Theory, research, and application* (pp. 93–109). Westport, CT: Praeger.

Cohen, S., & McKay, G. (1984). Social support, stress, and the buffering hypothesis: A theoretical analysis. In A. Baum, J. E. Singer, & S. E. Taylor (Eds.), *Handbook of psychology and health* (Vol. 4, pp. 253–267). New York: Wiley.

Cohen, S., Tyrell, D. A., & Smith, A. P. (1991). Psychological stress and susceptibility to the common cold. *New England Journal of Medicine, 325,* 606–612.

Cooper, C. L. (Ed.). (1996). *Handbook of stress, medicine, and health.* Boca Raton, FL: CRC Press.

Craig, T. J. K. (1989). Abdominal pain. In G. W. Brown & T. O. Harris (Eds.), *Life events and illness* (pp. 233–259). New York: Guilford Press.

Craig, T. J. K., & Brown, G. W. (1984). Goal frustrating aspects of life events stress in the etiology of gastrointestinal disorder. *Journal of Psychosomatic Research, 28,* 411–421.

Craufurd, D. I. O., Creed, F., & Jayson, M. D. (1990). Life events and psychological disturbance in patients with low-back pain. *Spine, 15,* 490–494.

Creed, F. (1981). Life events and appendicectomy. *Lancet, 1,* 1381–1385.

Creed, F., Craig, T., & Farmer, R. (1988). Functional abdominal pain, psychiatric illness, and life events. *Gut, 29,* 232–242.

Ellard, K., Beaurepaire, J., Jones, M., Piper, D., Tennant, C. (1990). Acute chronic stress in duodenal ulcer disease. *Gastroenterology, 99,* 1628–1632.

Folkman, S. (1992). Making the case for coping. In B. N. Carpenter (Ed.), *Personal coping: Theory, research, and application* (pp. 31–46). Westport, CT: Praeger.

Freud, S. (1955). Further remarks on the neuro-psychoses of defence. In J. Strachey (Ed. & Trans.), *The standard edition of the complete psychological works of Sigmund Freud: Vol. 3.* (pp. 43–62). London: Hogarth Press. (Original work published 1896)

Goldberger, L., & Breznitz, S. (Eds). (1993). *Handbook of stress: Theoretical and clinical aspects* (2nd ed.). New York: Free Press.

Grant, I., McDonald, W. I., Patterson, T., & Trimble, M. R. Multiple sclerosis. In G. W. Brown & T. O. Harris (Eds.), *Life events and illness* (pp. 295–311). New York: Guilford Press.

Hamilton, V. (1980). An information processing analysis of environmental stress and life crisis. In I. Sarason & C. Spielberger (Eds.), *Stress and anxiety* (Vol. 7, pp. 13–29). New York: Hemisphere.

Irwin, M., Patterson, T., Smith, T. L., Caldwell, C., Brown, S. A., Gillan, J. C., & Grant, I. (1990). Reduction of immune function in life stress and depression. *Biological Psychiatry, 27,* 22–30.

Jerusalem, M., & Schwarzer, R. (1992). Self-efficacy as a resource factor in stress appraisal processes. In R. Schwarzer (Ed.), *Self-efficacy: Thought control of action* (pp. 195–213). Washington, DC: Hemisphere.

Lavallo, W. R. (1997). *Stress and health: Biological and psychological interactions.* Thousand Oaks, CA: Sage.

Lazarus, R. S. (1966). *Psychological stress and the coping process.* New York: McGraw-Hill.

Lazarus, R., & Folkman, S. (1984). *Stress, appraisal, and coping.* New York: Springer.

Mandler, G. (1982). Stress and thought processes. In L. Goldberger & L. Breznitz (Eds.), *Handbook of stress: Theoretical and clinical aspects.* New York: Free Press.

Moos, R. H., & Schaefer, J. A. (1993). Coping resources and processes: Current concepts and measures. In L. Goldberger & S. Breznitz (Eds.), *Handbook of stress: Theoretical and clinical aspects* (2nd ed., pp. 234–257). New York: Free Press.

Neilson, E., Brown, G. W., & Marmot, M. (1989). Myocardial infarction. In G. W. Brown & T. O. Harris (Eds.), *Life events and illness* (pp. 314-342). New York: Guilford Press.

Parker, J. D. A., & Endler, N. S. (1996). Coping and defense: A historical overview. In M. Zeidner & N. S. Endler (Eds.), *Handbook of coping: Theory, research, applications* (pp. 3–23). Oxford, England: Wiley.

Ruscio, A. M., Ruscio, J., & Keane, T. M. (2002). The latent structure of posttraumatic stress disorder: A taxometric investigation of reactions to extreme stress. *Journal of Abnormal Psychology, 111,* 290–301.

Schwarzer, R. (Ed.). (1992). *Self-efficacy: Thought control of action.* Washington, DC: Hemisphere.

Seligman, M. E. P. (1975). *Helplessness: On depression, development, and death.* New York: W. H. Freeman.

Selye, H. (1993). History of the concept of stress. In L. Goldberger & S. Breznitz (Eds.), *Handbook of stress: Theoretical and clinical aspects* (2nd ed., pp. 7–17). New York: Free Press.

Skinner, E. A. (1992). Perceived control: Motivation, coping, and development. In R. Schwarzer (Ed.), *Self-efficacy: Thought control of action* (pp. 91–106). Washington, DC: Hemisphere.

Vaillant, G. (1986). *Empirical studies of ego mechanisms of defense.* Washington, DC: American Psychiatric Press.

Zeidner, M. & Endler, N. S. (Eds.). (1996). *Handbook of coping: Theory, research, applications.* Oxford, England: Wiley.

Zeidner, M., & Hammer, A. L. (1992). Coping with missile attack: Resources, strategies, and outcomes. *Journal of Personality, 60,* 709–746.

CHAPTER 3

The Biopsychosocial Effects of Traumatic Stress

Introduction

Traumatic stress can transform an individual's life in profound ways, including how one's body functions, how one thinks and views the world and its dangers, and how one relates and interacts with people. The goal of this chapter is to outline just how people respond and react to traumatic stressors and delineate its various consequences for the human body, mind, and social relations. As you will see, both negative and positive reactions are possible. Before we get started, however, consider the following quote from Yule, Williams, and Joseph (1999, p. 1):

> All human beings are complex organisms who constantly strive to adapt to the demands placed on them by their physical and social environments. We constantly strive to make sense of what happens to us, and we build up internal models of the world as we experience it. When threatened, we react with distress and fear. This response serves a survival function for each individual and for our species. We learn from encounters with danger and hopefully we learn to deal with them or not to place ourselves in similar dangerous situations. Thus, once danger has passed, we may ponder over the characteristics of whatever threatened us. We may think about it or see or hear it in our imagination—all ways of helping us recognize signs of danger in the future. Having done so, we can better avoid such dangers or prepare ourselves to face them.

This long quote is too good and too clear to have been paraphrased. It represents an important concept of understanding PTSD and trauma, which is that in order to understand abnormal reactions to threat, we should have some understanding or concept of what normal reactions to threat actually look like.

The Yule and colleagues quote presents us with an understanding of basic human functioning within our world of demands and potential threats, PTSD being just one possible reaction or outcome.

Case Study—Symptom Complexity

Joe was a delivery driver who passed by a number of schools on his route. One day, while waiting at a crosswalk for children to cross to school, Joe watched in horror as a car failed to yield and struck several children, killing three of them and critically injuring two. Joe witnessed the entire event. Joe rushed to the aid of the victims but was unable to provide much assistance other than comfort. As Joe got back into his truck he realized he was shook up, but he did not realize the extent of the impact of the trauma. The next day, Joe was unable to complete his route as it involved passing by the school. Joe's supervisor was sympathetic and changed his route, but Joe found that he could not drive past any school. Eventually Joe was placed on disability for PTSD. He began to have severe headaches and began to abuse alcohol. He felt depressed, as he was unable to leave his house without experiencing severe distress. Joe and his wife began to fight more often, and eventually she left and moved in with her sister. Joe's downward spiral continued. One day Joe had a severe panic attack and called 911. When the paramedics arrived, they cleared Joe medically and directed him to treatment. That day, Joe had a revelation of sorts. His gratitude toward the paramedics stirred in him thoughts and feelings that he, too, would like to help people the way these paramedics did. After seeking treatment, Joe started paramedic school and is now in his second semester, preparing to graduate.

This vignette is very illustrative of the complexity of the human response to traumatic events. Joe's responses included avoidance, substance abuse, depression, relationship difficulties, and physical problems. Joe's story is also illustrative of the potential positive impact of traumatic events that we sometimes see. In a possible attempt to master his memories and experience, Joe decided to learn how to help people in a way that he himself really appreciated.

Crisis, Acute Stress Disorder, and PTSD

Before we get into the details of the effects of exposure to traumatic stress, a quick word needs to be said about the difference between the immediate response to a traumatic stressor and more long-term responses.

Certainly, when we are in the midst of a situation of extreme and potentially traumatic stress, the potential for psychological crisis to emerge is high. A *crisis* is defined as a temporary state of upset and disorganization, characterized by an inability to cope with a particular situation or stimulus using customary methods. The crisis literature is extensive, and for more information the reader is directed to Slaikeu (1990). However, PTSD is about the aftermath of such a crisis, both the relatively short-term effects (acute—more than 1 month but less than 3 months), long-term effects (3 months or more), or even the delayed effects (onset of symptoms 6 months after an event).

Responses to traumatic stressors can be as varied as there are people in the world. A crisis may not necessarily lead to a mental disorder or psychiatric diagnosis. Some severe responses that would certainly constitute a crisis but not necessarily a diagnosable mental disorder are referred to as *peritraumatic reactions*—reactions that occur during the impact or immediate phase of a stressor (Shalev, 1996). Some peritraumatic responses are agitation, stupor, panic, numbing, freezing up, disorganization, and even dissociation. The key thing to remember is that these responses are *temporary* and *transient* and may occur in isolation. They go away, and they don't cluster together into Acute Stress Disorder (ASD).

Acute Stress Disorder is a formal mental disorder identified in the *DSM-IV-TR*. If someone meets criteria A1 and A2 and experiences qualified symptoms, he or she may meet criteria for ASD. Their symptoms have to last a minimum of 2 days and a maximum of 4 weeks, after which PTSD will be diagnosed. Three of the following dissociative symptoms must be present: a subjective sense of numbing, detachment, or absence of emotional responsiveness; a reduction in awareness of his or her surroundings (e.g., being in a daze); derealization; depersonalization; or dissociative amnesia (an inability to recall an important aspect of the trauma). They must also have at least one reexperiencing symptom, one avoidance symptom, and marked symptoms of anxiety or arousal, such as difficulty sleeping, irritability, poor concentration, or exaggerated startle. Research has shown that as much as 80 percent of those who suffer from ASD will develop PTSD (Brewin, Andrews, Rose, & Kirk, 1999).

Consequences of Exposure to Traumatic Stressors

For the purposes of this chapter, the various responses or consequences of exposure to traumatic stress will be divided into two large categories: (1) consequences identified by the American Psychiatric Association in the *DSM-IV-TR*, consisting of formalized diagnostic criteria and symptoms and (2) the biological, psychological, and social effects identified by researchers independent of the *DSM-IV-TR*.

The pathological or abnormal responses to exposure to a traumatic stressor identified in the *DSM-IV-TR* are grouped into three large categories: symptoms of reexperiencing, symptoms of avoidance, and symptoms of arousal.

DSM-IV-TR Identified Responses and Consequences

The consequences of exposure to traumatic stress manifesting as a mental disorder are formally outlined in the *DSM-IV-TR* (2000, pp. 467–468) as follows:

Diagnostic Criteria for Posttraumatic Stress Disorder

A. The person has been exposed to a traumatic event in which both of the following were present:

1. The person experienced, witnessed, or was confronted with an event or events that involved actual or threatened death or serious injury, or a threat to the physical integrity of self or others.

2. The person's response involved intense fear, helplessness, or horror. Note: In children, this may be expressed instead by disorganized or agitated behavior.

B. The traumatic event is persistently reexperienced in one (or more) of the following ways:

1. Recurrent and intrusive distressing recollections of the event, including images, thoughts, or perceptions. Note: In young children, repetitive play may occur in which themes or aspects of the trauma are expressed.

2. Recurrent distressing dreams of the event. Note: In children, there may be frightening dreams without recognizable content.

3. Acting or feeling as if the traumatic event were recurring (includes a sense of reliving the experience, illusions, hallucinations, and dissociative flashback episodes, including those that occur on awakening or when intoxicated). Note: In young children, trauma-specific reenactment may occur.

4. Intense psychological distress at exposure to internal or external cures that symbolize or resemble an aspect of the traumatic event.

5. Physiological reactivity on exposure to internal or external cures that symbolize or resemble an aspect of the traumatic event.

C. Persistent avoidance of stimuli associated with the trauma and numbing of general responsiveness (not present before the trauma), as indicated by three (or more) of the following:

1. Efforts to avoid thoughts, feelings, or conversations associated with the trauma.

2. Efforts to avoid activities, places, or people that arouse recollections of the trauma.

3. Inability to recall an important aspect of the trauma.

4. Markedly diminished interest or participation in significant activities.

5. Feeling of detachment or estrangement from others.

6. Restricted range of affect (e.g., unable to have loving feelings).

7. Sense of foreshortened future (e.g., does not expect to have a career, marriage, children, or a normal life span).

D. Persistent symptoms of increased arousal (not present before the trauma), as indicated by two (or more) of the following:

1. Difficulty falling or staying asleep.

2. Irritability or outbursts of anger.

3. Difficulty concentrating.

4. Hypervigilance.

5. Exaggerated startle response.

E. Duration of the disturbance (symptoms in Criteria B, C, and D) is more than one month.

F. The disturbance causes clinically significant distress or impairment in social, occupational, or other important areas of functioning.

Specify if:

Acute: If duration of symptoms is less than 3 months.

Chronic: If duration of symptoms is 3 months or more.

Specify if:

With Delayed Onset: Onset of symptoms is at least 6 months after the stressor.

Reexperiencing (Criterion B)

If one had to pick one symptom or sign that was the hallmark of PTSD, reexperiencing may very well be it. Hollywood and television portrayals of the disorder commonly depict the war veteran having a flashback, believing he is back in the combat zone, fighting for his life. When a trauma victim has a reexperience, he or she is in a state similar to the acute stress phase of the traumatic stress or stressor. Individuals may feel that they are in danger in the immediate moment. They may panic and want to escape. They may become aggressive or assaultive in order to protect themselves from the reexperience of threat.

Intrusive thoughts, images, and perceptions are considered major features of PTSD. Kardiner (1941) states that even prior to the formal recognition of PTSD, accounts of traumatic experiences always included features of intrusive imagery and thinking. In literature, intrusive thoughts, images, and perceptions are collectively referred to as *intrusive cognitions*. Salkovskis (1990, p. 91) defines *intrusive cognitions* as "mental events which are perceived as interrupting a person's stream of consciousness by capturing the focus of attention." An individual's thinking or mental activity is disrupted. Intrusive recollections can be triggered by stress or seemingly unprompted. (For more on the etiology or cause of intrusive recollections, see Chapters 5 to 7.) They are considered relatively common in individuals suffering from PTSD and occur more frequently than dreams or experiences of recurrence. An example of an intrusive cognition might be a visual image or memory of watching someone being struck by a car. Researchers,

Professional Alert

Accurate assessment of the exact nature of intrusive cognitions may be relevant to treatment strategies! As de Silva and Marks (1999) point out, exposure-based treatments may be better for intrusive images, while cognitive techniques may be better suited for intrusive thoughts.

de Silva and Marks (1999) give the following good examples: image of a car accident, lying on the road, with leg at an angle, blood around him; vivid memory of jacket ablaze, and his frantic movements as he tries to take it off; recollection of her body shaking, with the electric cable stuck to her hand, trying to scream but no sound coming out. Research has shown that visual images are a more common form of intrusive cognition than thoughts in verbal form.

In addition to images and thoughts, sounds can be reexperienced. Examples of hearing explosions, breaking glass, or screams are not uncommon. Feelings, tastes, and smells can also be reexperienced but are less common.

A type of memory known as a *flashbulb memory* has been used to describe the types of intrusive visual images reexperienced in PTSD. Flashbulb memories seemingly come out of nowhere, are very vivid and fresh, and give a sense of having recently occurred. Brown and Kulik (1977) suggest that public and personal events that are highly surprising and shocking are conducive to the formation of flashbulb memories. Certainly, traumatic stressors qualify as surprising and shocking.

As J. F. Pagel (2000) states, "nightmares are a defining symptom of PTSD." They are also considered a very common symptom amongst many clinicians. Pagel defines a *nightmare* as a vivid and terrifying nocturnal-sleep episode. The content of nightmares typically involves the traumatic experience and occurs during REM sleep but has been observed during sleep onset. Complications from nightmares can include insomnia, daytime memory impairment, and anxiety. Alan Siegel holds that PTSD nightmares are different than non-PTSD nightmares in that PTSD nightmares are considered more "emotionally intrusive and anxiety provoking."

Imagine driving to work in the morning, turning on the radio, and hearing a helicopter fly over your car, with machine-gun fire rattling. You swerve to avoid the bullets and end up in the drainage ditch next to the road. As witnesses come to the car you ask them if they saw the helicopter. Their answer of "no" lets you know you've had another flashback—a recurrence of a memory, feeling, or perceptual experience. Although this example may seem dramatic, it is exactly the kind of thing PTSD sufferers may experience. They are different than intrusive images or sounds in that they are perceived as a real experience of the trauma. Illusions are smaller forms of flashbacks that involve the misperception or misinterpretation of a real stimulus, such as perceiving a door slam as an explosion.

Hallucinations can also occur within the context of PTSD. A flashback is an actual memory that comes back into consciousness as a sight, smell, sound, or a complete scene. It has actually happened. Hallucinations are perceptions that seem real but occur without an external stimulus, as is the case with illusions. Within the context of PTSD, flashbacks happened, and hallucinations have not.

Hallucinations can be visual (e.g., seeing a dead person), auditory (e.g., hearing a baby crying), gustatory (e.g., tasting something bad), tactile (e.g., feeling worms under one's skin), olfactory (e.g., smelling rotting flesh), or somatic (e.g., feeling electricity in one's body). Lindley, Carlson, and Sheikh (2000) report that 30 to 40 percent of combat veterans with PTSD report auditory or visual hallucinations or delusions. These occur in the absence of an identifiable Psychotic Disorder or Mood Disorder with psychotic symptoms. They are often considered linked to more severe cases of PTSD, and symptoms include increased levels of paranoia, violent thoughts, and higher depression. They are typically nonbizarre and related to the trauma. Auditory hallucinations may involve hearing a voice of a dead enemy calling to them or even hearing their name called. Delusions can also be trauma related or nontrauma related, such as believing someone is attempting to poison them. In addition to hallucinations occurring within PTSD exclusively, PTSD sufferers also have higher rates of other Psychotic Disorders that involve hallucinations as well, such as Schizophrenia, Substance-Induced Psychotic Disorder, and Personality Disorders such as Borderline Personality Disorder.

The fourth component of Criterion B involves the experience of intense distress at exposure to internal or external stimuli that symbolize or resemble the trauma. A PTSD sufferer may cry uncontrollably at hearing a trumpet play, resembling the playing of taps. Becoming out of breath from running too fast may trigger intense fear in a recent near-drowning survivor. Along with the intense distress in component number four, a PTSD suffer may experience intense physiological reactivity to cues resembling the trauma, such as an increased heart rate, increased respiration, or intense sweating.

Avoidance (Criterion C)

Posttraumatic Stress Disorder also involves a significant change in an individual's responsiveness to his or her environment and the degree to which a person is engaged or detached. Certainly, one way to attempt to cope with a trauma is to try to avoid talking about it or ever thinking about it again. Avoiding thoughts, feelings, conversations, activities, places, or people that arouse recollection is common. People may move out of the town where an event occurred. One's memory for the event may be vague or even absent. "I don't want to think or talk about it" is a common reprise.

Emotional numbing and marked reduction in interest or participation in activities can also occur. For example, a tornado survivor may avoid feeling fear by expressing anger toward the government for not warning her and her family in time. Emotional numbing has been called *alexithymia*, the inability or difficulty in describing or being aware of one's emotions or moods. In response to the ever-present therapy question, "How does that make you feel?" a patient may respond, "I don't know what I feel!" and actually mean it.

"I feel like a stranger when I'm with my wife. I feel like she's on the other side of the world, even though she's lying right next to me in bed." These statements capture the experience of feeling detached or estranged from other people. It is not uncommon for a PTSD sufferer to feel intensely alone and alienated. He or she may have difficulty feeling love toward anyone, even people the PTSD sufferer can state he or she loves verbally, but without affect.

Finally, PTSD can involve a feeling that one might never grow up, get old, or have a future. They may engage in risk taking because they "know they won't live past 25 anyway." They can't imagine themselves grown up. Lenore Terr discusses this in length in her excellent book about PTSD in children, *Too Scared to Cry*.

Perhaps considered an ironic twist on the symptoms of avoidance, PTSD sufferers can sometimes engage in the exact opposite of avoidance and immerse themselves in trauma-related activities or stimuli. A Vietnam veteran may obsessively collect and compulsively view movies about the war, for example. van der Kolk (1996) identifies thee ways in which this immersion, or what he calls *compulsive reexposure*, (p.10) might occur: (1) Inflicting harm on others as a form of reenactment of the original trauma, (2) self-destructiveness such as self-mutilation or parasuicidal behavior, and (3) revictimization or being traumatized again and again in the same manner as before.

Arousal (Criterion D)

Posttraumatic Stress Disorder sufferers' minds and bodies can be in a constant state of alert and arousal. They can suffer sleep difficulties, exaggerated responses to being startled, irritability, outbursts of anger, poor concentration, and hypervigilance (always ready for something to occur). They are viewed as overreacting and can see their world as a dangerous or threatening place, reacting intensely to relatively nonintense stimuli. War veterans suffering from PTSD might find themselves on "patrol" of their neighborhoods, looking to "protect" and react to some impending danger. A hyperaroused parent of a child who nearly died from a serious illness might pull out the thermometer at the slightest sign of increased temperature and has the pediatric emergency doctor on speed-dial. Hyperaroused individuals can be "jumpy," becoming startled from the backfire of a passing car. Quite simply, these individuals have lost the ability to downregulate their mind's and body's danger response system. They cannot "turn it off" so to speak. This experience can sometimes lead to intense feelings of demoralization and powerlessness as a sufferer may become overwhelmed by both the intense arousal and by the inability to deescalate. It can feel as if one's body is "out of control" and they might fear they are "losing their minds."

Other Biological, Psychological, and Social Responses and Consequences

Physical Health

Research has consistently shown that individuals diagnosed with PTSD have higher rates of medical services use and increased levels of fatigue, headaches, chest pains, gastrointestinal disorders, cardiovascular disorders, and impaired immunity functioning when compared to individuals not diagnosed with PTSD. There is also a tendency for such individuals to rate themselves as less physically healthy overall when asked. Keep in mind that the jury is still out as to the exact nature of the relationship between PTSD and physical health problems and disease. Some researchers propose the existence of mediating variables such as drug or alcohol abuse to be responsible for the observed relationships thus far. It is not clear from the research so far whether physical health problems associated with PTSD are the result of somatization; physical health problems resulting from the actual physical aspects of the event (e.g., smoke inhalation from a fire, starvation as a prisoner of war, or exposure to Agent Orange); nonspecific physical responses associated with PTSD but not caused by it; or associated behaviors related to PTSD, such as alcohol abuse, smoking, or medication side effects.

Here is a list of some identified health problems related to PTSD:

- Greater frequency of medically explained and unexplained symptoms (Golding, 1994)

- More chronic physical limitations and a higher likelihood of a chronic medical condition (Ullman & Siegel, 1996)

- Increased risk for obesity (Felitti et al., 1998)

- Increased cardiovascular reactivity, disturbed sleep physiology, and adrenergic dysregulation (Friedman & Schnurr, 1995)

- For rape or incest survivors, more frequent gastrointestinal distress, recurrent headaches, dysuria, vaginal discharge, and chronic abdominal pain (Felitti, 1991; Rimsza, Berg, & Locke, 1988)

- For ex-POWs, higher rates of tuberculosis, cardiovascular disease, respiratory disease, and both gastric and duodenal ulcers (Eitinger, 1973)

- Increased occurrence of unspecified pain complaints and disorders (Wolfe et al., 1994)

- Enhanced thyroid functioning and altered hippocampal-pituitary-adrenal axis activity (Friedman & Schnurr, 1995)

Friedman and Schnurr (1995) have proposed that the pathophysiology associated with PTSD is directly implicated in the development of physical health problems, including excessive sympathetic reactivity, adrenergic dysregulation, endocrinological abnormalities, and a dysregulated immune system. They also hold that psychological states such as hostility, anger, and behavioral avoidance through alcohol or drug use have dire health consequences as well.

In addition to actual physical health problems and complications, exposure to traumatic stress sometimes leads to *somatization*, which is the occurrence of numerous bodily or physical complaints without an underlying disease process or physical illness to account for them. Symptoms reported under the heading of *somatization* are considered associated with psychological problems and, in a classic sense, are viewed as conversions of psychological difficulties or stress into physical complaints. Examples of somatization complaints are pain (head, neck, chest), diarrhea, nausea, erectile dysfunction, localized limb weakness, double vision, or fainting.

Neurological and Psychophysiological Consequences

Numerous investigators have observed alterations in the brain's neurochemistry in response to exposure to traumatic stressors. In general, the findings suggest that neurochemical alterations occur within specific locations in the brain, particularly those involved in arousal and memory. For example, investigators have found increased noradrenergic levels and sensitivity in the locus coeruleus, hypothalamus, hippocampus, amygdala, and cerebral cortex and increased nor-epinephrine levels in the locus coeruleus, which has been shown to interfere with memory consolidation for long-term memory storage.

Under conditions of acute stress, dopamine levels can be altered, and an observed increase in metabolism in conditions of acute stress can be seen. Specifically, an increase in dopamine enervation in the prefrontal cortex (PFC) is thought to play a role in a victim's sensitivity to future stress (Charney, Deutch, Southwick, & Krystal, 1995). Further, the PFC is implicated in working memory functioning and attention and is thought to contribute to hypervigilance because of its neural connectivity to the amygdala, the entorhinal cortex, and the locus coeruleus.

The comorbid presence of depression in those who suffer from PTSD may be connected to decreased monoamine oxydase inhibitor (MAOI) activity. In addition to depression, trauma victims sometimes complain of increased pain sensitivity or, conversely, a decrease in their overall pain tolerance levels. A decrease in endogenous opioids has been found that may account for these complaints.

Posttrauma alterations in brain chemistry have been implicated in actual anatomical or structural neural damage. The posttraumatic release of gluco-corticoids and other neurotransmitters has been shown to lead to actual damage to the hippocampus, which has been connected to verbal memory deficits (Bremner, Krystal, Southwick, & Charney, 1995).

Increased sympathetic nervous system response to acute stress and threat is considered a normal, expectable, and adaptive response. But researchers have found that once the stressor has dissipated or the threat has been reduced, sympathetic nervous system activation may continue, such as increased resting and reactive heart rate, increased resting and reactive blood pressure, increased resting muscle tension, altered electroencephalogram (EEG) alpha rhythms, and increased resting and reactive respiration (Blanchard, Kolb, Pallmeyer, & Gerardi, 1982; Dobbs & Wilson, 1960; Wenger, 1948). An individual may remain in a state of acute physiological activation as a response to a present stressor that is not actually present. Such high baseline levels of arousal are observable in the exaggerated startle reflex often seen in PTSD.

Sleep disturbance is a common problem found in those exposed to traumatic stressors. Friedman (1995) states that there can be a disruption in the sleep

Professional Alert

A patient's or client's comorbid sleep disturbance should be a priority in treatment. Sleep disturbance can lead to numerous complicating factors, such as irritability, suppressed immune functioning, and poor attention and concentration that may impede recovery and successful treatment. If necessary, seek a consult from a sleep expert or a sleep clinic.

architecture, with changes in the generally predictable patterns of sleep. Stage 1 and Stage 2 sleep are longer than typical. Delta rhythm sleep and rapid eye movement (REM) latency is decreased, while the overall REM percentage of sleep is increased.

Personality Changes

When one thinks of *personality*, the ideas of a stable, predictable, and consistent pattern of behavior and mental processes come to mind. A good working definition of *personality* is given by Allport (1961) as a dynamic organization, inside a person, of psychophysical systems that create the person's characteristic patterns of behavior, thoughts, and feelings.

So can a traumatic stressor and the development of PTSD really alter someone's personality? Research seems to suggest that this is possible. Ruth Williams (1999) states the perception that personality changes in those who suffer from PTSD is common among families and the victims themselves.

Sherwood, Funari, and Piekarski (1990) propose a connection between PTSD and certain abnormal or pathological personality styles: Passive-Aggressive Personality Disorder, Avoidant Personality Disorder, Schizoid Personality Disorder, and Borderline Personality Disorder. (For more on Borderline Personality Disorder and PTSD, see Chapter 8.) Hyer, Woods, and Boudewyns (1991) developed the concept of the *traumatic personality*, which is very similar to but less severe than Borderline Personality Disorder. Most notable are an individual's ambivalence and needy, but suspicious, behavior.

Talbert et al. (1993), using the Neuroticism, Extraversion, Openness–Personality Inventory (NEO–PI), a personality assessment instrument, found higher levels of the personality features of Neuroticism and low levels of Agreeableness. *Neuroticism* refers to a person's degree of emotionality and excitability. People high in neuroticism are more easily upset and considered more high strung. *Agreeableness* refers to an individual's social warmth and friendliness. Openness was also in the low range, which refers to a tendency to be open to new ideas and experiences and to be curious. Conscientiousness was average, which refers to a person's sense of responsibility, planfulness, and concern. The excitement-seeking feature of the Extraversion scale was very high. Finally, there were low levels of warmth, gregariousness, and positive emotions. However, it is important to note that this research was conducted with Vietnam veterans with chronic PTSD and histories of high levels of social and occupational dysfunction. Critics have argued that these individuals may have displayed these personality characteristics before they were traumatized.

In their work with severe burn victims, Roca, Spence, and Munster (1992) suggest the existence of what they call a *scar syndrome* to depict long-term changes in personality. Individuals with scar syndrome express less Openness, lower Extraversion, and higher Neuroticism.

Trauma victims have been known to struggle with their views of themselves after the trauma. The shame some experience after suffering from something they may view as their fault can be intense. Social rejection can complicate these issues. Feelings of self-hatred, self-loathing, lack of competence, and inner worth can result. They may feel unlovable, despicable, or weak. A trauma victim may escape with his or her life only to feel that he or she cannot rely on his or her abilities to cope successfully with the aftermath, including the PTSD symptoms themselves. Not being able to calm oneself down or to relax may have a demoralizing effect. They doubt their ability to cope with upcoming stress or strain in a successful and consistent manner. This can lead to isolation, withdrawal, failures to protect oneself in the future, and poor self-care.

Perhaps van der Kolk (1996) states it best:

> What is striking about the impact of trauma on character is that, regardless of pre-existing vulnerabilities, a previously well-functioning traumatized adult can experience an overall sharp deterioration in his or her functioning.

Cognitive and Neuropsychological Consequences

Deficits in learning and memory are commonly reported difficulties in PTSD sufferers. Poorer recall of both verbal and visual information as well as poorer verbal learning overall has been observed. Overall memory deficits in recalling specific memories from long-term memory and vague, convoluted recollections are also common, specifically for autobiographical information such as important events or dates. Memories for trauma can be exceptionally vivid or fragmented. Some researchers believe that traumatic memories are distinctly different from normal memories. Perceptual and emotional elements may be more prominent than with nontraumatic memories (Grinker & Spiegel, 1945; Kardiner, 1941; Terr, 1995). Environmental triggers do not typically evoke vivid images, sounds, smells, or other sensory experiences the way traumatic memories can and often do. Traumatic memories are thought to be recorded differently, in an almost dissociated state, typically unavailable to everyday consciousness in the form of a clear, integrated narrative or story. It is only with time that these memories begin to be organized in a coherent fashion. This is considered one of the tasks of recovery and treatment—to put the pieces of these fragmented memories together into a meaningful whole. (For more on this goal in treatment, see the discussion of narrative treatment in Chapter 15.)

Professional Alert

Keep in mind that over the last 15 to 20 years or so there has been a significant amount of controversy regarding the issue of recovered memories of trauma. This issue has typically arisen when a patient or client reports that he or she is remembering for the first time as an adult being physically or sexually abused as a child. Some professionals have claimed that these recollections are false memories that were created or implanted by a zealous therapist. Still others claim that recovered memories are legitimate. Samuel Knapp and Leon VandeCreek (2000, Table 1, p. 2) derived professional consensus statements for dealing with the issue of recovered memories in therapy: (1) Continuous memories of abuse are likely to be accurate; (2) "Some memories of past traumas can be lost and later recovered"; (3) "Memories from infancy are highly unreliable"; (4) "False memories of abuse can be created"; (5) Magnification and minimization may be better ways to conceptualize memory recall with some patients; (6) It is difficult to separate accurate memories if memory recovery techniques have been used. Repeated suggestion, confrontation, and highly suggestive techniques such as hypnosis can cause the creation of false memories. Ultimately, a clinician should maintain his or her standard of care and ethical boundaries when working with such issues and stay clear of controversial techniques. (For more on this issue, see Knapp and VandeCreek [2000].)

Trauma victims' memories seem biased toward the recall or remembering of traumatic information overall. That is, they tend to have better memories for trauma material than for nontrauma material despite poorer memory functioning overall as cited earlier.

In addition to exhibiting a biased memory system, trauma sufferers have been found to suffer from *attentional biases*. Research done with the Stroop Task has suggested that trauma victims are biased toward or fixated on traumatic stimuli in their environment. They are more vigilant or aware of such information relative to nontrauma information. The Stroop Task is a procedure that involves showing subjects words with differing emotional content in varying colors. The subjects are asked to name the color of the word and ignore what the actual word is or means. For trauma victims, response times to colored trauma-related words were slower or longer, indicating that the word itself or its meaning interfered with the simple color-naming task. Attention is more attentive, if you will, to trauma-related stimuli, thus interfering with the everyday, nontrauma related attention functioning.

Vasterling, Brailey, Constans, and Sutker (1998) found significant deficiencies in sustained attention, mental manipulation of information, initial acquisition of information, and retroactive interference in PTSD sufferers. They propose that symptoms of hyperarousal and frontal-cortical brain dysfunction contribute to these cognitive difficulties. In essence, PTSD sufferers have difficulty acquiring new information. They also have trouble remembering old information in part because they are distracted by newer, incoming information. They have trouble performing tasks in the immediate moment, such as mental arithmetic (math "inside one's head") and staying focused.

Hagh-Shenas, Goldstein, and Yule (1999) argue that these Stroop Task findings lend support to Mardi Horowitz's (1997) theory that traumatic information remains in active memory as incompletely processed material. It is too readily accessible and interferes with a patient's ongoing activity. This is also akin to the intrusiveness of traumatic memories, thoughts, images, and perceptions identified in the *DSM-IV-TR*. (For more about Horowitz's theory, see Chapter 5.)

Dissociation

Dissociation can be an integral part of posttraumatic reactions. There are numerous accounts of individual's "leaving their bodies" or "observing" the trauma from a "distance." For a more in-depth discussion of dissociative phenomenon in PTSD, see Chapter 5. For now, it is important to note that *dissociation* is defined as a disruption in the usually integrated functions of consciousness, memory, and identity; and altered perception of the environment that can occur during or after a traumatic stressor (peritraumatic dissociation). Examples of dissociative experiences or symptoms can take the form of an altered sense of time going faster or slowing down, feeling as if one is dreaming or that what is happening is not real, confusion, or disorientation.

Suicide and Self-Harm

According to the suicide expert Edwin Schneidman, suicide is often considered a response to the psychic pain of being completely overwhelmed and of feeling as if one has absolutely no resources. This description resonates with the phenomenology and subjective experience of PTSD sufferers. Are PTSD sufferers at greater risk for suicide than those diagnosed with the other mental disorders or the general population? To date there is no good available data to answer this question, yet some estimates have claimed as many as 150,000 Vietnam veterans have committed suicide since returning from the war. The experience of alienation, readjustment problems, disturbing images, feelings of unfairness, helplessness, unexpressed rage, and feeling dead are identified as common experiences associated with suicide risk in PTSD sufferers. Individuals that suffer from depression are commonly evaluated for suicidality. A safe approach for professionals would be to evaluate all clients and patients for suicidality, especially those presenting with PTSD.

Self-harm is defined to be the intentional or deliberate destruction of body-tissue through means of cutting, burning, or other means. It is not seen as an attempted suicide. Zlotnick, Mattia, and Zimmerman (1999) report 33 percent of PTSD sufferers in an outpatient psychiatric setting engaged in self-harm such as cutting or burning themselves. Higher rates in victims of childhood sexual abuse have also been identified. Some researchers and clinicians consider this behavior an attempt to bring one back to reality from a dissociative state through the experience of pain. Still others believe it is a deliberate attempt to induce a dissociative state in order to avoid other PTSD symptoms. van der Kolk (1996) reports that in children, self-harm in the form of head-banging, self-biting, self-burning, self-cutting, or self-starving can be considered attempts at dealing with dissociation or numbing.

Social and Relationship Consequences

The social or interpersonal costs of exposure to trauma can be immense. For example, scholars studying and writing about the development of Israeli society in response to the Holocaust have long proposed that the long-term effects of this collective trauma run deep in the very structure and fabric of modern Israeli society. Americans post-September 11, 2001 may feel a deep sense of change, such as lost innocence. War and disaster can lead to dislocation and a complete disruption of the structure and functioning of a community. Such large-scale changes are paralleled on the smaller scales of family and of the individual.

Posttraumatic Stress Disorder sufferers may struggle with fulfilling typical family roles. A father returning home from combat may struggle to provide financially. Family and other interpersonal realms of functioning may be impacted, for example, increased intimacy issues, increased intrafamilial irritability, increased fighting, decreased enjoyment of shared activities, increased marital discord, and increased intrafamilial and interpersonal violence.

Trust is an area of particular risk in PTSD sufferers who have been exposed to violence. Victims of interpersonal violence such as rape, child physical abuse, and torture may find themselves acutely attuned to even the slightest suggestion of dishonesty, betrayal, or distortion in their relationships. Such interpersonal suspicion is a hallmark of Borderline Personality Disorder, considered a consequence of childhood trauma by some professionals.

One's ability to be appropriately assertive may suffer. A PTSD sufferer may be inappropriately aggressive or hostile in social situations perceived as threatening. Interpersonal cruelty may result. Dysfunctional family patterns from childhood may be repeated in ways that replay victim-perpetrator dynamics. This is sometimes referred to as a *behavioral reenactment* (p.199) involving victimizing others. van der Kolk (1996) refers to this as the "compulsion to repeat the trauma" (p. 199). Lewis et al. (1988), for example, found that 12 out of 14 juveniles condemned to death for murder were brutally physically abused, and 5 were sodomized by relatives.

The issue of identifying with the perpetrator is complicated and goes well beyond the scope of this section. However, it has been recognized that some PTSD sufferers engage in increased attachment behavior in the face of danger. Attachment is an attempt by an individual to keep primary caregivers within close proximity in the face of danger or threat. In some cases, trauma victims have been known to form close relationships with those perpetrating the trauma. They may believe they are seeking protection from those who are perceived as in control or powerful. This identification with the traumatizing person or group has sometimes been called *Stockholm Syndrome*.

Other Consequences

The comorbid occurrence of other mental disorders is considered the rule rather than the exception. Generalized Anxiety Disorder and depression are considered some of the most common residual symptoms and disorders. (For more on co-occurring disorders, see Chapter 8.) Here is a quick list of common co-occurring disorders: Alcohol Abuse or Dependence (estimated 51 percent), Major Depressive Disorder (47.0 percent), Conduct Disorders (43.3 percent), Substance Abuse or Dependence (48.5 percent), Simple Phobia (29 percent), and Social phobias (28.4 percent).

Another consequence of survival guilt can occur when someone who survives a traumatic experience in which other people died feels intensely guilty for having lived. They may doubt their worthiness of survival. These feelings can trigger intense depressions. Pathological grief can occur as well in which someone is unable to come to terms with his or her loss of a loved one or friend. Finally, a phenomenon known as immersion can occur in which an individual with PTSD becomes almost obsessed with the trauma itself and anything thematically or directly related to it. A Vietnam veteran may become an obsessed collector of war memorabilia and an avid viewer of war films, for example.

The Course of PTSD

After the traumatic stressor has abated, the hurricane is over, the battle has ceased, or the fire has been put out by heroic firefighters, what does a person in the midst of a developing PTSD episode experience? Understanding the course of an illness is a vital aspect of medical science and clinical work. By course, we mean how a disorder behaves or looks over time. How do the symptoms emerge? What pattern do they take? Do some go away and then come back again? And so on.

The first phase of PTSD is referred to as the *acute phase*. This is different than Acute Stress Disorder as identified in the *DSM-IV-TR*. The acute phase of PTSD refers to the acuteness of the symptoms within a 3-month period posttrauma. If those symptoms continue longer than 3 months, the disorder is considered *chronic*. If the onset of symptoms occurs at least 6 months after the stressor, the disorder is considered *delayed*. Delayed onset PTSD is considered relatively uncommon.

Blank (1993) identifies six patterns of PTSD. Acute, chronic, and delayed have already been discussed. He identifies three more: *intermittent, residual,* and *reactivated. Intermittent* PTSD refers to an "on-again–off-again" type of PTSD, with symptoms being present at one point but not at another. *Residual* PTSD refers to subthreshold PTSD symptoms that may be triggered by subsequent stress in a diathesis-stress model. That is, the PTSD was not delayed per se, but rather not severe enough until subsequent stressors or other problems experienced by an individual allowed for these symptoms to blossom into a full-blown PTSD episode or syndrome. Finally, *reactivated* PTSD refers to a situation in which an original episode of PTSD that has either resolved itself or has been successfully treated becomes reactivated by some new stressor or trigger.

Posttraumatic Stress Disorder symptoms will typically begin to emerge in the immediate aftermath of the stressor or event. However, the exact pattern of symptom emergence in PTSD is considered independent of the acute pattern of response (McFarlane & Yehuda, 1996). That is, an individual may show one symptom pattern during an event and yet another in the more chronic phase of the disorder. The exception to this is the relationship that some researchers have shown between dissociative symptoms and later pathology and severity. (For more on dissociative symptoms, see the previous section on dissociative symptoms.)

The symptom picture or presentation can fluctuate over time. However, disordered arousal is considered a relatively prominent symptom that pervades the course of the disorder. Blank (1993) reports that the prominence of intrusive symptoms gradually decreases over a 2-year period poststressor, while avoidance symptoms increase over that same period. Still other researchers state that with severe PTSD, symptoms may be stable but exist in less intense forms over time, the intrusive and avoidance symptoms decreasing, and affective and arousal symptoms remaining relatively stable. Still other researchers have found that those individuals that begin to show severe distress very early in the acute phase of the disorder show a more stable and enduring symptom pattern over time. Ultimately, the variability of the course is shaped by features of the precipitating event (e.g., Judith Herman [1995] has argued that the consequences of child abuse are different than those following natural disaster), characteristics of the victim, and the nature of the recovery environment. In short, it is a complex diathesis-stress relationship.

Summary

To concisely cover the range of human responses to trauma is a nearly impossible task. Just as there are millions of traumatized individuals on the planet, there may exist millions of different types of reactions and subtle forms of PTSD. Remembering that a traumatized person is more than his or her symptoms or consequences is important while recognizing the regularities and expected outcomes that often do occur. Posttraumatic Stress Disorder has proven to be a model disorder of sorts for abnormal psychology and the study of mental disorders in that it is a truly biological, psychological, and social disorder with profound effects in all of these areas. Keep in mind that any one of these areas could have been covered in a chapter or an entire book devoted exclusively to each. Hopefully, Chapter 3 has provided those interested with a good overview and start.

Quick Review

- Surviving trauma and responding effectively to future stressors is a vital aspect of human functioning.

- A traumatic stressor cannot be adequately defined without considering the subjective interpretation of the target event(s).

- Posttraumatic Stress Disorder is only one of many possible reactions to exposure to a traumatic stressor; others are Acute Stress Disorder, depression, or no disorder at all.

- The *DSM-IV-TR* groups abnormal posttraumatic reactions into three large categories: reexperiencing phenomenon, avoidance phenomenon, and arousal phenomenon.

- Other consequences of exposure to a traumatic stressor include physical health problems, memory problems, attention difficulties, personality problems, social functioning deficits, suicidal or self-harm difficulties, dissociative responses, and even obsessive or immersion experiences.

References

Allport, G. W. (1961). *Pattern and growth in personality*. New York: Holt, Rinehart, and Winston.

American Psychiatric Association. (2000). *Diagnostic and Statistical Manual of Mental Disorders* (4th ed., text revision). Washington, DC: Author.

Blanchard, E. B., Kolb, L. C., Pallmeyer, T. P., & Gerardi, R. J. (1982). A psychophysiological study of Post Traumatic Stress Disorder in Vietnam veterans. *Psychiatric Quarterly, 54,* 220–229.

Blank, A. S., Jr. (1993). Vet centers: A new paradigm in delivery of services for victims and survivors of traumatic stress. In J. P. Wilson & B. Raphael (Eds.), *International handbook of traumatic stress syndromes* (pp. 915–923). New York: Plenum Press.

Bremner, J. D., Krystal, J. H., Southwick, S. M., & Charney, D. S. (1995). Functional neuroanatomical correlates of the effects of stress on memory. *Journal of Traumatic Stress, 8,* 527–553.

Brewin, C. R., Andrews, B., Rose, S., & Kirk, M. (1999). Acute Stress Disorder and Posttraumatic Stress Disorder in victims of violent crime. *American Journal of Psychiatry, 156,* 360–366.

Brown, R., & Kulik, J. (1977). Flashbulb memories. *Cognition, 5,* 73–99.

Charney, D. S., Deutch, A. Y., Southwick, S. M., & Krystal, J. H. (1995). Neural circuits and mechanisms of Post-Traumatic Stress Disorder. In M. J. Friedman, D. S. Charney, & A. Y. Deutch (Eds.), *Neurobiological and clinical consequences of stress: From normal adaptation to Post-Traumatic Stress Disorder* (pp. 271–287). Philadelphia: Lippincott, Williams, & Wilkins.

de Silva, P., & Marks, M. (1999). Intrusive thinking in Post-Traumatic Stress Disorder. In W. Yule (Ed.), *Post-Traumatic Stress Disorders: Concepts and therapy* (pp. 161–175). New York: Wiley.

Dobbs, D., & Wilson, W. P. (1960). Observations on persistence of war neurosis. *Disorders of the Nervous System, 21,* 40–46.

Eitinger, L. (1973). A follow-up study of the Norwegian concentration camp survivors' mortality and morbidity. *Israel Annals of Psychiatry & Related Disciplines, 11,* 199–209.

Felliti, V. J. (1991). Long-term medical consequences of incest, rape, and molestation. *Southern Medical Journal, 83,* 328–331.

Felliti, V. J., Anda, R. F., Nordenberg, D., Williamson, D. F., Spitz, A. M., Edwards, V., Koss, M. P., et al. (1998). Relationship of childhood abuse and household dysfunction to many of the leading causes of death in adults: The Adverse Childhood Experiences (ACE) Study. *American Journal of Preventive Medicine, 14,* 245–258.

Friedman, M. J. (1995). Biological approaches to the diagnosis and treatment of Post-Traumatic Stress Disorder. In G. S. Everly & J. M. Lating (Eds.), *Psychotraumatology: Key papers and core concepts in post-traumatic stress* (pp. 171–194). New York: Plenum Press.

Friedman, M. J., & Schnurr, P. P. (1995). The relationship between trauma, Post-Traumatic Stress Disorder, and physical health. In M. J. Friedman, D. S. Charney, & A. Y. Deutch (Eds.), *Neurobiological and clinical consequences of stress: From normal adaptation to Post-Traumatic Stress Disorder* (pp. 507–524). Philadelphia: Lippincott, Williams, & Wilkins.

Grinker, R. R., & Spiegel, J. P. (1945). *Men under stress.* Philadelphia: Blakiston.

Golding, J. M. (1994). Sexual assault history and physical health in randomly selected Los Angeles women. *Health Psychology, 13,* 130–138.

Hagh-Shenas, H., Goldstein, L., & Yule, W. (1999). Psychobiology of Post-Traumatic Stress Disorder. In W. Yule (Ed.), *Post-Traumatic Stress Disorders: Concepts and therapy* (pp. 139–160). New York: Wiley.

Herman, J. L. (1995). Complex PTSD: A syndrome in survivors of prolonged and repeated trauma. In G. S. Everly & J. M. Lating (Eds.), *Psychotraumatology: Key papers and core concepts in post-traumatic stress* (pp. 87–100). New York: Plenum Press.

Horowitz, M. J. (1997). *Stress response syndromes: PTSD, grief and adjustment disorders* (3rd ed.). Lanham, MD: Jason Aronson.

Hyer, L., Woods, M. G., & Boudewyns, P. A. (1991). A three tier evaluation of PTSD among Vietnam combat veterans. *Journal of Traumatic Stress, 4,* 165–194.

Kardiner, A. (1941). *The traumatic neuroses of war.* New York: National Research Council.

Knapp, S., & VandeCreek, L. (2000). Recovered memories of childhood abuse: Is there an underlying professional consensus? *Professional Psychology: Research and Practice, 31,* 365–371.

Lewis, D. O., Pincus, J. H., Bard, B., Richardson, E., et al. (1988). Neuropsychiatric, psychoeducational, and family characteristics of 14 juveniles condemned to death in the United States. *American Journal of Psychiatry, 145,* 584–589.

Lindley, S. E., Carlson, E. B., & Sheikh, J. (2000). Psychotic symptoms in Posttraumatic Stress Disorder. *CNS Spectrums, 5,* 52–58.

McFarlane, A. C., & Yehuda, R. A. (1996). Resilience, vulnerability, and the course of posttraumatic reactions. In B. A. van der Kolk, A. C. McFarlane, & L. Weisaeth (Eds.), *Traumatic stress: The effects of overwhelming experience on mind, body, and society* (pp. 155–181). New York: Guilford Press.

Pagel, J.F. (2000). Nightmares and disorders of dreaming [Electronic Version]. *American Family Physician, 61/7,* 2037-2042.

Rimsza, M. E., Berg, R. A., & Locke, C. (1988). Sexual Abuse: Somatic and emotional reactions. *Child Abuse & Neglect, 12,* 201–208.

Roca, R. P., Spence, R. J., & Munster, A. M. (1992). Posttraumatic adaptation and distress among adult burn survivors. *American Journal of Psychiatry, 149,* 1234–1238.

Salkovskis, P. M. (1990). Obsessions, compulsions, and intrusive cognitions. In David F. Peck & Colin M. Shapiro (Eds.), *Measuring human problems: A practical guide* (pp. 91–118). Oxford, England: Wiley.

Schneidman, E. S. (1981). A psychological theory of suicide. *Suicide and Life-Threatening Behavior, 11,* 221–231.

Shalev, A. Y. (1996). Stress vs. traumatic stress: From acute homeostatic reactions to chronic psychopathology. In B. A. van der Kolk, A. C. McFarlane, & L. Weisaeth (Eds.), *Traumatic stress: The effects of overwhelming experience on mind, body, and society* (pp. 77–101). New York: Guilford Press.

Sherwood, R. J., Funari, D. J., & Piekarski, A. M. (1990). Adapted character styles of Vietnam veterans with Posttraumatic Stress Disorder. *Psychological Reports, 66,* 623–631.

Siegel, A. (2003). *A mini-course for clinicians and trauma workers on posttraumatic nightmares.* The Association for the Study of Dreams. Retrieved from http://www.asdreams.org.

Slaikeu, K. A. (1990). *Crisis intervention: A handbook for practice and research* (2nd ed.). Needham Heights, MA: Allyn & Bacon.

Talbert, F. S., Braswell, L. C., Albrecht, J. W., Hyer, L. A., et al. (1993). NEO–PI profiles in PTSD as a function of trauma level. *Journal of Clinical Psychology, 49,* 663–669.

Terr, L. (1990). *Too scared to cry: Psychic trauma in childhood.* New York: Harper & Row.

Terr, L. C. (1995). Childhood traumas: An outline and overview. In G. S. Everly, Jr. & J. M. Lating (Eds.), *Psychotraumatology: Key papers and core concepts in post-traumatic stress* (pp. 301–320). New York: Plenum Press.

Ullman, S. E., & Siegel, J. M. (1996). Traumatic events and physical health in a community sample. *Journal of Traumatic Stress, 9,* 703–719.

van der Kolk, B. A. (1996). The complexity of adaptation to trauma: Self-regulation, stimulus discrimination, and characterological development. In B. A. van der Kolk, A. C. McFarlane, & L. Weisaeth (Eds.), *Traumatic stress: The effects of overwhelming experience on mind, body, and society* (pp. 182–213). New York: Guilford Press.

Vasterling, J. J., Brailey, K., Constans, J. I., & Sutker, P. B. (1998). Attention and memory dysfunction in Posttraumatic Stress Disorder. *Neuropsychology, 12,* 125–133.

Wenger, M. A. (1948). Studies of autonomic balance in army air forces personnel. *Comparative Psychology Monographs, 19.*

Williams, R. M. (1999). Personality and Post-Traumatic Stress Disorder. In W. Yule, William (Ed.), *Post-Traumatic Stress Disorders: Concepts and therapy* (pp. 92–115). Chichester, England: Wiley.

Wolfe, J., Schnurr, P. P., Brown, P. J., & Furey, J. (1994). Posttraumatic stress disorder and war-zone exposure as correlates of perceived health in female Vietnam war veterans. *Journal of Consulting and Clinical Psychology, 62,* 1235–1240.

Yule, W. (Ed.). (1999). *Post-Traumatic Stress Disorders: Concepts and therapy.* Chichester, England: Wiley.

Yule, W., Williams, R., & Joseph, S. (1999). Post-Traumatic Stress Disorders in adults. In William Yule (Ed.), *Post-Traumatic Stress Disorders: Concepts and therapy* (pp. 1–24). Chichester, England: Wiley.

Zlotnick, C., Mattia, J. I., & Zimmerman, M. (1999). Clinical correlates of self-mutilation in a sample of general psychiatric patients. *Journal of Nervous and Mental Disease, 187,* 296–301.

CHAPTER 4

Exposure to Trauma and Risk for Posttraumatic Stress Disorder

The world is getting to be such a dangerous place, a man is lucky to get out alive.

—W. C. Fields

Posttraumatic stress disorder is one of many reactions to danger. Traumatic events signal danger to life, limb, and even one's sanity. Just how dangerous is our world? How risky is it to just wake up in the morning? Accidents represent the fifth leading cause of death in the United States, ahead of diabetes, influenza, pneumonia, and Alzheimer's disease, according to the National Center for Health Statistics. What about violence? Violence, including war, is one the most common sources of traumatic stress.

There are many dangerous places in the world. The United States Department of State issues travel advisories for dangerous countries. The United States Department of Justice reports that in 2003 for every 1,000 persons aged 12 or older, there occurred one rape or sexual assault, one assault with injury, and two robberies. There occurred about 6 murder victims per 100,000 persons in 2002, and in 2003 there were 5.4 million crimes of violence. With all this danger, the risk for exposure to traumatic stressors is real, and so is the risk for PTSD.

Personally, I have some experience in one region that many people consider extremely dangerous—the Middle East. I have visited family and friends in Israel several times, each time witnessing combat, suicide bombings, bomb threats, and other dangerous situations. My friends and family in the United States always treat me like I am crazy for going back there. Once there, however, an interesting thing happens—you adjust, as have the people who live there. I have heard many times from Israelis and Palestinians alike, "There is no such thing as security." Yet

- In 2000, 57,000 children or adolescents were murdered worldwide.
- Collective violence by groups, states, or nations have claimed 191 million victims in the twentieth century.
- There were 300,000 direct victims of violence in 2000.
- In high-income countries, 1 in 100,000 people are victims of violent death.
- In low- and middle-income countries, 6.2 in 100,000 people are victims of violent death.
- Africa has the highest violent death risk, with 32 out of 100,000 people being a victim of a violent death.
- The percentage of female murder victims killed by their husbands or boyfriends is 40 to 70 percent.
- In 2000, 199,000 youth were murdered globally.
- In 2000, 565 children or adolescents were killed per day.

they continue with their day-to-day lives, acting relatively immune on a moment-by-moment basis to the threat around them. They acknowledge the danger but keep on living. In many ways, the daily stress they encounter is not necessarily traumatic. One would think that everyone would be walking around with PTSD, but that simply is not the case. This speaks directly to the complexity of PTSD and who develops it after being exposed to traumatic events. If war, suicide bombings, missile attacks, and combat are not traumatic, then what is?

What Exactly Is a Traumatic Stressor?

The truth is that even though we are all exposed to high levels of stress, including some of us who have been exposed to war, combat, and related stressors that would be defined as *traumatic stressors*, research has continued to show that most individuals exposed to stressors that would meet the definition of a *traumatic stressor* fail to develop PTSD, much like the citizens of Israel and Palestine. According to Breslau, Andreski, Federman, and Anthony (1998) only 9 percent of those exposed to traumatic stressors develop PTSD. It was once widely held that a direct linear relationship between the intensity of a stressor and symptom development existed. That is, if you were exposed to a traumatic stressor, you would develop PTSD. This is referred to as the *dose-response model;* the more intense a stressor, the more likely PTSD will develop. Research has not supported this strict direct correlation (McNally, 2003). From this we can conclude that a traumatic stressor alone is necessary but not sufficient for PTSD to develop. Before we get into the other necessary components, let's take a closer look at this traumatic stressor issue.

The following are the most common types of traumatic stressors related to PTSD (*DSM-III-R*; National Center for PTSD):

In general:

Threats to one's life or physical integrity

A serious threat or harm to one's children, spouse, relative, or close friend

Sudden destruction of one's home or community

Seeing another person injured or killed due to physical violence

For Men:	*For Women:*
Combat exposure	Rape
Rape	Sexual molestation
Childhood neglect	Physical attack
Childhood physical abuse	Being threatened with a weapon
	Childhood physical abuse

Defining a traumatic stressor is tricky. Certainly not all severe stressors are traumatic. The *DSM-IV-TR* defines a *traumatic stressor* in its diagnostic Criteria A for PSTD as "an event or events that involve actual or threatened death or serious injury, or a threat to the physical integrity of self or others" (p. 467).

Criterion A indicates that an individual can experience, witness, or be confronted with such a stressor in order to meet this criterion. Criteria A accounts for the *subjective element* of definition of a *traumatic stressor*. Criteria A states that in order for a stressor to qualify for traumatic status, it not only needs to fit with the previous criteria but must also involve "[a] person's response [that] involved fear, helplessness, or horror" (p. 467).

Researchers have also found that in addition to these characteristics, stressors that are very sudden, very intense, very dangerous, and perceived as uncontrollable and unpredictable are likely to be experienced as traumatic.

Eve Carlson and Constance Dalenberg (2000) propose three defining features that classify a stressor as traumatic: *negative valence, lack of controllability,* and *suddenness.* Carlson and Dalenberg propose that restricting the definition of a *traumatic stressor* to only those events that involve injury or death excludes other traumatic stressors, such as losing one's home due to a flood, which may not necessarily lead to fears of death or injury but is nonetheless traumatic. In order to capture the traumatizing nature of the traumatic stressor, it is vital to get inside the mind and experience of a traumatized individual. How did he or she psychologically experience the event in question?

An event with *negative valence* is an event that has negative consequences. Events with severe negative consequences can result in death or serious injury, and events with less negative valence can involve lesser degrees of pain or discomfort. Carlson and Dalenberg (2000) propose that the negative valence of an event can be the result of physical pain, emotional pain, or because of the perception that an event is likely to cause physical pain, injury, or emotional pain or death. It is important to point out their inclusion of emotionally painful events in their work. Emotional pain can produce extreme fear and activate issues related to one's sense of self or psychic integrity. A man who has always known himself to be a physically fit professional athlete could be traumatized by news that he may never walk again after a car accident. Carlson and Dalenberg state it best: "the perception of the event is more important that the actual danger associated with the event" (p. 8).

Oftentimes following a traumatic event, we find ourselves thinking or saying, "If only I had done . . ." or "I should have done. . . ." This is an excellent example of how important the perceived *controllability* of an event is in determining our reaction and eventual adjustment. These sorts of questions represent post hoc attempts to control an event, at least psychologically, and to give both a sense of controllability in the aftermath and in potential future events of the same nature. In essence, the more uncontrollable an event is experienced as, the more likely it will be experienced as traumatic. Ultimately, control over one's life and limb is a critical component to the perception of trauma.

Finally, the time frame of a stressor plays a key role in the perception of trauma. Events that are more imminent are more stressful. This is in part because the amount of time one may need to muster an effective response is smaller, and thus the negative valence of the event is higher as a consequence (Carlson & Dalenberg, 2000). If you know that a stressor is coming, you can prepare for it, you can experience it in smaller doses if you will. This is one of the key components of stress inoculation therapy (SIT; for more on SIT, see Chapter 12). One can see that the negativity, controllability, and suddenness of an event are all interrelated and work together to either produce a traumatic experience or not.

Why Do Some Develop PTSD and Some Do Not?

Figuring out why some people develop PTSD and some do not after exposure to a traumatic stressor requires an understanding of the *risk factors*. Is it personality? Could it be genetic? Why do some people seem to be traumatized over and over again? Some seemingly trivial events have led to PTSD. When this is the case, personal vulnerability and risk factors become tantamount. A stressor alone is rarely enough to produce psychopathology.

There are three large categories of risk factors, pretrauma, peritraumatic, and posttraumatic. It is also important to keep in mind that the risk factor issue is not as clear-cut as it might at first seem. Certainly, if someone possesses risk factors, he or she would be considered more likely to develop PTSD. But what if someone has 2, 3, or 10 risk factors? Is he or she 2 times or 10 times more likely to develop PTSD? The answer is we don't know. The risk factor issue is not a simple additive model, with the more risk factors you have adding up to PTSD. This may be the case, and it does make sense logically and even clinically. A clinician or professional working in prevention might want to operate on this assumption. But for now, most research looks at the various risk factors in isolation, and each should be considered an individual risk factor in and of itself.

Exposure Risk

Some people are exposed to traumatic stressors more than others. Certainly, a soldier serving combat is at a higher risk than a gardener. Being at a higher risk for exposure to a traumatic stressor is an obvious but sometimes overlooked risk factor. The lifetime prevalence of exposure to a traumatic stressor or event in a general population sample has been estimated to be 39.1 percent (Breslau, Davis, Andreski, Federman, & Anthony, 1998). Almost 40 percent of us have been exposed.

Exposure risk can be broken down into more specific categories. Exposure rates for men are higher than for women in general, but exposure rates to sexual violence are higher for women, and the lifetime prevalence of PTSD is higher in women. Persons with lower education levels, especially those who have not finished high school, have higher exposure rates than college graduates.

The most dangerous jobs, according to a CNN poll, include the following: timber cutters, fishers, pilots and navigators, structural metal workers, driver-sales workers, roofers, electric power installers, farm workers, construction laborers, and truck drivers. The literature, however, shows no research has been done on PTSD in many of these occupations, with the exception of motor vehicle accident–related PTSD. One study done with construction workers exposed to a fatal work accident showed that 26.8 percent of 41 subjects met criteria for PTSD postaccident (Hu, Liang, Hu, Long, & Ge, 1999).

According to Haslam and Mallon (2003), emergency workers are at high risk for developing PTSD. Emergency workers are exposed to traumatic stressors on a daily or weekly basis. Consider Table 4.1, adapted from Figley (1995).

Clohessy and Ehlers (1999) found that 21 percent of ambulance drivers in their study of 56 persons met criteria for PTSD. Robinson, Sigman, and Wilson (1997) found that 13 percent of a sample of 100 suburban police officers met criteria for PTSD. A study done with resident physicians found that 13 percent met criteria for PTSD. Eriksson, van de Kemp, Gorsuch, Hoke, and Foy (2001) found that approximately 30 percent of international relief and development workers showed significant symptoms of PTSD. Ultimately, one can conclude from these studies that certain occupations put participants at increased risk for PTSD, above the expected prevalence rates ranging from 1 to 14 percent in the *DSM-IV*.

TABLE 4.1

Secondary Traumatic Stress Exposure

Occupation	Personal direct exposure to life-threatening trauma	Body handling	Direct or indirect secondary exposure
Firefighters	Yes	Yes	Weekly–Daily
Paramedics	Yes	Yes	Daily
Law enforcement officers	Yes	Yes	Daily
Rescue workers	Yes	Yes	Daily

Are some people more exposed to violence than others? A history of criminal victimization is a significant risk factor for subsequent victimization (Koss & Dinero, 1989; Norris & Kaniasty, 1992; Sorenson, Siegel, Golding, & Stein, 1991; Steketee & Foa, 1987; Wyatt, Guthrie, & Notgrass, 1992).

The personality trait of sensation seeking has been implicated in increased exposure risk. Zuckerman et al. (1979) define *sensation seeking* as the need for varied, novel, and complex sensations and experiences and the willingness to take physical and social risk for such experiences. This has been associated with Substance Abuse, which itself is an exposure risk factor. The personality traits of Extroversion and Neuroticism are exposure risk factors (Breslau, Davis, & Andreski, 1995). McNally (2003) states, "outgoing, stress prone people were exposed to trauma more often than retiring, calm people."

An interesting question has been researched asking whether having a pre-existing mental disorder increases one's risk for exposure to traumatic stressors or events. Research has shown that someone with a prior history of major depression and illicit drug use is at a higher risk for exposure to traumatic stressors.

Finally, Dohrenwend (1998) and McNally (2003) report that being African American, having a family history of psychiatric illness, having a childhood history of conduct problems, having a history of prior traumatic event exposure, having a history of Major Depression, and having a history of drug or Alcohol Abuse puts someone at greater risk for exposure. This issue of race has been found to be significant with respect to combat exposure. Minority status has been shown to be a risk for combat and war exposure and thus higher risk for PTSD (Green, Grace, Lindy & Leonard, 1990; MacDonald, Chamberlain, & Long, 1997).

Individual Risk Factors for PTSD

Ozer, Best, Lipsey, and Weiss (2003) reviewed 23 studies that showed a small but significant relationship between history of prior trauma and PTSD symptoms or diagnosis. This relationship differed significantly depending on the type of stressor: When the trauma was noncombat, interpersonal violence such as assault, rape, or domestic violence was more strongly related to future PTSD than combat exposure was.

People with a lifetime history of PTSD typically have at least one other mental disorder (Breslau, Davis, et al., 1998). Specifically, preexisting Major Depression and any Anxiety Disorder increase the risk for PTSD following exposure to a traumatic event.

Prior adjustment problems including previous mental health treatment, pretrauma emotional problems, pretrauma Anxiety Disorder or affective disorders, and Antisocial Personality Disorder prior to military service are risk factors (Ozer et al. 2003). Further, having prior adjustment problems was more related to PTSD when the trauma was noncombat interpersonal violence or accident than combat exposure and when the adjustment problems were closer in time to the trauma. In the same review, psychopathology in family of origin in 9 studies showed a relationship to future PTSD, especially with noncombat interpersonal violence.

Are people who suffer from serious physical health problems, injuries, or terminal illness at risk for PTSD? Some research suggests that the rates of PTSD in persons with specific illnesses are higher than general rates. Kelly et al. (1998) report that 30 percent of 61 men informed that they were human immunodeficiency virus (HIV) positive met criteria for PTSD in response to their diagnosis. That is more than twice the rate prevalence rate in the *DSM-IV*. In 100 post-myocardial infarction patients, 16 percent were suffering from PTSD (Kutz, Shabtai, Solomon, & Neumann, 1994). In women with breast cancer studied by Leiderman-Cerniglia (2002), 9 to 14 percent of women with cancer met criteria for PTSD. In 109 survivors of serious physical injury requiring hospitalization, 32 percent met criteria for high levels of PTSD (Richmond & Kauder, 2000).

Pretrauma personality features such as certain types of personal schemas about the self, others, or the world have been implicated in the course of PTSD. Elliot and Lassen (1997) identified inflexible schemas, and Riggs and Foa (1993) identified overvalued schematic representations, which are rigid beliefs in one's absolute safety of the world and the invulnerability of the self. There are negative pretrauma schemas (Beck, Rush, Shaw, & Emery, 1979). Mardi Horowitz (2004) implicates pretrauma personality types with the basic idea that people with balanced pretrauma schemas of world, self, and others that are not too overvalued and not too negative will go through a healthier readjustment process. After an initial period of disruption and posttraumatic symptomology, there is a normative and gradual assimilation of trauma-related information and ultimate resolution without development of PTSD. Overvalued schemas lead to vulnerability and more posttraumatic distress.

The personality factors of Extroversion and Neuroticism as measured by the Eysenck Personality Inventory have been found to be relevant premorbid factors in which PTSD groups are higher in Neuroticism and lower in Extroversion than non-PTSD individuals (McFarlane, 1988).

Studies done with the Minnesota Multiphasic Personality Inventory have found that characteristics of psychopathic deviancy, and hypochondriasis, were relevant premorbid factors measured many years before the occurrence of a traumatic stressor(s) (Schnurr, Friedman, & Rosenberg, 1993).

In research looking at the genetic risk, PTSD is more prevalent in monozygotic twins versus dizygotic twins (Skre et al., 1993). True and Lyons (1999) report that 13 to 30 percent of the variance in reexperiencing symptoms, 30 to 34 percent in avoidance symptoms, and 28 to 32 percent in arousal symptoms can be accounted for by genetics.

Perhaps some people have a psychobiological vulnerability to PTSD. Carlson and Dalenberg (2000) propose the existence of a nongenetic biological predisposition that determines varied responses to the same stressor. Biological changes in response to prior trauma can shape responses to future traumas. Vaiva et al. (2004) found that individuals with low plasma–gamma-aminobutyric acid levels involved in the regulation of the intensity and the duration of the central hyperadrenergic response in times of high stress were more prone to PTSD following exposure to a traumatic stressor.

Carlson and Dalenberg (2000) report that children at earlier stages of development will have more extreme responses because of their lack of coping resources. The emotional developmental stage can be important; has the child has formed a secure attachment. Insecure attachment is a risk factor, especially if the trauma involves an attachment figure. Better cognitive, behavioral, and social skills can enable better coping, social support acquisition, and control and help prevent future trauma through better planning and avoidance. Traumatic experiences earlier on have a more pervasive impact, and symptoms can interfere with healthy development, thus having a twofold effect on future trauma reactions.

Group Risk Factors

Are there certain groups or sociological categories that being a member of puts one at an increased risk for PTSD? Norris et al. (2003) hypothesized that in poor countries, factors such as physically demanding and dangerous work; inferior and overcrowded housing; extreme subsistence hardship; and high power differentials between rich and poor, women and men, and adults and children put people in these countries at a higher risk for exposure to traumatic bereavement, life-threatening accidents, interpersonal violence, and, thus, higher rates of PTSD. In their study of four cities in Mexico, lifetime prevalence of exposure was 76 percent, and prevalence of PTSD was 11.2 percent. Risk for PTSD was highest in the poorest city, persons of lower socioeconomic status (SES), and women. Although still within the range of 1 to 14 percent from the *DSM-IV*, subjects in this study were at the higher end of this range. Davidson, Hughes, Blazer, and George (1991) sampled approximately 3,000 subjects in one community and found that of those sampled who had PTSD-related symptoms, they had higher rates of job instability and parental poverty.

Although men are exposed to traumatic stressors overall more often, women are more likely than men to develop PTSD (Kessler et al., 1995). Women are more likely to develop chronic forms of the disorder as well (Breslau, Kessler, et al., 1998). Different hypotheses as to why this is the case have been put forward with inconclusive empirical results: greater physiological reactivity in women; different levels of interpersonal violence in women; higher levels of poverty, discrimination, and oppression in women (Breslau, Kessler, et al., 1998; Shalev, Orr, & Pitman, 1993; Wolfe & Kimerling, 1997).

Being a victim of violence and crime increases one's chance of PTSD (Norris, 1992; Kilpatrick et al., 1989; Resnick et al., 1993). A history of rape is one of the highest risk factors of PTSD (Breslau, Davis, Andreski, & Peterson, 1991; Resnick et al., 1993). Elevated risk for PTSD can vary with the type of crime to which one is exposed. In essence, however, a victim's perception that his or her life is threatened or that he or she is actually injured is associated with increased risk (Kilpatrick et al., 1989).

Finally, Brewin, Andrews, and Valentine (2000) conducted a meta-analysis of risk factors and found that female gender, greater social disadvantage, greater educational disadvantage, greater intellectual disadvantage, psychiatric history, and various types of personal adversity are all significant risk factors. These investigators note, however, that the effect size for each of these is relatively low when compared to factors happening during or immediately after the trauma, such as trauma severity, lack of social support, and additional life stress posttrauma.

Peritraumatic Risk Factors

How one acts, thinks, and feels during an actual traumatic event have been found critical in predicting the future development of PTSD. When dissociative symptoms emerge or a person has a dissociative experience during the actual event, known as *peritraumatic dissociation*, the risk of future PTSD development is higher (Candel & Merckelbach, 2004). Ozer et al. (2003) state that peritraumatic dissociation is the strongest predictor of future PTSD symptoms.

Research has also found that the degree to which someone perceives his or her life to be at risk during the actual stressor is a peritraumatic risk factor. Ozer et al. (2003) reviewed 12 studies showing a significant and strong relationship between perceived life threat and future PTSD diagnosis or symptoms.

In a review of studies looking at peritraumatic emotional responses, Ozer et al. (2003) found that persons who report having very intense negative emotional responses during or immediately after a traumatic event had higher levels of PTSD symptoms. The emotions reported in the studies were fear, helplessness, horror, guilt, and shame.

Posttrauma Risk Factors

O'Brien and Hughes (1991) propose that there is a general agreement that events following exposure to a traumatic stressor play a significant role in determining whether someone develops PTSD or PTSD-related symptoms.

Many Vietnam veterans report that when they came home from the war they encountered a hostile and unwelcoming environment. This report and similar observations by people have in part spurred mobilizations to be more support-ive of United States military personnel in subsequent conflicts. Research has shown that negative homecoming experiences were found to be more associated with PTSD than positive homecoming experiences (Butler et al., 1988). The same finding was made with British soldiers returning home from the Falkland Islands (O'Brien & Hughes, 1991).

Posttraumatic Stress Disorder has been repeatedly associated with lower lev-els of perceived social support in both civilian and veteran populations (Barrett & Mizes, 1988; Bowler, Mergler, Huel, & Cone, 1994; Solomon, Mikulincer, & Avitzur, 1988). Ozer et al. (2003) state that perceived social support is one of the strongest predictors.

According to McFarlane and Yehuda (1996), how one adapts to disruption of the acute and chronic symptoms of PTSD is a risk factor: "The ability to toler-ate suffering is therefore a critical determinant of long-term adaptation" (p. 157). The ability to tolerate fear and loss and to effectively cope with the demoraliza-tion of hyperarousal and the progressive disruption of the individual's neurobi-ological functioning play an increasing role in understanding the nature and course of PTSD above and beyond the original traumatizing event or events.

Summary

Who develops PTSD after being exposed is a complex issue. The perception of the stressor or event is one critical factor. People can look at the same stressor and have different reactions. That is the challenging and great thing about the human mind. Individual differences play a large role. Even something as traumatizing as war does not produce PTSD in everyone that is exposed. There are three different types of risk factors; pretrauma risk factors, peritraumatic risk factors, and posttrauma risk factors. Each of these types has been shown to be very important in the *how, why,* and *whom* questions of PTSD.

Quick Review

- Breslau, Andreski, Federman, and Anthony (1998) report that only 9 per-cent of those exposed to traumatic stressors develop PTSD, and a traumatic stressor alone is necessary but not sufficient for PTSD to develop.

- The *DSM-IV-TR* defines a *traumatic stressor* in its diagnostic Criteria A for Posttraumatic Stress Disorder as an event or events that involve actual or threatened death or serious injury or a threat to the physical integrity of self or others.

- The most common types of traumatic stressors related to PTSD are threats to one's life or physical integrity; a serious threat or harm to one's children, spouse, relative, or close friend; sudden destruction of one's home or community; and seeing another person injured or killed due to physical violence

- Three defining features that classify a stressor as traumatic are *negative valence, lack of controllability,* and *suddenness.*

- There are three large categories of risk factors: pretrauma, peritraumatic, and posttraumatic.

- Some people are exposed to traumatic stressors more than others, which is known as *exposure risk.*

- Personality characteristics, history of trauma, mental health history, psychobiology, and genetics are good examples of pretrauma risk factors.

- Some group factors put people at higher risk for PTSD, such as being a woman and being poor.

- Peritraumatic reactions involving dissociation and intense emotions are risk factors.

- Posttraumatic social support and the ability to cope with the symptoms of PTSD themselves are risk factors.

References

American Psychiatric Association (1987). *Diagnostic and Statistical Manual of Mental Disorders* (3rd ed., revised). Washington, DC: Author.

American Psychiatric Association. (2000). *Diagnostic and Statistical Manual of Mental Disorders* (4th ed., text revision). Washington, DC: Author.

Barrett, T. W., & Mizes, J. S. (1988). Combat level and social support in the development of Posttraumatic Stress Disorder in Vietnam veterans. *Behavior Modification, 12,* 100–115.

Beck, A., Rush, J., Shaw, B., & Emery, G. (1979). *Cognitive therapy of depression.* New York: Guilford.

Bowler, R. M., Mergler, D., Huel, G., & Cone, J. E. (1994). Psychological, psychosocial, and psychophysiological sequelae in a community affected by a railroad chemical disaster. *Journal of Traumatic Stress, 7,* 601–624.

Breslau, N., Davis, G. C., & Andreski, P. (1995). Risk factors for PTSD-related traumatic events: A prospective analysis. *American Journal of Psychiatry, 152,* 529–535.

Breslau, N., Davis, G., Andreski, P., Federman, B., & Anthony, J. C. (1998). Epidemiological findings on Posttraumatic Stress Disorder and co-morbid disorders in the general population. In B. P. Dohrenwend (Ed.), *Adversity, stress, and psychopathology* (pp. 319–330). New York: Oxford University Press.

Breslau, N., Davis, G. C., Andreski, P., & Peterson, E. (1991). Traumatic events and Posttraumatic Stress Disorder in an urban population of young adults. *Archives of General Psychiatry, 48,* 216–222.

Breslau, N., Kessler, R. C., Chilcoat, H. D., Schultz, L. R., Davis, G. C., & Andreski, P. (1998). Trauma and Posttraumatic Stress Disorder in the community: The 1996 Detroit Area Survey of Trauma. *Archives of General Psychiatry, 55,* 626–632.

Brewin, C. R., Andrews, B., & Valentine, J. D. (2000). Meta-analysis of risk factors for Posttraumatic Stress Disorder in trauma-exposed adults. *Journal of Consulting and Clinical Psychology, 68,* 748–766.

Butler, R. W., Foy, D. W., Snodgrass, L., Hurwicz, M., et al. (1988). Combat-related Posttraumatic Stress Disorder in a nonpsychiatric population. *Journal of Anxiety Disorders, 2,* 111–120.

Candel, I., & Merckelbach, H. (2004). Peritraumatic Dissociation as a Predictor of Post-Traumatic Stress Disorder: A critical review. *Comprehensive Psychiatry, 45,* 44–50.

Carlson, E. B., & Dalenberg, C. J. (2000). A conceptual framework for the impact of traumatic experiences. *Trauma, Violence, & Abuse, 1,* 4–28.

Clohessy, S., & Ehlers, A. (1999). PTSD symptoms, response to intrusive memories and coping in ambulance service workers. *British Journal of Clinical Psychology, 38,* 251–265.

Davidson, J. R., Hughes, D., Blazer, D. G., & George, L. K. (1991). Post-Traumatic Stress Disorder in the community: An epidemiological study. *Psychological Medicine, 21,* 713–721.

Dohrenwend, B. P. (Ed.). (1998). *Adversity, stress, and psychopathology.* New York: Oxford University Press.

Elliott, C. H., & Lassen, M. K. (1997). A schema polarity model for case conceptualization, intervention, and research. *Clinical Psychology: Science and Practice, 4,* 12–28.

Eriksson, C. B., Vande Kemp, H., Gorsuch, R., Hoke, S., & Foy, D. W. (2001). Trauma exposure and PTSD symptoms in international relief and development personnel. *Journal of Traumatic Stress, 14,* 205–219.

Figley, C. R. (Ed.). (1995). *Compassion fatigue: Coping with secondary traumatic stress disorder in those who treat the traumatized.* Philadelphia: Brunner/Mazel.

Green, B. L., Grace, M. C., Lindy, J. D., & Leonard, A. C. (1990). Race differences in response to combat stress. *Journal of Traumatic Stress, 3,* 379–393.

Haslam, C., & Mallon, K. (2003). A preliminary investigation of post-traumatic stress symptoms among firefighters. *Work & Stress, 17,* 277–285.

Horowitz, M. J. (2004). *Stress response syndromes: Personality styles and intervention* (4th ed.). Northvale, NJ: Jason Aronson.

Hu, B. S., Liang, Y. X., Hu, X. Y., Long, Y., & Ge, L. N. (1999). Anxiety symptoms of Post-Traumatic Stress Disorder after work accident among construction workers. *Homeostasis in Health and Disease, 39,* 203–208.

Kaniasty, K., & Norris, F. H. (1992). Social support and victims of crime: Matching event, support, and outcome. *American Journal of Community Psychology, 20,* 211–241.

Kelly, B., Raphael, B., Judd, F., Kernutt, G., Burnett, P., & Burrows, G. (1998). Posttraumatic Stress Disorder in response to HIV infection. *General Hospital Psychiatry, 20,* 345–352.

Kessler, R. C., Sonnega, A., Bromet, E., Hughes, M., et al. (1995). Posttraumatic Stress Disorder in the National Comorbidity Survey. *Archives of General Psychiatry, 52,* 1048–1060.

Kilpatrick, D. G., Saunders, B. E., Amick-McMullan, A., Best, C. L., et al. (1989). Victim and crime factors associated with the development of crime-related Post-Traumatic Stress Disorder. *Behavior Therapy, 20,* 199–214.

Koss, M. P., & Dinero, T. E. (1989). Discriminant analysis of risk factors for sexual victimization among a national sample of college women. *Journal of Consulting and Clinical Psychology, 57,* 242–250.

Kutz, I., Shabtai, H., Solomon, Z., Neumann, M., et al. (1994). Post-Traumatic Stress Disorder in myocardial infarction patients: Prevalence study. *Israel Journal of Psychiatry and Related Sciences, 31,* 48–56.

Leiderman-Cerniglia, L. J. (2002). Psychological factors associated with resistance to PTSD symptoms in women with breast cancer. *Dissertation Abstracts International: B. The Physical Sciences and Engineering, 62*(10), 4792B. (UMI No. AAI3030506)

MacDonald, C., Chamberlain, K., & Long, N. (1997). Race, combat, and PTSD in a community sample of New Zealand Vietnam War veterans. *Journal of Traumatic Stress, 10,* 117–124.

McFarlane, A. C. (1988). The longitudinal course of posttraumatic morbidity: The range of outcomes and their predictors. *Journal of Nervous and Mental Disease, 176,* 30–39.

McFarlane, A. C., & Yehuda, R. A. (1996). Resilience, vulnerability, and the course of posttraumatic reactions. In B. A. van der Kolk, A. C. McFarlane, & L. Weisaeth (Eds.), *Traumatic stress: The effects of overwhelming experience on mind, body, and society* (pp. 155–181). New York: Guilford Press.

McNally, R. J. (2003). Progress and controversy in the study of Posttraumatic Stress Disorder. *Annual Review of Psychology, 54,* 229–252.

National Center for Health Statistics. (2005). *Death-Leading Causes.* Retrieved February 16, 2005, from http://www.cdc.gov.

Norris, F. H. (1992). Epidemiology of trauma: Frequency and impact of different potentially traumatic events on different demographic groups. *Journal of Consulting and Clinical Psychology, 60,* 409–418.

Norris, F. H., & Kaniasty, K. (1992). A longitudinal study of the effects of various crime prevention strategies on criminal victimization, fear of crime, and psychological distress. *American Journal of Community Psychology, 20,* 625-648.

Norris, F. H., Murphy, A. D., Baker, C. K., Perilla, J. L., Rodriguez, F. G., & Rodriguez, J de J (2003). Epidemiology of trauma and Posttraumatic Stress Disorder in Mexico. *Journal of Abnormal Psychology, 112,* 646–656.

O'Brien, L. S., & Hughes, S. J. (1991). Symptoms of Post-Traumatic Stress Disorder in Falklands veterans five years after the conflict. *British Journal of Psychiatry, 1159,* 135–141.

Ozer, E. J., Best, S. R., Lipsey, T. L., & Weiss, D. S. (2003). Predictors of Posttraumatic Stress Disorder and symptoms in adults: A meta-analysis. *Psychological Bulletin, 129,* 52–73.

Resnick, H. S., Kilpatrick, D. G., Dansky, B. S., Saunders, B. E., et al. (1993). Prevalence of civilian trauma and Posttraumatic Stress Disorder in a representative national sample of women. *Journal of Consulting and Clinical Psychology, 61,* 984–991.

Richmond, T. S., & Kauder, D. (2000). Predictors of psychological distress following serious injury. *Journal of Traumatic Stress, 13,* 681–692.

Riggs, D. S., & Foa, E. B. (1993). Obsessive Compulsive Disorder. In D. H. Barlow (Ed.), *Clinical handbook of psychological disorders: A step-by-step treatment manual* (2nd ed., pp. 189–239). New York: Guilford.

Robinson, H. M., Sigman, M. R., & Wilson, J. P. (1997). Duty-related stressors and PTSD symptoms in suburban police officers. *Psychological Reports, 81,* 835–845.

Schnurr, P. P., Friedman, M. J., & Rosenberg, S. D. (1993). Preliminary MMPI scores as predictors of combat-related PTSD symptoms. *American Journal of Psychiatry, 150,* 479–483.

Shalev, A. Y., Orr, S. P., & Pitman, R. K. (1993). Psychophysiologic assessment of traumatic imagery in Israeli civilian patients with Posttraumatic Stress Disorder. *American Journal of Psychiatry, 150,* 620–624.

Skre, I., Onstad, S., Torgersen, S., Lygren, S., et al. (1993). A twin study of *DSM-III-R* Anxiety Disorders. *Acta Psychiatrica Scandinavica, 88,* 85–92.

Solomon, Z., Mikulincer, M., & Avitzur, E. (1988). Coping, locus of control, social support, and combat-related Posttraumatic Stress Disorder: A prospective study. *Journal of Personality and Social Psychology, 55,* 279–285.

Sorenson, S. B., Siegel, J. M., Golding, J. M., & Stein, J. A. (1991). Repeated sexual victimization. *Violence and Victims, 6,* 299–308.

Steketee, G., & Foa, E. B. (1987). Rape victims: Post-traumatic stress responses and their treatment: A review of the literature. *Journal of Anxiety Disorders, 1,* 69–86.

True, W. R., & Lyons, M. J. (1999). Genetic risk factors for PTSD: A twin study. In R. Yehuda (Ed.), *Risk factors for Posttraumatic Stress Disorder* (pp. 61–78). Washington, DC: American Psychiatric Association.

Vaiva, G., Thomas, P., Ducrocq, F., Fontaine, M., Boss, V., Devos, P., et al. (2004). Low posttrauma GABA plasma levels as a predictive factor in the development of acute Posttraumatic Stress Disorder. *Biological Psychiatry, 55,* 250–254.

Wolfe, J., & Kimerling, R. (1997). Gender issues in the assessment of Posttraumatic Stress Disorder. In J. P. Wilson & T. M. Keane (Eds.), *Assessing psychological trauma and PTSD* (pp. 192–238). New York: Guilford.

World Health Organization. (2003). *Report on violence and health.* Retrieved February 15, 2005, from http://www.who.int.

Wyatt, G. E., Guthrie, D., & Notgrass, C. M. (1992). Differential effects of women's child sexual abuse and subsequent sexual revictimization. *Journal of Consulting and Clinical Psychology, 60,* 167–173.

Zuckerman, M., et al. (1979). Determinants of information-seeking behavior. *Journal of Research in Personality, 13,* 161–174.

CHAPTER 5

Cognitive and Behavioral Theories and Models of Posttraumatic Stress Disorder

There is nothing more practical than a good theory.

–Kurt Lewin

The advancement of any field or knowledge enterprise occurs when individual observations and bits of data are brought together into a coherent, organized theory or model. Parsimony is an important principle in all of science. In order for one to understand PTSD, for instance, he or she could have a grasp of all the individual findings, observations, and discussion versus only having a firm grasp on a particular model that is parsimonious and comprehensive. In Chapter 3 we discussed the various effects that exposure to a traumatic stressor can have on us in isolation. In Chapters 5, 6, and 7, we turn to the *how* question of PTSD and pull those individual consequences together in an attempt to explain just how PTSD develops.

Cognitive Theories and Models

All cognitive theories of Posttraumatic Stress Disorder have the following features or components in common, according to Dalgleish (1999):

- Individuals have pretrauma beliefs and models of the world, self, and others that come into play when a trauma occurs.

- Traumatic stressors provide salient and typically incompatible information relative to these beliefs and models.

- Such information cannot be easily ignored nor integrated or assimilated into these existing belief structures and models.

- The process of attempting to integrate this difficult and problematic information leads to what is observed as the PTSD phenomena (i.e., symptoms and signs of the disorder).

- Successful resolution results in integration. Unsuccessful resolution occurs when the traumatic information cannot be brought into line with the pretrauma cognitive environment.

Cognitive theories or models are also known as *information processing models*. Litz and Hearst give a good description of the relevant concepts from an information processing perspective, which include:

> hypothetical [mental] constructs, derived from experimental cognitive psychology, that address how individuals perceive, selectively attend to, and retrieve personally relevant information from memory. Information processing . . . addresses how life experiences are organized in memory in a manner that facilitates the utilization of past experience. Past experience is organized in memory in functional units called networks or schemas . . . Information processing theories of PTSD posit that traumatic life experiences influence how new information relevant to the trauma is processed. (p. 4)

Key words or concepts in this chapter will be *memory, networks,* and *schemas*. Each of these are essential constructs in the cognitive conceptualization of PTSD.

Mardi Horowitz's Stress Response Syndrome

The psychiatrist Mardi Horowitz has been an integral part of the PTSD field for decades. His theoretical work was a critical component in the development of the *DSM-III* version of PTSD. Horowitz's model of PTSD has its theoretical roots in Freudian and psychodynamic theory. However, his is essentially a cognitive-processing model in which individuals are seen as active processors of incoming information from their environment, working to integrate, assimilate, or accommodate, à la Jean Piaget, the new or novel information into existing psychological structures, schemas, or models of the world.

Initially, we start with a traumatic stressor. From here an individual engages in the cognitive processing of the incoming trauma-related information. At the center of this process is a basic human tendency called the *completion tendency*, which Horowitz defines as the need to match new information with inner models based on older information and the revision of both until they agree (Horowitz, 1986). Dalgleish (1999) states that this process helps the mind make effective decisions and choose courses of action by staying in touch with reality. In other words, the partaking in processing is preferable over simply shutting down or totally shutting out the incoming traumatic stimuli, as the latter would result in ineffectual responding.

Horowitz (1986) states that traumatic stress requires a person to process incoming information as threatening. He cites the work of Lazarus (1966; see Chapter 2 for more on Lazarus), which emphasizes the role of cognitive appraisal in determining idiosyncratic stress responses. Different people interpret different stimuli differently. Once a stressor is determined to be traumatic, we engage in the integration process, alternating between periods of intrusion and engagement of denial-based defensive mechanisms. *Intrusion* refers to the awareness of the traumatic stimuli, and *denial* refers to the lack of conscious acknowledgment. This process allows for the natural titration of traumatic stress, and ideally ends in integration and resolution. Intrusion periods involve symptoms of reexperiencing and hyperarousal. Intrusion then gives way to denial, numbing, and avoidance symptoms.

Horowitz proposes that processing occurs in a multistage process that we engage in and pass through on our way to resolution or integration. They are as follows:

1. *A crying out or stunned reaction occurs.*

2. *An information overload occurs.* Thoughts, memories, and images of the trauma cannot be integrated, and there is a failure to integrate (Dalgleish, 1999).

3. *An engagement of defense mechanisms occurs.* Despite defense mechanisms, the completion tendency maintains the traumatic information in active memory, leading to intrusive symptoms such as flashbacks, dreams, or intrusive thoughts. There is an oscillation between defense and completion tendency, accompanied by gradual integration. Failures of integration lead to partial processing of trauma information and their remaining in active memory, thus leading to symptom production.

As intrusion is processed and is properly integrated, normal adaptation occurs. Appropriate and effective defensive functioning facilitates this process. If the defensive functions fail to facilitate this process, traumatic information is only partially processed and is maintained in active memory, readily accessible, easily activated, and overt symptoms emerge.

Janoff-Bulman's Cognitive Appraisal Model

The core of this model rests on the idea that humans have basic ideas or mental models of the world and themselves in that world that allow them to plan, make decisions, react, and generally function. They can be seen as primary programs or operating systems that guide our thoughts, emotions, and actions. In the cognitive appraisal model of Janoff-Bulman (1992), PTSD is the consequence of the shattering of basic assumptions or models about ourselves or the *self* and the *world*.

There are three critical core assumptions that are affected with PTSD. The first assumption is that we are personally invulnerable or safe. This is characterized by statements or beliefs such as, "It won't happen to me," or "That only happens to people who . . .," and so on. The second assumption involves the perception that the world is meaningful and comprehensible. In other words, nothing happens without a reason and the world is understandable and makes sense. Finally, the third assumption is that the self is viewed in a positive way. That is, we generally see ourselves in a positive light. Our self-concept is not generally negative. Dalgleish (2004) proposes that these beliefs provide structure and meaning to our experience, and when they are challenged or shattered, the world is experienced as chaotic, confusing, intrusive, and to be avoided or escaped from. We become overstimulated and hyperaroused. I would add that the very human need to live in a predictable world is powerfully challenged by traumatic stress. Car accidents happen despite our best preparation against them. Unthinkable atrocities are committed all over the world, everyday. "Strong" people break down when under stress, surprising themselves and those around them.

Edna Foa's Fear Network

Edna Foa and her colleagues (1989) proposed a model that is based on the activation of particular components of our memory, which subsequently lead to symptom expression. The groundwork for this work was laid by researcher Peter Lang. Lang (1985a, 1985b, 1987) proposed that stimuli that are fear-relevant are arranged and stored in highly organized, semantic, *fear networks* in memory. Information about cues that elicit fear; information about cognitive, motor, and psychophysiological responses; and information about the meaning of cues and responses are all part of these networks. Fear stimuli activate these networks and all its related components. Lang (1985a, 1985b, 1987) proposed that Anxiety Disorders as a class are characterized by stimuli-sensitive and stable fear networks that can be triggered more easily in patients with Anxiety Disorders than in patients without Anxiety Disorders. Quite simply, Anxiety Disorder patients react to a broader range of stimuli.

In line with Lang, Foa and her colleagues (1989) proposed that in PTSD, the trauma-related information stored in a fear network could be activated and brought into conscious awareness by cues or cue stimuli in the current biopsychosocial environment. When this happens, we engage in defense attempts to avoid or suppress this conscious recollection. Successful resolution of this cycle comes from integration of the information into more stable, less volatile memory structures. Foa and colleagues (1989) identifies some mediating variables for determining successful or unsuccessful integration. The more unpredictable and uncontrollable a stressor is perceived to be, the more resistant to integration it will be. Severe trauma that alters memory and attention functioning in a way that disorganizes and fragments the fear network makes trauma information resistant to integration. Peritraumatic dissociation is an example of a process that can interfere with the organization of trauma-related information and increase the fragmentation of memory.

Cognitive Action Theory

Chemtob et al. (1988) have developed a model similar to Foa et al.'s (1989) fear network model. It is significantly different, however, in that the fear network is considered permanently activated, resulting in the PTSD sufferer essentially being in a perpetual state of trauma and survival mode. This survival mode is characterized as the typical functional response mode to traumatic stress. In Foa et al.'s (1989) model, the fear network required cueing. This model has no such requirement but still allows for it. The fear network is simply on all the time. This perpetual activation leads to observed symptoms of hyperarousal and intrusiveness. There is a constant state of alert and interpretation of a stimulus as such. Even neutral stimuli can be interpreted as threatening.

In addition to the ongoing or perpetual activation process, there are parallel processes that further account for symptoms. With each episode of arousal, there is a decrease in the interval between each episode. Episodes are then experienced more often. It's akin to the decreasing radius of a tornado as one gets closer to its core. Along with this change in interval and frequency of occurrence, the magnitude of activation increases with each episode. In essence, the fear network feeds back onto itself, becoming more common and more intense. Thus, an initially cued activation becomes virtually independent of cues, and as the episodes take on virtual lives of their own, the result is perpetual activation.

Cognitive Processing Model

Creamer, Burgess, and Pattison's (1992) cognitive processing model combines the work of Horowitz (1986), Foa et al. (1989), and Chemtob et al. (1988) into a model that explains recovery and the possible therapeutic mechanism in therapy. The activation of fear networks is seen as a necessary component for recovery from trauma. This process is called *network resolution processing*. There is an initial period of intrusion because the fear network is activated or stimulated. This initial intrusiveness, however, is followed by the use of defense mechanisms and avoidance. The higher the level of intrusion at the end of the acute stressor period, the better the outcome for the individual and the better the chances for healthy adaptation and recovery. The less denial, avoidance, and dissociation up front, the quicker the recovery process. It's as if the mind has less to dig up and process on a conscious level.

Dual Representation Theory

Brewin, Dalgleish, and Joseph (1996) proposed their dual representation theory in line with others' work and with emphasis on memory and the storage of trauma-related information. They proposed that trauma information is stored on two levels of memory, one on a conscious memory level called *verbally accessible memories* (VAMs) and one that is susceptible to cues but is unconscious called *situationally accessible memories* (SAMs). Verbally accessible memories can be deliberately accessed and processed, perhaps, for example, in response to a therapist asking a client to talk about what they remember from a trauma. On the other hand, SAMs cannot be deliberately accessed but can be activated by cues.

Each level of storage gives rise to different PTSD symptom phenomenon. Verbally accessible memories give rise to intrusive memories, emotions, and selective recall of particular aspects of an event or events. Situationally accessible memories give rise to flashbacks, dreams, and situational arousal. Posttraumatic Stress Disorder sufferers need to consciously integrate VAM information into preexisting beliefs and models of the world and "restoring a sense of safety and control, by making appropriate adjustments to expectations about the self and world" (p. 8). From this will follow the integration of SAM information as new but ultimately nonthreatening information and the eventual creation of new SAMs.

Chronic PTSD symptoms occur when the discrepancy between the trauma and prior assumptions is very large, resulting in chronic emotional processing. The system keeps working to process and integrate the VAM and SAM information, but the discrepancy is too large. Processing and integration can also be stalled by avoidance of stimuli, resulting in an insufficient level of activation necessary for integration to properly occur.

Ehlers and Clark's Model of the Maintenance of PTSD

Posttraumatic Stress Disorder is a disorder in which a past threat is experienced as a current threat. How an event is interpreted and how trauma memory is represented are key factors. Ehlers and Clark (2000) propose that the integration of traumatic memory with existing memory is critical for stabilization and health. Trauma memories are strong and cohesive, leading to a broad range of trauma stimuli and overgeneralization and in essence, many stimuli are infected, if you will, by the trauma (Ehlers and Clark, 2000). Coping behavior based on threat stands in the way of cognitive resolution and serves to perpetuate symptoms. Sufferers never test their belief that there is a threat in the current moment if they are constantly avoiding or enacting their alert status (Ehlers & Clark, 2000).

Dalgleish and Power's SPAARS Approach

The schematic, propositional, analogue, and associative representational systems (SPAARS) model (Dalgleish, 1999; Power & Dalgleish, 1997, 1999) is a model of emotion used as a comprehensive attempt to integrate the emotional or, more specifically, fear processing aspects of PTSD with the memory-based approaches discussed so far. The schematic, propositional, analogue, and associative representational model represents the system and architecture involved in the storage of information, the interaction and relationship of this information, and how this information is processed. Schematic information is higher order–linguistic and conceptual representations of the self, the world, and goals. Propositional information consists of memory bits, such as beliefs, objects in the world, and concepts. Associative information consists of the relationships between both schematic and prepositional information. Analogue representation consists of the more primitive or basic perceptual units of a trauma, such as visual, olfactory, or auditory information.

The experience of trauma within the SPAARS system works in a simple fashion characterized by Figure 5.1.

Ultimately, all trauma information—after proceeding through the different levels of schematic, propositional, analogical, and associative levels—are appraised at the schematic level, which gives rise to emotion in the face of current stimuli, and emotions can be generated in relation to past experiences.

At the center of the SPAARS model is a theory of emotions that proposes that emotions are tools used for the resolution of problems and the reaching of goals. If the problem faced by a human is a threat, then the emotion of fear is experienced, and the cognitive system that deals with current and future threat is engaged. Emotions are central cognitive orienting or organizing constructs that adaptively reorganize a person's cognitive system in various and different ways to deal with changes in the internal and external environments. When this process goes awry, disorder or pathology ensues.

Traumatic stimuli produce intense fear after being processed at the schematic level and are represented or stored in the analogical, propositional, and associative levels in the SPAARS model.

When posttraumatic processing of trauma information is processed at the various SPAARS levels but not successfully integrated, symptoms are produced. Trauma can challenge one's sense of self at the schematic level, for example. Trauma can result in the lack of integration between the different levels of the system.

Meaning at the schematic level is maintained by the processing of other-level information yet to be integrated. As long as the information is processed as incompatible or unintegrated, an individual will be in a constant state of fear activation.

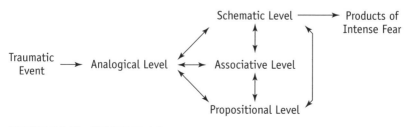

FIGURE 5.1 *The SPAARS Model.*

Foa's Integrated Emotion Processing Theory

Edna Foa and colleagues expanded upon the earlier theory of fear networks in a number of works (Foa & Meadows, 1998; Foa & McNally, 1996; Foa & Riggs, 1993; Foa & Rothbaum, 1998) by placing more emphasis on the disorganized nature of the traumatic memories. Dalgleish (2004) considers this later work as one of the most comprehensive cognitive theories of PTSD in the literature. There are three components to this model: memories, schemas, and posttraumatic reactions of self and others.

Posttraumatic memories are disorganized because of the disrupted and altered information processing at the time of the traumatic event or stressor. The disruption is a consequence of the intense peritraumatic emotions, which leads to what Dalgleish (2004) calls, "disorganized and unbalanced memory records." Research support for this has come from analyzing the narratives of trauma victims before and after treatment. The more organized trauma narratives were or are, the less symptom intensity and vice versa (Foa, Molnar, & Cashman, 1995; van Minnen, Wessel, Dijkstra, & Roelofs, 2002).

Another memory phenomenon involves the number of stimulus-danger associations stored in memory. A large network of information is tied to signs or signals of danger. This is akin to a stimulus overgeneralization process. Just about anything, then, can be associated with danger and set off an alarm. Trauma memories are also varied in the number of responses they possess. Nontrauma–fear-related memories do not have the same number of physiological, cognitive, and behavioral responses that trauma-related memories do. This is cited as possibly related to the trauma victim's subject experience of being out of control of him- or herself.

Traumatic stressors violate existing schematic knowledge similar to the types of violations outlined in Janoff-Bulman's (1992) work. Schemas related to a person's ability to cope and be safe and the general safety and predictability of the world are important. This process leads to a collection of intrusive and avoidance symptoms. There must, however, be a high discrepancy between pretrauma schemas and traumatic stressor–related information.

Finally, traumatic stressors and posttraumatic events can alter one's sense of self and others. The interpretation of symptoms, for example, can activate pretrauma schemas that exacerbate difficulties. Victims can develop views of themselves as weak or as failures. This leads to a vicious cycle that maintains PTSD symptoms. Also, unsympathetic responses from others or being blamed may also contribute to problematic schema development, such as schemas of incompetence.

Individual Processes and Variables

The previous sections have addressed attempts at relatively comprehensive models of PTSD. In this section, individual research findings and theoretical work are discussed. Some of these may fit into one or more model discussed in preceding sections, but each is represented in the literature as relatively independent. These concepts are important to be aware of because new research directions and a more complete picture of the etiological cognitive factors will necessarily involve addressing all the relevant research findings and theoretical work.

Attribution Processes and Perceptions of Control

Researchers and theorists have argued that it is a general human need to predict the future and have a sense of control over events. In fact, researchers have shown many positive mental and physical health benefits to the perception of control, even if it is slightly illusory. We live in our world as if it is predictable and orderly. When this perception is violated or tested, we seek answers. The more out of control we perceive our world to be, the poorer our adjustment overall.

In addition to our need to predict our world, we have a need to maintain our sense of self-worth and self-esteem. Brewin (1989) and Steele (1988) indicate that one way we do this is by attempting to understand why events have occurred. Greenberg and colleagues (1993) feel that self-esteem serves a stress-buffering function. (For more on stress buffers, see Chapters 2 and 4.)

Abramson et al. (1989) derived hopelessness theory to help us understand what happens when this need is thwarted. When we perceive a stressor as long-lasting and wide ranging in its effects, this can lead to an orientation of hopelessness. This theory has its theoretical roots in Albert Bandura's (1997) work in learned helplessness, which states that in the face of uncontrollable stress, individuals tend to develop an orientation that leads to giving up.

How may we go about the process of regaining that feeling of control, predictability, and hope? It seems that utilizing blame is one such technique. Stephen Joseph (1999) identifies two types of blame that are implicated here: self-blame and other-blame.

In blaming ourselves, we engage in a process of finding the ways and means that lead to a particular situation, giving us a sense of control and a sense that had we engaged in other behaviors or made other choices, we could have prevented whatever it was that happened. This works for future events as well. We may say to ourselves such things as "Next time I wont . . ." or "If this ever happens again, I'll be sure to . . ." Keep in mind, however, that overusing the blaming-oneself method can put one at risk for depression and increase our focus on our perceived weaknesses rather than strengths. Intrusive and avoidant symptoms of PTSD have been theoretically connected to self-blame and shame. Shame may lead to avoidance coping, such as denial or social distancing. Guilt may lead to problem-seeking reparative action, which is typically a positive attempt at coping. However, when direct reparation is not possible, trauma stimuli may linger in active memory and be more easily activated involuntarily, leading to the experience of intrusiveness.

Conversely, blaming other people may contribute to our sense of powerlessness because we placed the perceived control over the event's occurrence in the hands of another person or persons. Although ironically we may be preserving our self-esteem by blaming others, we paradoxically increase our sense that the cause was out of our personal control. Research and clinical experience suggest that a balance between blaming oneself and blaming others is preferable.

Similar to self-blame versus other-blame, the concept of *locus of control* (Rotter, 1966) refers to the belief that control over events can be attributed *internally* ("I am in control") or *externally* ("Control resides outside or externally to me"). Research with combat veterans has shown poorer overall adjustment in individuals with a more external locus of control orientation, indicating that a belief in one's own sense of control is a more adaptive and positive orientation to events.

Attention Bias

Attention deficits that result from trauma exposure were discussed in Chapter 3. However, in addition to the effects of trauma, attention deficits have been implicated in the etiology and maintenance of PTSD symptomology. Research has continued to show that trauma victims have an attentional bias toward trauma-related information.

According to Buckley, Blanchard, and Neill (2000), in PTSD, attentional resources are allocated toward threatening stimuli. Research, done with the broad class of Anxiety Disorders and not PTSD specifically, have led some to believe that Anxiety Disorder patients process negative information more quickly than positive or neutral information. They also do this faster than nonanxiety-disordered patients.

Research using a well-known technique called the *Stroop Task* has consistently shown that PTSD sufferers are poised and biased toward the perception of trauma-relevant information. The Stroop Task measures how much attention resources are being reserved or allocated to trauma-related information. This is done by measuring how much trauma-related information interferes with the processing of neutral information. Generally, findings show that when trauma-related information is presented simultaneously with neutral information, the processing of neutral information is slower as a consequence of the interference.

Summary

As we have seen from the various cognitive etiological models, the understanding of the roles of basic psychological processes such as memory and attention are crucial to our understanding what causes PTSD. Cognitive models show how PTSD can be viewed as a disorder of memory and attention and how the human trauma response can persist and be stimulated long after the traumatic stressor has abated. When traumatic information is processed, stored, and subsequently stimulated in a particular manner or fashion, PTSD can result.

Quick Review

- Litz and Hearst (1994) state, "Information processing [cognitive] theories of PTSD posit that traumatic life experiences influence how new information relevant to the trauma is processed" (p. 5).

- Mardi Horowitz's (1986) stress response syndrome model proposes that the symptoms of PTSD are indicative of an oscillating integration process between the defensive avoidance of traumatic information and the active processing of traumatic information. Successful resolution is facilitated by effective defensive functioning.

- Janoff-Bulman's (1992) cognitive appraisal model proposes that fundamental alterations in one's sense of the world and his or her self account for the symptoms of PTSD.

- Edna Foa and colleagues' (Foa & McNally, 1996; Foa & Meadows, 1998; Foa & Riggs, 1993; Foa & Rothbaum, 1998) fear network and integrated emotion processing theories propose that threat-related information is stored in our memories in a manner that makes them more easily stimulated, thus leading to symptom expression.

- Cognitive action theory proposes that the symptoms of PTSD are the consequence of being in a perpetual cognitive state of survival, with its relevant consequences for memory and attention processes.

- The cognitive processing model proposes that the activation of fear-related or threat-related information is a necessary component of getting over a trauma and becoming healthy.

- Dual representation theory proposes that memories for trauma information are stored in two different ways: VAMs and SAMs. Verbally accessible memories are consciously accessible, and SAMs are not. Each level of storage gives rise to different PTSD symptoms.

- Ehlers and Clark's (2000) model of the maintenance of PTSD proposes that traumatic memory is organized in such a way that it infects other memories and stimuli and is therefore more easily triggered by a broad range of stimuli.

- Dalgleish and Power's (Dalgleish, 1999; Power & Dalgleish, 1997, 1999) SPAARS approach expands on the dual representation theory to include multiple levels of memory storage for traumatic information, each with its own contribution to the symptom picture.

- Attributional biases toward oneself, having an internal locus of control relevant to trauma, and attentional biases toward trauma-related information are all very important factors to consider when trying to understand the etiology of PTSD.

References

Abramson, L. Y., Alloy, L. B., Hogan, M. E., Whitehouse, W. G., Donovan, P., Rose, D. T., et al. (1999). Cognitive vulnerability to depression: Theory and evidence. *Journal of Cognitive Psychotherapy, 13,* 5–20.

Abramson, L. Y., Metalsky, G. I., & Alloy, L. B. (1989). Hopelessness depression: A theory-based subtype of depression. *Psychological Review, 96,* 358–372.

Bandura, A. (1997). *Self-efficacy: The exercise of control.* New York: W. H. Freeman.

Brewin, C. R. (1989). Cognitive change processes in psychotherapy. *Psychological Review, 96,* 379–394.

Brewin, C. R., Dalgleish, T., & Joseph, S. (1996). A dual representation theory of Post-traumatic Stress Disorder. *Psychological Review, 103,* 670–686.

Buckley, T. C., Blanchard, E. B., & Neill, W. T. (2000). Information processing and PTSD: A review of the empirical literature. *Clinical Psychology Review, 20,* 1041–1065.

Chemtob, C. M., Roitblat, H. L., Hamada, R. S., Carlson, J. G., et al. (1988). A cognitive action theory of Post-Traumatic Stress Disorder. *Journal of Anxiety Disorders, 2,* 253–275.

Creamer, M., Burgess, P., & Pattison, P. (1992). Reaction to trauma: A cognitive processing model. *Journal of Abnormal Psychology, 101,* 452–459.

Dalgleish, T. (1999). Cognitive theories of Post-Traumatic Stress Disorder. In W. Yule (Ed.), *Post-Traumatic Stress Disorders: Concepts and therapy* (pp. 193–220). New York: Wiley.

Dalgleish, T. (2004). Cognitive approaches to Posttraumatic Stress Disorder: The evolution of multirepresentational theorizing. *Psychological Bulletin, 130,* 228–260.

Ehlers, A., & Clark, D. M. (2000). A cognitive model of Posttraumatic Stress Disorder. *Behaviour Research and Therapy, 38,* 319–345.

Foa, E. B., & McNally, R. J. (1996). Mechanisms of change in exposure therapy. In R. M. Rapee (Ed.). *Current controversies in the anxiety disorders* (pp. 329–343). New York: Guilford.

Foa, E. B., & Meadows, E. A. (1998). Psychosocial treatments for posttraumatic stress Disorder. In R. Yehuda (Ed.), *Review of psychiatry: Vol. 17. Psychological trauma* (pp. 179–204). Washington, DC: American Psychiatric Association.

Foa, E. B., Molnar, C., & Cashman, L. (1995). Change in rape narratives during exposure therapy for Posttraumatic Stress Disorder. *Journal of Traumatic Stress, 8,* 675–690.

Foa, E. B., & Riggs, D. S. (1993). Post-traumatic stress disorder in rape victims. In J. Oldham, M. B. Riba, & A. Tasman (Eds.), *Review of psychiatry* (Vol. 12, pp. 273–303). Washington, DC: American Psychiatric Association.

Foa, E. B., Riggs, D. S., Massie, E. D., & Yarczower, M. (1995). The impact of fear activation and anger on the efficacy of exposure treatment for posttraumatic stress disorder. *Behavior Therapy, 26,* 487-499.

Foa, E. B., & Rothbaum, B. O. (1998). *Treating the trauma of rape: Cognitive behavioral therapy for PTSD.* New York: Guilford.

Foa, E. B., Steketee, G., & Rothbaum, B. O. (1989). Behavioral/cognitive conceptualizations of Post-Traumatic Stress Disorder. *Behavior Therapy, 20,* 155–176.

Greenberg, J., Pyszczynski, T., Solomon, S., Pinel, E., et al. (1993). Effects of self-esteem on vulnerability-denying defensive distortions: Further evidence of an anxiety-buffering function of self-esteem. *Journal of Experimental Social Psychology, 29,* 229–251.

Horowitz, M. J. (1986). *Stress response syndromes.* Lanham, MD: Jason Aronson.

Janoff-Bulman, R. (1992). *Shattered assumptions: Towards a new psychology of trauma.* New York: Free Press.

Joseph, S. (1999). Attributional processes, coping and Post-Traumatic Stress Disorders. In W. Yule (Ed.), *Post-Traumatic Stress Disorders: Concepts and therapy* (pp. 51–70). New York: Wiley.

Lang, P. J. (1985a). Cognition in emotion: Concept and action. In C. E. Izard, J. Kagan, & R. B. Zajonc (Eds.), *Emotions, cognition, and behavior* (pp. 192–226). New York: Cambridge University Press.

Lang, P. J. (1985b). The cognitive psychophysiology of emotion: Fear and anxiety. In A. H. Tuma & J. D. Maser (Eds.), *Anxiety and the Anxiety Disorders* (pp. 131–170). Hillsdale, NJ: Erlbaum

Lang, P. J. (1987). Fear and anxiety: Cognition, memory, and behavior. In D. Magnusson & A. Öhman (Eds.), *Psychopathology: An interactional perspective* (pp. 159–176). San Diego: Academic Press.

Lazarus, R. S. (1966). *Psychological stress and the coping process.* New York: McGraw-Hill.

Litz, B. T., & Hearst, D. (1994). Clinical implications and applications of information processing models of Post-Traumatic Stress Disorder. In L. Hyer (Ed.), *Trauma victim: Theoretical issues and practical suggestions* (pp. 423–443). Muncie, IN: Accelerated Development.

Power, M. J., & Dalgleish, T. (1997). *Cognition and emotion: From order to disorder.* Hove, England: Psychology Press.

Power, M. J., & Dalgleish, T. (1999). Two routes to emotion: Some implications of multi-level theories of emotion for therapeutic practice. *Cognitive and Behavioural Psychotherapy, 27,* 129–142.

Steele, C. M. (1988). The psychology of self-affirmation: Sustaining the integrity of the self. In L. Berkowitz (Ed.), *Advances in experimental social psychology: Vol. 21. Social psychological studies of the self: Perspectives and programs* (pp. 261–302). San Diego: Academic Press.

Rotter, J. B. (1966). Generalized expectancies for internal versus external control of reinforcement. *Psychological Monographs: General & Applied, 80,* 1–28.

van Minnen, A., Wessel, I., Dijkstra, T., & Roelofs, K. (2002). Changes in PTSD patients' narratives during prolonged exposure therapy: A replication and extension. *Journal of Traumatic Stress, 15,* 255–258.

CHAPTER 6

Biological Theories and Models of Posttraumatic Stress Disorder

At the center of the danger and threat of traumatic stressors is the human body. After all, it is the body that is at risk of death or injury. The body has to run, fight, or freeze when threatened. Energy needs to be mobilized by the brain and the heart to get the muscles moving. The lungs need to get oxygen to the heart, and the heart needs to get blood out to the periphery.

The biological approaches to understanding PTSD discussed in this chapter focus on the brain and body's protective responses to danger and threat of death or substantial injury. Although the physiology of danger and threat responding involves many organs and body systems, such as the lungs and heart, the focus on the biological understanding of PTSD is on the brain and central nervous system. Biological models of PTSD necessitate an understanding of the brain. The basis for a biological understanding of PTSD depends on the idea that the normal brain processes and mechanisms involved in danger and threat responding, self-preservation behavior, and protection behavior become dysfunctional, thus producing the various core symptoms of the syndrome. At the center of this dysfunction or malfunction is the process of learning. In PTSD (from a biological perspective at least), the hallmark of the disorder is continuing fear and danger responding in the absence of danger. The underlying brain systems are working when they shouldn't be. Essentially, individuals with PTSD have been biologically trained to respond to danger when no credible danger exists.

Before we go on, let's quickly address this issue of protection behavior. We know from Chapter 1 that someone can develop PTSD even if they are not the direct target of a threat and are only witnesses. Why? A discussion of this is an entire book in and of itself. However, simply put, witnessing trauma can stimulate fear for oneself in a physical sense ("I might be next," "An airplane might crash into my building," etc.) and in a very profound psychological sense ("I can't live without my wife," "My children are my life," etc.). Keep in mind that the psychoanalytic and psychodynamic models of PTSD spend a great deal of time on the issue of psychic or psychological threat. Even when we are not the specific targets of danger, our danger response behaviors can be activated and employed. This is probably most obvious in maternal or parental protection behavior where we are protecting our genetic investment in our offspring.

Conceptual Foundations of the Biological Models

When trying to understand the biology of PTSD, it can be easy to get lost in the reductionism of the brain and its various systems and biochemical processes and lose sight of the big picture. The big picture represents the ultimate behavior of reacting or responding to danger, the protection of life and limb, and the training or learning occurring within the nervous system. In this chapter, we will be looking at the various brain processes, structures, and systems that underlie these processes.

It might help to simplify things by referring to all of the various responses and underlying process that save or protect an organism and its valued cohorts as *danger responses*. The following list outlines some of these:

Fear–the emotional response to the perception of threat.

Memory–the knowledge and memories of what represents danger in our worlds.

Arousal–being on alert, vigilance in perception, and mobilization of resources.

Fighting, fleeing (flight), or freezing–aggression in self-defense and protection, avoidance of threat, or reducing threat you generate yourself.

Various other psychic or psychological processes involved in protection, such as dissociation and various psychoanalytic defense mechanisms. (For more on dissociation, see Chapter 8, and for more on psychoanalytic defense mechanisms, see Chapters 2 and 7.)

Restoring or returning to baseline–maintaining organismic balance.

The emotion of fear is a characteristic emotional response to danger or threat, and, in turn, our memory determines what in our internal and external environments represent danger or threat. They work hand in hand. Arousal keeps us alert and gets us going. Fighting eliminates the danger through force. Fleeing gets us away from the danger. Freezing might help us hide or communicate that we come in peace. Dissociation protects our consciousness.

Finally, restoration processes such as homeostasis and allostasis keep us balanced and capable of responding to the next danger. Homeostasis is the process of maintaining organismic balance and stability under normal stress loads. Allostasis, on the other hand, is the process of maintaining or restoring organismic balance under heavy stress loads, such as the fear of death or significant bodily injury. After all, what could be more allostatically stressing or loading than fear of death or significant injury? In allostasis, the body works to maintain stability when stressors place a load on the body system, challenging it to maintain adaptive biological functioning under significant demands, such as the demand for survival (Wilson, Friedman, & Lindy, 2001). When the processes involved in allostasis are not adequately activated in response, shut down after a response, or are overburdened, biological wear and tear on the body and brain occur (McEwan, 2004).

Before we get into the biological details of PTSD, something needs to be said about methodology and the issue of the "level of study." The ideas and models discussed in this chapter will address numerous neurobiological processes including neuroanatomical structures and systems, neurotransmitter systems, neurophysiology, functional brain systems, neuropsychological functions, and endocrine and hormonal functioning. Each of these reflects a different level of analysis within the brain and body, much the same way Newtonian physics represents a different level than quantum physics for the analysis of the physical reality of the universe. The differing analyses at different levels *all* address the biological reality of PTSD. Partly as a function of pragmatics, the brain in PTSD gets divided up and analyzed from all these different levels. But it is essential to understand that the brain is a complex system that typically defies such gross divisions, and perhaps these divisions only reflect our limited ability to grasp the complexity of the brain beyond a componential level. Nonetheless, in this chapter, we are going to discuss brain structures, circuits, and neurochemical phenomena. At the core we are talking about learned alterations in the brain, changes in brain structure, changes in brain circuitry or connectivity, and changes in brain chemistry. Brain circuits are interconnected brain areas that are connected by the synaptic patterns and neurotransmitter systems subserving them. Ultimately, the symptoms of PTSD reflect changes in the neurochemical functioning of the brain within specific circuits. Neural circuits are altered by changes in connectivity, a consequence of synaptic change. Neurochemicals are involved in the transmission and modulation of synaptic activity, which is shown in Figure 6.1.

Alterations in Neurochemicals

    ↘

    Alterations in Connectivity

       ↘

      Alterations in Circuitry

        ↘

        Alterations in Behavior and Mental Processes

FIGURE 6.1 *Neurobiological Alterations.*

Confused? Let's hope not! But in case you are, perhaps psychiatrist Bessel A. van der Kolk can clarify things. Bessel A. van der Kolk (1996) proposes that PTSD can be accounted for by looking at how traumatic stress impacts multiple psychobiological systems in three critical ways:

1. Abnormal arousal (e.g., vigilance and hyperarousal).

2. Failure to appropriately monitor and regulate physiologic reactivity.

3. Emotional dysregulation.

He states that individuals with PTSD are in a state of a "chronically disordered pattern of arousal" (p. 218). Avoidance symptoms make sense from this view as attempts to manage such abnormal arousal by shutting down or shutting out stimuli. Further, individuals with PTSD are reactive to both internal stimuli (i.e., memories) and external stimuli (sounds, sights, etc.). Finally, normal emotional functioning that involves distinguishing between what is relevant and important and what is not is impaired. Krystal (1978) reports that in PTSD, emotions fail to alert us to what is relevant, with a subsequent breakdown in adaptive responding. Arousal and adaptation responding are disconnected from each other as van der Kolk (1996) proposes that emotional cues fail to modulate more reactive and primitive stimulus-response patterns. In PTSD, time is not taken to analyze, only to react! As emotions take on this disconnected and functionally useless role, they can then plague and remind the PTSD sufferer of his or her sense of being in danger and ineffectualness in gaining control and feeling safe. Sufferers of PTSD have intense reactions to specific reminders of the trauma. They also overreact to intense stimuli that have nothing to do necessarily with the initial traumatic stressor and suffer from what van der Kolk refers to as a *failure in stimulus discrimination*. Trigger stimuli acquire reactive status through fear conditioning.

Neurobiology of the Fear Response and Learning

Over the years, one thing that I have realized in both my clinical practice and in my academic work is that in order to understand pathological functioning, it is critical to have a firm grasp on what constitutes normal functioning. In the case of PTSD, understanding abnormal or pathological reactions to traumatic stressors involves understanding the typical processes by which the human mind and body respond to fear. For instance, McEwan (1998) proposes that PTSD pathology is the consequence of the normal systems of allostatic maintenance failing to shut off once the load of an actual stressor is gone. Posttraumatic Stress Disorder, then, might be understood as a consequence of the organism's inability to shut off its fear-response mechanisms.

Fear Learning and the Amygdala

Joseph LeDoux identifies the amygdala as the brain structure at the center of our defense or danger responding system. It lies at the center of fear. The amygdala is critical to emotional processing in general and is crucial to fear-conditioning, involved in associating stimuli that elicit fear with stimuli that do not normally elicit fear. This fear-learning process involves the development of a conditioned emotional response or a classically conditioned fear response. As LeDoux states, "amygdala activation, in other words, turns a plain perceptual experience into a fearful one" (2002, p. 225). When this occurs, our consciousness is adaptively and understandably dominated by amygdala activation for the purpose of orienting us for appropriate action. LeDoux identifies what he calls the *motive circuit* in which emotional arousal plays a central role in shaping our motivated and intentional acts. Emotional arousal gives rise to a motivational state, leading to coordinated brain activity in the service of the motivation and arousal and guidance of behavior toward positive goals and away from aversive stimuli. With fear conditioning, our motive circuit is motivated toward survival.

When the amygdala is active, we are in defense or danger mode. Overstimulation of the amygdala has been shown to potentiate an animal's startle response. They are more reactive. Stimulation of the amygdala in general has been shown to lead to hyperarousal and hyperreactivity, increased heart rate, increased blood pressure, increased muscle tension, activation of the stress response system, and subjective experiences of fear and anxiety.

The brain systems that send input to the amygdala and the systems to which the amygdala sends output are all critical. The amygdala receives input from the sensory cortex, the medial temporal lobe memory system (the hippocampus), and the frontal lobe (specifically, the medial prefrontal cortex and the orbitofrontal cortex), which is shown in Figure 6.2.

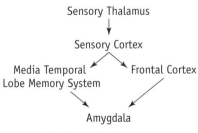

FIGURE 6.2 *Inputs to Amygdala.*

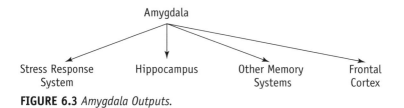

FIGURE 6.3 *Amygdala Outputs.*

The amygdala then sends output to the stress response system, the hippocampus, various other memory systems, and the frontal cortex, which is shown in Figure 6.3.

Fear Learning, the Amygdala, and the Hippocampus

As one can see, the hippocampus both sends information to and receives information from the amygdala. The hippocampus helps shape or determine what the amygdala responds to. It provides contextual information about stimuli, such as location in space and time (i.e., the sites, sounds, and time frames within which a fear-conditioned event occurred). It provides memory-based information about fear-inducing situations.

The amygdala has been implicated in the assigning of emotional valence or qualitative importance to explicit memories. The central nucleus of the amygdala triggers the release of adrenal hormones, which ultimately provide feedback to the brain. The amygdala's connections to the hippocampus (and other memory systems) can strengthen memory consolidation in the hippocampus, subsequently rendering these memories more vivid and more easily retrieved (LeDoux, 2002). However, in states of high arousal, our memory systems are impaired.

Other processes and connections of the hippocampus are critical to understanding fear-learning in their own right. For example, by virtue of its connections to the frontal cortex, the hippocampus provides contextual information to our working memory system as it processes current and active threat. Of critical importance to fear learning is memory. Without memory, there is no learning.

Therefore, we cannot understand PTSD without knowing about memory. After all, memory is central to PTSD, either failing to forget danger or being reminded of danger on a relentless and persistent basis. Posttraumatic Stress Disorder is about fear and the memories of fear-inducing stimuli and the psychobiological underpinnings of fear and memory.

From a neurobiological perspective, many theorists and researchers view memory as essentially synonymous with a process called long-term potentiation (LTP). Long-term potentiation is a process in which relatively permanent changes occur at the synapse level of neurons in response to stimulation. After a neuron is stimulated, it will return to its prefiring baseline activation point. But LTP shows us that as a neuron is repeatedly stimulated by a particular stimulus, the neurophysiology of that neuron is altered, resulting in the firing of that neuron now being differentially or characteristically associated with a particular stimulus. It remains poised and ready for activation, potentiated to respond to a particular stimulus. This process is thought to be the neural basis of memory reflecting relatively permanent changes in our neurons from repeated stimulation from a specific input. As long as a neuron remains potentiated, a memory remains.

Let's return now to the hippocampus. Long-term potentiation has been demonstrated repeatedly in the hippocampus. In addition to the hippocampus, explicit memory processes (e.g., events, distinct episodes, and conscious memory processes) have been associated with the rhinal cortex, the amygdala, and the prefrontal cortex. Each of these areas has extensive neural connections with the thalamus, the forebrain, and the sensory areas of the neocortex. Hence, it is not surprising that the hippocampus, with its demonstrated LTP, is a critical brain structure in PTSD.

The hippocampus is important in the formation of explicit memories; short-term memory; temporal aspects of experience; assessing reward, punishment, and novelty; and learning from experience. Research has shown that when an animal is subject to fear conditioning to a particular stimulus, it will respond to cues in the environment with the same response. That is, the stimulus has been contextualized, and the hippocampus is crucial to this process. Lesions in the hippocampus result in canceling or eliminating the role of these contextual cues. The hippocampus anchors the fear response in time and space; without this, we see free-floating and decontextualized fear responses as we see in PTSD. The subjective experience is one of being overreactive and, always and in all places, in fear. Nowhere is safe because fear is not anchored to a time or place. As van der Kolk (1996) mentioned, this accounts for the heightened state of arousal to a broad range of essentially unrelated stimuli.

Intense amygdala activity can suppress hippocampus functioning, and stress-induced corticosterone suppresses hippocampus activity. Increases in glucocorticoids for prolonged periods can lead to cell death. Numerous studies have substantiated reductions in hippocampus volume in those with PTSD and other subjects who have experienced either very intense acute stressors and went on to develop PTSD or individuals who have been exposed to prolonged periods of intense stress, such as victims of child physical abuse or domestic violence. Some studies have found that the hippocampus may, in fact, be able to regenerate cells after damage. However, high stress levels have been found to inhibit this process. At least theoretically, a reduction in hippocampus volume results in a limited ability of the hippocampus to consolidate memories and a reduction in its ability to provide useful or even accurate information to the amygdala.

Branching out from the hippocampus for just a minute, research with epilepsy patients has found that stimulation of the temporal lobe (where the hippocampus is located) can result in symptoms and experiences similar to flashbacks in PTSD. These include complex visual hallucinations or illusions, déjà vu, and emotional distress.

The Amygdala and the Prefrontal Cortex

In turn, the amygdala is partially controlled or regulated by its connections to the medial prefrontal cortex. This is another reciprocal relationship in which when one is active, the other is inhibited, and so on. The prefrontal cortex (PFC) is part of the ever so important executive control systems of the frontal lobe. It is a critical structure in the planning and organization of behavior. The PFC serves as a check or monitor of amygdala reactivity, when it is not functioning properly, the amygdala is more reactive and less inhibited by the reality of current input from working memory and from the controlling features of rationality and appropriate planning. In turn, the amygdala can interrupt the selective attention and working memory processes of the frontal cortex in order to alert the organism to a threat.

The orbitofrontal cortex, a section of the PFC, has been implicated in the failure of extinction in fear learning. Lesion research with the orbitofrontal cortex has also shown symptoms of intense fear and even visual hallucinations akin to the flashbacks of PTSD. When the orbitofrontal cortex is damaged, animals have been found to have poor extinction and, therefore, are perpetually responsive to old stimuli to which they should have habituated.

Stress Responding and the Locus Coeruleus

The locus coeruleus (LC) has long been understood to play a role in stress responding. Norepinephrine is prominent in the LC (see norepinephrine section below). The LC is connected to multiple brain regions also involved in stress and fear responding, such as the amygdala and the hippocampus. The LC is regulated by both neurotransmitters and neuropeptides (hormones). Corticotrophin releasing factor (CRF) and glutamate stimulate the LC, while norepinephrine, epinephrine, the endogenous opiates, gamma-aminobutyric acid (GABA), and serotonin have been found to inhibit its function. Bremner (1999) identifies the LC as a central relay station that receives information from multiple inputs and responds with norepinephrine release. Novel stimuli can stimulate the LC, and subsequent sympathetic nervous system activation occurs. Fear and stress response behaviors occur with LC activation. Research has shown that animals that have a prior exposure to chronic stress have an exaggerated norepinephrine response under current threat conditions (Bremner, 1999). Researchers have also found that chronic stress results in more active LC firing. Ultimately, Bremner, Southwick, Johnson, Yehuda, et al. (1993) conclude that increased LC firing and responsiveness and subsequent norepinephrine release may represent the neural substrate of stress sensitization and hyperreactivity in PTSD.

Posttraumatic Stress Disorder and Neurochemical Processes

As was mentioned earlier, what lies at the root of brain alterations in PTSD are alterations in neurochemicals such as neurotransmitters, hormones, and neuropeptides. These alterations ultimately lead to changes at the synaptic level, which lead to changes in circuitry and connectivity and the way different brain areas interact with and influence each other. These neural changes occur within the larger behavioral and neurobiological context of the stress response and the fear response and its various brains structures and systems outlined in the preceding section. In the stress response, there is a release of stress hormones and activation of stress-related neurotransmitters systems. Figure 6.4 outlines the brain regions involved in this process.

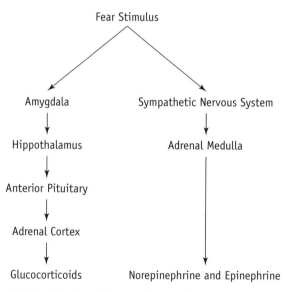

FIGURE 6.4 *Neurobiology of Stress Response.*
Notes: The amygdala is activated, which activates the hypothalamus, which releases CRF (or CRH). The anterior pituitary releases adrenocorticotropic hormone (ACTH). The adrenal cortex releases glucocorticoids (e.g., cortisol), which effect glucose metabolism by helping break down proteins and converting them to glucose, making fat available for energy, increasing blood flow, and stimulating responsive behavior. The sympathetic nervous system activates the adrenal medulla, which releases norepinephrine and epinephrine. Epinephrine activates glucose metabolism, which provides the brain and body energy to respond to the threat and serves to increase blood flow to muscles by increasing heart output. Norepinephrine is both a stress hormone and a neurotransmitter and is involved in the stimulation of heart activity, dilation of blood vessels, and increase in respiration.

Research has shown that PTSD involves the activity of the following neuro-chemicals:

Catecholamines (norepinephrine and dopamine)

Serotonin

Hormones and peptides (glucocorticoids (e.g., cortisol) and corticotropin-releasing factor)

Endogenous opiates

The benzodiazepine system and GABA

Catecholamines

Catecholamine levels in the brain are responsive to stress. They are among the critical neurochemicals involved in stress and fear responding. When there are exaggerated catecholamine levels there are increases in physiological and behavioral reactivity (Southwick, Krystal, Johnson, & Charney, 1995; Zigmond, Finlay, & Sved, 1995). Southwick, Rasmusson, Barron, and Arnsten (2005) refer to this as *stress sensitization*. As catecholamines become subsequently activated either by repeated stress or very intense stimuli, their sensitization results in a heightened state of reactivity. This reactivity is reflected in the arousal symptoms and vigilance of PTSD.

Catecholamines are also involved in the regulation of the amygdala. An increase in catecholamines increases amygdala functioning, promoting fear conditioning and the formation, or *stamping in,* of emotionally important memories. Again, catecholamine function is implicated in the hyperarousal of PTSD.

In turn, the amygdala influences catecholamine release in the prefrontal cortex. Increases in catecholamines (and glucocorticoids) suppress cognitive functioning in the PFC, such as planned and organized behavior. The amygdala stimulates the release of catecholamines and cortisol for better functioning, but this process suppresses the prefrontal cortex. This leads to an inability of the PFC to appropriately inhibit the amygdala, and thus the amygdala operates unchecked. As the amygdala goes unchecked, it is more reactive, again a process reflected in the hyperarousal of PTSD.

The catecholamines are also implicated in memory functioning. Generally, the catecholamines have an inverted *U relationship* with memory formation. They are involved in memory consolidation and have been shown to amplify explicit memory during emotional arousal. However, at very low levels or at very high levels of catecholamines, memory consolidation is impaired. PTSD sufferers have fragmented memories for the traumatic events specifically and also have generally impaired memory functioning.

So individuals with PTSD should show elevations in catecholamines, right? Elevated levels of norepinephrine in 24-hour blood plasma measures have been found in combat veterans with PTSD when compared to combat veterans without

PTSD; civilians living next to Three Mile Island following the nuclear-meltdown scare; and women with histories of child abuse (Davidson & Baum, 1986; Limieux & Coe, 1995; Yehuda, 1998a, 1998b). Other studies, using sophisticated biochemical manipulations to produce functional increases in norepinephrine, have shown that such experimental manipulation of norepinephrine can cause panic attacks and increases in specific PTSD symptoms such as hypervigilance, intrusive memories, and full-blown flashbacks in subjects diagnosed with PTSD (Southwich et al., 1993).

Norepinephrine

Norepinephrine is a specific catecholamine that has been implicated in PTSD pathology. It is a critical neurotransmitter in the amygdala fear circuit. Brain regions that have high concentrations of norepinephrine have been implicated in behaviors that orient an organism to its environment. Activation of norepinephrine stimulates alertness and vigilance. Attention resources are also activated, and responses to novel stimuli are increased. Finally, norepinephrine is involved in mobilizing the body for action and responding to danger.

The LC contains the vast majority of norepinephrine-producing cell bodies. It is involved in processing relevant sensory information and facilitates fear-related physiological, motor, cognitive, and neuroendocrine responses. Experimental stimulation of the LC produces fear-related behavior and increases release of norepinephrine in numerous brain areas, including the amygdala, hippocampus, hypothalamus, and the PFC (Southwick et al., 2005). Research has shown that animals that are intensely or repeatedly stressed will respond with exaggerated norepinephrine responsivity and reflect stress sensitization effects. Southwick and colleagues (2005) cite that this increased sensitivity is more typical in episodes of uncontrollable stress as opposed to controllable stress. This is certainly consistent with the types of traumatic stressors associated with PTSD.

Dopamine

Stimulation of the ventral tegmentum by the amygdala after a fear stimulus has been perceived results in the activation of dopamine stimulation. This leads to activation of the nucleus accumbens and subsequent activation and invigoration because dopamine facilitates synaptic transmission in the pathway from the nucleus accumbens and the pallidum, which is ultimately involved in the control of movement and motor responses.

It has long been thought that dopamine is involved in the reward system of the brain (i.e., learning from reinforcement). Stimulation of a particular region of the hypothalamus as fibers to the brainstem are activated results in stimulation of targeted neurons that make dopamine in the ventral tegmentum. They then project to the forebrain, releasing dopamine widely throughout the brain.

Research has shown that emotional numbing, anhedonia, and social disconnection are associated with dopamine dysfunction in the mesocortical and mesolimbic systems (Bremner, Southwick, & Charney, 1999). Also, dopamine is implicated in anticipatory behavior and may be implicated in the hypervigilance of PTSD because dopamine projections to the amygdala facilitate fear conditioning, leading to possible overreactivity of the amygdala subsequent to dopamine dysfunction.

Serotonin

Posttraumatic Stress Disorder symptoms have been associated with alterations in serotonin levels in the brain. Serotonin is an important neurotransmitter in multiple brain systems including the amygdala, the orbitofrontal cortex, the LC, the hippocampus, and the nucleus accumbens. Although the amygdala sits at the center of the fear circuit and receives and projects to many brain regions, it is thought to typically ignore most information coming to it. It has a reaction point or set point, and it is not simply reactive. Its reaction point is controlled or determined by many processes (see the discussion of the medial prefrontal cortex), but it also has an internal control mechanism mediated by its internal neurochemical makeup. Danger signaling stimuli overcome the amygdala's typical set point. The neurochemical set point of the amygdala can be significantly altered in two ways: by inputs having been altered upstream in the circuits sending input projections to it and if its own internal properties are altered. Serotonin levels have been implicated in altering the set point. When serotonin levels are sufficient, the set point functions adequately, but significant drops in functional serotonin levels result in less inhibition of the amygdala, lowering its trigger point and resulting in more reactivity. The stress hormone cortisol has been found to interfere with serotonin's ability to inhibit the amygdala as well.

Serotonin in the orbitofrontal cortex is involved in filtering and processing social and emotional information. Dysfunction here can result in poor decision making, poor recognition of emotion of others (resulting in attribution errors), and even aggression. The orbitofrontal cortex is sensitive to serotonin effects with depletions in serotonin causing dysfunction. Finally, reductions in serotonin levels have been shown to increase the firing rate of norepinephrine neurons in the LC.

Under stress, the medial prefrontal cortex increases serotonin metabolism, but with chronic stress, there can be decreases or reductions in functional serotonin levels. Low serotonin can be related to difficulties in modulating arousal, as is seen in exaggerated startle responding. Serotonin checks norepinephrine's responsiveness and norepinephrine-related arousal as well. There can also be higher levels of hostility, aggressiveness, impulsivity, and depression. All of these are common comorbid conditions with PTSD. van der Kolk (1996) proposes that serotonin plays a role in an organism's ability to monitor the environment and react flexibly to stimulation with situation-appropriate responses instead of reacting to internal stimuli that may be unrelated to current demands.

The Hypothalamic-Pituitary-Adrenal Axis, Neuropeptides, and Neurohormones

As previously outlined, three brain areas—the hypothalamus, the pituitary, and the adrenal cortex—have been specifically implicated in the biology of PTSD because of their role in neuropeptide and neurohormone activity. These brain areas are part of what is called the *hypothalamic-pituitary-adrenal axis* (HPA axis). When the amygdala is activated, it in turn activates or stimulates the hypothalamus. The hypothalamus is stimulated to release the neuropeptide: corticotropin-releasing factor (CRF). Release of CRF leads to the release of adrenocorticotropin-releasing factor by the pituitary, which leads to the release of the glucocorticoids, specifically cortisol, from the adrenal cortex.

Corticotropin-Releasing Factor (CRF)

As was previously mentioned, CRF is a critical component in the stress response. In addition to its role in the eventual release of cortisol, CRF itself has been implicated in PTSD pathophysiology. Corticotropin-releasing factor is distributed in numerous brain areas that are involved in stress responding, such as the amygdala, hippocampus, PFC, and LC. Stress increases levels of CRF in the hypothalamus. Bonne et al. (2004) report that exposure to stress early in life can produce long-term elevations in CRF and sensitization of CRF neurons with future stress. Brunson, Avishai-Eliner, Hatalski, and Baram (2001) have implicated CRF elevations in hippocampal damage. Further, research has shown that patients with PTSD have elevations of CRF in their cerebral spinal fluid (Baker et al., 1999).

Cortisol

During the stress response, the adrenal cortex secretes cortisol. It is considered a glucocorticoid because it has an impact on glucose metabolism by helping to break down proteins and converting them to glucose, making fats available for energy, increasing blood flow, and providing needed energy for danger responding. Cortisol's other roles in the stress response include inhibition of growth and sexual reproductive systems and modulation of inflammatory responses of the immune system. Cortisol is essential to the activation of the relevant systems of fight or flight and eventual survival.

Cortisol also modulates the effects of serotonin on GABA in the amygdala, which can result in altering the sensitivity of the amygdala. Cortisol's relation to fear responding is somewhat complex. In addition to its modulation of GABA in the amygdala, its release eventually can also lead back to the amygdala for increased function. This same process, however, suppresses PFC function. As was already discussed, PFC dysfunction is implicated in PTSD with dysfunction in working memory and ultimately in amygdala dysregulation.

Secretion of stress hormones can affect how memories are laid down and established. For instance, traumatic memories are more easily accessed and recalled under states of high arousal, even generic arousal. Conversely, oxytocin and endorphins have been found to interfere with memory for traumatic events.

Endogenous Opiates

Part of the stress response is the mobilization of resources to cope with or ignore pain. Stress-induced analgesia is caused by endogenous opiates. In addition, endogenous opiates are involved in modulating the stress responses of CRF and norepinephrine. Although endogenous opiates serve positive and adaptive functions under stress, they may have negative effects related to PTSD symptoms. It is thought they may be responsible for emotional blunting or flattening. This may also be related to dissociation as memory formation has been found to be affected by these substances as well.

The Benzodiazepine System and GABA

There are specific receptor sites for both benzodiazepines and GABA in the brain that are widely distributed. Benzodiazepines enhance and extend the synaptic actions of the neurotransmitter GABA. Gamma-aminobutyric acid is seen as an inhibitory neurochemical in the brain. Benzodiazepine receptors and GABA receptors are often considered jointly in what is sometimes called the *GABA-benzodiazepine receptor complex* (Maksay & Ticku, 1985). Animal research has shown that when subjects are exposed to acute or chronic inescapable shock, there is a reduction in benzodiazepine binding in the frontal lobe, the hippocampus, and the hypothalamus. These decreases have been associated with changes in memory, deficits in learning, and decreased release of GABA.

Alternations in GABA have subsequent effects as well. Gamma-aminobutyric acid is involved in inhibiting the amygdala from responding to unimportant stimuli. If GABA functioning is compromised, danger could be anywhere or represented by anything due to an uninhibited amygdala and hyperresponsiveness.

Imaging Studies and Anatomical Changes

Lisa Shin, Scott Rauch, and Roger Pitman (2005) discuss three specific brain regions with structural and functional abnormalities related to PTSD pathology: the amygdala, the medial prefrontal cortex, and the hippocampus.

PET (positron emission tomography) scan and SPECT (single photon emission computed tomography) span studies analyzing regional cerebral blood flow of the amygdala have shown increased blood flow—an index of activity—in the amygdala (Hendler et al., 2003; Liberzon et al., 1999; Pissiota et al., 2002; Rauch, van der Kolk, Fisler, & Alpert, 1996; Semple et al., 2000). This research shows increased amygdala activation in reaction to trauma reminders and fear-inducing stimuli alike.

Using magnetic resonance imaging (MRI), researchers have revealed reduced gray matter volume in the medial prefrontal cortex (Carrion et al., 2001; De Bellis et al., 2002; Fennema-Notestine, Stein, Kennedy, Archibald, & Jernigan, 2002).

Also, researchers have found reduced activity in the medial prefrontal cortex as measured by regional cerebral blood flow.

Finally, as was briefly mentioned previously, changes in the hippocampus have been shown. Researchers have found reduced hippocampal activation in response to trauma imagery and memory tasks as measured by regional cerebral blood flow, and reductions in hippocampal volume have also been found.

Lateralization

Lateralization refers to differential functioning between the two cerebral hemispheres. Although there are very few studies in this area, consistent findings have emerged. Research has shown that there are marked differences in the activity of the right hemisphere relative to the left, with increases in the right. This hemisphere is broadly considered involved in the evaluation of emotional stimuli for significance and in autonomic regulation and hormone responses. All of these are critical to fear and stress responding.

Reductions in left-hemispheric activity of Broca's area have been found. Broca's area is a critical brain structure in speech and language processing and the organization of experience and may play a role in the disorganized and fragmented state of PTSD memory processes and functioning.

Professional Alert

This research might be of particular interest to clinicians working from the narrative or constructivist therapy perspectives.

Electrophysiological Findings in PTSD

A relatively newer paradigm for investigating neurobiological abnormalities in PTSD has emerged in the measurement of brain wave activity with a special kind of electroencephalogram (EEG) measure called event-related potentials (ERPs). Event-related potentials measure changes in EEG activity in response to stimuli and serve as indices of reactivity and habituation and learning against background resting-state activity. An ERP, for example, serves as a measure of the brain's reaction to novel stimuli, with a reduction in activity as information is habituated to and is deemed repetitive or noninformative.

Arciniegas and colleagues (2000) have proposed that the symptoms of hypervigilance and attention deficits in PTSD are consequences of a reduction in sensory gating. Boutros and Belger (1999) define sensory gating as follows:

> [T]he ability of the brain to modulate its sensitivity to incoming sensory stimuli. This definition allows the concept of gating to include both the capacities to minimize or stop responding to incoming irrelevant stimuli (gating out) and to respond when a novel stimulus is presented or a change occurs in ongoing stimuli (gating in). (p. 917, abstract)

Metzger, Gilbertson, and Orr (2005) propose that in PTSD, selective attention is impaired because of a failure to filter out irrelevant environmental stimuli. They state, "Instead, they [PTSD sufferers] interpret or respond to repetitive stimuli as though they might maintain some significance." In other words, all stimuli are considered potentially relevant and, perhaps, dangerous because of their novelty.

Other researchers have found that not only do PTSD sufferers respond to a broader range of stimuli as novel for a longer period of time, but they also have an increased sensitivity to stimulus intensity. Under normal conditions and functioning, there is an increase in brain response with corresponding increases in stimulus intensity. But if the stimulus is too intense, there should be a smaller, more circumscribed brain response. This is viewed as a protective mechanism against overstimulation. In PTSD, this protective mechanism is engaged at lower stimulus thresholds than for non-PTSD sufferers. This research suggests rather direct biological evidence for the phenomenon of reactivity in PTSD.

Finally, in addition to poor habituation and lowered thresholds, researchers have found heightened sensitivity to stimulus change and novelty. Event-related potentials sensitive to this process have shown that in PTSD this process is amplified, leading to increased sensitivity to novelty and monopolization of attention resources.

Quick Review

- The central idea of the biological understanding of PTSD is that normal brain processes and mechanisms involved in danger and threat responding, self-preservation behavior, and protection behavior become dysfunctional, thus producing the various core symptoms of the syndrome.

- Sufferers of PTSD are stuck in the biological mode of responding to danger and threat, with subsequent alterations in alertness to threat cues and preferential processing of threat reminders and memories.

- The neurobiological mechanisms underlying fear conditioning and learning are critical to the biological account of PTSD.

- The symptoms of PTSD reflect changes in the neurochemical functioning of the brain within specific circuits.

- Alterations in specific brain structures such as the amygdala, the PFC, the hippocampus, the LC, and others are critical to the biology of PTSD.

- Alterations in specific neurochemicals such as the catecholamines, serotonin, neuropeptides, neurohormones, GABA, and endogenous opiates have been found to underlie the symptoms of PTSD.

- Alterations in the anatomy of the brain in the medial prefrontal cortex and hippocampus are implicated.

- Alterations in the brain's general responsiveness to novel stimuli and habituation as measured by ERPs have been connected to hyperresponsiveness and reactivity.

References

Arciniegas, D., Olincy, A., Topkoff, J., McRae, K., Cawthra, E., Filley, C. M., et al. (2000). Impaired auditory gating and P50 nonsuppression following traumatic brain injury. *Journal of Neuropsychiatry & Clinical Neurosciences, 12,* 77–85.

Ben-Shachar, M., Hendler, T., Kahn, I., Ben-Bashat, D., & Grodzinsky, Y. (2003). The neural reality of syntactic transformations: Evidence from functional magnetic resonance imaging. *Psychological Science, 14,* 433–440.

Baker, D. G., West, S. A., Nicholson, W. E., Ekhator, N. N., Kasckow, J. W., Hill, K. K., et al. (1999). Serial CSF corticotropin-releasing hormone levels and adrenocortical activity in combat veterans with Posttraumatic Stress Disorder. *American Journal of Psychiatry, 156,* 585–588.

Bonne, O., Grillon, C., Vythilingam, M., Neumeister, A., & Charney, D. S. (2004). Adaptive and maladaptive psychobiological responses to severe psychological stress: Implications for the discovery of novel pharmacotherapy. *Neuroscience & Biobehavioral Reviews, 28,* 65–94.

Boutros, N. N., & Belger, A. (1999). Midlatency evoked potentials attenuation and augmentation reflect different aspects of sensory gating. *Biological Psychiatry, 45,* 917–922.

Bremner, J. D. (1999). Does stress damage the brain? *Biological Psychiatry, 45,* 797–805.

Bremner, J. D., Southwick, S. M., & Charney, D. S. (1999). The neurobiology of Posttraumatic Stress Disorder: An integration of animal and human research. In P. A. Saigh & J. D. Bremner (Eds.), *Posttraumatic Stress Disorder: A comprehensive text* (pp. 103–143). Needham Heights, MA: Allyn & Bacon.

Bremner, J. D., Southwick, S. M., Johnson, D. R., Yehuda, R., et al. (1993). Childhood physical abuse and combat-related Posttraumatic Stress Disorder in Vietnam veterans. *American Journal of Psychiatry, 150,* 235–239.

Brunson, K. L., Avishai-Eliner, S., Hatalski, C. G., & Baram, T. Z. (2001). Neurobiology of the stress response early in life: Evolution of a concept and the role of corticotropin releasing hormone. *Molecular Psychiatry, 6,* 647–656.

Carrion, V. G., Weems, C. F., Eliez, S., Patwardhan, A., Brown, W., Ray, R. D., et al. (2001). Attenuation of frontal asymmetry in pediatric Posttraumatic Stress Disorder. *Biological Psychiatry, 50,* 943–951.

Davidson, L. M., & Baum, A. (1986). Chronic stress and Posttraumatic Stress Disorders. *Journal of Consulting and Clinical Psychology, 54,* 303–308.

De Bellis, M. D., Keshavan, M. S., Shifflett, H., Iyengar, S., Beers, S. R., Hall, J., et al. (2002). Brain structures in pediatric maltreatment-related Posttraumatic Stress Disorder: A sociodemographically matched study. *Biological Psychiatry, 52,* 1066–1078.

Fennema-Notestine, C., Stein, M. B., Kennedy, C. M., Archibald, S. L., & Jernigan, T. L. (2002). Brain morphometry in female victims of intimate partner violence with and without Posttraumatic Stress Disorder. *Biological Psychiatry, 52,* 1089–1101.

Hendler, T., Goshen, E., Zwas, S. T., Sasson, Y., Gal, G., & Zohar, J. (2003). Brain reactivity to specific symptom provocation indicates prospective therapeutic outcome in OCD. *Psychiatry Research: Neuroimaging, 124,* 87–103.

Krystal, H. (1978). Trauma and affects. *Psychoanalytic Study of the Child, 33,* 81–116.

LeDoux, J. (2002). *Synaptic self. How our brains become who we are.* New York: Penguin Books.

Lemieux, A. M., & Coe, C. L. (1995). Abuse-related Posttraumatic Stress Disorder: Evidence for chronic neuroendocrine activation in women. *Psychosomatic Medicine, 57,* 105–115.

Liberzon, I., Taylor, S. F., Amdur, R., Jung, T. D., Chamberlain, K. R., Minoshima, S., et al. (1999). Brain activation in PTSD in response to trauma-related stimuli. *Biological Psychiatry, 45,* 817–826.

Maksay, G., & Ticku, M. K. (1985). CNS depressants accelerate the dissociation of 35s-TBPS binding and GABA enhances their displacing potencies. *Life Sciences, 43*(16), 1331–1337.

McEwen, B. S. (1998). Stress, adaptation, and disease: Allostasis and allostatic load. In S. M. McCann, J. M. Lipton, E. M. Sternberg, G. P. Chrousos, P. W. Gold, et al. (Eds.), *Annals of the New York Academy of Sciences: Vol. 840. Neuroimmunomodulation: Molecular aspects, integrative systems, and clinical advances* (pp. 33–44). New York: New York Academy of Sciences.

McEwen, B. S. (2004). Protective and damaging effects of the mediators of stress and adaptation: Allostasis and allostatic load. In J. Schulkin (Ed.), *Allostasis, homeostasis, and the costs of physiological adaptation* (pp. 65–98). New York: Cambridge University Press.

Metzger, L. J., Gilbertson, M. W., & Orr, S. P. (2005). Electrophysiology of PTSD. In J. J. Vasterling & C. R. Brewin (Eds.), *Neuropsychology of PTSD: Biological, cognitive, and clinical perspectives* (pp. 83–102). New York: Guilford.

Pissiota, A. F., Fernandez, M., von Knorring, L., Fischer, H., & Fredrikson, M. (2002). Neurofunctional correlates of Posttraumatic Stress Disorder: A PET symptom provocation study. *European Archives of Psychiatry and Clinical Neuroscience, 252,* 68–75.

Rauch, S. L., van der Kolk, B. A., Fisler, R. E., & Alpert, N. M. (1996). A symptom provocation study of Posttraumatic Stress Disorder using positron emission tomography and script-driven imagery. *Archives of General Psychiatry, 53,* 380–387.

Semple, W. E., Goyer, P. F., McCormick, R., Donovan, B., Muzic, R. F., Jr., Rugle, L., et al. (2000). Higher brain blood flow at amygdala and lower frontal cortex blood flow in PTSD patients with comorbid Cocaine and Alcohol Abuse compared with normals. *Psychiatry: Interpersonal and Biological Processes, 63,* 65–74.

Shin, L. M., Rauch, S. L., & Pitman, R. K. (2005). Structural and functional anatomy of PTSD: Findings from neuroimaging research. In J. J. Vasterling & C. R. Brewin (Eds.), *Neuropsychology of PTSD: Biological, cognitive, and clinical perspectives* (pp. 59–82). New York: Guilford.

Southwick, S. M., Krystal, J. H., Johnson, D. R., & Charney, D. S. (1995). Neurobiology of Post-Traumatic Stress Disorder. In G. S. Everly, Jr. & J. M. Lating (Eds.), *Psychotraumatology: Key papers and core concepts in post-traumatic stress* (pp. 49–72). New York: Plenum Press.

Southwick, S. M., Krystal, J. H., Morgan, C. A., Johnson, D., et al. (1993). Abnormal noradrenergic function in Posttraumatic Stress Disorder. *Archives of General Psychiatry, 50,* 266–274.

Southwick, S. M., Rasmusson, A., Barron, J., & Arnsten, A. (2005). Neurobiological and neurocognitive alterations in PTSD: A focus on norepinephrine, serotonin, and the hypothalamic-pituitary-adrenal axis. In J. J. Vasterling & C. R. Brewin (Eds.), *Neuropsychology of PTSD: Biological, cognitive, and clinical perspectives* (pp. 27–58). New York: Guilford.

van der Kolk, B. A. (1996). The body keeps the score: Approaches to the psychobiology of posttraumatic stress disorder. In B. A. van der Kolk, A. C. McFarlane, & L. Weisaeth (Eds.), *Traumatic stress: The effects of overwhelming experience on mind, body, and society* (pp. 214–241). New York: Guilford.

Wilson, J. P., Friedman, M. J., & Lindy, J. D. (Eds.). (2001). *Treating psychological trauma and PTSD.* New York: Guilford.

Yehuda, R. (1998a). Neuroendocrinology of trauma and Posttraumatic Stress Disorder. In R. Yehuda (Ed.), *Psychological trauma* (pp. 97–131). Washington, DC: American Psychiatric Association.

Yehuda, R. (1998b). Psychoneuroendocrinology of Post-Traumatic Stress Disorder. *Psychiatric Clinics of North America, 21,* 359–379.

Zigmond, M. J., Finlay, J. M., & Sved, A. F. (1995). Neurochemical studies of central noradrenergic responses to acute and chronic stress: Implications for normal and abnormal behavior. In M. J. Friedman, D. S. Charney, & A. Y. Deutch (Eds.), *Neurobiological and clinical consequences of stress: From normal adaptation to Post-Traumatic Stress Disorder* (pp. 45–60). Philadelphia: Lippincott, Williams, & Wilkins.

CHAPTER 7

Psychodynamic, Psychosocial, Alternative, and Integrated Theories and Models of Posttraumatic Stress Disorder

Because of the wide range of approaches used to investigate the etiology of PTSD, PTSD perhaps represents the prototype for the use of the Biopsychosocial approach to understanding mental disorders. Although many other mental disorders have been approached from each of these three areas (e.g., depression or Schizophrenia), PTSD stands out as one of the most broadly investigated and multidisciplinary-involved disorders in the *DSM-IV-TR*. PTSD has been heavily investigated by physicians, psychologists, and even sociologists. As we have seen in Chapters 5 and 6, cognitive theories and biological models alike have given us powerful insights into the experience and etiology of PTSD on an individual basis. But like all psychological phenomena, these cognitive and biological processes occur within an interpersonal and social context that plays a powerful role in determining the development and presentation of the disorder. In this chapter, we will look at PTSD with the social and interpersonal perspectives in mind and conclude with some promising attempts at integration and construction of comprehensive understandings of its etiology.

Safety, Security, and Attachment—Psychodynamic Approaches to PTSD

Most students of psychology are familiar with psychodynamic theories of human psychological functioning, from the works of Sigmund Freud to W. Bion. *Psychodynamic* is the modern name for what most people would recognize as psychoanalytic. Psychodynamic theories are bound together by their rich history and tradition as well as by their core themes and conceptual focus. Psychodynamic theories of psychopathology have in common a focus on the internal struggle of the mind for the expression and management of impulses, wishes, fears, and instincts by the defensive functions and other mental operations.

According to Ulman and Brothers (1988), there are three main schools of psychoanalytic or psychodynamic thought on trauma: (1) classical, (2) neoclassical, and (3) revisionist.

The classical school begins with Sigmund Freud, who recognized that traumatic events could produce *traumatic neuroses,* conditions recognized by Freud to consist of intrusive imagery, physiological hyperactivity, active reliving the event as if it was recurring in the here and now (Wilson, 1995). A traumatic event threatens the ego with destruction or annihilation, and in order to cope with this threat, repression is employed as a defense. Freud characterizes traumatic stressors as overwhelming for the protective shield of the ego. There is a disruption in normal functioning and the ability to cope effectively with current stressors. Traumatic stressors and current stressors combine to overwhelm the ego and its defenses, thus leading to symptom expression. The strong affects related to the trauma press for expression in emotional or behavioral form.

Freud developed a second model of trauma that served as an important predecessor to the neoclassical and revisionist schools. In this model, trauma is viewed as a stimulus that activates deep unconscious processes and memories of deep conflict. A traumatic event has meaning and power only in that it activates and is subsequently derived from dormant pathology and repressed memories. As unconscious memories and conflicts become activated by the intrusiveness of the traumatic stimulus, it results in overstimulation and symptomatic breakthroughs.

The work of Phyllis Greenacre (1969) and Edith Jacobson (1949) characterize the neoclassical school. Both theorists rely heavily on Freud's second model. For Greenacre, trauma results from stimulation of deep unconscious conflict, but she adds that the response is organized as a sadomasochistic fantasy. That is, the trauma is dealt with as a purely mental phenomenon as it is connected to deep unconscious processes. The drama of the traumatic stress reaction is played out, coped with, and resolved as our mental defenses transform it into a fantasy that is both out of our control and simultaneously under our control.

Edith Jacobson (1949) proposed that traumatic stressors represent an assault on our ego and result in a "narcissistic disturbance inside the ego involving conflicts between self-representations" (Ulman & Brothers, 1988, p. 52). Conflict arises between views of oneself as safe and secure versus being weak and unsafe. There are problems with the formulation and maintenance of a healthy self-image. Decompensation and regression develop as responses to the assault on a person's dignity and pride. There is an unacceptable and painful sense of self or a self that has been "degraded, humiliated, and worthless" (Ulman & Brothers, 1988, p. 53). This can lead to dissociation. Again, the key point to remember in the works of Freud, Greenacre, and Jacobson is that trauma comes not directly from the event but from a stimulation of unconscious conflict and our coping and defensive responses to the conflict.

Big names from the revisionist school are Rado (1942), Kardiner (1941), and Kelman (1945). For both Rado and Kardiner (1941), trauma is characterized as a disturbance in adaptational functioning in which there is a pathological alteration in one's sense of self and how it relates to the outer world. For Kelman, trauma is caused by the loss of and failure to revive a neurotic character- or personality-organizing structure that gives rise to a core sense of self. Symptoms come from extreme personality decompensation, and some people are more vulnerable than others due to underlying character pathology that is overly focused on a view of oneself as strong, unique, inviolate, invulnerable, and having a strong need for self-control and external control of the environment. Trauma is the result of these images of oneself breaking down.

Ulman and Brothers (1988) have developed a self-psychology model of trauma based to a large degree on the work of psychoanalyst Heinz Kohut. In essence, trauma shatters the self, with *the self* defined as the "subject's experience of mental being and physical existence" (Ulman & Brothers, 1988, p. 5). With trauma, there is a disturbance in self-functioning that contributes to the sense of trauma, there is damage to one's view of the self, and there is a failure to restore the self to the center of one's psychological organization of the world. One's ability to maintain an organized sense of experience breaks down. This, in part, may account for the disorganized and fragmented nature of traumatic memories and cognitions. Trauma is a significant challenge to narcissistic fantasies of personal uniqueness, entitlement, and invulnerability. As a victim responds to these insults and features of disorganization, symptoms ensue.

Lemma and Levy's Perversion of Loss

Allessandra Lemma and Susan Levy (2004) give us a very contemporary psychodynamic approach to understanding PTSD. At its core, PTSD is about loss—symbolic loss, actual loss (e.g., death or almost dying), or both. Exactly how the experience of loss is processed is crucial as are the relationships between traumatic responses and a victim's capacity to mourn the loss in question. A traumatic stressor presents a victim with a very powerful and unbelievable experience. The normal mourning process used in coping with loss is altered in response to traumatic stress as a way to manage the "unbearable and unthinkable nature of the traumatic loss" (Lemma & Levy, 2004, p. xvi). Internal and unconscious mental functioning is altered.

The mental representation and symbolism of interpersonal relations and representations of self are critical components in this theory. There is a breakdown in the symbolic functioning of the mind and its identifications that result in the trauma victim's being locked or stuck in a chronic state of melancholia or a related unresolved posttraumatic response. With the onset of a traumatic stressor, an individual engages in defensive functioning, central to which is one's connection to an attachment figure or object. With trauma, there is an attack on attachment in which both internal mental representations and external relationships at the time of the trauma are taxed and challenged. A trauma is experienced as an attack on this symbolic mental representation and the quality of one's identifications with attachment figures. It is as if traumatic stressors lead to one questioning his or her very connection to the people they feel closest to and safest with. Further, a trauma is an attack on one's sense of identity and security in relation to the world. The world is experienced as having turned against the victim, leaving them perpetually afraid and hyperresponsive to everything. The ego and its functioning is compromised as the trauma's severity breaks through and breaks down typical defenses. The ego and the self are penetrated and can no longer be trusted for protection. Hypervigilance results, and perceptual and other stimuli cease to be mere symbols but are mistaken as actual signals of danger.

There are four main themes to Lemma and Levy's (2004) work. The first theme, mentioned earlier, is that trauma is an attack on attachment. There is an attack on and damage done to one's ability to share and engage with others. There is also an attack on one's ability to mentally structure a story or narrative about the event–an attack on one's ability to put what happened into words, "both in relation to another person and also in terms of the construction of an inner dialogue with our subject" (Levy & Lemma, 2004, p. 5).

The second theme holds that there is a breakdown in the ability to adequately mourn the loss in question. This process leads to the *perversion of loss* in which emotional pain and guilt overwhelm the victim and result in identifying with the perpetrator of the trauma as a means to control or cope with these powerful emotions. Also, a current trauma can reshape memories of attachment and give a victim a sense that good objects (i.e., mental representations of people) will not endure or prevail under the stress and strain. This is the breakdown in the capacity to mourn.

The third theme involves consequent oscillating identifications between internal psychological themes of goodness, survival, and safety and the destructive identification or perverted loss identification. The fourth and final theme involves the breakdown of symbolic functioning in which the traumatic stressor undermines the facility to think and reflect on current, conscious, lived experience. Posttrauma images, thoughts, and feelings are represented in a manner that distorts reality testing and are not stored as typical memories. They emerge in concrete form as flashbacks and intrusive thoughts, and the mind is vulnerable to overstimulation.

Psychosocial and Alternative Models

Judith Herman's Work

In her book *Trauma and Recovery*, Judith Herman (1992) takes a very humanistic and sociopolitical approach to understanding posttraumatic stress and reactions. Her work is based in part on psychodynamic theory but also on a sophisticated and humane understanding of the role that traumatized people play in the social order, society, and our culture. She has combined both a clinical and social approach. Herman believes that trauma is an almost taboo subject and experience in most societies and that trauma victims suffer not only from the direct effects of the traumatic stressor themselves but also from a type of social trauma. She states, "The ordinary response to atrocities is to banish them from consciousness" (p. 1). That is, victims and those around them, including society as whole, wish to forget. For Herman, healing from trauma for both the individual victim and society requires that the events be acknowledged and their reality validated. We must bear witness if healing is to occur. This process is extremely difficult and often consists of oscillating periods between open acknowledgment and denial, a process she calls the *dialectic of trauma.*

A basic understanding of trauma requires that a political movement and sociopolitical context of support exist in order to combat the natural forces of denial, repression, and avoidance. Herman (1992) is adamant about the role that discrediting trauma victims plays in increasing their suffering and symptomology. Forgetting what happened, whether it is on an individual level, a family or group level, or at the level of society, is a critical feature in maintaining the syndrome. Herman states that perpetrators of trauma want everyone to forget and use secrecy, silence, and attacks on a victim's credibility to help this process along. Posttraumatic Stress Disorder is seen as an affliction of the powerless accompanied by extremely strong subjective experiences of helplessness and of being overpowered and overwhelmed. When the natural or normal responses to danger fail to bring safety and security, thus comes the experience of trauma.

The intrusive symptoms of PTSD are a consequence of the way traumatic stimuli are encoded in memory. Because of abnormal levels of sympathetic (fight or flight) arousal, the normal pathways of iconic and linguistic memory are not established, and memories associated with the stimuli are not organized in a manner easily talked about or discussed. Victims lack verbal narrative and context. Memories are stored in the form of vivid sensations and images. This is, perhaps, why talk therapy can be so effective with trauma survivors.

In keeping with her emphasis on the social context in which a trauma occurs, Herman (1992) focuses on the role played by a victim's sense of disconnection from other people and from his or her environment in PTSD. Trauma can challenge one's sense of attachment, especially in situations in which the trauma is a consequence of human action, such as violence. One can become disconnected from oneself as his or her ties to others bring into question a sense of having a stable identity as it relates to other people. Belief systems related to an orderly and stable social order and even the world at large can lead to strong feelings of instability and of experiencing the world as unpredictable. The sense of disconnection then can be felt in relation to others, oneself, and even the world as a whole.

With trauma, our sense of basic safety is significantly challenged. Herman reminds us that our sense of basic trust is initially established in our interactions with our primary caregiver, à la Erik Erikson's work on basic trust versus mistrust. Our basic sense of trust enables us to engage the world. Herman (1992) states, "the original experience of care makes it possible for human beings to envisage a world in which they belong, a world hospitable to human life" (p. 51). Trauma challenges this and leads to an experiencing of relationships as alien and fraught with abandonment. In keeping with her psychoanalytic roots and similar to the work of Freud, Herman states that trauma reactivates old psychodynamic conflicts and our struggles related to autonomy, initiative, competence, identity, and intimacy. As our autonomy fails to triumph over the powerful traumatic stimulus, our ability to self-regulate our emotions and levels of arousal breaks down. Trauma, with its invasiveness, injuries, damage, and potential for death, violates our very basic bodily integrity, according to Herman. Finally, strong feelings of guilt and shame come from the passing of judgment of the victim upon oneself for having failed to be safe and avoid the overwhelming stimulus.

Disconnection does not just refer to a victim's orientation to the outside world but also to their intrapsychic or mental organization. Symptoms can become disconnected from the original stimulus or event and can become fragmented, leading to a sense of chaos and disorganization. They can take on a life of their own of sorts, and the purposeful action and responses of everyday living are disrupted and break down. Perception becomes untrustworthy, false, and fear-based despite no evidence of danger. Judgment and decision making fail as a consequence of bad data. The nervous system is reconditioned, resulting in a perpetual state of alert with no or very little habituation.

Herman (1992) adds that traumatic reactions are individualized and unique to each person with no two people necessarily reacting the same. Individual differences, with some people being relatively immune to PTSD and still others being vulnerable, are important factors. Stress-resilient people are typically highly social people who are thoughtful, have an active coping style, and have a strong sense of being able to control their own destinies. Interestingly, true belief in the concept of having good luck for having survived a trauma intact seems to be an important buffer. Social support is also a mitigating factor. Coming full circle, Herman states that the community reaction is an extremely important factor with importance being placed on acknowledgment and assigning blame and responsibility to perpetrators with recognition and restitution being necessary to "rebuild a survivor's sense of order and justice" (p. 70).

Feminist Theory

Coinciding with the theoretical and empirical development and investigation of PTSD in Vietnam veterans was the painstaking work of feminist-oriented therapists and their experiences with women survivors of sexual assault, domestic violence, childhood abuse, and sexual harassment. Similar to the work of Judith Herman, feminist practitioners, theoreticians, and researchers took a more contextual and social view of trauma, and, as Laura Brown (2004) states, "moved the locus of the problem of interpersonal violence from its historical location in the victim's personality to the misogyny of the culture expressed through the actions of perpetrators of violence" (p. 464). Trauma is framed within its social, emotional, and political environments, and Brown (2004) summarizes the feminist theory of trauma best:

> [The] feminist theory of trauma argues that what is traumatizing to a person is not simply the experience of threat to life or safety. Rather, it is what will be symbolically evoked by this experience and the manner in which the social context responds to the person who has been traumatized. (p. 465)

Trauma, specifically interpersonal violence, is seen as an individualized representation of societal or institutional forms of discrimination, repression, and oppression such as racism, sexism, or heterosexism. Vulnerability is set up by the presence of unjust "hierarchies of value in the culture," according to Laura Brown (2004, p. 465). Thus, trauma is a violation that serves to uphold the oppressive cultural status quo.

Root (1992) proposed the concept of *insidious traumatization* in which persons of target and marginalized groups experience subthreshold traumatic stressors on a daily basis. Three examples are cited: (1) news that a member of one's group has been the target of bias-based violence or discrimination, (2) negative and stigmatizing images of one's group in media, textbooks, and discourse of peers and coworkers, and (3) various forms of institutionalized racism, heterosexism, and other exclusionary systems of value in which the individual is denied access to material or human resources solely on the basis of group membership. Such subthreshold stressors are cumulative and "serve as constant reminders of the precariousness of one's safety in contexts where one's group is the target of bias" (Brown, 2004, p. 466). This can lead to relatively small stressors leading to PTSD symptom expression. In my own practice, I have evaluated numerous individuals, who seem to have a dormant form of PTSD, thats' become activated by a serious, but certainly not dangerous or life-threatening, situation or event. One such patient began to have both PTSD symptoms and debilitating panic attacks after being yelled at by her boss and after he jumped up out of his seat and pointed his finger at her. Roots believed that what is traumatic in such situations is the representation of a threat to one's safety.

Lay Person Alert

Don't let the word *feminist* get in the way of the power and importance of such models of trauma. In fact, the work of feminist-oriented professionals might be extremely important if someone finds him- or herself in a situation at work or in a relationship that he or she finds extremely troubling but does not understand why. If someone finds that he or she may be having what most people think is an extreme reaction to a minor event, consider the concepts of insidious traumatization. Confusion, doubt, and strong feelings of shame and guilt might be indications of something more serious going on, something that before the work of feminists might have been disregarded, ignored, dismissed, or just forgotten.

The Constructivist Narrative Perspective

Social scientists and psychologists from the constructivist perspective hold central the tenet that people actively construct their individual realities and "create their own representational models of the world" (Meichenbaum & Fitzpatrick, 1993, p. 707). We don't respond to the world in its pure form but rather to our interpretations of the information we receive about the world and to the implications of that information.

The meaning of information is constructed in a narrative process or stories that we "tell ourselves to others, as well as to ourselves" (Meichenbaum & Fitzpatrick, 1993, p. 707). Narrative psychology is the study of such stories. We make sense and meaning of the world in terms of such stories. Victor Frankl was a famous psychologist and survivor of a Nazi concentration camp in World War II. In his book *Man's Search for Meaning,* Frankl spoke of the importance of finding meaning in life as crucial to both physical and psychological survival, but implicit in his work was the idea that meaning could be derived almost despite the adverse circumstances in which one finds himself. Meichenbaum and Fitzpatrick (1993) proposed that meaning making through narrative often occurs in response to disruptions in a person's routine and when reacting or adjustment is necessary, "especially when their physical or psychological well-being is judged to be at stake" (p. 708). Stressful events or traumatic stressors would certainly qualify as such. The process of posttraumatic adjustment is thought to be critically influenced by how a person goes through the narrative construction process and that, ultimately, good adjustment and health emerge from what Schafer (1981) called *narrative repair.*

Traumatic stimuli and events have the effect of challenging or damaging one's personal reality—one's *assumptive world* (Epstein, 1991). Thus, constructing a new narrative and assumptive world that assimilates the traumatic experience is crucial to recovery. Engaging in the *why* process is a natural example of a question that fuels the narrative construction process. Many posttrauma survivors have even questioned their "god," sometimes finding answers in religious and spiritual revelation. Baumeister, Stillwell, and Wotman (1990) report that whether a survivor defines himself as a victim or perpetrator will influence distress levels and symptom expression. Even the symptoms of intrusive imagery are thought of as an attempt to make sense of the event. Posttraumatic Stress Disorder and chronic distress can result from an inability to construct meaning from an event, leaving one feeling chronically overwhelmed and fragmented. Although a search for meaning and narrative construction are seen as health-generating processes, Tait and Silver (1989) found that a persistent search for meaning for an event was inversely related to psychological health and well-being when there was no final resolution or conclusion. It would seem that telling a story about what happened can help if the story has an ending but not if it just goes on and on.

Integrated Theories and Models

Yule's, Williams, and Joseph's Integrated Psychosocial Model

Yule, Williams, and Joseph present what they call a multifactorial model of PTSD that includes numerous components from other models and combines them into a complex of interrelated variables. Perhaps, the easiest way to approach an understanding of their model is to first present it as shown in Figure 7.1.

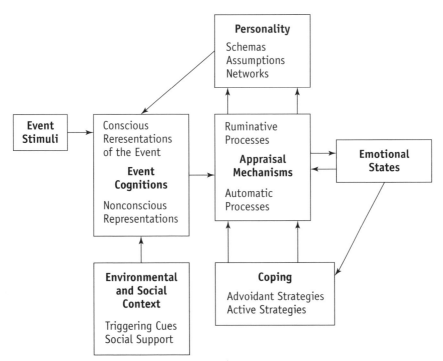

FIGURE 7.1 *An Integrated Psychosocial Model.*

To understand the model, begin with the traumatic event, and go clockwise through event cognitions, appraisals, emotional states, coping, appraisal with cognitions influenced by personality or memory representations, and the social environment, with a final state of either continued cycling or resolution.

This is a complicated model, and, perhaps, the best way to represent it is to simply define the components in a listwise fashion:

- *Event stimuli.* A traumatic stressor.

- *Event cognitions.* Mental representations that are either not available for conscious inspection or information is intentionally retrievable. These are the basis for reexperiencing symptoms of PTSD.

- *Appraisal cognitions.* These are thoughts about the stressor information and memories it evokes. Its two forms are automatic thoughts associated with schemas and emotional states and reappraisals or conscious thinking through alternative meanings. This aspect reflects rumination and intrusive cognition.

- *Personality.* An individual's schemas and personality characteristics that exert influence on both appraisals and cognitions about the event.

- *Emotional states.* Emotional states that can also be appraised or reappraised.

- *Coping.* This component includes any and all coping responses, such as avoidance, rumination, emotional suppression, and so on.

- *Environmental and social context.* This component represents the context in which all of this takes place and the ongoing environmental stimuli that might serve to trigger a traumatic cognition.

In essence, what Yule's, Williams and Joseph's model is saying is that an event triggers a cognitive response that is determined by a person's personality and appraisal outcomes. Appraisal outcomes are determined by personality, emotion, and coping in a cyclical feedback loop. The environment and social context are both independent but are influenced by the person's coping responses. The model, although complex, takes a sophisticated approach in its attempt to capture all the components in PTSD etiology and how they interact with each other. What stands out is their focus on the interaction of each of the components and how they influence each other. This model is an excellent representation of the complexity of both PTSD specifically and psychological processes in general.

George Everly's Integrative Two-Factor Model

Everly's (1995) approach combines a biological and psychological explanation of PTSD. Its attempt at integration combines the core *DSM-IV-TR* symptom groups into a single psychophysiological construct. As one might discern from its title, there are two factors, conceptualized within a neurocognitive framework. A diagram of the model is shown in Figure 7.2.

Factor one consists of an underlying sensitized nervous system with three main features. The first feature involves the augmentation of excitatory neurotransmitters, such as norepinephrine, dopamine, and glutamate. The second feature involves a functional reduction in inhibitory neurochemicals, such as gamma-aminobutyric acid (GABA). The third and final feature involves changes in neural structure and intraneuronal functioning that biases the nervous system toward excitability, such as postsynaptic sensitivity or a reduction in neurotransmitter reuptake mechanisms. Ultimately, all of this results in an individual being in a state of extreme, chronic, and intense arousal. It is as if the nervous system is set, poised, and fixated in a state of alert, survival, and security.

Factor two refers to the hypersensitivity of the psychological components of the model. At the core of this factor is the underlying concept that human beings have as a basic need and are constantly striving toward an understanding and cognitive or mental grasp on their world and their self. What essentially happens is that a traumatic stressor or event results in a significant challenge and violation of a person's worldview and a subsequent inability to assimilate the new information into one's view of the world and one's view of oneself. Ultimately, as Maslow (1970) and Horowitz (1976) have stated, once a person's sense of basic safety and security is so significantly challenged or threatened, he or she becomes fixated on the task of trying to restore it, constantly seeking resolution or integration.

Bessel van der Kolk and McFarlane's Model

Bessel van der Kolk characterizes the range of Biopsychosocial consequences or responses to traumatic stress as a process of adaptation to trauma. Trauma can have at least three very large effects on an individual. First problems with regulation of affective states, including problems with anger and anxiety, can arise. Victims overreact to emotional stimulation and may experience anhedonia and numbing as a consequence.

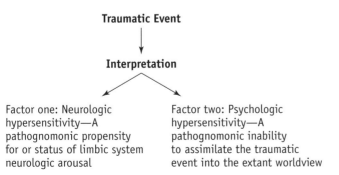

Traumatic Event

Interpretation

Factor one: Neurologic hypersensitivity—A pathognomonic propensity for or status of limbic system neurologic arousal

Factor two: Psychologic hypersensitivity—A pathognomonic inability to assimilate the traumatic event into the extant worldview

FIGURE 7.2 *Two-Factor Model of PTSD.*

A second consequence leads to vulnerability to engage in pathological attempts at self-regulation, such as self-mutilation, Eating Disorders, or Substance Abuse. In an individual's attempts to regain control, he or she may resort to unhealthy means to do so. There is a breakdown in an individual's capacity to consider a range of actions before acting. They may have problems with fantasy and playing with options. van der Kolk and McFarlane (1996) state that fantasizing may allow previously blocked memories to emerge. In order to avoid this, emotions are restricted and one's fantasy life is limited. This leads to the avoidance of recollection. They may also have significant difficulty sorting out important stimuli from unimportant stimuli, finding themselves unable to filter what is unimportant and reacting by shutting down and shutting out stimuli. This leads to less contact with daily life and a subsequent increase in ruminating about the trauma.

"What distinguishes people who develop PTSD from people who are merely temporarily distressed is that they organize their lives around the trauma," according to van der Kolk and McFarlane (1996, p. 6).

Third, extreme arousal is accompanied by dissociation, alexithymia, somatization, and a failure to establish a sense of security and safety, leading to characterological issues with self-efficacy, shame, self-hatred, dependence, and isolation and relationship issues. One's attachment security is considered a primary defense against trauma-induced pathology. This is seen as especially important with traumatized children, and research has shown that the quality of the parental bond may be the most important factor in whether PTSD develops (McFarlane, 1987a, b, c, d) in kids.

A Diathesis-Stress Model

Victoria McKeever and Maureen Huff (2003) have attempted to construct a single model to address the various influences contributing to the development of PTSD. They reason that because the majority of persons exposed to traumatic stressors do not develop PTSD, this variation can be accounted for by the presence or lack of certain etiological risk factors per individual. They categorize all the various etiological risk factors into three large groups: residual or situation stress, ecological diatheses, and biological diatheses. They state that all of these mutually influence each other. Figure 7.3 represents the model

The residual category represents the primary pathway for the development of PTSD, being augmented or attenuated by the other two groups of etiological diatheses and biological diatheses. A diathesis can be conceptualized as a relatively dormant set of risk factors that blossom, if you will, when triggered by a sufficient stimulus. McKeever and Huff (2003) make an important point about the relationship between intensity of a stressor and the level of diatheses present in an individual. They call this the *psychological break point*, the point at which PTSD emerges. Basically, the higher the degree of premorbid risk factors or diatheses is present, the smaller a stressor has to be to push someone toward

PTSD and vice versa. *Residual stress* was defined by Foy, Donahoe, and Carroll (1987) as a negative psychological condition resulting from the experience of a traumatic event. The more severe the trauma, the higher the level of residual stress. The diagnostic qualifiers of intense fear, helplessness, and horror capture this feature of the model in the *DSM-IV-TR*.

As was discussed in Chapter 4, research has demonstrated a great number of risk factors for the development of PTSD. McKeever and Huff's (2003) model addresses nonbiological risk factors in the ecological component of their model. A history of childhood abuse, being a member of a discriminated against group, poor social support, or personality factors are all examples of ecological diatheses.

Finally, biological diatheses such as altered neuronal functioning, altered brain volume, and altered hormone functioning are the final key component in this triarchic diathesis stress model. (For more on the various biological complications resulting from trauma, see Chapter 3.)

The Holistic-Organismic Approach

Wilson, Friedman, and Lindy (2001) have proposed a complex model of PTSD that attempts to go beyond the *DSM-IV* and the core symptoms of PTSD to capture the multidimensional aspects of the disorder as it affects individuals across a wide range of biopsychosocial areas. At the core of their model rests Bruce McEwan's concept of allostatic load. *Allostasis* refers to an organism's regulation of biopsychosocial functioning in the face of stress and strain, or *allostatic load*. Many of us are familiar with the concept of homeostasis, in which an organism attempts to maintain a balance between internal and external or ecological and environmental demands. Similarly, allostasis works to maintain balance through similar mechanisms of input and feedback but more specifically when impinged or impressed upon by significant load.

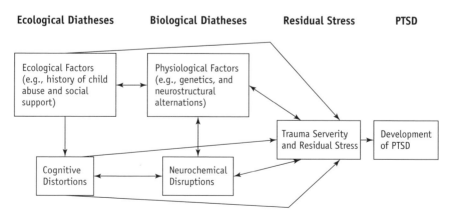

FIGURE 7.3 *Diathesis-Stress Model of PTSD.*

Posttraumatic Stress Disorder is broadly conceptualized as a holistic or total organism (i.e., organismic) process of allostatic management. When an individual is exposed to a traumatic stressor, subsequent failure to resolve or integrate the trauma within a healthy baseline biopsychosocial repertoire leads to subsequent vulnerability to cues and triggers that leads to abnormal adjustment and nonresolution of the original trauma long after the original threat no longer exists. This reflects a failure or breakdown in allostasis. Posttraumatic Stress Disorder sufferers are vulnerable to abrupt changes in organismic status, including emotion and arousal so that states of relative calm can be abruptly disrupted by intense fear, anger, depression, or vigilance.

PTSD is essentially viewed as altered *psychobiological allostasis* in eight domains:

1. *Altered thresholds of response:* hypervigilance, altered appraisals, increased threat appraisal, proneness to reenactment, and lower stress tolerance overall.

2. *Hyperreactivity or allostatic dysregulation:* irritability, proneness to aggression, exaggerated startle, insomnia, avoidance, and poor modulation of arousal and affect.

3. *Altered initial response patterns:* decreased safety appraisals, overreaction to cues, proneness to fight or flight.

4. *Altered capacity of internal monitoring:* decreased capacity for accurate self-monitoring and increased vulnerability of cognitive and emotional responses.

5. *Altered feedback based on distorted information:* decreased capacity for accurate monitoring of interpersonal events and interactions, altered cognitive schemas, and distortions of view of self and world.

6. *Altered continuous response:* increased proneness to avoidance and dissociative phenomena, hyperarousal, cognitive dysregulation, and somatic expressions of distress.

7. *Failure to habituate:* increased proneness to reenactment, traumatic memories, fluctuating levels of arousal, and acting out.

8. *Establishment of new level of allostatic steady-state adaptations:* encompassing all areas of 1 to 7.

Wilson, Friedman, and Lindy (2001) privilege ego functioning or what they call *ego states* as a primary level of psychological functioning in order to understand PTSD. Ego states are viewed as "epiphenomenonal manifestations of the psychobiology of PTSD." These ego states can be understood as the consciously and verbally accessible code to the underlying psychobiological mechanisms in operation in the disorder, akin to the lines of quasi-linguistic code used to program the hardware and physical attributes of a computer system. Ultimately, the organism is thought to respond to trauma with adaptations in five interrelated areas:

1. Emotional regulation.

2. Cognitive processes and information processing at different levels of consciousness.

3. Motivational predispositions, such as need-based, goal-directed behaviors.

4. Psychobiological processes (i.e., fight-or-flight responses).

5. Ego defenses, coping patterns, and systems of belief, meaning, and spirituality.

In an attempt to represent PTSD as a "multidimensional construct of stress response syndromes," Wilson et al. (2001, p. 30) created what they call the *tetra-hedral model*, a holistic representation of an organism with five symmetric post-traumatic states. For a visual representation of the model, the reader is referred to Chapter 2 in *Treating Psychological Trauma and PTSD* (Wilson 2001). This figure is far too complex and intricate to be visually represented here, but a verbal description of the model follows.

The tetrahedral model is essentially a five-sided figure with a multilayer embedded system within it that represents the interactions of the various components of ego and psychobiological processes. There are three basic dimensions of psychological functioning outlined: the entire organism; the triad of core PTSD symptoms per the *DSM-IV;* and internal ego processes, including ego states, self-structure, and identity configuration. Internal ego processes directly impact somatic and integrated biological-organismic system functioning. Post-traumatic Stress Disorder symptoms in turn influence ego processes, cognition, self-reference, ego-identity, and the operation of the ego-defense mechanisms. The psychobiological processes are represented in these ego states, ego processes, elements of self-structure, individual persona, and the "entire range of dynamics in personality processes"(Wilson et al., 2001, p. 34). An easy way to approach this model is to think of the ego functions, personality characteristics, cognitions, emotional responses, and interpersonal functioning of a person with PTSD as representing underlying neurobiological alterations. In many ways, as they themselves state, their model represents a good attempt at a mind-body model of PTSD. Perhaps that is what they meant by the *holism* component of their model's title? In many ways, this model is not an etiological account as much as it is a solid attempt to bring together the psychological and biological knowledge bases within the PTSD research and clinical tradition.

Summary

Perhaps the moral of the story for this chapter is that in order to gain a full appreciation of the individual suffering from PTSD, a serious application of the biopsychosocial model of human behavior and mental processes must be attempted. Posttraumatic Stress Disorder occurs within a mental and intrapsychic context and its complex dynamics. It occurs within a social and political matrix replete with roles, expectations, and identities. Finally, a respect for the complexity of PTSD and the people who suffer from it will necessarily entail trying to understand a four-dimensional concept with two-dimensional tools. Ultimately, we may never see the proverbial elephant except from our different perspectives of tail or ears, but if the tail and ear observers talk to each other, integration might be possible.

Quick Review

- Freud characterizes traumatic stressors as overwhelming the *protective shield* of the ego with a disruption in normal functioning and the ability to cope as traumatic stressors and current stressors combine to overwhelm the ego and its defenses and lead to symptom expression.

- Other psychoanalytic theorists (e.g., Greenacre [1969] or Jacobson [1949]) hold that trauma comes not directly from a traumatic event proper but by a stimulation of unconscious conflict and our coping and defensive responses to the conflict.

- Allessandra Lemma and Susan Levy (2004) state that PTSD is about loss—symbolic loss, actual loss (e.g., death or almost dying), or both, and the normal mourning process used in coping with loss is altered in response to traumatic stress as a way to manage the "unbearable and unthinkable nature of the traumatic loss" (p. xvi).

- Psychiatrist Judith Herman holds that at the core of PTSD symptom expression and treatment is forgetting and remembering on both social and individual levels. The loss of a safe and validating "other" to help us organize and make sense of our experience lies at the center of the disorder.

- Feminist theory helps us understand traumatic stress on individual levels as microcosmic manifestations of larger, societal and cultural forces involving power, domination, and victimization.

- The constructivist narrative account of PTSD puts the telling of the trauma story at the center of the disorder. A lack of a coherent and organized narrative to place a traumatic event within allows its effects to persist in a chaotic and intrusive fashion.

- The integrated models serve to pull the various models from the differing perspectives together in a manner that are likely the most accurate and real-world accounts of PTSD phenomenology.

References

American Psychiatric Association. (2000). *Diagnostic and statistical manual of mental disorders* (4th ed., text revision). Washington, DC: Author.

Baumeister, R. F., Stillwell, A., & Wotman, S. R. (1990). Victim and perpetrator accounts of interpersonal conflict: Autobiographical narratives about anger. *Journal of Personality and Social Psychology, 59,* 994–1005.

Brown, L. S. (2004). Feminist paradigms of trauma treatment. *Psychotherapy: Theory, Research, Practice, Training, 41,* 464–471.

Epstein, S. (1991). The self-concept, the traumatic neurosis, and the structure of personality. In D. J. Ozer, J. M. Healy, Jr., & A. J. Stewart (Eds.), *Perspectives in personality: Vol. 3. Part A: Self and emotion; Part B: Approaches to understanding lives* (pp. 63–98). Philadelphia: Jessica Kingsley.

Everly, G. S., Jr. (1995). An integrative two-factor model of post-traumatic stress. In G. S. Everly & J. M. Lating (Eds.), *Psychotraumatology: Key papers and core concepts in post-traumatic stress* (pp. 27–48). New York: Plenum Press.

Foy, D. W., Donahoe, C. P., & Carroll, E. M. (1987). Posttraumatic Stress Disorder. In L. Michelson & L. M. Ascher (Eds.), *Anxiety and Stress Disorders: Cognitive-behavioral assessment and treatment* (pp. 361–378). New York: Guilford.

Greenacre, P. (1969). *Trauma, growth, and personality.* Oxford, England: International Universities Press.

Herman, J. L. (1992). *Trauma and recovery.* New York: Basic Books.

Horowitz, M. J. (1976). *Stress response syndromes.* Oxford, England: Jason Aronson.

Jacobson, E. (1949). Observations on the psychological effect of imprisonment on female political prisoners. In K. R. Eissler (Ed.), *Searchlights on delinquency: New psychoanalytic studies* (pp. 341–368). Oxford, England: International Universities Press.

Jacobson, E. (1961). Adolescent moods and the remodeling of psychic structures in adolescence. *Psychoanalytic Study of the Child, 16,* 164–183.

Kardiner, A. (1941). *The traumatic neuroses of war.* New York: National Research Council.

Kardiner, A., & Spiegel, H. (1947). *War stress and neurotic illness* (2nd ed., revised ed.). Oxford, England: P. B. Hoeber.

Kelman, H. (1945). Character and the traumatic syndrome. *Journal of Nervous and Mental Disease, 102,* 21–153.

Lemma, A., & Levy, S. (2004). The impact of trauma on the psyche: Internal and external processes. In S. Levy & A. Lemma (Eds.), *The perversion of loss: Psychoanalytic perspectives on trauma* (pp. 1–20). Philadelphia: Whurr.

Maslow, A. H. (1970). *Motivation and personality.* New York: Harper & Row.

McFarlane, A. C. (1987a). Family functioning and overprotection following a natural disaster: The longitudinal effects of post-traumatic morbidity. *Australian and New Zealand Journal of Psychiatry, 21,* 210–218.

McFarlane, A. C. (1987b). Life events and psychiatric disorder: The role of a natural disaster. *British Journal of Psychiatry, 151,* 362–367.

McFarlane, A. C. (1987c). Posttraumatic phenomena in a longitudinal study of children following a natural disaster. *Journal of the American Academy of Child & Adolescent Psychiatry, 26,* 764–769.

McFarlane, A. C. (1987d). The relationship between patterns of family interaction and psychiatric disorder in children. *Australian and New Zealand Journal of Psychiatry, 21,* 383–390.

McKeever, V. M., & Huff, M. E. (2003). A diathesis-stress model of Posttraumatic Stress Disorder: Ecological, biological, and residual stress pathways. *Review of General Psychology, 7,* 237–250.

Meichenbaum, D. (1977). *Cognitive behavior modification: An integrative approach.* New York: Plenum Press.

Meichenbaum, D., & Fitzpatrick, D. (1993). A constructivist narrative perspective on stress and coping: Stress inoculation applications. In L. Goldberger & S. Breznitz (Eds.), *Handbook of stress: Theoretical and clinical aspects* (2nd ed., pp. 706–723). New York: Free Press.

Rado, S. (1942). Pathodynamics and treatment of traumatic war neurosis (traumatophobia). *Psychosomatic Medicine, 4,* 362–368.

Root, M. P. P. (1992). Reconstructing the impact of trauma on personality. In L. S. Brown & M. Ballou (Eds.), *Personality and psychopathology: Feminist reappraisals* (pp. 229–265). New York: Guilford.

Schafer R. (1981). *Narrative actions in psychoanalysis.* Worcester, MA: Clark University.

Tait, R., & Silver, R. C. (1989). Coming to terms with major negative life events. In J. S. Uleman & J. A. Bargh (Eds.), *Unintended thought* (pp. 351–382). New York: Guilford.

Ulman, R. B., & Brothers, D. (1988). *The shattered self: A psychoanalytic study of trauma.* Hillsdale, NJ: Analytic Press.

van der Kolk, B. A., & McFarlane, A. C. (1996). The black hole of trauma. In B. A. van der Kolk, A. C. McFarlane, & L. Weisaeth (Eds.), *Traumatic stress: The effects of overwhelming experience on mind, body, and society* (pp. 3–23). New York: Guilford.

Wilson, J. P. (1995). The historical evolution of PTSD diagnostic criteria: From Freud to *DSM-IV.* In G. S. Everly & J. M. Lating (Eds.), *Psychotraumatology: Key papers and core concepts in post-traumatic stress* (pp. 9–26). New York: Plenum Press.

Wilson, J. P., Friedman, M. J., & Lindy, J. D. (2001). A holistic, organismic approach to healing trauma. In J. P. Wilson, M. J. Friedman, & J. D. Lindy (Eds.), *Treating psychological trauma and PTSD* (pp. 28–56). New York: Guilford.

Yule, W., Williams, R., & Joseph, S. (1999). Post-Traumatic Stress Disorders in adults. In W. Yule (Ed.), *Post-Traumatic Stress Disorders: Concepts and therapy* (pp. 1–24). New York: Wiley.

CHAPTER 8

Other Trauma-Related Disorders and Complications

As we know, most people exposed to traumatic stress do not develop PTSD. This is a function of the interaction of many complex factors, of course. This finding, however, should not be taken to mean that those who do not develop PTSD do not develop pathological reactions altogether. There are varied types of reactions to traumatic stress, some pathological, some not. In this chapter, we will discuss some of the pathological conditions that can develop in response to traumatic stress other than PTSD. Consider the following case illustration:

Officer Johnson, a correctional officer at a prison, was on duty when an inmate bludgeoned one of her colleagues, a fellow correctional officer, to death. She responded to the incident and helped transport her colleague's dead body to the local evacuation hospital. For several days after the attack, Officer Johnson went without sleep as she frantically worked to put together a donation for the family of the victim to help with funeral expenses. When asked if she had time to eat lunch with other staff, she claimed that she was not hungry. When asked how she was doing by the institutional mental health staff, she responded in a very detached, "Fine." This went on for 2 weeks. One day, while at her post at the medical clinic, a fight broke out between an inmate and a staff member. Officer Johnson was the closest officer to the incident but the last to respond. Some of her colleagues accused her of being too scared to respond. She later said in an interview with employee assistance staff, "I swear I didn't realize there was a fight. I feel like I've been dreaming for the last week. I can't believe he's gone. I can't believe all of this has happened." She referred to her dreamlike state as occurring for the "last week" despite observers reporting it had been going on for 2 weeks.

Acute Stress Disorder

The correctional officer in the preceding vignette displays many of the signs and symptoms consistent with Acute Stress Disorder (ASD). She was clearly having a difficult time adjusting after her exposure to the traumatic stressor of witnessing her colleague being murdered. She was not returning to a normal level of functioning, and her levels of stress were problematic enough to cause significant functional impairment. Acute Stress Disorder is sometimes considered the precursor to PTSD. Both of these disorders share a great many symptoms, although ASD includes more dissociative symptoms than PTSD. The main difference between the two is that ASD can only be diagnosed within the first 2 days to 4 weeks after a traumatic stressor, and PTSD can only be diagnosed after 4 weeks following exposure to a traumatic stressor. In essence, ASD is PTSD for 4 weeks; after that, if symptoms persist, it *becomes* PTSD. The main symptom clusters of ASD are the same as for PTSD: reexperiencing, avoidance, and hyperarousal. Acute Stress Disorder has the additional symptom cluster of dissociation as separate, and an individual has to exhibit three symptoms in order to meet criteria for this cluster. Examples of dissociative symptoms are numbing, reduced awareness of one's surroundings, depersonalization, derealization, and amnesia.

An important question regarding ASD is what distinguishes a normal or expected reaction to a traumatic stressor and a more pathological one such as ASD? After all, aren't people entitled to emotional turmoil, shock, and distress after a traumatic event? With the existence of the diagnosis of ASD, it would seem that we are all expected to get back to business after only 2 days and return to our baseline level of functioning. This is why PTSD is not diagnosed until after 4 weeks, in order not to "pathologize transient and normative stress reactions" (Harvey & Bryant, 2002, p. 86). One way to answer this question is to rely on the criterion for all *DSM-IV-TR* disorders that symptoms must be significant enough to cause significant impairment. This, however, is not a perfect remedy. Ultimately, the issue of whether the existence of ASD pathologizes normal and transient stress reactions is to know that its existence as a diagnosis is considered controversial within the field of mental health for this very reason. Acute Stress Disorder perhaps represents the prototypical example of what critics of the mental health field consider the pathologizing of all variation in human behavior and mental processes. This is one disorder where clinical judgment should be exercised with extreme care, carefully analyzing the nature of the exposure, the symptoms being displayed, and the severity of the functional impairment when considering giving an individual the diagnosis. Ultimately, professionals should be keenly aware of the purposes of diagnosis as a practice to aid in treatment. If an individual is exhibiting ASD-symptoms posttrauma, would a diagnosis of a formal mental disorder aid this person and help them be helped.

Rates of ASD collected in research range from 6 percent to 33 percent. In returning to the issue of the controversy for a moment, these rates should at least partially answer the question of whether normative stress reactions are being pathologized. Taking these rates as indicators, the answer to that question would be *no* because even in the case of the 33 percent, the large majority, 67 percent of people exposed to traumatic stressors, will not develop ASD symptoms, and 67 percent certainly represents a *normative* sample size. Individuals that have been found to be at risk for ASD include those with previous PTSD, premorbid psychological problems, previous depression, previous mental health treatment, and those who are prone to dissociate in the face of extreme stress (Barton, Blanchard, & Hickling, 1996; Bryant, Guthrie, & Moulds, 2001; Bryant & Harvey, 2000).

Theoretical models of ASD include dissociative, cognitive, and biological explanations (Harvey & Bryant, 2002). From the dissociative perspective, ASD develops as a consequence of dissociation interfering with the integration and resolution of traumatic memories and affect (Koopman, Classen, Cardeña, & Spiegel, 1995). From the cognitive perspective, ASD may be the consequence of individuals having difficulties in accessing and resolving trauma memories due to retrieval breakdown or schematic disorganization (Harvey & Bryant, 2002). Also, from the cognitive perspective, ASD is considered linked to an individual's cognitive distortion of the probability of future negative events (Warda & Bryant, 1998). Finally, from the biological perspective, ASD is related to disrupted catecholamine functioning and hypothalamic-pituitary-adrenal axis (HPA-Axis) dysfunction.

Finally, ASD treatment can be approached from either a cognitive-behavioral approach or with earlier interventions such as crisis intervention, psychological first aid, critical incident stress debriefing, and other forms of secondary prevention.

Substance Abuse and Dependence

Researchers using something called an odds ratio, which measures the odds of having one disorder if an individual has the other disorder, have measured the rates of comorbid Substance Abuse and PTSD. Studies have revealed the range of odd ratios for comorbid Alcohol Dependence or Abuse is 2.06 to 4.25. This means that if someone has PTSD, his or her odds of having an Alcohol Abuse or Dependence Disorder is anywhere from two to four times higher than if they did not have PTSD. Regarding Substance Abuse or Dependence, the range of odds ratios from various studies is 2.48 to 8.68. Again, this means that the odds of someone with PTSD also having a comorbid Substance Abuse or Dependence Disorder is anywhere from 2.5 times to 8.5 times higher than if he or she did not have PTSD.

Posttraumatic Stress Disorder patients with comorbid Substance Abuse or Dependence Disorders have been found to have higher levels of pathology in both disorders, more stressors, higher rates of health care utilization, less effective coping skills, and poorer responses to treatment than either disorder alone (Meichenbaum, 2003). Additionally, comorbid disorders of Panic Disorder, Major Depressive Disorder, Personality Disorders, Antisocial Behavior, and violence exist at higher rates. A quick summary of the *DSM-IV-TR* criteria for Substance Abuse are characterized by at least one of the following:

1. Recurrent substance use resulting in failure to fulfill major role obligations.

2. Recurrent substance use in situations in which it is physically hazardous.

3. Recurrent substance-related legal problems.

4. Continued substance use despite having persistent and recurrent social or interpersonal problems caused or exacerbated by the effects of the substance.

The criteria for Substance Dependence are represented by the presence of three or more of the following:

1. Tolerance as defined by either a need for increased amounts of the substance in order to achieve intoxication or the desired effect or markedly diminished effect of continued use of the same amount.

2. Withdrawal as manifested by either a characteristic withdrawal syndrome or the same substance is taken to relieve or avoid withdrawal symptoms.

3. The substance is taken in larger amounts or over a longer period than was intended.

4. There is a persistent desire or unsuccessful efforts to cut down or control use.

5. A great deal of time is spent in activities necessary to obtain the substance.

6. Important life activities are given up or reduced.

7. The use is continued despite knowledge of having persistent or recurrent physical or psychological problems likely caused or exacerbated by the substance use.

There have been three main hypotheses put forward to explain the comorbid relationship between PTSD and Substance Abuse Disorders: (1) the *self-medication hypothesis*, (2), the *high-risk hypothesis*, (3) and the *susceptibility hypothesis*. We will cover the self-medication hypothesis in more detail in the following section. The high-risk hypothesis holds that individuals that use drugs live lives that are riskier and that bring them into higher frequency contact with traumatic stressors. The susceptibility hypothesis holds that individuals with Substance Abuse Disorders are at higher risk for developing PTSD once they have been exposed to a traumatic stressor because of the psychophysiological and psychological effects of substance abuse. This is a model of vulnerability to PTSD. Chilcoat and Menard (2003) remind us that there could also be a fourth, unrelated factor that accounts for the high comorbidity, something that both disorders and dually diagnosed individuals have in common. Stewart and Conrod (2003), for example, have proposed that this fourth factor could be that once the baseline symptoms of the two disorders are mutually established, the symptoms reinforce each other and develop into a vicious cycle. Ultimately, however, despite the plausibility of any one of these models, no one model has emerged as more empirically reliable to this date.

In returning to the self-medication hypothesis, research has shown that in the comorbid population, the development of PTSD typically precedes Substance Abuse or Dependence. Some research has shown that PTSD sufferers who have high levels of anxiety sensitivity (i.e., are very sensitive to low levels of anxiety) and who catastrophize about the consequences of their anxiety are more likely to cope with drugs that reduce arousal, such as central nervous system suppressants (Stewart & Conrod, 2003). This suggests that hyperarousal symptoms may be the link for the self-medication hypothesis. Alcohol and certain drugs that are particularly effective at inhibiting activity in anxiety-related brain circuitry have been found effective at reducing the startle response. Alcohol, for example, has been shown to reduce the startle response and has particular effects on the amygdala and the prefrontal cortex (for more on the biological underpinnings of PTSD, see Chapter 6). Although substances are sought to reduce symptoms, they may have the paradoxical effect of worsening other symptoms. For example, substances that interfere with hippocampus and prefrontal cortex functioning may interfere with extinction of trauma memories that would normally occur with long-term memory processing and consolidation of traumatic memories. Further, physiological withdrawal may worsen the symptoms that the individual was initially trying to escape, perhaps leading to increased use.

Treatment Issues

Ouimette, Moos, and Brown (2003, p. 93) state that a "fundamental concern voiced by providers who treat SUD-PTSD patients is when in the treatment course to address substance use and when to address PTSD." They cite that most clinical researchers suggest concurrent treatment. Ouimette, Moos, and Brown make the following four recommendations for an empirically based comorbid PTSD-Substance Abuse/Dependence practice:

1. Substance Abuse or Dependence patients should be routinely screened for PTSD.

2. Comorbid patients should be referred for concurrent trauma or PTSD treatment or for psychological treatment with the recommendation that trauma or PTSD issues be addressed.

3. Comorbid patients should be referred for concurrent participation in self-help groups and, when indicated, for family treatment.

4. Providers should offer comorbid patients continuing outpatient mental health care.

Dissociative Disorders

Dissociation has long been considered an integral part of PTSD and posttraumatic reactions. After a traumatic event, survivors have often reported "leaving their bodies" or of "observing themselves from the outside". One's sense of time can be distorted, and there can be a sense of unreality. *Dissociation* can be defined as a disruption in the usually integrated functions of consciousness, memory, identity, or perception of the environment. Bessel van der Kolk has proposed that at least in one sense, dissociation may be functional by allowing a trauma victim to observe the experience from a safe, less intense distance, protecting his or her awareness from the trauma. In this sense it may serve as a form of psychological shock, a form of protective detachment.

Peritraumatic dissociation refers to a state of immediate dissociation at the time of the actual event (Marmar et al., 1997). Marmar et al. provides the following list of peritraumatic experiences:

Altered time sense

Feelings of unreality

Out-of-body experiences

Bewilderment

Confusion/disorientation

Altered pain perception

Altered body image

Feeling disconnected from body

Tunnel vision

van der Hart, van der Kolk, and Boon (1998) identify three variations of dissociation: (1) primary dissociation, (2) secondary dissociation, and (3) tertiary dissociation. *Primary dissociation* refers to a state in which percepts are fragmented. Sounds, smells, images, and so on can be experienced partially or in pieces. There is a lack of integration into consciousness and memory. This is a state in which concrete perceptions are separate from actual experiences. *Secondary dissociation* refers to a state in which the mind engages in distancing maneuvers, such as out-of-body experiences, with feelings and emotions beings separated from awareness, actual experience, and conscious memory. There are alterations in time, place, or space, and person with a feeling of unreality, confusion, and even periods of memory loss or amnesia, which are sometimes called blackouts. *Tertiary dissociation* refers to the state most commonly known as multiple personalities or Dissociative Identity Disorder (DID). In this state of dissociation, distinct ego states develop, each with its own personality, to such a profound sense that the consciousness of the actual person may or may not be aware of this state of mental operation.

Jon G. Allen discusses the concept of a continuum of dissociation he calls the *continuum of detachment*. Detachment refers to relatively milder forms of dissociation in which one feels disconnected from the outside world. He states,

> When you are in a state of alert consciousness, you can be fully aware of the external environment, as well as having a sense of self that includes awareness of your body and your own actions. In a state of alert consciousness, you remain grounded by flexible awareness of both the outer and inner worlds. I contrast alert consciousness with three levels of detachment: mild (absorption), moderate (depersonalization and derealization), and extreme (unresponsiveness). (p. 177)

Mild detachment or absorption is characterized by a breakdown in the ability to notice external events and sometimes experiencing an altered sense of self. Moderate detachment involves having the experience of unreality and may include depersonalization or derealization. *Depersonalization,* as defined in the *DSM-IV-TR* (p. 822), refers to a state in which a person feels "detached from, and as if one is an outside observer, of one's mental processes or body (e.g., feeling like on is in a dream)." Derealization refers to a feeling that the world is unreal or strange in a significant sense. Allen states,

> Some clients complain about feeling spacey, foggy, or fuzzy. They feel as if they are floating or drifting. Others feel as if they are acting in a play, watching themselves from a distance, or dreaming. Some feel isolated as if in a shell, a bubble, or behind glass. (p. 178)

Allen (2001) describes extreme detachment as a state of unresponsiveness in which a person might sit, stare blankly, act comatose or catatonic, or have no sense of self-awareness and no sense of time. This can occur for minutes, hours, or even days.

Allen (2001) discusses a form of dissociation beyond these milder forms of detached that is related to Dissociative Amnesia, Dissociative Fugue, and DID called *compartmentalization*. Compartmentalization refers to a form of dissociation that "goes beyond detachment in excluding whole realms of experience from consciousness" (p. 183). Compartmentalization is seen as a form of dissociation that preserves some sense of coherence and unity in consciousness.

According to Allen (2001), *Dissociative Amnesia* "exemplifies compartmentalization" (p. 186). Dissociative Amnesia is defined in the *DSM-IV-TR* as "one or more episodes of inability to recall important personal information, usually of a traumatic or stressful nature" (p. 519). Another example of a compartmentalization disorder is *Dissociative Fugue,* defined by the *DSM-IV-TR* as "sudden, unexpected travel away from home or one's customary place of work, with inability to recall one's personal past" (p. 519).

Allen proposes that DID represents the most dramatic example of compartmentalization. The *DSM-IV-TR* defines *Dissociative Identity Disorder* as "presence of two or more distinct identities or personality states. . . [which] recurrently take control of the person's behavior" (p. 519). Dissociative Identity Disorder is often associated with severe trauma from child abuse. It is important to note that DID is considered a controversial disorder, and its very existence is challenged by some in the field. As was mentioned previously, DID represents a form of tertiary dissociation consistent with van der Hart et al.'s (1998) classification. Dissociative Identity Disorder represents a somewhat rare disorder in mental health practice in that a large percentage of mental health practitioners have very little experience with this disorder. Dissociative Identity Disorder is a very complex disorder, and its treatment equally complex and extensive. A thorough discussion of DID can fill several volumes of books in and of itself. However, a brief mention of treatment recommendations is warranted here. van der Hart et al. (1998) outline the treatment for DID in the following steps:

1. Psychoeducation about DID.
2. Fostering cooperation between identities participating in daily life.
3. Building a working alliance with persecutory states of mind.
4. Contacting identities.
5. Teaching techniques for coping with reactivated traumatic memories.
6. Cognitive therapy techniques for cognitive distortions.
7. Family and couples therapy if implicated.
8. Medication, including antidepressants, anxiolytics, and anticonvulsants.
9. Developing a protocol for crisis intervention, including short-term psychiatric admissions.
10. Overcoming the phobia of traumatized memories.
11. Overcoming the phobia of everyday life.

Dissociative failure to integrate traumatic memories, perceptions, cognitions, and bodily memories during the acute stage and the immediate posttrauma period is a risk factor for developing PTSD. Prior episodes of dissociation increase the likelihood of recurrence and a lowered threshold for dissociation in the future. Risk factors for dissociation include younger age of victim, higher levels of stress exposure, greater subjective experiences of threat, poorer general psychological health and adjustment, weaker or more vulnerable identity formation, greater sense of external locus of control, and more use of escape-avoidance and emotion-focused coping strategies (Marmar, Weiss, Metzler, & Delucchi, 1996). van der Kolk considers a reliance on the external world for a sense of security as a risk factor. Spiegel, Hunt, and Dondershire (1988) propose that dissociation may be related to a heritable trait for a tendency to dissociate under extreme stress that is "aggravated by early trauma exposure and correlated with hypnotizability" (Marmar et al., 1997, p. 419).

With regard to treatment, there is very little research on treatment for dissociation specifically. Kluft (1993) recommends individual psychodynamic psychotherapy and some use of hypnosis and medication. The use of hypnosis is suggested as a means to induce a state of calm under which processing of trauma material can be undergone. van der Hart et al. (1998) recommend a three-phase treatment model that includes (1) stabilization and symptom reduction, including establishing a therapeutic relationship and psychoeducation, (2) treatment of traumatic memories, and (3) reintegration and rehabilitation.

Posttraumatic Grief

Alfred Adler was among the first to propose that pathological grief and bereavement can stem from the trauma of the death of a loved one or significant other. In this sense, it can be considered a type of PTSD. Jacobs (1999, p. 23) states, "The disorder is one of a class of disorders, including Post-traumatic Stress Disorder and Acute Stress Disorder that occur after an event in a person's life which opens a period of risk for the disorder...[it] may prove to be an adult form of Separation Anxiety Disorder." Mardi Horowitz and colleagues (Horowitz et al., 2003) added to Adler's work and along with colleagues has introduced criteria for a disorder called *complicated grief disorder*. Jacobs (1999) refers to posttraumatic grief more simply as *traumatic grief*. Jacobs states that this term is preferable because it avoids confusing it with other forms of grief that are not particularly related to trauma and because it better captures the two underlying dimensions of the disorder—*separation distress* and *traumatic distress*. Jacobs (1999, p. 24) defines traumatic grief as follows: "Traumatic Grief is a disorder that occurs after the death of a significant other. Symptoms of separation distress are the core of the disorder and amalgamate with bereavement specific symptoms of being devastated and traumatized by death."

The symptoms must be marked, persist for 2 months, and cause clinically significant impairment in functioning.

Treatment of traumatic grief may consist of the use of a variety of techniques and modalities, including medication, individual psychotherapy, psychoeducation, and group psychotherapy. Jacobs (1999) proposes that a useful approach is to conceptualize traumatic grief as a form of Separation Anxiety Disorder, and treatments that have been found useful for this disorder in children may prove useful in adaptation to adults.

Borderline Personality Disorder

Sometimes trauma, particularly repeated trauma, is considered to lead to long-term alterations in personality development, structure, and functioning. Some professionals postulate that personality disorders can develop. Some have proposed the concept of the "posttraumatic personality" to characterize these more pervasive and integrated forms of posttraumatic reactions. Allen (2001) cites that research has revealed a "global relationship between trauma and personality disorders." He states that patients with a diagnosis of Personality Disorder are more likely to report a history of childhood physical abuse, sexual abuse, or both. Borderline Personality Disorder (BPD) is the most common disorder found. He states, "Those with BPD were more likely to have experienced multiple abuses by multiple perpetrators and to have been abused by both parents. Sexual abuse, verbal abuse, physical abuse, and being adopted all contributed independently to the likelihood of a BPD diagnosis."

Gabbard (2000) cites that childhood maltreatment is considered an etiological factor in BPD. The symptoms of BPD include fears of abandonment, unstable and intense relationships, disturbance in identity, self-destructive behavior, recurrent suicidal and self-injurious behavior, unstable affect, feelings of emptiness, intense anger, transient psychosis, and dissociation (Allen, 2001). The causal or precise etiological relationship between trauma and BPD has not been fully delineated yet, but promising lines of research indicate that the same biological underpinnings of PTSD may be active in BPD. Marsha Linehan and colleagues' diathesis-stress model is considered a good model although it requires more empirical investigation.

When professionals think of treatment for BPD, many of them know that the treatment will be long, intense, very organized, and complex, and have a guarded prognosis. These thoughts may or may not be supported by research. Nonetheless, the treatment of BPD often takes the form of psychodynamic therapy. However, Kroll (1993) warns that overreliance on a psychodynamic model for BPD for etiology and treatment may detract from its connection to trauma and render treatment less effective overall. To date, the most comprehensive and empirically supported treatment for BPD is Linehan's cognitive-behavioral treatment for BPD.

Traumatic Brain Injury and PTSD

It seems logical that many events that would lead to the potential for death or physical injury may also have high potential for traumatic brain injury (TBI). This is true for car accidents, combat exposure (e.g., bomb-blasts concussion), and even physical abuse. In my own clinical practice, I have worked with many victims of violent crime who suffered head injuries, some with TBI (e.g., from being hit with a pipe or baseball bat) and some with relatively mild difficulties (e.g., a mild concussion). However, the coexistence of PTSD and TBI is a controversial topic (Harvey, Kopelman, & Brewin, 2005) because oftentimes TBI patients have amnesia for a particular event, which would make the development of PTSD virtually impossible. How can someone reexperience something they don't remember, for example? Earlier research showed a concordance rate of 0 percent for TBI and PTSD (Warden et al., 1997). However, more recent research has shown rates of comorbid PTSD and TBI to be anywhere from 14 percent to 27 percent. They can coexist.

The TBI and PTSD picture is somewhat complicated. Traumatic brain injury patients, for example, may not experience the classic set of PTSD symptoms, and instead there may be differences in symptom experience and expression. An example of this is that intrusive memories may emerge much later in TBI patients than in non-TBI patients with PTSD. This is because posttraumatic amnesia fades with time, thus allowing for the emergence of intrusive memories at some point. Also, disruptions in cognitive processes may affect the form in which memories are recalled, as they may be more reconstructed and present within the context of common memory problems seen in TBI. That is, TBI patients often have memory deficits in general, and PTSD memories will not be exempt from these effects.

It is important to not confuse the clinical manifestations of neuropsychological deficits associated with PTSD in general with other mild signs of cognitive deficit secondary to TBI. These overlapping deficits include attention and concentration problems and speed of information processing. More severe TBI and its sequelae are probably less mistakable, such as severe memory deficits and major deficits in problem solving, executive functions, and speed of processing. This, of course, is a question of differential diagnosis, and the use of neuropsychological testing is highly recommended in such instances. Basso and Newman (2000) suggest operating from an initial stance that a client's initial presentation is the consequence of both PTSD and TBI and working to rule either out through thorough assessment and evaluation.

Complex PTSD and DESNOS

Treatment professionals and researchers have long recognized that reactions to trauma can include PTSD, but other sequelae of trauma can be just as problematic. These other complications represent perhaps a more severe or complicated form of PTSD that is now being recognized as Complex PTSD (CPTSD). Others sometimes refer to this form of complex posttraumatic reaction as disorders of extreme stress not otherwise specified (DESNOS). Judith Herman (1992) proposed the term Complex PTSD to capture the "panopoly of psychopathology frequently observed in the wake of extreme and repeated interpersonal trauma." Courtois (2004) defines it as "a type of trauma that occurs repeatedly and cumulatively, usually over a period of time and within specific relationships and contexts." Complex PTSD can be conceptualized by seven problem areas associated with early interpersonal trauma (Courtois, 2004; Herman, 1992):

1. Alterations in the regulation of affective impulses, including difficulty with modulation of anger and self-destructiveness.

2. Alterations in attention and consciousness leading to amnesias and dissociative episodes and depersonalization.

3. Alterations in self-perception, such as a chronic sense of guilt and responsibility, and ongoing feelings of intense shame.

4. Alterations in perception of the perpetrator, including incorporation of his or her belief system.

5. Alterations in relationships to others, such as not being able to trust and not being able to feel intimate with others.

6. Somatization or medical problems.

7. Alterations in systems of meaning, including feelings of hopelessness about finding anyone to understand his or her pain.

Complex PTSD is considered an associated feature of PTSD-proper as identified in the *DSM-IV-TR* but is not formally recognized as such currently. That is, it is conceivable that an individual could have PTSD and CPTSD or DESNOS. Courtois (2004) outlines a treatment model for CPTSD founded on development of self-management skills and safety. Cognitive-behavioral techniques and methods are employed. Research is showing that many of the treatment issues and methods used for PTSD are applicable to CPTSD. Courtois proposes using a meta-model approach to treatment "that encourages careful sequencing of therapeutic activities and tasks, with specific initial attention to the individual's safety and ability to regulate his or her emotional state." It is considered a three-stage oriented model with the following stages:

1. Pretreatment issues, treatment frame, alliance building, safety, affect regulation, stabilization, skill building, education, self-care, and support.

2. Deconditioning, mourning, resolution, and integration of trauma.

3. Self- and relational development-enhanced daily living.

The length of treatment will vary per individual but can last anywhere from 6 months to 12 months. Termination issues that apply to therapy in general and PTSD should be paid close attention to with CPTSD due to its connection to interpersonal issues.

Summary

Human responses to traumatic stress can range from mild distress to long-lasting changes and alterations in personality. Posttraumatic Stress Disorder as a concept and diagnosis only captures a portion of this variation. Trauma can lead to a variety of disorders. When working with trauma survivors, it is important to assess for the possibility for these various other reactions and plan and treat accordingly. A respect for the variation in human minds and bodies will hopefully help keep us open to these possibilities and hopefully prevent us from too narrowly focusing on what we think we already know.

Quick Review

- Posttraumatic Stress Disorder is but one of many possible pathological reactions to exposure to traumatic stress.

- Acute Stress Disorder includes PTSD symptoms and the additional symptom cluster of dissociation (e.g. Dissociative Amnesia, depersonalization, or derealization).

- An individual with PTSD has a higher chance of having a Substance Abuse or Dependence Disorder and vice versa.

- Dissociative Disorders are part of PTSD and can develop as separate and severe pathological reactions to traumatic stress.

- Traumatic grief is considered a specific type of grief reaction that follows from the traumatic loss of a loved one or significant other.

- Borderline Personality Disorder has been connected to a history of childhood maltreatment and shares many common features with PTSD.

- Posttraumatic Stress Disorder and TBI may coexist in patients. Differential diagnosis is important because of the neuropsychological deficit and symptom overlap of these two disorders.

- Complex PTSD or DESNOS is a form of posttraumatic reaction that involves more complex interpersonal difficulties and disturbances in identity and can coexist with PTSD or exist on its own.

References

Adler, A. (1924). *The practice and theory of individual psychology* (2nd ed. rev.). Oxford, England: Humanities Press.

Allen, D. M. (2001). Integrating individual and family systems psychotherapy to treat Borderline Personality Disorder. *Journal of Psychotherapy Integration, 11,* 313–331.

Allen, J. G. (2001). *Traumatic relationships and serious mental disorders.* New York: Wiley.

American Psychiatric Association. (2000). *Diagnostic and statistical manual of mental disorders* (4th ed., text revision). Washington, DC: Author.

Barton, K. A., Blanchard, E. B., & Hickling, E. J. (1996). Antecedents and consequences of Acute Stress Disorder among motor vehicle accident victims. *Behaviour Research and Therapy, 34,* 805–813.

Basso, M. R., & Newman, E. (2000). A primer of closed head injury sequelae in Post-Traumatic Stress Disorder. *Journal of Personal and Interpersonal Loss, 5,* 125–147.

Bryant, R. A., Guthrie, R. M., & Moulds, M. L. (2001). Hypnotizability in Acute Stress Disorder. *American Journal of Psychiatry, 158,* 600–604.

Bryant, R. A., & Harvey, A. G. (2000). *Acute Stress Disorder: A handbook of theory, assessment, and treatment.* Washington, DC: American Psychological Association.

Chilcoat, H. D., & Menard, C. (2003). Epidemiological investigations: Comorbidity of Posttraumatic Stress Disorder and Substance Use Disorder. In P. Ouimette & P. J. Brown (Eds.), *Trauma and Substance Abuse: Causes, consequences, and treatment of comorbid disorders* (pp. 9–28). Washington, DC: American Psychological Association.

Courtois, C. A. (2004). Complex trauma, complex reactions: Assessment and treatment. *Psychotherapy: Theory, Research, Practice, Training, 41,* 412–425.

Gabbard, G. O. (2000). Psychodynamic psychotherapy of Borderline Personality Disorder: A contemporary approach. *Bulletin of the Menninger Clinic, 65,* 41–57.

Harvey, A. G., & Bryant, R. A. (2002). Acute Stress Disorder: A synthesis and critique. *Psychological Bulletin, 128,* 886–902.

Harvey, A. G., Kopelman, M. D., & Brewin, C. R. (2005). PTSD and Traumatic Brain Injury. In J. J. Vasterling & C. R. Brewin (Eds.), *Neuropsychology of PTSD: Biological, cognitive, and clinical perspectives* (pp. 230–246). New York: Guilford.

Herman, J. L. (1992). Complex PTSD: A syndrome in survivors of prolonged and repeated trauma. *Journal of Traumatic Stress, 5,* 377–391.

Horowitz, M. J., Siegel, B, Holen, A., Bonanno, G. A., Milbrath, C., & Stinson, C. H. (2003). Diagnostic criteria for complicated grief disorder. *Focus, 1,* 290–298.

Jacobs, S. C. (1999). *Traumatic grief: Diagnosis, treatment, and prevention.* Philadelphia: Brunner/Mazel.

Kluft, R. P. (1993). The treatment of Dissociative Disorder patients: An overview of discoveries, successes, and failures. *Dissociation: Progress in the Dissociative Disorders, 6,* 87–101.

Koopman, C., Classen, C., Cardeña, E., & Spiegel, D. (1995). When disaster strikes, Acute Stress Disorder may follow. *Journal of Traumatic Stress, 8,* 29–46.

Kroll, J. (1993). *PTSD/Borderlines in therapy: Finding the balance.* New York: W. W. Norton.

Linehan, M. M., Cochran, B. N., & Kehrer, C. A. (2001). Dialectical behavior therapy for borderline personality disorder. In David H. Barlow (Ed.), *Clinical handbook of psychological disorders: A step-by-step treatment manual* (3rd ed., pp. 470–522). New York: Guilford.

Marmar, C. R., Weiss, D. S., & Metzler, T. J. (1997). The Peritraumatic Dissociative Experiences Questionnaire. In J. P. Wilson & T. M. Keane (Eds.), *Assessing psychological trauma and PTSD* (pp. 412–428). New York: Guilford.

Marmar, C. R., Weiss, D. S., Metzler, T. J., & Delucchi, K. (1996). Characteristics of emergency services personnel related to peritraumatic dissociation during critical incident exposure. *American Journal of Psychiatry, 153,* 94–102.

Meichenbaum, D. (2003). Cognitive-behavior therapy: Folktales and the unexpurgated history. *Cognitive Therapy and Research, 27*, 125–129.

Ouimette, P., Moos, R. H., & Brown, P. J. (2003). Substance Use Disorder-Posttraumatic Stress Disorder comorbidity: A survey of treatments and proposed practice guidelines. In P. Ouimette & P. J. Brown (Eds.), *Trauma and substance abuse: Causes, consequences, and treatment of comorbid disorders* (pp. 91–110). Washington, DC: American Psychological Association.

Spiegel, D., Hunt, T., & Dondershine, H. E. (1988). Dissociation and hypnotizability in posttraumatic stress disorder. *American Journal of Psychiatry, 145*, 301–305.

Stewart, S. H., & Conrod, P. J. (2003). Psychosocial models of functional associations between Posttraumatic Stress Disorder and Substance Use Disorder. In P. Ouimette & P. J. Brown (Eds.), *Trauma and substance abuse: Causes, consequences, and treatment of comorbid disorders* (pp. 29–55). Washington, DC: American Psychological Association.

Warda, G., & Bryant, R. A. (1998). Cognitive bias in Acute Stress Disorder. *Behaviour Research and Therapy, 36*, 1177–1183.

Warden, D. L., Labbate, L. A., Salazar, A. M., Nelson, R., et al. (1997). Posttraumatic Stress Disorder in patients with traumatic brain injury and Amnesia for the event. *Journal of Neuropsychiatry & Clinical Neurosciences, 9*, 18–22.

van der Hart, O., van der Kolk, B. A., & Boon, S. (1998). Treatment of Dissociative Disorders. In J. D. Bremner & C. R. Marmar (Eds.), *Trauma, memory, and dissociation* (pp. 253–283). Washington, DC: American Psychiatric Association.

van der Kolk, B. A. (1996). The complexity of adaptation to trauma: Self-regulation, stimulus discrimination, and characterological development. In B. A. van der Kolk, A. C. McFarlane, & L. Weisaeth (Eds.), *Traumatic stress: The effects of overwhelming experience on mind, body, and society* (pp. 182–213). New York: Guilford.

CHAPTER 9

Cross-Cultural Issues and International Perspectives

The Importance of Ethnicity and Culture

Psychologists, researchers, and mental health professionals live in an ethnically and culturally diverse world. This is an undeniable fact that forces us to question our positions, thoughts, theories, and entire worldviews regarding our knowledge base. Theories and models of psychological functioning, psychopathology, and treatment of mental disorders must all be analyzed across cultural contexts. Culture is a variable of undeniable importance in the study of all psychological phenomena.

For the purpose of this chapter, the variables of *culture* and *ethnicity* will be referred to as *ethnocultural*. Marsella (1988, p. 10) provides a good working definition of *culture:*

> [Culture is] shared learned behavior which is transmitted from one generation to another to promote individual and group adjustment and adaptation. Culture is presented externally as artifacts, roles, and institutions and is represented internally as values, beliefs, attitudes, cognitive styles, epistemologies, and conscious patterns.

Culture is an extremely important dimension of human experience. Within the last 20 or so years, a self-consciousness of sorts has developed in the social and medical sciences. Scientists and practitioners in the United States and Western Europe have come to the inevitable conclusion that their way of seeing the world is not the only way of seeing the world. In line with Marsella's respect for culture and its role in human experience, these seekers of truth and knowledge have been obliged to question their worldviews with respect to nonwestern contexts. The reasons for this go well beyond the scope of this chapter and book, but for a more in-depth discussion of these issues, see Berry, Poortinga, Segall, and Dasen (1992) and their work on cross-cultural research.

A critical issue in the scientific enterprise is the *generalizability* of research findings. That is, does a researcher's findings in his or her lab or clinic actually translate to the real world? Do the findings generalize from the specific to the broad or more general? When a finding does in fact translate, this is taken as a form of confirmation and is viewed as a critical step in the scientific validation of knowledge. If it was otherwise, scientists could be creating elaborate fictions to explain the world, even if the world he or she is explaining is only in their lab, or worse, in his or her head. Just as theory and experiments have to translate to the real world, so, too, do they need to translate all of the different contexts of the real world. Obviously, variation in ethnocultural contexts is a reality of the world I am speaking of, and inasmuch as science addresses reality, it must therefore address all reality in all its variations. A theory that only works in some places some of the time is not a very powerful theory. However, it can remain respectable as long as its parameters and limitations are acknowledged. But as long as psychology is touted as a human science for all people, psychologists must strive for more universal validation of their work. This necessarily involves cross-ethnocultural inquiry.

Professionals and researchers have come to accept that such concepts as depression, PTSD, or even the mind or psyche cannot be taken for granted across all ethnocultural contexts. Ironically, perhaps, the search for scientific objectivity has led us to the acknowledgment of ethnocultural variation and subjectivity as critical variables in our search.

From a clinical perspective, this issue is extremely important. As stated in Gergen, Gulerce, Lock, and Misra (1996), "the culturally engaged psychologist might help to appraise various problems of health, environment, industrial development, and the like in terms of the values, beliefs, and motives that are particular to the culture at hand" (p. 1). In other words, efficacious and ethical psychological treatment and intervention will depend on the consideration of ethnocultural variables. Perhaps the goal will be to build local knowledge bases rather than universal models of psychopathology and treatment. Perhaps conducting psychotherapy in Brazil for PTSD will mean something very different than it will in Wisconsin. The names for techniques and treatment modalities as well as disorders may vary. Professionals may observe similar symptoms with different linguistic and ethnocultural forms of expression or different symptoms that result from similar etiological sources and events. Etiologies may vary. Disorders as expressed may vary. Cures or treatments may vary.

However, before you throw your hands up in confusion feeling that there may never be an end to this seeming relativism, you should know that dedicated researchers and professionals have been working hard to clarify these muddy waters. The process of gaining cross-cultural and ethnocultural knowledge is ongoing, and perhaps the journey itself is the most important part.

Professional Alert

My own clinical training regarding issues of ethnocultural differences between therapist and client has taught me that when working with patients or clients of a different ethnocultural background than oneself, the clinician should engage in an active effort to understand the client's ethnocultural frame of reference. Few assumptions should be made, and the process of listening and learning is tantamount. This is true, of course, for all patients and clients, even if he or she is of the same ethnocultural background. The issue of differences should be an explicit part of the treatment but not overemphasized. The process of learning about the client's ethnocultural background is a critical clinical tool in the development of empathy, the therapeutic alliance, and the facilitation of treatment through the establishment of a common language and conceptual backdrop.

Ethnocultural Aspects of Psychopathology in General

Draguns (1994) states that despite the presence of some psychiatric disorders, such as Schizophrenia and depression, across numerous ethnocultural contexts, there is an extremely wide variety of expressions of symptoms of virtually all other mental disorders. From this perspective, a mental disorder is a "mix of universal and culture-specific factors" (Stamm & Freidman, 2000, p. 71).

The *DSM-IV-TR* recommends that ethnocultural factors be carefully considered in diagnosis, including addressing the following:

1. The cultural identity of the patient.

2. Cultural explanations of the individual's illness.

3. Cultural factors related to the psychosocial environment and levels of functioning.

4. Cultural elements of the relationships between the individual and the clinician.

5. Overall cultural assessment for diagnosis and care.

Ethnocultural Aspects of PTSD

At the outset of this book, I made the point that trauma is a near universal human experience. But as I have just finished saying, psychologists are increasingly questioning the concept of universality. Is trauma a universal experience? Can all human beings be psychologically traumatized? Some researchers argue that the very concept of psychological trauma is culturally constructed and, therefore, might be very different from one ethnocultural context to another. In fact, the very existence of psychological trauma might be called into question. For example, in Israel during its long history of military conflict and turmoil, there was a point in time in which the concept of psychological trauma was considered virtually nonexistent. Amidst the struggle for national survival and growth, the government and military establishment seemed to not have time for the concept of trauma. They were too busy building and defending a country. Israeli Brigadier General, Dr. M. Kordova was quoted as saying, "We do not have this problem and cannot afford this 'American luxury'" (cited in Witzum & Kotler, 2000, p. 106). The point is that the concept of psychological trauma cannot be taken for granted across ethnocultural contexts. Etiology, symptom development, symptom expression, and eventual treatment are all potentially variable across ethnocultural contexts.

However, consideration of ethnocultural variables does not automatically imply that universals do not exist. Stamm and Friedman argue that, "all humans have the capacity to experience and express fear, helplessness, or horror when exposed to traumatic stress" (2000, p. 70). My position for the purpose of the *CGPTSD* is the same. Despite ethnocultural variation in the etiology, development of, and expression of psychological trauma, all human beings possess the capacity to meet the Criterion A2 in the *DSM-IV-TR*. Variation might arise when addressing specific stressors or stimuli, of course. Further, Stamm and Friedman (2000) argue that all humans must have or possess an ability to cope with stress. Characteristic responses of stress reactions related to the psychobiological response of fight or flight are also considered universals from their perspective.

Certainly in the United States, psychological trauma is understood primarily from a mental health perspective in the form of PTSD. Posttraumatic Stress Disorder symptoms have been identified in various other ethnocultural contexts, such as Southeast Asia and Central America. But is the American construct of PTSD the best way to conceptualize the psychological impact of traumatic stress for individuals of various other ethnocultural groups?

Remember again from Chapter 1 that acceptance of the PTSD construct into the official nomenclature of modern psychiatry and clinical psychology was dependent on the recognition that PTSD actually existed as a distinct clinical entity. In other words, the mental health community finally acknowledged the reality of psychological trauma. Posttraumatic Stress Disorder was formally recognized as a distinct set of reactions in response to exposure to a traumatic event or events. However, working from an ethnocultural perspective, the reality of PTSD once again comes into question.

Consider this; just as everyone exposed to a traumatic stressor does not develop PTSD symptoms, not everyone exposed to such stressors develops the PTSD symptoms outlined in the *DSM-IV-TR*. That being said, there is a consensus that exposure to traumatic stressors may result in pathological reactions of both an acute and chronic nature even if there is variation in the expression of posttraumatic reactions and even if they do not map neatly onto the *DSM-IV-TR* PTSD concept.

Research has consistently documented ethnocultural variations in PTSD in the following areas:

Perceptions of threat and subjective experience of traumatic stressors

Etiology

Expression of symptoms

Comorbidity

Course

Outcome

Treatment

Marsella, Friedman, Gerrity, and Scurfield (2001) focus the ethnocultural study of PTSD on the following questions:

1. Is the PTSD construct valid across cultures?

2. Can PTSD be accurately diagnosed across ethnocultural contexts?

3. Are there ethnocultural variations in the rates and distributions of PTSD?

4. Are certain ethnocultural groups at greater risk for the development of PTSD?

5. Does culture impact interpretations of trauma and responses to it?

6. Is there variation in responses to various forms of treatment, including pharmacological treatment?

7. Is it possible to render successful treatment independently of the patient's cultural construction of their illness experience, or are there alternative therapies that may be more appropriate for particular groups?

If the clinical goal of identifying and treating psychological trauma is to be accomplished, we have to know how to see it (diagnosis of PTSD) and fix it (treatment of PTSD). I often ask my students in my abnormal psychology course, "How do you know a depression when you see it?" After the puzzled looks fade a little, they usually begin to list the perceivable manifestations of depression. The same goes for PTSD, and for the purposes of this chapter, the questions are asked, "When working with clients of varying ethnocultural backgrounds or across ethnocultural backgrounds, how do you know PTSD when you see it?" and "How do you know a posttraumatic reaction of a pathological nature when you see it?" A patient may come to you with a presenting problem and symptom presentation (e.g., somatic complaints) that fails to conform to your *DSM-IV-TR* conceptual schema. Yet they may describe to you an experience similar to Criterion A2 in the *DSM-IV-TR* for traumatic stimuli. If you lack the necessary skills or knowledge to work from an ethnocultural perspective, you may very well fail that particular patient.

In this journey to grasp the ethnocultural manifestations of PTSD, keep in mind that it is a process that oscillates between the identification of universals and variations. For instance, research continues to show intense posttraumatic symptoms across a wide range of cultures: Sri Lankans exposed to civil war (Somasundaram, 2004); civilian survivors of the war in Afghanistan (Scurfield et al., 1993); and volcano eruption survivors in Colombia (Lima, Pai, Santacruz, Lozano, & Luna, 1988). These are just a few examples of the universality of posttraumatic reactions. But variations exist nonetheless.

Epidemiological Issues

The International Federation of the Red Cross (IFRC) produces a "World Disaster Report," detailing both human-made and natural disasters across the world. Generally speaking, their data have shown that disaster is a common traumatic stressor across cultures but there are geographic variations as well. The following is the distribution of disasters across global regions:

Asia	42 percent (of global totals)
Americas	22 percent
Africa	15 percent
Europe	15 percent
Oceania	6 percent

Disasters tend to be more frequent in the most economically disadvantaged regions. These regions are also more severely impacted by disaster. The safety net of government protection and nongovernmental organizations is weaker and less developed. From 1967 to 1991, 117 million people in developing countries were affected by disaster compared to 700,000 in developing countries (de Girolamo & McFarlane, 1996). Some research has suggested that population density in hazard-prone areas (e.g., housing in flood plains) contributes to this imbalance. These statistics strongly suggest that one's geographic and subsequent national locale can increase one's risk of developing PTSD as a consequence of exposure to disaster.

We've seen that the frequency and impact of disasters vary across the globe, but what about other forms of traumatic stress, for instance, violence? Certainly, by almost any formal measure of violence, there are some ethnocultural contexts or societies that are more violent than others, especially when it comes to war. The IFRC estimates that approximately 40 million people have been killed in wars and conflicts since World War II. Developing countries, again, experience a disproportionate number of wars. There is also the usual consequence of refugees in war-torn regions with its high levels of distress due to displacement. Violent deaths appear to be a more common and prevalent cause of death in developing countries.

Identification and Assessment Issues

The following are some general findings in understanding the relationship between culture and PTSD (de Girolamo & McFarlane, 1996):

Level of acculturation is an issue with respect to diagnosis and symptom manifestation.

The stress of minority status can possibly complicate PTSD and treatment issues such as compliance (e.g., bicultural identity, racism, language issues, mistrust of members of majority culture, stereotypes, etc.).

The degree to which persons identify with their apparent ethnocultural group is an issue.

Researchers addressing the diagnosis and assessment of PTSD across ethnocultural contexts have concluded that there is a generally accepted biological response to traumatic events of psychophysiological activation and disregulation in adrenergic, opioid, and hypothalamic-pituitary-adrenal axis (HPA-axis) functioning, with a variety of symptoms that cut across cultures. But as this response may not vary, there may be considerable variation in recognizable expression of symptoms. Concepts of self, personhood, social systems, concepts of health, and concepts of disease all mediate the expression of posttraumatic reactions. For example, there appears to be considerable variation in the occurrence of avoidance or numbing and hyperarousal symptoms.

Identification of posttraumatic reactions must take into account the idioms of distress that individuals of different ethnocultural contexts use to discuss problematic aspects of their lives and functioning. These are the words and phrases used to express their problems. They tend to be highly specific and idiosyncratic. It has long been known that non-Westerners use somatic or bodily complaints to discuss all sorts of problems not of a physical nature rather than using a more psychological language, for example.

Treatment Issues

One unmistakable feature of psychological trauma is its powerful push to be known. Judith Herman (1981) states that bearing witness to trauma is a key component in the healing process (for more on Judith Herman's treatment technique, see Chapter 15). People who are traumatized seem compelled to tell the story, as it were. I believe this urge to tell is an ethnocultural universal. As I was buying life insurance one day, the salesman told me he was from Uganda and had witnessed the brutal repression of Idi Amin. His pain was apparent despite his obvious strength and years of learning to cope in virtual silence. This simple gesture of telling me, a psychologist, of his past was an attempt at healing. He went on to talk about how he felt about the political system in the United States and how being from Uganda and witnessing what he had gave him such a different perspective. I believe his story illustrates the point that an individual who finds him- or herself growing up or living as an adult in a society and culture that is not congruent with his or her own cultural identity and experience may exhibit conflicts around issues of belonging, trust, safety, approach-avoidance, and isolation. The patient may find him- or herself thinking, "I'm all alone" or "Nobody understands me." These thoughts are common cognitive sequelae in PTSD and can serve to exacerbate symptoms and interfere with treatment.

Gusman et al. (1996) propose the use of their three-way mirror model as a therapy heuristic. This model purports to help with the interaction of multiple forms of self and social identification and traumatic variables and factors. It helps the clinician explore the connections between pretrauma, trauma, and the accumulation of life experiences both prior to and posttruama.

Pretrauma contexts include cultural practices, control, power, vulnerability, fear, relationships, intimacy, family, gender roles, sexuality, and religion. Trauma contexts and topics include attempts to suppress traumatic recollections in order to escape stress or anxiety, aggression as an attempt to gain control over the experience and emotions, and survival coping mechanisms that can be interpreted as appropriate during the traumatic experience but lead to maladaptive behavior in the long run. The final panel in the mirror refers to how the individual integrates these various components into his or her current functioning and behavioral repertoire.

Ultimately, this model is intended to help patients explore their self-concepts in relation to the trauma with respect to the many ways they identify themselves, be it nationally, ethnically, or religiously, for example.

Based on the work of Catherall (1989), Gusman et al. (1996) proposes that one possible outcome of trauma is a "disorder of the multicultural self." According to Catherall (1989) the two central clinical issues are outlined as (1) conflicts in self-integration and (2) the loss of self-cohesion. With the first issue, a patient does not suffer a loss of his or her sense of self, but the feelings and emotions associated with the trauma cannot be assimilated or tolerated. In the second issue, there is a misalignment between a victim and his or her social environment and his or her ability to assimilate or tolerate traumatic feelings and emotions, which results in additional problems with mistrust, alienation, identity disturbance, and interpersonal problems.

Kinzie (1978) proposes a model with three main principles to be used in cross-ethnocultural treatment. The first principle involves the appropriate use of the medical or psychiatric model of PTSD. A focus on the medical model is suggested because it is viewed as generic, value-free, and nonjudgmental and allows for the presentation of and acknowledgment of somatic complaints. Second, there must be recognition on the part of the clinician of the nonverbal modes of communication. Finally, the clinician must be sensitive and attentive to the subjective meaning-making processes of the patient. These general orienting or guiding principles are considered more important than the actual treatment techniques employed, as a technically valid treatment may be ineffective when presented in an inappropriate context.

Juris Draguns (2001) provides the following *universal components of effective intervention in Posttraumatic Stress Disorder,* which are suggested for all posttrauma treatment:

1. Intervene immediately or promptly after the traumatic event.
2. Focus on presenting complaints or current distress.
3. Use specific and possibly directive techniques.
4. Deal with any guilt or self-blame early and directly.
5. Experience and communicate empathy readily.
6. Strengthen the client's sense of competence, autonomy, and self-worth.
7. Help clients make sense of the traumatic event in the context of their lives (including culture).
8. Deal with any object losses early and directly.

Draguns (2001) augments this model with the following *culturally variable components of intervention* to work within an ethnocultural model:

1. Use of interpretations and their rationale and basis.
2. Extent and nature of verbal interaction between the client and therapist.
3. Role of verbal communication.
4. Role differentiation between client and therapist.
5. Respective weights of physical and somatic and psychological distress.
6. Role of ritual in psychotherapy.
7. Use of metaphor, imagery, myth, and storytelling in psychotherapy.
8. Nature of relationship between therapist and client.

With regard to psychopharmacological issues in treatment, research has shown interethnic differences in response to various psychotropic drugs. Differences have been found in the following:

Pharmacogenetics: the interplay between genetic factors in the metabolism of a particular medication

Pharmacodynamics: the mechanism of action of pharmacologic compounds affecting the physiological system

Environmental factors: variation that occurs when drugs are exposed to different diets, environmental toxins, and other drugs

Posttraumatic Stress Disorder and Specific Ethnocultural Groups

Before we begin to look at the various ethnocultural factors of some specific groups, a disclaimer needs to be made. Certainly, a discussion of all the various ethnocultural groups in the United States (and elsewhere for that matter) would by encyclopedic. The groups discussed in this section were chosen for a couple of reasons. Studies with these particular groups constitute the largest proportion of studies. Further, these three groups constitute the largest ethnic minority groups in the United States. It is not my intention to communicate that other groups' experiences are not as important. For more information on various other groups and an in depth discussion of ethnocultural factors and PTSD, please see *Ethnocultural Aspects of Posttraumatic Stress Disorder: Issues, Research, and Clinical Applications* (2001), edited by Anthony Marsella, Matthew Friedman, Ellen Gerrity, and Raymond Scurfield. What is important to get from this section is that depending on historical factors, certain ethnocultural groups may be at increased risk for exposure to traumatic events and subsequent development of PTSD. For now, these groups have been identified, but these groups' statuses as high-risk groups are not frozen in time or carved in stone. Traumatic stress does not respect cultural or national boundaries, and for now our focus is on these groups, but nobody knows the fates of other groups.

Posttraumatic Stress Disorder and African Americans

The African American community has an unmistakably unique social and cultural history in the United States. The ethnocultural approach requires that such uniqueness be treated with the utmost importance when approaching PTSD within the African American community. In essence, the African American experience is one of stress—historically and contemporarily. This experience of heightened stress has been viewed to have a unique effect on both the occurrence and prevalence of traumatic stressors within the African American community and the epidemiology, manifestation, and treatment of PTSD.

The legacy of slavery, past and ongoing racism, high rates of poverty, high rates of incarceration, and high rates of violent death among male adolescents and young adults are considered critical stressors in the African American community. Moreover, Allen (1996) proposes that such an adverse and challenging environment has created life circumstances requiring a constant search and struggle for meaning, purpose, and pressure within the African American community. These circumstances serve as moderating variables that may lead to greater or more long-lasting effects of traumatic stress than in other groups.

Research seems to suggest a positive relationship between being African American and an increase in the frequency and degree of PTSD. However, Allen (1996) again goes on to state that we should be cautious against a bias that views African Americans as living more pathological lives than others and adds the following caveat: "The majority of African Americans do not suffer from PTSD nor do they consider themselves traumatized as individuals. . . Many have learned to cope and survive despite difficult life experiences" (p. 210). Or, as W. Nobles (1991) states,

> African American psychology is something more than the psychology of so-called underprivileged peoples, more than the experience of living in ghettoes or having been forced into the dehumanizing condition of slavery. It is more than the "darker" dimension of general psychology. Its unique status is from the positive features of basic African psychology which dictate the values, customs, attitudes, and behavior of Africans in Africa and the New World. (p. 47)

Despite both of these positive and powerful positions, some investigators and researchers still struggle with the question of whether the African American experience in the United States is inherently *traumatogenic*. Racism and its expression in social and political policies create circumstances that make trauma and deprivation "endemic facts of life" (Allen, 1996, p. 216). Hacker (1992) has identified numerous circumstances or factors: higher unemployment rates than European Americans; social problems, such as higher rates of teen pregnancies, higher rates of single-parent households, higher rates of incarceration, lower life expectancy, higher rates of low birth-weight newborns, higher rates of postneonatal mortality, higher rates of tuberculosis, hypertension, stroke, diabetes, and heart disease; and inequality in education and schools. This is certainly a daunting list and in as much as these factors can be viewed as traumatogenic or increasing one's risk for developing PTSD, the answer to the question of whether the African American experience in the United States is traumatogenic is a resounding *yes*. Irving Allen (1996, p. 221) states, "racism is the ideological foundation for excessive stress in the lives of African Americans."

Research from an ethnocultural perspective with African Americans is typically divided into research with African American Vietnam veterans and research with civilian populations.

African American Vietnam veterans have been consistently found to have higher rates of PTSD than those of European descent. As soldiers, they were 12 percent more likely to be assigned to combat duty and, therefore, had higher rates of combat exposure. The National Vietnam Veterans Readjustment Study of 1990 (Kulka et al., 1990) found that 20.6 percent of African American soldiers suffered from PTSD, compared to 13.7 percent for European Americans and 27.9 percent for Hispanic Americans.

Civilian studies have found that African American children reported higher rates of symptoms following Hurricane Hugo than European American children (Lonigan et al., 1991). Norris (1992), in a study of four Southern cities in the United States, found that African Americans showed higher levels of trauma-related distress. Researchers have cited that SES was a significant confounding factor in these studies, however.

Now that we know that African Americans are at increased risk for exposure to PTSD and of developing PTSD, what issues are important in treatment? To begin with, it is extremely important to keep in mind that African American clients or patients don't leave their experience at the door when they enter treatment. Conflicts and issues that occur in the broader society can be played out in any treatment setting (clinic, therapy office, or hospital). Reenactments of such conflicts have the potential to retraumatize patients or, at the very least, add to their disillusionment. As we have been warned by Allen (1996) and Nobles (1991), there is the risk of overpathologizing behavior or of failing to recognize symptoms by being quick to label *hostility* or a sense of being *entitled*.

African American clients and patients may be less open with non-African American professionals and professionals working in settings identified with the larger, conflict-ridden society and culture. Therapist neutrality is contraindicated as patients or clients may expect some acknowledgment of their background and unique experiences. There has been some suggestion that group therapy is a preferred modality for psychotherapy (Prothrow-Stith, 1991). For a more in depth discussion of treatment, see Elaine Pinderhughes' 1989 book, *Understanding Race, Ethnicity, and Power*.

Posttraumatic Stress Disorder and Southeast Asians

Abueg and Chun (1996) cite that the body of literature studying PTSD with Asians and Asian Americans is relatively small and is focused primarily on Asian refugees in the United States. The region of Southeast Asia including Vietnam, Cambodia, and Laos is considered a highly war-torn area, and the peoples of this region have been extensively exposed to traumatic events and stressors. Abueg and Chun (1996) have developed a schema for understanding stress and traumatic stress in Southeast Asian refugees. They identify four distinct periods of stress: premigration, migration, encampment, and postmigration stress.

Premigration stressors include exposure to war, brutalization, death of family and friends, and loss of property. Migration period stressors include separation from family, travel barriers, and assaults by border police and guards. Encampment stressors include detainment in unsafe, overcrowded and unsanitary conditions plus high levels of uncertainty about one's future. Postmigration stressors include having to learn a new language and skills, loss of loved ones, and loss of cultural and social familiarity.

Vietnamese refugees have been exposed to all such stressors in their experience of war and migration to the United States following the Vietnam War. There were long periods of refugee encampment in Thailand, Hong Kong, Indonesia, Malaysia, and the Philippines. Research has continued to show high levels of vulnerability to depression, anxiety, and poor general health in the general Vietnamese refugee population. Groups that are considered particularly at risk are divorced or widowed female heads of households, individuals older than

46 years old, individuals younger than 21 years old, and women between the ages of 21 and 45 years old. (For more on PTSD and women, see the last section of this chapter.)

Prevalence rates for PTSD vary from study to study but are still considerably higher than the general non-Vietnamese population: 11 percent at a refugee clinic (Mollica, Wyshak, & Lavelle, 1987), 8.1 percent at a psychiatric outpatient clinic (Kroll et al., 1989), and 54 percent at another psychiatric outpatient clinic (Kinzie et al., 1990).

Cambodian refugees have experienced horrendous premigration stress with the political terror and genocide of Pol Pot's Khmer Rouge regime. These people have experienced mass executions, forced separations of family members, confinement to work camps, forced labor, torture, beatings, starvation, and disease. Cambodians have consistently shown higher levels of anxiety and depression than even Vietnamese refugees. They have also been found to see themselves as more different than Americans than do Vietnamese, Laotian, and Hmong refugees (Mollica, 1994; Nicassio, 1983). The following prevalence rates for PTSD have been found: 57 percent in a psychiatric outpatient clinic (Mollica et al., 1987), 22 percent in a clinic population (Kroll et al., 1987), and 92 percent in another clinic population (Kinzie et al., 1990).

Abueg and Chun (1996) argue that understanding that Cambodian, Hmong, and Mien refugees have the highest rates of traumatization among Southeast Asian refugee groups is a crucial factor in effective clinical work, especially in the establishment of empathic connections and encouraging help seeking and disclosure.

Posttraumatic Stress Disorder and Hispanics

Hispanics in the United States represent the largest ethnic minority group. Immigration from Mexico, Central America, and South America continues at an unprecedented pace, with the consequence of people bringing their traumatic experiences with them, not to mention their experience as immigrants and the stressors that come with such. There is also a substantial group of Hispanic Americans whose presence in what is now known as the United States far outdates most European Americans. Just as the groups discussed so far, their history and ongoing experience is unique to them and are important variables with respect to PTSD.

Immigrants and refugees from Latin America have experienced high rates of political repression in the latter half of the twentieth century. Children from both Chile and Argentina have shown increased levels of withdrawal, generalized fear, increased startle response, increased levels of depression, an increased sense of impotence, and an increased sense of vulnerability, for example.

Hispanics living in the United States, whether recent immigrants or long-time inhabitants, may have experiences that add to their vulnerability to PTSD. Disadvantaged sectors of even developed nations may have higher prevalence rates of trauma. This group has higher rates of exposure to crime, exposure to violence, immigration issues, prejudice, discrimination, fewer social resources, and language barriers (Hough, Canino, Abueg, & Gusman, 1996).

Research with nonimmigrant Mexican Americans has shown increased risk for PTSD. Following the San Ysidro McDonald's Massacre in the early 1980s, Hough et al. (1990) found general vulnerabilities significant in predicting later onset of PTSD, such as old age, low income, and medical illness. These researchers suggest that in tightly knit Hispanic communities, trauma may spread throughout the social network.

From the positive side, research shows that in the case of disaster, the strong focus on social and family support within Mexican American communities has proven to provide a stress- or trauma-buffering effect. On the negative side, however, social networks can also place demands or burdens that have shown to be related to a higher number of posttraumatic symptoms (Solomon, the Federman Foundation, & the Israeli Ministry of Defense, 1993).

Although variation in symptom expression can been seen, Guarnaccia, DeLa-Cancela, and Carrillo (1989) found a significant dissociative feature to *ataques de nervios* (a cultural label for stress reactions) However, research has failed to find an increased level of dissociation than in other populations.

Numerous studies have shown that Hispanics tend to report significantly more somatic symptoms than non-Hispanics. There are also higher levels of unexplained physical symptoms. In the case of comorbidity, PTSD is more typically seen in conjunction with a host of other *DSM-IV-TR* diagnoses even though Hispanics with PTSD have been found to be less likely (8.4 percent compared to 37.3 percent for European Americans and 13.6 percent for African Americans) to be diagnosed with a Mood Disorder than individuals from other groups.

When it comes to treatment with the Hispanic ethnocultural group, keep in mind that this population does not use mental health services as much as other groups. When they do seek formal treatment, they may have had experiences that have left them feeling that treatment programs, clinics, and professionals are culturally insensitive. These factors increase their risk for chronicity of PTSD and other mental disorders as well.

Posttraumatic Stress Disorder and Women

It may at first seem out of place to be discussing gender issues as they relate to PTSD in this chapter, but consider the following story from Amy Goodman, infamous journalist and radio talk show host on Pacifica Radio. Amy was speaking of the defense of her dissertation for her PhD in anthropology, stating that she conducted a study of health care delivery for women in the Southern region of the United States. A member of the committee asked her if she knew that anthropology was the study of cultures other than one's own and questioned why she would conduct a study within the United States. Amy's response was powerful;

she stated that as a woman in a male-dominated society, she did not typically think of the United States as her "own culture" and, therefore, was not violating the tenets of anthropology. The committee member responded, "Carry on."

This story is not to arouse the reader's political sensibilities but simply to illustrate the point that within the context of considering the importance of ethnocultural factors and their relation to PTSD, gender and, certainly, being a woman is a cultural factor worth discussing.

The exploration of PTSD and the other groups within this chapter has revealed that certain groups are at increased risk for being exposed to traumatic stressors or stimuli and for developing PTSD. This is also the unfortunate case for women but in a more specific sense. Maria Root (1996) makes the powerful point that women are at a considerably higher risk for exposure to violence. As the other groups in this chapter are at greater risk for natural disaster, refugee stressors, and racism, women are exposed to disproportionate levels of interpersonal violence. Consider the following statistics from Root (2001):

Annually, 2,000 women are murdered by their husbands.

Each year, 1.8 million wives are physically battered by their husbands.

One woman is raped every 60 seconds.

One out of four adult women report being the target of sexual abuse as a child.

These statistics are serious and daunting and make a powerful argument that women are virtual victims of a war consisting of murder, assault, sexual assault, and many other forms of violent trauma. Many, if not most, women are acutely aware of these risks and find themselves altering and adjusting their everyday lives in order to protect themselves. These circumstances have led to very real pragmatic limitations on women's freedom. The cumulative effects of abuse of power, male domination, economic inequality, and sexism have been powerful. Researchers (Ho, 1990; Sorenson & Siegel, 1992) have argued that the roots of the traumatogenic nature of being a women stems from a larger cultural endorsement of violence and ultimately results in impacting women's well-being physically, psychologically, and spiritually.

Women are raped more than men. Koss (1992) reports that one out of five women have experienced a *completed rape*. The trauma of rape is therefore more likely in women than men. Herman (1981) found that one out of three to one out of five women has had a sexual encounter as a child with an adult male. In a large study, Straus and Gelles (1986) found that 28 percent of women and men reported physical violence within their intimate relationships, but 75 percent of the incidents were male perpetrators to female victims.

Even with these shocking statistics, the mental health community has been relatively slow to acknowledge the psychological and psychiatric effects of such experiences in women. Researchers have found that a significant number of women admitted to emergency psychiatric facilities have histories of sexual assault (Carmen, Rieker, & Mills, 1984), ranging from almost half to 81 percent (Beck & van der Kolk, 1987; Jacobson & Richardson, 1987). It has been proposed that the common nature of violence against women and girls has been suppressed and denied in the United States. Such denial may have led many women to seek mental health treatment for trauma-related problems and symptoms without a direct acknowledgment of their traumatic experiences. Certain psychiatric diagnoses that are more commonly given to women than to men have been associated with higher incidences of violence and sexual violence, such as Eating Disorders, Dissociative Disorders, and Borderline Personality Disorder.

Perhaps one of the more infamous scandals with regard to this phenomenon came from the work of Sigmund Freud. Some critics have argued that Freud's Oedipal complex was invented as a cover-up to hide the fact that many of his female patients' discussions of sexual encounters with their fathers were in fact real and did actually occur. Given that many of Freud's patients were the daughters of his colleagues and the powerful members of Viennese society at the time, it is alleged that Freud concocted the notion of fantasized encounters rather than expose the epidemic of sexual abuse. Of course, this has never been actually proved or substantiated, but it is very interesting in light of the current discussion.

There are numerous clinical issues related to the high risk of women to the traumatic stimulus of violence. Women may be more reluctant to seek treatment for PTSD secondary to violence or sexual assault, instead presenting for treatment for depression, panic attacks, or relationship problems instead. This situation is fraught with the risk of misdiagnosis and the possibility of failing to form an empathic clinical relationship. From this situation, treatment drop out may be more common. Cross-gender treatment situations may also lead to difficulties. Feminist therapists have long argued about the unique nature of conducting psychotherapy with women. As with ethnicity, the larger society is never left at the clinic door. Gender stereotypes and sexist beliefs can be significant barriers to effective treatment.

Summary

In this world of global exchange and communication it has become impossible for mental health professionals and researchers to ignore the importance of culture and ethnocultural variation. Important differences exist alongside similarities that challenge comprehensive knowledge and effective treatment. Being a member of a particular ethnocultural or gender group plays a significant role in the manifestation of PTSD.

Quick Review

- Culture is a variable of undeniable importance in the study of all psychological phenomena. Theories and models of psychological functioning, psychopathology, and treatment of mental disorders must all be analyzed across cultural contexts.

- Efficacious and ethical psychological treatment and intervention will depend on the consideration of ethnocultural variables.

- Draguns (1994) states that despite the presence of some psychiatric disorders, such as Schizophrenia and depression, across numerous ethnocultural contexts, there is an extremely wide variety of expressions of symptoms of virtually all other mental disorders.

- Despite ethnocultural variation in the etiology, development of, and expression of psychological trauma, all human beings possess the capacity to meet the Criterion A2 in the *DSM-IV-TR*.

- Research has consistently documented ethnocultural variations in PTSD in the following areas: perceptions of threat and subjective experience of traumatic stressors, etiology, expression of symptoms, comorbidity, course, outcome, and treatment.

- Disasters tend to be more frequent in the most economically disadvantaged regions. These regions are also more severely impacted by disaster. The safety net of government protection and nongovernmental organizations is weaker and less developed.

- The IFRC estimates that approximately 40 million people have been killed in wars and conflicts since World War II. Developing countries, again, experience a disproportionate number of wars. There is also the usual consequence of refugees in war-torn regions, with high levels of distress due to displacement. Violent deaths appear to be a more common and prevalent cause of death in developing countries.

- Draguns's (2001) *culturally variable components of intervention* works within an ethnocultural model and includes the following: use of interpretations and their rationale and basis; extent and nature of verbal interaction between the client and therapist; role of verbal communication; role differentiation between client and therapist; respective weights of physical and somatic and psychological distress; role of ritual in psychotherapy; use of metaphor, imagery, myth, and storytelling in psychotherapy; and nature of relationship between therapist and client.

- Research with African Americans, Southeast Asian refugees, and Hispanics has revealed important differences relevant to epidemiology, etiology, diagnosis, and treatment.

- The exploration of PTSD and the other groups within this chapter has revealed that certain groups are at increased risk for being exposed to traumatic stressors or stimuli and for developing PTSD. This is also the unfortunate case for women but in a more specific sense. Maria Root (1996) makes the powerful point that women are at a considerably higher risk for exposure to violence. As the other groups in this chapter are at greater risk for natural disaster, refugee stressors, and racism, women are exposed to disproportionate levels of interpersonal violence.

References

Abueg, F. R., & Chun, K. M. (1996). Traumatization stress among Asians and Asian Americans. In A. J. Marsella, M. J. Friedman, E. T. Gerrity, & R. M. Scurfield (Eds.), *Ethnocultural aspects of Posttraumatic Stress Disorder: Issues, research, and clinical applications* (pp. 285–299). Washington, DC: American Psychological Association.

Allen, I. M. (1996). PTSD among African Americans. In A. J. Marsella, M. J. Friedman, E. T. Gerrity, & R. M. Scurfield (Eds.), *Ethnocultural aspects of Posttraumatic Stress Disorder: Issues, research, and clinical applications* (pp. 209–238). Washington, DC: American Psychological Association.

American Psychiatric Association. (2001). *Diagnostic and Statistical Manual of Mental Disorders* (4th ed., text revision). Washington, DC: Author.

Beck, J. C., & van der Kolk, B. A. (1987). Reports of childhood incest and current behavior of chronically hospitalized psychotic women. *American Journal of Psychiatry, 144,* 1474–1476.

Berry, J. W., Poortinga, Y. H., Segall, M. H., & Dasen, P. R. (1992). *Cross-cultural psychology: Research and applications.* New York: Cambridge University Press.

Carmen, E. H., Rieker, P. P., & Mills, T. (1984). Victims of violence and psychiatric illness. *American Journal of Psychiatry, 141,* 378–383.

Catherall, D. R. (1989). Differentiating intervention strategies for primary and secondary trauma in Post-Traumatic Stress Disorder: The example of Vietnam veterans. *Journal of Traumatic Stress, 2,* 289–304.

de Girolamo, G., & McFarlane, A. C. (1996). The epidemiology of PTSD: A comprehensive review of the international literature. In A. J. Marsella, M. J. Friedman, E. T. Gerrity, & R. M. Scurfield (Eds.), *Ethnocultural aspects of Posttraumatic Stress Disorder: Issues, research, and clinical applications* (pp. 33–85). Washington, DC: American Psychological Association.

Draguns, J. G. (1994). Pathological and clinical aspects. In L. L. Adler & U. P. Gielen (Eds.), *Cross-cultural topics in psychology* (pp. 165–177). Westport, CT: Praeger.

Draguns, J. G. (2001). Psychopathological and clinical aspects of personal experience: From selves and values to deficits and symptoms. In L. L. Adler & U. P. Gielen (Eds.), *Cross-cultural topics in psychology* (2nd ed., pp. 247–262). Westport, CT: Praeger.

Gergen, K. J., Gulerce, A., Lock, A., & Misra, G. (1996). Psychological science in cultural context. *American Psychologist, 51,* 496–503.

Guarnaccia, P. J., DeLaCancela, V., & Carrillo, E. (1989). The multiple meanings of *ataques de nervios* in the Latino community. *Medical Anthropology, 11,* 47–62.

Gusman, F. D., Stewart, J., Young, B. H., Riney, S. J., Abueg, F. R., & Blake, D. D. (1996). A multicultural developmental approach for treating trauma. In A. J. Marsella, M. J. Friedman, E. T. Gerrity, & R. M. Scurfield (Eds.), *Ethnocultural aspects of Posttraumatic Stress Disorder: Issues, research, and clinical applications* (pp. 439–457). Washington, DC: American Psychological Association.

Hacker, A. (1992). *Two nations: Black and white, separate, hostile, unequal.* New York: Scribner.

Herman, J. (1981). Father-daughter incest. *Professional Psychology, 12,* 76–80.

Ho, C. K. (1990). An analysis of domestic violence in Asian American communities: A multicultural approach to counseling. In L. S. Brown & M. P. Root (Eds.), *Diversity and complexity in feminist therapy* (pp.129–150). New York: Haworth Press.

Hough, R. L., Vega, W., Valle, R., Kolody, B., et al. (1990). Mental health consequences of the San Ysidro McDonald's massacre: A community study. *Journal of Traumatic Stress, 3,* 71–92.

Hough, R. L., Canino, G. J., Abueg, F. R., & Gusman, F. D. (1996). PTSD and related Stress Disorders among Hispanics. In A. J. Marsella, M. J. Friedman, E. T. Gerrity, & R. M. Scurfield (Eds.), *Ethnocultural aspects of Posttraumatic Stress Disorder: Issues, research, and clinical applications* (pp. 301–338). Washington, DC: American Psychological Association.

Jacobson, A., & Richardson, B. (1987). Assault experiences of 100 psychiatric inpatients: Evidence of the need for routine inquiry. *American Journal of Psychiatry, 144,* 908–913.

Kinzie, J. D. (1978). Lessons from cross-cultural psychotherapy. *American Journal of Psychotherapy, 32,* 510–520.

Kinzie, J. D., Boehnlein, J. K., Leung, P. K., Moore, L. J., et al. (1990). The prevalence of Posttraumatic Stress Disorder and its clinical significance among Southeast Asian refugees. *American Journal of Psychiatry, 147,* 913–917.

Koss, M. P. (1992). The underdetection of rape: Methodological choices influence incidence estimates. *Journal of Social Issues, 48,* 61–75.

Kroll, J., Habenicht, M., Mackenzie, T., Yang, M., et al. (1989). Depression and Posttraumatic Stress Disorder in Southeast Asian refugees. *American Journal of Psychiatry, 146,* 1592–1597.

Kulka, R., et al. (1990). *Trauma and the Vietnam War generation: Report of findings from the National Vietnam Veterans Readjustment Study.* New York: Brunner/Mazel.

Lima, B. R., Santacruz, H., Lozano, J., & Luna, J. (1988). Planning for health/mental health integration in emergencies. In M. Lystad (Ed.), *Mental health response to mass emergencies: Theory and practice* (pp. 371–393). Philadelphia: Brunner/Mazel.

Lonigan, C. J., Shannon, M. P., Finch, A. J., Daugherty, T. K., et al. (1991). Children's reactions to a natural disaster: Symptom severity and degree of exposure. *Advances in Behaviour Research & Therapy, 13,* 135–154.

Marsella, A. J., Friedman, M. J., Gerrity, E. T., & Scurfield, R. M. (Eds.). (1996). *Ethnocultural aspects of Posttraumatic Stress Disorder: Issues, research, and clinical applications.* Washington, DC: American Psychological Association.

Marsella, A. J., Friedman, M. J., Gerrity, E. T., & Scurfield, R. M. (1996). Ethnocultural aspects of PTSD: Some closing thoughts. In A. J. Marsella, M. J. Friedman, E. T. Gerrity, & R.M. Scurfield (Eds.), *Ethnocultural aspects of posttraumatic stress disorder: Issues, research, and clinical applications* (pp. 105–129). Washington, DC: American Psychological Association.

Marsella, A.J. (1988). Cross-cultural research on severe mental disorders: Issues and findings. *Acta Psychiatrica Scandinavica Supplementum, 344,* 7–22.

Mollica, R. (1994). Southeast Asian refugees: Migration history and mental health issues. In A. J. Marsella, T. Bornemann, S. Ekblad, & J. Orley (Eds.), *Amidst peril and pain: The mental health and well-being of the world's refugees* (pp. 83–100). Washington, DC: American Psychological Association.

Mollica, R. F., Wyshak, G., & Lavelle, J. (1987). The psychosocial impact of war trauma and torture on Southeast Asian refugees. *American Journal of Psychiatry, 144,* 1567–1572.

Nicassio, P. M. (1983). Psychosocial correlates of alienation: Study of a sample of Indochinese refugees. *Journal of Cross-Cultural Psychology, 14,* 337–351.

Nobles, W. W. (1991). African philosophy: Foundations for Black psychology. In R. L. Jones (Ed.), *Black psychology* (3rd ed., pp. 47–63). Berkeley: Cobb & Henry.

Norris, F. H. (1992). Epidemiology of trauma: Frequency and impact of different potentially traumatic events on different demographic groups. *Journal of Consulting and Clinical Psychology, 60,* 409–418.

Pinderhughes, E. (1989). *Understanding race, ethnicity, and power: The key to efficacy on clinical practice.* Florida: Free Press.

Prothrow-Stith, D. (1991). *Deadly consequences: How violence is destroying our teenage population and a plan to begin solving the problem.* New York: Harper Perennial.

Root, M. P. (1996). Women of color and traumatic stress in "domestic captivity": Gender and race as disempowering statuses. In A. J. Marsella, M. J. Friedman, E. T. Gerrity, & R. M. Scurfield (Eds.), *Ethnocultural aspects of Posttraumatic Stress Disorder: Issues, research, and clinical applications* (pp. 363–387). Washington, DC: American Psychological Association.

Scurfield, R. M., Hunter, E. J., Orner, R. J., Kinzie, J. D., Solomon, Z., Somasundaram, D. J., et al. (1993). Section B: Research from World War II to the present. In J. P. Wilson & B. Raphael (Eds.), *International handbook of traumatic stress syndromes* (pp. 285–394). New York: Plenum Press.

Shalev, A. Y., Yehuda, R., & McFarlane, A. C. (Eds.). (2000). *International handbook of human response to trauma.* Dordrecht, Netherlands: Kluwer Academic.

Solomon, Z., Federman Foundation, & Israeli Ministry of Defense. (1993). *Combat stress reaction: The enduring toll of war.* New York: Plenum Press.

Somasundaram, D. (2004). Short- and long-term effects on the victims of terror in Sri Lanka. *Journal of Aggression, Maltreatment & Trauma, 9,* 215–228.

Sorenson, S. B., & Siegel, J. M. (1992). Gender, ethnicity, and sexual assault: Findings from a Los Angeles study. *Journal of Social Issues, 48,* 93–104.

Straus, M. A., & Gelles, R. J. (1986). Societal change and change in family violence from 1975 to 1985 as revealed by two national surveys. *Journal of Marriage & the Family, 48,* 465–479.

Stamm, B. H., & Friedman, M. J. (2000). Cultural diversity in the appraisal and expression of trauma. In A. Y. Shalev, R. Yehuda, & A. C. McFarlane (Eds.), *International handbook of human response to trauma* (pp. 69–85). Dordrecht, Netherlands: Kluwer Academic.

Witzum, E., & Kotler, M. (2000). Historical and cultural construction of PTSD in Israel. In A. Y. Shalev, R. Yehuda, & A. C. McFarlane (Eds.), *International handbook of human response to trauma* (pp. 103–114). Dordrecht, Netherlands: Kluwer Academic.

Evaluating, Assessing, and Treating Posttraumatic Stress Disorder

THE WILEY
CONCISE GUIDES
TO MENTAL HEALTH

Posttraumatic
Stress
Disorder

CHAPTER 10

Clinical Evaluation and Assessment of Posttraumatic Stress Disorder

General Evaluation and Assessment Issues

When I teach abnormal psychology, I often start out by asking my students to brainstorm various symptoms and signs of the particular disorder we are discussing for that lesson. This has gone a lot less smoothly than I initially thought. Students come up with a few key components, but not many or even most signs or symptoms. They typically are unable to paint me a picture of what a particular disorder actually looked like in the real world. Of course, I realize that my job as their professor is to teach them how to do this. A few guiding questions are usually helpful such as, "What exactly does PTSD look like?" or "How would someone with PTSD behave, think, or feel differently than someone without PTSD?" After we derive a fairly comprehensive list of indicators, I put a crucial and core question of psychology right back to them:

Professor: How do you *know* that these people are behaving, thinking, or feeling the way you describe? This usually elicits a long silence with many strange looks.

Students: What do you mean?

Professor: How do you know your uncle the Vietnam veteran acts wound up and irritable?

Students: He yells a lot, he tells us he is pissed off all the time, and he's always jumpy, looking over his shoulder or out the window.

Professor: That's what I mean. You know that people are behaving, thinking, or feeling in a particular way because you have observed, recorded, or measured these variables in some way.

At the heart of psychology and clinical practice is systematic and scientific measurement, and psychological assessment is the means by which this is achieved. What is being measured? Human psychological phenomena within a biopsychosocial model are being measured (thoughts, feelings, personality characteristics, physiological reactivity, etc.). There are numerous data gathering and measurement methods and procedures, including the following:

Interviews (e.g., structured or semistructured interviews)

Observation (e.g., behavioral observation or mental status exam)

Questionnaires (e.g., self-report, clinician administered, or third-party sources)

Projective tests (e.g., TAT or the Rorschach Inkblot Test)

Objective tests (e.g., intelligence, neuropsychological, personality, cognitive)

Psychobiological measures (e.g., EEG, MRI, blood tests, or electrophysiological)

Before we go on, a key distinction needs to be made between psychological evaluation and psychological assessment. *Psychological evaluation* is a broader term and a procedure that may or may not include psychological assessment. The evaluation process involves collection of relevant data and subsequent case formulation for the purpose of arriving at a diagnosis, setting up a treatment plan, making recommendations, or answering relevant referral questions. Psychological assessment involves the use of psychological instruments, such as questionnaires and tests, and is a subcomponent of the evaluation process. Not all evaluations include psychological assessment, however. Psychological assessment as part of the evaluation process is considered a critical component to the study and treatment of PTSD. Clarity in identification and diagnosis is often difficult with PTSD because of the complex nature of symptoms and difficulties of individual patients or clients. As was discussed in Chapters 3 and 8, the wide range of posttraumatic consequences and complications, including comorbid disorders, taxes researchers' and clinicians' abilities to grasp what exactly they are dealing with in any particular case. Human psychological functioning is extremely complex, and the naked clinical eye often requires help in seeing clearly or seeing what cannot be seen upon initial presentation. Here, power and utility of psychological assessment is demonstrated. Psychological assessment is simply a more formal and systematic approach to evaluation as Maloney and Ward (1976) state: "[Psychological assessment is] an extremely complex process of solving problems (answering questions) in which psychological tests are often used as one of the methods of collecting relevant data" (p. 5).

Relevant questions are derived from your general clinical model and orientation and your typical clinical method. Let me make a quick point about clinical method. Formal evaluation and psychological assessment is a particular method of psychological science. Other sciences and practices have different methods, techniques, and tools for evaluation. Psychologists use psychological tests as tools of observation. Orthopedists use X-rays. Microbiologists use microscopes. Astronomers use telescopes.

Let's get back to the issue of orientation for a minute. Consider that different clinicians of different orientations may not want to measure the same variables or gather the same data. Of course, sound clinical practice dictates that some information should be universally gathered, but we will return to this issue in a moment. A cognitive therapist may not want to measure a patient's object relations the way a psychodynamic-oriented clinician might. The key thing to remember is that the purpose of assessment should drive the particular variables being measured.

Assessment aids in the establishment of an accurate diagnosis and facilitates professional communication and reliability. This is particularly important in forensic evaluations when the presence of PTSD in a particular individual may be in dispute and a professional's method for arriving at his or her conclusions are closely scrutinized.

Psychological assessment and testing is a complicated endeavor that should only be undertaken and utilized by qualified professionals. Evaluation and assessment results should always be safeguarded against abuse or misuse, and issues of confidentiality and test security should always be observed and maintained. The following is quick summary of established ethical guidelines:

- Only valid, reliable, and appropriately normed instruments should be used.

- Only qualified professionals should administer, score, and interpret instruments.

- Test results should be safeguarded against abuse or misinterpretation.

- Professionals should respect the privacy of persons being evaluated and assessed and only examine what is clinically relevant. No psychological voyeurism!

- Persons being evaluated should be properly informed and formally consent to the evaluation process, with the ability to withdraw or stop the process at any time.

- Confidentiality shall be observed and maintained at all times.

- Results shall be presented and communicated in a meaningful, effective, and useful manner to the consumer of the results.

The Importance of Norms, Validity, and Reliability

All assessment instruments are developed by administering a particular procedure or set of questions to a given group of people, the *norm*, to establish a comparative and distributive performance level for that particular instrument. An instrument developed on veterans for use with veterans should not be used with children, for example. Using a test on persons that are not part of the norming sample yields meaningless and useless results. Always be aware if you are comparing apples to oranges or oranges to apples, and so on! If an instrument's norming parameters are not observed, the results are essentially not valid.

Validity refers to the issue of whether a particular instrument is measuring what it purports to be measuring. If I develop a test to measure intelligence but it is never put through the rigors of establishing its validity, I may not be measuring intelligence at all but some other variable. Or I might not be measuring anything at all.

That brings us to the issue of reliability. *Validity* refers to measuring what we think we are measuring, and *reliability* refers to the issue of whether a person's performance or score on a particular instrument reflects their actual performance or some source or error inherent in the test. We want to measure the person taking the test, not the test's inability to capture the person's performance. Test scores and performances tell us the measurable difference between person A and person B. If a test is unreliable, then we may not be able to trust that the difference between person A and person B is due to the actual measured construct or due to some error produced by factors inherent in the instrument or method. If I measure the height of a wall three times and get three different measurements each time, I am not a very reliable wall-height measurer. This is, unfortunately, a true example!

Getting Started

Getting started first requires the selection of a given method, technique, and instrument. In order to do so, the clinician needs to consider the following questions and issues:

1. What is the setting? (clinic, school, jail, etc.)

2. What questions are being asked, by whom are the questions being asked, and what is the purpose of the evaluation?

3. What is the person reporting?

The setting in which a particular evaluator or assessor works will determine the extent, degree, and particular method utilized in the process. If I am a crisis worker in the field going door to door looking for people who might need psychological first aid, crisis intervention, or more comprehensive treatment, I am not going to carry around with me a suitcase full of psychological tests and sit each person down for 2 to 4 hours of testing. I might bring a simple questionnaire or no instruments at all. In addition to the issues of norms, validity, and reliability, the appropriateness of a particular method, technique, or tool is determined by the setting, the urgency of which the relevant questions need to be answered, and the ability of the person or persons being evaluated to engage in the process. Time frames are important and so is the ability of a particular person to engage in the evaluation and assessment process. Whether you have the required time and whether the examinee is actually testable (e.g., are they hearing impaired, visually impaired, acutely psychotic, etc.?) are very important determinants in the process. Make sure you can get the information you are looking for in the time allowed, and make appropriate adaptations and adjustments. Whether you choose to use an informal, unstructured interview or a 2-hour pencil-and-paper test will be determined by these factors. A test that requires a patient to read may be useless if the person in question does not read at a requisite level, for example.

The second question addresses the issue of the referral question and referral source. The method employed by a clinician (or even a researcher) will depend on what the important and relevant parties want to know. The referring party can be the patient (i.e., self-referral); you, the clinician; or some third party, such as an employer, judge, or agency. Don't measure personality if you're asked for mental status, for example.

Finally, in the third question—what the person(s) being evaluated presents in observation, self-report, report by third party, or through documentation or records—will determine the method and instrument(s) used. You may assess for depression if someone presents with anxiety, but if they are reporting anxiety, your focus in going to center on the most salient issues and only then work your way out from there. Start with what is central and then work your way outward.

Once the clinician has the answers to these questions and methods and instruments have been selected, the actual process can begin in a stepwise fashion, employing relevant techniques and arriving at appropriate and valid conclusions.

Evaluation And Assessment of PTSD

So far we have discussed the general issues of psychological evaluation and assessment that are important for any and all psychological and psychiatric problems. We now turn specifically to the evaluation and assessment of PTSD. Although the clinical evaluation of PTSD should be similar to the evaluation of other disorders, there are specific issues, approaches, and techniques especially relevant to PTSD. This is important to consider because a generic approach to the assessment of PTSD might leave many questions unanswered and ultimately lead to a client or patient not receiving the help he or she needs. John Wilson (2004) proposes a very useful and comprehensive approach to the evaluation and assessment of PTSD in order that these issues might be avoided. Wilson's (2004) comprehensive model of assessment includes two large areas of assessment, symptom clusters and adaptive behavioral considerations. There are five symptom clusters: (1) reexperiencing, (2) avoidance, numbing, and coping, (3) hyperarousal, (4) self and ego, and (5) interpersonal affiliation patterns of attachment, bonding, intimacy, and love. The adaptive behavioral configurations include dysregulated affects, personality alterations (self, ego, etc.), altered interpersonal processes (detachment, loss of intimacy, alienation), psychosocial functioning (school, work, etc.), comorbidity, health, life-course trajectory (changes in epigenetic developmental patterns), and recovery and healing. Using Wilson's approach, comprehensive assessment with the PTSD patient should involve measuring each of the areas listed. Wilson calls his approach an *organismic* approach encompassing the complete functioning of an individual's biopsychosocial functioning. Specifically, a complete assessment involves an encompassing set of psychological and psychosocial functions, such as are presented in the following:

1. Addressing of the etiology of the disorder in the five subsystems and affected functioning for a particular patient or client.

2. Understanding the changes in pretraumatic baseline functioning.

3. Assessment of profile configurations in terms of frequency, periodicity, severity, intensity, and duration of symptoms within the five clusters.

4. Knowledge of how core inner dimensions of the self are altered in ways that are associated with posttraumatic self-typologies that fall along a continuum of fragmentation to integration and transformation.

5. Understanding of how the trauma has affected his/her biopsychosocial functioning in terms of epigenetic development and personality functioning in the life cycle.

Also included in Wilson's model is a comprehensive trauma history, a prior history of abuse, victimization, and an evaluation of preexisting Axis I or II disorders.

Newman, Kaloupek, and Keane (1996) also suggest a comprehensive and multimethod approach to the clinical evaluation and assessment of PTSD. They state, "The challenge in the clinical assessment of PTSD is to combine appropriate measure so as to distinguish individuals who, once exposed to potentially traumatic events, have gone on to develop the disorder from those who have not" (p. 245). They promote a flexible approach that yields the highest level of diagnostic utility, that is, the extent to which a particular assessment approach or instrument accurately differentiates one group from another. Test batteries are suggested to maximize sensitivity and the power of the assessment process. Unfortunately, there has been no specific battery of instruments identified for PTSD. At this point, battery construction is left up to the individual clinician or researcher for his or her particular purposes.

Newman et al. (1996) recommend using a comprehensive structured or semistructured interview in order to "insure that all PTSD symptomatology is reviewed in detail" (p. 247). The strength of a semistructured format over a structured one is its flexibility while maintaining its structure. A weakness of this method is its dependence on the clinical skill of the administrator. Another component of the multimethod approach is the self-report measure, providing a patient's eye view of their experience and symptoms. A third component to the multimethod approach is the use of empirically derived psychometric measures of PTSD. Finally, psychometric instruments not specifically designed for PTSD but that can help in assessing other concomitant issues can be employed, such as the MMPI-2, the Beck Anxiety Inventory, or the various Wechsler scales of intelligence and memory.

Getting Started—Global Assessment

All clinical evaluations begin with identifying the presenting problem of a given patient or patients. Individuals with PTSD rarely come in and state, "Hey, I have PTSD and here are my symptoms." Instead, much like most people presenting for mental health services, they complain of less core symptoms and of more peripheral problems. Here is a quick guide to common PTSD presenting problems:

- Memory, attention, and concentration problems
- Irritability, agitation, and anger
- Feeling stressed out or keyed up
- Feeling fearful, as if something bad is going to happen
- Feeling numb, wanting to avoid people, and relationship problems
- Nightmares
- Depression

Individuals with PTSD will often present with memory, attention, and concentration problems. They will report, or their family members will report, that they forget conversations, where they placed objects, and common daily events. They act spaced out. Agitation or irritability is also a common complaint. They report feeling keyed up or stressed out all the time. They might complain of feeling emotionally numb and disconnected from people. They might be having nightmares. No matter what the presenting problems are, once enough information has been ascertained by the clinician to suspect that the patient might be suffering from PTSD, a PTSD-relevant background and history taking needs to be performed.

All clinicians have training and favored methods to use in their general approach to the generic patient. To one extent or another, clinicians employ a structured or semistructured interview method in beginning to grasp and develop an understanding of a particular patient's issues. With respect to PTSD presentations, there exist a number of structured and semistructured clinical interview methods or instruments.

The Structured Clinical Interview for *DSM-IV* Axis I Disorders, Clinical Version (SCID-I) is a very widely used and trustworthy structured interview for all psychiatric disorders. It is considered a sensitive instrument in accurately identifying persons with PTSD versus those who do not have PTSD. A weakness of this instrument is considered to be its reliance on the interviewee's memory and recollection of symptom severity over a long period of time. This may result in distorted or inaccurate measurement.

Other structured or semistructured interview techniques of note are the PTSD Interview (Watson, Juba, Manifold, Kucala, et al., 1991) and the Clinician-Administered PTSD Scale (CAPS; Blake et al., 1990, 1995). The PTSD Interview has shown strong reliability features and good sensitivity. It is brief and does not require a professional to administer. Its weaknesses are its face validity and potential for bias due to reporter distortion. The CAPS was developed for use with veterans and is considered a solid instrument because of its psychometric properties and its rating of both the intensity and frequency of symptoms. It is considered an accurate and efficient instrument. Its weaknesses are its administration length and its limited use with nonveterans.

Background and History

When working with PTSD patients, the first order of business is to get a *trauma history* to determine whether a traumatic event has occurred. Simply ask the patient when his or her symptoms and problems began. Next, ask if he or she has been exposed to a traumatic event or stressor per the *DSM-IV-TR criteria:* "Have you ever experienced, witnessed, or been confronted with an event that involved actual or threatened death or serious injury, or a threat to the physical integrity of you or others?"

Clinician Alert

The phrasing of this question is an extremely important issue. If this question is asked too formally, patients might get confused. It always helps to ask the question in a language the patient can understand. Sometimes it is better to just ask, "Have you ever almost died?" or "Have you ever seen anyone get killed or die right in front of you?" These questions are fairly specific and, therefore, might not cover the range of qualified traumatic stressors, but they are often useful in stimulating the patients' thinking about traumatic events in their lives. They might bring up events or examples that don't qualify in a strict sense, but all responses to this question should be investigated further. If an event is salient enough to produce trauma symptoms, simple questions will often stimulate patients just enough to yield good information.

If there was an event or events, are the symptoms or problems contiguous with the event or stressor? Also, ask about past traumatic events that occurred long before the appearance of symptoms or dysfunction. Patients' recollections of when signs and symptoms began are not always accurate, and their difficulties may have begun much earlier than they realize. Careful and thorough questioning will help pinpoint when signs and symptoms began and whether they appear to be related to a traumatic event.

Background and history information relevant to a trauma history can be ascertained in any number of ways, ranging from structured clinical interviews, questionnaires, nonstructured clinical interviews, and standardized self-report measures. Norris and Hamblen (2004) reviewed seven quality self-report measures designed to ascertain the presence of qualified traumatic events in a patient's history. Two standout instruments are both questionnaires: the Traumatic Life Events Questionnaire (TLEQ), developed by Edward Kubany et al. (2000) and the Stressful Life Events Questionnaire (SLESQ), developed by Goodman, Corcoran, Turner, Yuan, and Green (1998). The TLEQ assesses the occurrence of 23 traumatic events (e.g., natural disasters, motor vehicle accidents, or combat), is useful for both research and clinical practice, is clinician-administered, and has good psychometric properties. It is a comprehensive questionnaire covering a wide range of traumatic events. The SLESQ is a self-report screening instrument that assesses lifetime exposure to potentially traumatic events and, like the TLEQ, has good reliability statistics. It provides such useful information as the age, frequency, and degree of life threat of a particular trauma.

Core Symptom Assessment of PTSD

Once the presence of a traumatic event has been established and it appears that the patient's problems are contiguous with the event, the presence, intensity, and duration of the core symptoms of PTSD need to be evaluated.

Is the patient demonstrating *reexperiencing* phenomena occurring in at least one of the following ways?

1. The patient experiences recurrent and intrusive distressing recollections of the event, including images, thoughts, or perceptions. Note that in young children, repetitive play may occur in which themes related to the event are reflected.

2. The patient experiences recurrent distressing dreams of the event. Note that in children, there may be frightening dreams without recognizable content.

3. The patient acts or feels as if the traumatic event were recurring (includes a sense of reliving the experience, illusions, hallucinations, and dissociative

flashback episodes, including those that occur on awakening or when intoxicated). Note that in young children, trauma-specific reenactment may occur.

4. The patient experiences intense psychological distress at exposure to internal or external cures that symbolize or resemble an aspect of the traumatic event.

5. The patient experiences physiological reactivity on exposure to internal or external cures that symbolize or resemble an aspect of the traumatic event.

Is the patient experiencing persistent avoidance of stimuli associated with the trauma and a numbing of general responsiveness (not present before the trauma), as indicated by three (or more) of the following?

1. Efforts to avoid thoughts, feelings, or conversations associated with the trauma.

2. Efforts to avoid activities, places, or people that arouse recollections of the trauma.

3. Inability to recall an important aspect of the trauma.

4. Markedly diminished interest or participation in significant activities.

5. Feeling of detachment or estrangement from others.

6. Restricted range of affect (e.g., unable to have loving feelings).

7. Sense of foreshortened future (e.g., does not expect to have a career, marriage, children, or a normal life span).

Finally, is he or she experiencing persistent symptoms of increased arousal (not present before the trauma), as indicated by two (or more) of the following?

1. Difficulty falling or staying asleep.

2. Irritability or outbursts of anger.

3. Difficulty concentrating.

4. Hypervigilance.

5. Exaggerated startle response.

Norris and Hamblen (2004) also reviewed 17 instruments relevant to assessing the core symptoms of PTSD. Some strong instruments identified are the Posttraumatic Stress Diagnostic Scale, developed by Foa, Cashman, Jaycox, and Perry (1997) and the PTSD-Interview (PTSD-I), developed by Watson et al. (1991). The Posttraumatic Stress Diagnostic Scale inquires about *DSM-IV* symptoms occurring within the last month. Both validity (alpha = .92) and reliability (r = .83) are considered solid. The PTSD-I was developed for veterans, but Norris and Hamblen state it could be used for almost any population. The *DSM-IV* symptoms are identified as existing on a seven-point scale, ranging from "no" to "extremely" or "never" to "always." Again, validity (alpha = .92) and reliability (test-retest reliability = .95) are considered solid. The Mississippi Scale for Combat-Related PTSD is an empirically developed instrument specifically designed to assess PTSD in veterans but has been used with civilians and women as well. It is considered a good general measure of PTSD. Finally, the Impact of Event Scale–Revised has been identified as a useful and simple measure to assess the core PTSD symptoms across a range of different samples.

Psychophysiological Assessment of PTSD

The prominent role of psychophysiological mechanisms in PTSD etiology and course are undeniable. Most psychophysiological assessment of PTSD has been relegated to research purposes. There are a few clinical applications, specifically for prediction of adjustment and treatment outcomes.

Psychophysiological assessment typically involves measurement of one of four key physiological systems outlined by Orr, Metzger, Miller, and Kaloupek (2004): cardiovascular measurement, such as blood pressure and heart rate measurement, with electrocardiograms (ECG); electrodermal measurement of skin conductance; electromyographic measurement of muscle activity; and electrocortical measurement with electroencephalograms (EEG). Evidence of the various symptoms and components of PTSD has been provided. Reactivity to trauma-related cues, numbing of general responsiveness, sleep disturbance, irritability and anger, difficulty concentrating, hypervigilance, exaggerated startle responses, and persistent autonomic arousal have all been measurable and assessed using various psychophysiological techniques, lending solid evidence for many biological theories and models of PTSD. For now, however, the use of complex psychophysiological measures in the clinical setting is limited. For purposes of this chapter, only research findings relevant to potential clinical application will be discussed.

Altered baseline heart rate in traumatized individuals may be a good predictor of future PTSD development. Initial elevation in heart rate has been shown to be related to development of PTSD in motor vehicle accident victims (Bryant, Harvey, Guthrie, & Moulds, 2000). Blanchard, Hickling, Galovski, and Veazey (2002) made similar findings with elevated heart rate's predictive value.

It is proposed by Orr et al. (2004) that progress in treatment and treatment outcome can be psychophysiologically measured. Foa and Kozak (1986) propose that treatment gains are observable when patients rate their subjective distress to trauma cues as less distressing over time. In addition to subjective verbal ratings and reports, a patient's reactivity to trauma cues could be measured physiologically. Pitman, Orr, Altman, and Longpre (1996) found that measured reductions in heart rate, skin conductance, and facial electromyography (EMG) during treatment were correlated with a reduction in daily intrusive symptoms. Further, Shalev, Orr, and Pitman (1992) found that psychophysiological responses to imagery presentation were responsive to psychiatric improvements. Boudewyns and Hyer (1990) found that a decrease in skin conductance in response to trauma imagery was correlated with higher scores on an adjustment measure up to 3 months after treatment.

Ultimately, the utility and practicality of psychophysiological measures in clinical practice are limited at this time. However, with innovations in computer technology and more affordable technology becoming available, it might be that in just a few years pencil-and-paper tests of symptoms will be replaced or at least augmented by the types of psychophysiological measures mentioned here.

Functional Assessment of PTSD

Cognitive Functioning
Memory, Attention, and Concentration

Memory dysfunction is a common presenting problem from patients with PTSD and can be observed by third parties, such as family members, coworkers, or employers. Patients are told they are forgetting conversations they've had or tasks they were expected to perform. Memory problems can also be observed clinically in patients' inability to recall information from their pasts surrounding the traumatic event, missing appointment times, or forgetting to do between-session homework assignments, for example.

The assessment of memory in PTSD in some ways is no different from assessment of memory in general. The Wechsler Memory Scale–Third Edition (WMS-III) is a widely used instrument with a solid research base across clinical populations and sound psychometric properties. The WMS-III has not been identified as a specific instrument for use in PTSD assessment, but its clinical utility will help any clinician assess a PTSD patient's memory functioning, whether dysfunction is viewed as related to PTSD symptomotology.

Measurement of attention and concentration problems in PTSD patients follows along similar lines of memory assessment. Various non-PTSD specific measures of attention and concentration can be employed, such as the Trail Making Test Parts A and B or the Continuous Performance Test. To reiterate, these instruments are suggested as generic measures of attention and concentration deficits whether related to PTSD or not. Keep in mind, however, that the Trail Making Test Parts A and B is susceptible to anxiety effects, particularly performance anxiety, and that poor scores may reflect either the effects of anxiety or poor attention and concentration. Although this could be a confound in one's clinical formulation, it may, in fact, help a clinician see his or her examinee's attention and concentration functioning within the context of anxiety.

Dissociation

As has been discussed in Chapter 8, dissociative symptoms such as derealization, depersonalization, or psychogenetic amnesia are sometimes critical features of a PTSD patient's presentation. Research has shown considerable prevalence of dissociative symptoms in trauma victims. Sometimes these symptoms warrant a separate diagnosis of a Dissociative Disorder, but when assessing PTSD, they are a considered a necessary component to thorough assessment, and although formal assessment may ultimately be unnecessary, at the very least dissociative symptoms should be inquired about in the initial interview.

The *DSM-IV-TR* defines *dissociation* as the disruption in the usually integrated functions of consciousness, memory, identity, or perception . . . (p. 822). According to Steinberg (2004), there are five essentially measurable symptoms of dissociation that can be reliably and validly measured by the Structured Clinical Interview for *DSM-IV* Dissociative Disorders (SCID-D). They are amnesia, depersonalization, derealization, identity confusion, and identity alteration. The SCID-D is a clinician-administered instrument for either adults or adolescents and allows for the eventual diagnosis of the five Dissociative Disorders in the *DSM-IV-TR*: Dissociative Amnesia, Dissociative Fugue, Depersonalization Disorder, Dissociative Identity Disorder, and Dissociative Disorder Not Otherwise Specified.

Personality, General Psychological Functioning, and Comorbid Diagnoses

As was discussed in Chapter 3, PTSD patients may exhibit altered personality functioning and significant dysfunction in other aspects of their functioning, including coping, ego-defense mechanisms, relationships, and motivation. Specific instruments for use with PTSD patients have not been identified in the literature. However, a clinician can use any number of more generic available instruments to assess these areas.

Personality functioning can be very adequately assessed using the Minnesota Multiphasic Personality Inventory–Second Edition (MMPI-2), the Millon Clinical Multiaxial Inventory–Third Edition (MCMI-III), the NEO-Personality Inventory (Neuroticism, Extroversion, Openness), or the 16 PF (Personality Factors). The MMPI-2 is considered the gold standard in personality and psychological functioning assessment and is particularly useful for PTSD because of some specialized scales developed to detect and assess PTSD symptomology. Keane, Malloy, and Fairbank (1984) developed the PK scale, consisting of specific items on the MMPI-2 to detect PTSD symptoms, and it is considered a good initial screening tool. Schlenger and Kulka (1989) also developed a PTSD subscale for the MMPI-2 that can be used to differentiate between veterans who are experiencing PTSD, those with other mental disorders, and those with no mental disorder.

Luxenberg and Levin (2004) propose that the Rorschach is a useful instrument in PTSD assessment. Although the Rorschach is a controversial instrument within the psychological assessment community, Luxenberg and Levin propose that it is useful in providing not only information about PTSD symptoms but also information about a patient's sense of self, worldview, perceptions of others, and affective functioning. The Rorschach is considered a good tool by some for use with patients who have trouble consciously accessing thoughts, feelings, and memories related to their traumas because it can get (purportedly) around defense mechanisms and limits to conscious recollection and reporting.

Certainly a patient's general health status and any problems should be part of a comprehensive assessment. Some professionals are not licensed or qualified to perform a standard medical history and physical, but general inquiry should always be performed. Of particular interest when discussing health issues in PTSD assessment are cardiac functioning, general immunity or immune functioning, and neurological status. As was discussed in Chapter 3, trauma victims may suffer from neurological problems as a direct result of the traumatic event they experienced. Patients should be assessed for a history of traumatic brain injury; closed-head injury, such as anoxic injuries (for example, from drowning accidents or exposures to gases); neurotoxic or toxic exposures; and chronic Alcohol Abuse and its complications.

A thorough Substance Abuse assessment should be included in the PTSD evaluation. Ruling in or ruling out Substance Disorders will help in all phases of patient interaction, diagnosis, treatment, and follow up. Instruments of particular use are the Addiction Severity Index, the Michigan Alcohol Screening Test, or the Drug Abuse Screening Test.

Finally, the presence of other mental disorders in PTSD patients should be determined. Depression is a common comorbid condition and can be assessed using formal methods, such as the SCID-I or the Beck Depression Inventory. The MMPI-2 can be useful for this purpose as well. Ultimately, if a thorough assessment is conducted from the outset, paths for assessment will be revealed and will require further inquiry and follow up.

Summary

Psychological assessment is an invaluable tool in the research or evaluation and treatment of PTSD. In addition to a general or generic approach, specific instruments and techniques will help capture the complexity of a PTSD patient's experience and solidify diagnosis, treatment planning, and general understanding. Advances in assessment techniques and approaches will continue to yield rich information about our patients and study subjects in the future. The importance of empirically based evaluation in PTSD is not to be minimized and should be a critical component in all our work with PTSD patients.

Quick Review

- At the heart of psychology and clinical practice is systematic and scientific measurement, and psychological assessment is the means by which this is achieved.

- Psychological assessment as part of the evaluation process is considered a critical component to the study and treatment of PTSD.

- Only valid, reliable, and appropriately normed instruments should be used, and only qualified professionals should administer, score, and interpret instruments.

- The setting, the referral question, and the presenting problems will guide the assessment process.

- Wilson (2004) calls for an organismic approach to assessment encompassing the complete functioning of an individual's biopsychosocial functioning, including understanding etiology and affected functioning; understanding the changes in pretraumatic baseline functioning; assessment of frequency, periodicity, severity, intensity, and duration of symptoms; knowledge of core inner dimensions of the self and the ways it is altered; and understanding epigenetic development effects and personality functioning in the life cycle.

- Assessment techniques and instruments include formal testing, self-report questionnaires, and psychophysiological measures.

- Common presenting problems in PTSD patients include memory, attention, and concentration problems; irritability, agitation, and anger; feeling stressed out or keyed up; feeling fearful, as if something bad is going to happen; feeling numb; wanting to avoid people; and relationship problems, nightmares, and depression.

- General clinical assessment should be followed up by a thorough trauma history.

- Core symptoms of PTSD per the *DSM-IV-TR* must be assessed.

- Concomitant functional issues should be assessed, including general functioning, health status, Substance Abuse, and comorbid disorders.

References

American Psychiatric Association. (2000). *Diagnostic and statistical manual of mental disorders* (4th ed., text revision). Washington, DC: Author.

Blake, D. D., Keane, T. M., Wine, P. R., Mora, C., et al. (1990). Prevalence of PTSD symptoms in combat veterans seeking medical treatment. *Journal of Traumatic Stress, 3,* 15–27.

Blake, D. D., Weathers, F. W., Nagy, L. M., Kaloupek, D. G., et al. (1995). The development of a clinician-administered PTSD Scale. *Journal of Traumatic Stress, 8,* 75–90.

Blanchard, E. B., Hickling, E. J., Galovski, T., & Veazey, C. (2002). Emergency room vital signs and PTSD in a treatment seeking sample of motor vehicle accident survivors. *Journal of Traumatic Stress, 15,* 199–204.

Boudewyns, P. A., & Hyer, L. (1990). Physiological response to combat memories and preliminary treatment outcome in Vietnam veteran PTSD patients treated with direct therapeutic exposure. *Behavior Therapy, 21,* 63–87.

Bryant, R. A., Harvey, A. G., Guthrie, R. M., & Moulds, M. L. (2000). A prospective study of psychophysiological arousal, Acute Stress Disorder, and Posttraumatic Stress Disorder. *Journal of Abnormal Psychology, 109,* 341–344.

Foa, E. B., Cashman, L., Jaycox, L., & Perry, K. (1997). The validation of a self-report measure of Posttraumatic Stress Disorder: The posttraumatic diagnostic scale. *Psychological Assessment, 9,* 445–451.

Foa, E. B., & Kozak, M. J. (1986). Emotional processing of fear: Exposure to corrective information. *Psychological Bulletin, 99,* 20–35.

Goodman, L. A., Corcoran, C., Turner, K., Yuan, N., & Green, B. L. (1998). Assessing traumatic event exposure: General issues and preliminary findings for the Stressful Life Events Screening Questionnaire. *Journal of Traumatic Stress, 11,* 521–542.

Keane, T. M., Malloy, P. F., & Fairbank, J. A. (1984). Empirical development of an MMPI subscale for the assessment of combat-related Posttraumatic Stress Disorder. *Journal of Consulting and Clinical Psychology, 52,* 888–891.

Kubany, E. S., Leisen, M. B., Kaplan, A. S., Watson, S. B., Haynes, S. N., Owens, J. A., et al. (2000). Development and preliminary validation of a brief broad-spectrum measure of trauma exposure: The Traumatic Life Events Questionnaire. *Psychological Assessment, 12,* 210–224.

Luxenberg, T., & Levin, P. (2004). The role of the Rorschach in the assessment and treatment of trauma. In J. P. Wilson & T. M. Keane (Eds.), *Assessing psychological trauma and PTSD* (2nd ed., pp. 190–225). New York: Guilford.

Maloney, M. P., & Ward, M. P. (1976). *Psychological assessment: A conceptual approach.* Oxford, England: Oxford University Press.

Newman, E., Kaloupek, D. G., & Keane, T. M. (1996). Assessment of Posttraumatic Stress Disorder in clinical and research settings. In B. A. van der Kolk, A. C. McFarlane, & L. Weisaeth (Eds.), *Traumatic stress: The effects of overwhelming experience on mind, body, and society* (pp. 242–275). New York: Guilford.

Norris, F. H., & Hamblen, J. L. (2004). Standardized self-report measures of civilian trauma and PTSD. In J. P. Wilson & T. M. Keane (Eds.), *Assessing psychological trauma and PTSD* (2nd ed., pp. 63–102). New York: Guilford.

Orr, S. P., Metzger, L. J., Miller, M. W., & Kaloupek, D. G. (2004). Psychophysiological assessment of PTSD. In J. P. Wilson & T. M. Keane (Eds.), *Assessing psychological trauma and PTSD* (2nd ed., pp. 289–343). New York: Guilford.

Pitman, R. K., Orr, S. P., Altman, B., & Longpre, R. E. (1996). Emotional processing and outcome of imaginal flooding therapy in Vietnam veterans with chronic Posttraumatic Stress Disorder. *Comprehensive Psychiatry, 37,* 409–418.

Schlenger, W. E., & Kulka, R. A. (1989). *PTSD scale development for the MMPI-2.* Research Triangle Park, NC: Research Triangle Institute.

Shalev, A. Y., Orr, S. P., & Pitman, R. K. (1992). Psychophysiologic response during script-driven imagery as an outcome measure in Posttraumatic Stress Disorder. *Journal of Clinical Psychiatry, 53,* 324–326.

Steinberg, M. (2004). Systematic assessment of posttraumatic dissociation: The structured clinical interview for *DSM-IV* Dissociative Disorders. In J. P. Wilson & T. M. Keane (Eds.), *Assessing psychological trauma and PTSD* (2nd ed., pp. 122–143). New York: Guilford.

Watson, C. G., Juba, M. P., Manifold, V., Kucala, T., et al. (1991). The PTSD interview: Rationale, description, reliability, and concurrent validity of a *DSM-III*-based technique. *Journal of Clinical Psychology, 47,* 179–188.

Wilson, J. P. (2004). PTSD and complex PTSD: Symptoms, syndromes, and diagnoses. In J. P. Wilson & T. M. Keane (Eds.), *Assessing psychological trauma and PTSD* (2nd ed., pp. 7–44). New York: Guilford.

CHAPTER 11

Introduction and Overview of Treatment

In the previous chapters, the various models, theories, and research about the consequences and etiology of PTSD have been covered. This chapter serves as an introduction to the various treatments derived from such work and the treatment of PTSD in general. Before we get into the specific models of treatment, from the variety of psychotherapies to biological treatments to integrated and comprehensive treatments, it might be helpful to take a broader and foundational view of treatment of PTSD as a whole.

As trauma and its consequences come to disrupt the biological, social, psychological, and even spiritual functioning of trauma victims, society and its members are faced with a profound question, "How can I help?" This is the title of a not-so-famous but powerful book written by Ram Das and Paul Gorman (1985), *How Can I Help?* My reading of this book led me to the conclusion that in order to help, we must learn to connect to the common humanity in all of us. In other words, we must begin with a deep and profound commitment to empathy. Professionals treating trauma victims are faced with the challenging power of hearing about and confronting human suffering, sometimes from the wrath of nature or the callousness of other human beings, and make no mistake about it, this will challenge a clinician's ability to empathize. Treatment begins with a willingness to face trauma and to stay connected.

The costs of not helping victims of trauma are far reaching, on both a societal and individual scale. Entire groups and communities can develop entrenched and long-standing deficits that result in large-scale dysfunctions and ill health. For example, the American people have lived with the consequences of the Vietnam War veterans returning home with PTSD for almost 40 years. The effects of trauma, unacknowledged and untreated, can be seen in generation after generation following mass trauma as is seen in contemporary Israeli society and in El Salvador. When I was an intern at a local community college with a very large Vietnamese refugee population, I bore witness to several war survivors and their daily struggle with PTSD, 35 years later! The treatment sections of this book are an answer to Ram Das's and Gorman's call to empathy and a step toward answering the question, "How can I help?"

Just as PTSD has its biological, social, psychological, and spiritual consequences, there are equal attempts to address or treat each of these areas in its own right. A physician might address immunological compromise. A group such as the postapartheid Truth and Reconciliation Commission in South Africa might address social consequences. Psychological consequences might be addressed by psychotherapy or counseling. Spiritual consequences might be dealt with by working within one's religious tradition on such issues as trust in God or the forgiveness of perpetrators. For purposes of the *CGPTSD,* we are going to focus on the specific mental health treatments for PTSD, including psychotherapy in its various forms, psychopharmacological treatment, and more systemic or holistic treatment approaches and leave the other areas to the respective experts and professionals. In diagnostic nomenclature, I am *deferring.*

Mental health treatment for PTSD has probably been around as long as trauma itself has been around. I cannot imagine that before the advent of modern psychotherapy almost 100 years ago or the widespread popularity of psychopharmacological treatments in psychiatry that help or treatment did not exist. I am sure that as long as suffering was observed, help was available in any variety of forms.

Broadly, we are going to approach the mental health treatment of PTSD from the following perspective. *Treatment* is any specific procedure used for the cure or the amelioration of a disease or pathological condition (*Taber's Cyclopedic Medical Dictionary*). *Taber's* also defines *therapy* as any treatment of a disease or pathological condition (Thomas, 1993). In essence, treatment and therapy are synonymous in a broad sense.

More specifically, *psychological treatment* or *intervention* can be defined as any therapy that is intended to bring about change in an individual's mental processes, emotional functioning, and behavior (including social functioning, occupational functioning, etc.) for the purpose of improving overall functioning and subjective well-being. Although psychological interventions do not always target a mental disorder, when they do involve a mental disorder, their purpose is to alleviate and remove symptoms. Psychological treatment is often referred to as *psychotherapy*. L. R. Wolberg (1967) defined *psychotherapy* as:

> a form of treatment for problems of an emotional nature in which a trained person deliberately establishes a professional relationship with a patient with the object of removing, modifying, or retarding existing symptoms, of mediating

disturbed patterns of behavior, and of promoting positive personality growth and development. (p. 3)

The chapters that follow will introduce both psychological interventions in the classic sense and psychobiological interventions such as psychopharmacological interventions. With the ultimate goals of removing or at least reducing symptoms and their sequelae, each intervention can be understood in terms of the level of biopsychosocial functioning it operates on. For example, pharmacological treatment may operate at the level of neurochemical processes in the brain, but it still seeks to relieve one's subjective sense of vigilance and fear. Cognitive therapy may operate on the level of unconscious and automatic thought processes and content. The former operates at the most fundamentally reduced level and the latter at a more abstract and psychological level. Each level of therapy carries with it at least two sets of goals, the specific goals relevant to the model of treatment (thoughts, chemicals, behavior, etc.) and the broad goals of cure or reduction of PTSD.

General Treatment Goals and Principles

How can *helping* be defined with respect to PTSD? From a phenomenological perspective, PTSD can be understood to be about fear, vigilance, and arousal. Consider the following sentiment by a patient in therapy for PTSD:

> When I first started coming, I couldn't connect to anyone! I was numb all the time. I didn't care if my son cried. I couldn't feel his pain. I don't know if it was the lack of sleep that kept me feeling like I was in a dream or a daze all the time. I'd go to work, and if I needed gas, I wouldn't stop if I saw someone that looked suspicious, like they might rob me. I almost ran out of gas at least a dozen times. My wife was afraid to talk to me on most days because I kept yelling at her. I was pissed off all the time! But lately, I've realized that underneath all that anger and the numbness was a hell of a lot of fear. I don't want to die! I'm afraid I'm going to die all the time! When I'm not numb and angry, I can't stop thinking about running through that village with those two guys behind me shooting at me, catching up to me after I stumbled and shooting me in the back!

At the core of this patient's experience is the fear of death. This real-life example demonstrates the centrality of the *DSM-IV* diagnostic criteria. This patient was acutely afraid of being killed on a daily basis. At first he was not particularly conscious of it, but after some therapy sessions he began to see that underneath what he thought was a pretty good return to a normal life after returning home from war, he was afraid. He did not want to die!

Treatment for PTSD is about restoring one's sense of mastery, safety, and security in the world, from helping the brain break loose from fear conditioning to helping the mind break loose from its vigilant search for threat and to gain self-control.

The following are some principles that should guide PTSD treatment:

- *Process.* Help the client access traumatic material and be able to discuss it.
- *Integrate.* Help the client integrate their experience into a healthy and present- and future-oriented behavioral and emotional framework.
- *Deactivate.* Reduce or deactivate hyperactive stress response mechanisms.

Shalev, Friedman, Foa, and Keane (2000) provide the following suggestions for developing treatment goals in PTSD treatment, selecting a treatment, and addressing various complications that may arise:

1. Treatment should be informed by the patient's needs, abilities, and preferences.
2. Consider whether the treatment goals are attainable.
3. Define the focus. Is it stabilization, symptom reduction, or relapse prevention?
4. Does the patient first need to realize that he or she needs to address his or her PTSD and seek help?
5. Are there other adjustment-related or circumstantial issues that need to be addressed first, such as housing or medical care?

The following are seven guidelines for choosing from the various treatments available:

1. Expected efficacy against PTSD. (Does the treatment work for PTSD?)
2. Associated disorders and conditions.
3. Difficulties, side effects, and negative effects.
4. Acceptability and consent.
5. Cultural appropriateness.
6. Length, cost, and availability of resources.
7. Legal, administrative, and forensic implications.

Other complications and important issues include the following:

1. *Addressing treatment expectations and defining realistic goals.* A prospective patient's expectations should be addressed up front, and the reality of achieving them should be addressed. The focus should be on change and process rather than cure per se. Goals should be predefined, adhered to, and evaluated. If treatment fails or is not working, this can and should be addressed and subsequent alterations made. A long-term orientation should be maintained.
2. *Combining various treatment techniques.* Combined treatment is common. However, there should be a sound clinical rationale for doing so, with one form of treatment serving as the central-organizing feature. Individual psychotherapy might well serve this function. Additional treatments

should be considered, added, and terminated based on analysis of their efficacy. A clinician should not just throw everything available at a particular patient, and ineffective treatments should never continue out of pure momentum and without proper analysis.

3. *Addressing complex clinical pictures and comorbid conditions.* Ideally, practitioners should implement a treatment that can address the comorbid conditions and PTSD at the same time. If this is not possible, simultaneous treatment is recommended, particularly for Substance Abuse Disorders.

4. *Length that treatment should proceed.* There are no hard-and-fast guidelines for addressing this issue. Two helpful questions to guide this process are considering how long the beneficial outcomes can be expected to be sustained and whether therapeutic gains can be maintained with booster sessions or treatment.

5. *Features of PTSD that require special attention.* Special features of PTSD that must be addressed include respecting defenses; pacing assessment and interventions; being aware of issues of trust and security and whether the person seeks treatment for his or her trauma, particularly if the trauma is discovered in the course of addressing some other clinical issue.

6. *Issues in treatment resistance and failure.* PTSD is considered resistant to treatment generally. The reasons for such are similar to other disorders and include chronicity, comorbidity, poor compliance, and adverse life circumstances. The use of clinical wisdom is evoked in such cases.

In their edited volume *Treating Psychological Trauma and PTSD* (2001), John Wilson, Matthew J. Friedman, and Jacob Lindy provide an unbelievably comprehensive, powerful, and complex discussion of the whole of treatment for PTSD. The reader is directed to this excellent book for more detail. Much of what they and their authors have to say about treating PTSD will be covered in the sections that follow.

Wilson, Friedman, and Lindy (2001) introduce their *criteria for healing and recovery* from trauma and PTSD with multiple focal points for treatment goals. They begin with the very broad goals of (1) maximizing stabilization of symptoms and functioning, (2) a return toward optimal functioning, (3) integration of the traumatic experience, and (4) reduction of the client's sense of fragmentation and experience of ego-alien states. From these broad goals, they provide three more focused goals. However, before we go on, as was mentioned earlier, these authors' discussion and guidelines for treatment are extremely sophisticated and complex. Simplifying their approach proves very difficult. However, one helpful thing to keep in mind is to frame their work in terms of an embedded network of goals that start out very broad, with almost philosophical principles, and then branches down to very specific treatment issues for specific symptoms and clinical phenomenon.

Getting back to the three more focused goals. For Wilson et al. (2001), healing and recovery from trauma should be concerned with the following:

1. A patient's perception of trauma and its impact on their identity and personhood.

2. The allostatic (regulatory) disruption of their lives in terms of affect regulation and capacity, to reorganize and modify noneffective allostatic processes that perpetuate the syndrome. (Targets should be normalization of the stress response and attenuation of the allostatic load and processes that perpetuate maladaptive and prolonged psychobiological stress responses within the organism to alleviate anxiety, tension, and levels of distress and facilitate a reduction or elimination of maladaptive psychobiological processes that include cognitive distortion, hyperarousal processes, hypervigilance, startle responses, sleep disturbance, and affective instability, ranging on a continuum from anger to depression to diverse forms of anxiety.)

3. Restoration of a meaningful sense of self-sameness and self-continuity with warmth, dignity, wholeness, purpose, and vitality.

Wilson et al. (2001) state:

> The healed self that was once traumatized can project itself into the future with joy, serenity, and a measure of wisdom. Persons who have transformed trauma can do so because of an awareness that the boundary separating the fear of threat from quiescence is more often than not illusory and only creates allostatic load when induced by cognitive appraisals of threat to the psychological basis of existence. (p. 12)

Healing is characterized as "extraordinary changes that occur when those afflicted by trauma emerge with a human radiance, energy, and dignity that is the total antithesis of illness, despair, suffering, and fragmentation of personality" (Wilson et al., 2001).

In their holistic and organismic model, these authors summarize posttraumatic pathology into what they call the *five core dimensions of PTSD* from their pentahedral model: (1) psychobiological mechanisms, (2) traumatic memories, (3) avoidance, numbing, denial, and coping, (4) self-structure, ego states, and identity, and (5) interpersonal relations. The goals of the various treatment approaches (psychopharmacological, cognitive-behavioral therapy, analytic psychotherapy, etc.) should be understood by their relations to these five core dimensions. Table 11.1 is a heavily borrowed but simplified reproduction of Wilson et al.'s (2001, p. 411).

TABLE 11.1

Treatment Approaches for PTSD and Their Goals

Core treatment approaches	Treatment goals
Psychopharmacotherapy	Facilitate normalization toward homeostasis
Psychodynamic	Restore toward normal intrapsychic functioning
Acute interventions	Reestablish a normal stress response pattern
Cognitive-behavioral	Gain authority of traumatic experiences
Group psychotherapy	Facilitate normalization of PTSD responses and enhance capacity for healthy relationships
Complex PTSD	Restore a positive self-schema of effective coping
Dual diagnosis	Determine treatment that fosters recovery from Axis I and Axis II disorders
Cross cultural	Foster recovery from within an embedded cultural framework
Children	Foster trauma recovery to overcome interruption of normal development
Families and couples	Restore healthy attachments, relationships, and capacity for intimacy
Severe mental illness and PTSD	Facilitate social reintegration and support for activities of daily living

As if Wilson et al. (2001) have not provided enough direction, they have introduced 30 principles to guide trauma treatment, with 80 specific target goals for the five core dimensions. For purposes of space, the 30 principles will be listed, with a very brief description, but for the 80 specific goals, the reader is directed to Chapter 3 in Wilson et al.'s book (2001).

Guiding Principles

- Safety and protection—feelings of vulnerability should be kept to a minimum by providing a safe and secure facility and relationship.
- Nonjudgmental acceptance of the victim-client—unconditional positive regard should be communicated with an open-minded and flexible approach to really hearing the client.
- Trauma-specific transference and countertransference must be attended to.
- Traumatic memory recollection and integration should be approached with respect for ego-defense mechanisms and client readiness.
- Rapid intervention and the establishment of supportive resources should be implemented in order to aid the stress recovery process.
- Vulnerability, fear, and uncertainty should be addressed through nurturance support in order to facilitate healthy coping and mastery.
- Provide psychoeducational material for understanding and support.
- Recognize and be alert to changes in nonsymptom areas such as alterations in psychoinformative processes, self-schemas, and beliefs about human nature, justice, authority, and life's meaning.
- Promote the importance of effective boundary management, including striking a balance between appropriate openness and defensiveness.
- Promote basic self-maintenance and self-care through meditation, exercise, diet, and health monitoring.
- Identify and inventory specific traumatic stimuli triggers, such as particular situations, anniversaries, sounds, sights, etc.
- Recognize that anxiety, anger, and depression are interwoven in PTSD, and encourage management of each.
- Identify and address treatment for dual-diagnosis issues of alcohol and substance abuse and dependence.
- Address disturbances in sleep, nightmares, and physiological hyperarousal with specific interventions, such as relaxation training or sleep hygiene.
- Recognize the different forms of peridissociative and dissociative mechanisms, such as psychic numbing, emotional anesthesia, denial/disavowal, and splitting of object relations.
- Address the role of self-recrimination, posttraumatic shame, survivor guilt, and victim thinking in the perpetuation of symptoms and expression.

- Address traumatic effects on life-stage development.
- Work toward the requirement of transforming and integrating ego-alien, self-incongruent, and distressing components of the traumatic experience into a new cognitive framework.
- Recognize that PTSD waxes and wanes and that progress is determined by the pace and dose of treatment the client can manage at different stages and times.
- Work closely with a primary care physician to monitor the efficacy of any conjoint or co-occurring medical treatment, particularly in the case of alcohol or drug dependency.
- Carefully screen potential group therapy clients for personality, psychopathological expressions of symptoms, type of trauma exposure, and fitness for a particular group.
- Prioritize issues when traumatic grief, bereavement, and loss issues are involved.
- Address comorbid Axis I and Axis II issues, and design treatments accordingly.
- Recognize that there are at least seven distinct allostatic processes that reflect psychobiological alterations associated with hyperarousal mechanisms and their relation to symptoms.
- Implement appropriate acute stress interventions in order to quickly reestablish the normal stress response and environmental and intrapersonal supports.
- Acknowledge and address issues of childhood and adolescent victimization.
- Recognize reenactment behaviors in children as they manifest in play, fantasies, dreams, and symbolic forms of acting out.
- Recognize that the process of healing and overcoming pain caused by trauma may result in personal struggles with the meaning of life, justice, the existence of God, and the search for a purpose in living and a state of higher or heightened spirituality and capacity for self-actualization may emerge.
- Prosocial behavior, altruism, and caring for others should be promoted as appropriate and safe in order to facilitate recovery.
- Always work within a framework of holistic dynamic functioning.

As the final chapter in their book and perhaps as a final word, Wilson et al. (2001) make a call to all mental health professionals working with trauma survivors to "Do No Harm" and to "Respect the Trauma Membrane" (p. 432). The trauma membrane is conceptualized as the individual and social response to posttraumatic dysfunction that forms a membrane or protective skin of sorts around the victim-survivor. They warn us against overzealous and aggressive treatment and to be guided by the patients, taking their lead rather than the other way around. Treatment begins when "they invite us to enter the space covered by the trauma membrane" (p. 436). Once invited in, we can be assured that we will be tested for trustworthiness and knowledge and to witness ego defenses' protection of "their perceived and experienced sense of vulnerability" (p. 436). We are warned not to induce more trauma (sometimes referred to as *secondary traumatization*) and give the clients more than they can handle at the moment, which may result in damaging the working alliance and stress newly formed ego defenses and coping mechanisms that have been formed to replace the trauma membrane.

Perhaps I am beating the proverbial dead horse here, but I believe that it bears mentioning one last time. Posttraumatic Stress disorder treatment is about joining survivors and victims in their fear-laden chaos and arousal, acknowledging their experience, walking them through it, calming them down, seeing them through to a sense of safety, and witnessing their revitalization.

Issues in Treatment Planning

Treatment planning for any mental disorder or psychological issue or problem is an extremely important component to the healing process. In my own experience, this is perhaps the one professional skill or practice that separates the beginners from the novices and the novices from the experts. Having a well-thought-out plan is an invaluable tool. This is perhaps even more important when dealing with the all too typical complexity and chaos of PTSD.

Before we get into some of the specific treatment planning issues for PTSD, let's take a quick look at treatment planning from a more general perspective.

Before treatment begins and a clinician begins to penetrate the trauma membrane, he or she should consider in detail the current life circumstances and supports in which a potential patient or client finds him- or herself. At the most basic of levels, consider where you are in a physical sense. Can PTSD treatment be undertaken where you and the client find yourselves? For instance, if your job is to provide short-term–coping-based stabilization treatment to jail inmates, can you really engage in the complexity of PTSD treatment in that setting? Is there enough time? Is there enough outside or third-party support available? I am not suggesting that if the answer to these questions is *no* that

Professional Alert

This material is intended primarily for students and lay people, but a little brush up never hurt anyone!

you do not address PTSD at all, but, rather, that the answers to these questions be important factors in considering what to treat, how to treat, when to treat, and whether to treat at all.

Also consider whether the person coming to you wants treatment for PTSD or trauma. This may sound like a strange point, but if someone comes to you for test-taking anxiety and you start digging into their past for trauma and how it is currently affecting them, you may be guilty of psychological voyeurism. What are the patient's expectations? Does he or she expect you to heal or cure him or her? Are you simply going to ameliorate the patient's symptoms? Addressing these issues from the very beginning will facilitate communication and empathy and serve as a good foundation to work from when the inevitable ruptures in the working alliance between patient and clinician develop. Be cautious of going where you are not invited. Also, a patient's personality, current level of functioning, and both internal and external supports and coping resources should be important features of your treatment plan. Is the prospective patient motivated to enter into treatment, to face their trauma, or to make the necessary alterations in his or her life that might be required? Practical issues, such as language compatibility; communication barriers, such as hearing impairment or blindness; and, certainly, cognitive and intellectual deficits should be considered. Remember that issues such as the length of treatment; termination issues, including follow up if necessary; frequency of contacts; general format; patient and clinician's responsibilities; and, of course, cost should be discussed. Finally, it is always helpful to talk about the potential risks of going into treatment, such as discomfort, rage, and disruptions in relationships. Ultimately, the things I am mentioning are part of the informed consent process that empowers the patient to enter treatment with knowledge and willful participation.

> **Student Alert**
>
> If nobody in school has told you that you do not have to treat everyone that comes to you, then you can hear it from me first—you don't!

In any type of treatment or treatment setting, the most pressing issues should always be addressed first, with life-threatening issues being at the top of the list, such as suicidal or homicidal threat or grave disability. Restoration of basic functioning must begin before more complex treatment can proceed.

The initial contact with a patient should address such issues as the patient's expectations of treatment. Does he or she believe you are going to remove his or her problems, for instance? It is always helpful to explain what treatment is about and what it involves. Some helpful points to discuss with patients are as follows:

1. Treatment involves focusing on mental processes in which he or she will engage in discussions about thoughts, feelings or emotions, relationships, and behaviors.

2. Self-disclosure and openness are required and expected, albeit at his or her pace.

3. Emotional expression and release are often involved.

4. Oftentimes (but not always) there is an exploration of one's childhood.

5. Insight is encouraged.

6. Interpretation of current problems in light of past issues and development may occur.

7. A working relationship with the clinician or therapist is expected to form.

8. There are boundaries that exist within and define the limits to this working relationship. It is a professional relationship.

9. A range of treatment options are available and may be utilized, and he or she might be expected to take medication as a necessary component of treatment and be willing to take difficult steps during a crisis, such as being admitted to a hospital in the instances of suicidal ideation, homicidal ideation, or grave disability.

10. The patient has the right to terminate therapy at any time, except in circumstances of court-ordered treatment or within other legal constraints.

Now let's turn to some PTSD-specific treatment planning issues. As a clinician or a treatment team is formulating a treatment plan, they should consider the following issues: duration and repetition of the particular trauma, type of pathology, chronicity, concomitant diagnoses and comorbid conditions, and attempt to match the treatment approach with the PTSD core phenomenology (Wilson et al. 2001).

Wilson et al. (2001) suggest that a patient's treatment be approached through one of the core symptom cluster or clusters that presents as primary and most pressing. If a patient is most concerned with and is having significant relationship issues, then this might be the initial focus. If a patient presents with hyperarousal and physiological reactivity, psychopharmacological intervention may be the initial inroad. These authors also suggest that the source of referral is a critical issue in treatment planning, citing that referrals by family members may point toward the necessity to involve the family in treatment at a very central level, for example.

Where Can One Get Treatment?

Treatment for PTSD can be found broadly within the mental health service system that exists within one's community. Taking the limitations and restrictions on services that exist within any one setting, various degrees of treatment and types of treatment can be found in many different settings. The following is a list of places where one can seek treatment for PTSD:

Veteran's Administration hospitals (for veterans, of course)

Community mental health clinics

County mental health service centers

College and university counseling centers and psychological service clinics

Private practice mental health clinics and offices of psychologists, psychiatrists, or clinical social workers

Departments of psychiatry at medical centers

The American Red Cross (for emergency services, psychological first aid, and crisis services)

Behavioral health or psychiatric hospitals with either outpatient or inpatient programs

Who Performs the Treatment

Increasingly, PTSD is treated by a multitude of health and mental health disciplines, oftentimes within a treatment team and in a collaborative manner. The following is a list of professionals that one can seek help from:

Psychiatrists are medical doctors specially trained in the diagnosis and treatment of mental disorders, including the use and prescription of medication and psychopharmacological agents as well as other somatic therapies such as electroconvulsive therapy. Some psychiatrists are trained to conduct psychotherapy, but not all.

Clinical psychologists are doctors of psychology specifically trained in the diagnosis and treatment and rehabilitation of mental disorders, abnormal mental processes, abnormal behavior, and related biopsychosocial disorders and dysfunction. They have unique specialty training in psychological assessment and testing, and they are trained as psychotherapists in all aspects.

Clinical or psychiatric social workers are masters-level practitioners with specific training in working with the social and interpersonal consequences of mental disorders and abnormal behavior. They, too, are trained as psychotherapists and often have specialty training in social services provision and family, couples, and group therapy.

Collateral and adjunctive support and treatment for related dysfunctions and issues can be performed by marriage and family therapists, physicians such as internists or pediatricians, neuropsychologists, drug and alcohol counselors, counselors, clergy, and peer counselors.

Finally, if you are one listed in the preceding, you have to ask yourself whether you have the appropriate training, experience, or expertise to work with PTSD. (For resources on training, see Appendix A.) Consumers of mental health services, too, have the right to ask the person they are seeking help from about his or her experience, level of training, and level of expertise in working with PTSD.

A List of Therapies

Below is a list of therapies, some common and some uncommon, used in the treatment of PTSD. It is not exhaustive; James Prochaska and John Norcross (1994) have identified that there are several hundred forms of psychotherapy. However, it should serve as a good starting point.

Biofeedback

Cognitive-behavioral therapy (CBT)

Constructivist-narrative therapy

Creative therapies

Crisis intervention

Exposure therapy

Eye movement desensitization and reprocessing (EMDR)

Family therapy

Feminist therapy

Group therapy

Hypnosis

Inpatient treatment

Marital and couples therapy

Pharmacotherapy

Psychodynamic therapy

Psychoeducation

Psychological debriefing or critical incident stress debriefing (CISD)

Psychological first aid

Psychosocial rehabilitation

Relaxation training

Stress-inoculation training

Systematic desensitization

Commonalities among Therapies

Wilson et al. (2001) identify the following characteristics that PTSD and trauma therapies and treatments have in common. On a broad scale, they all focus on reducing symptoms, improving functioning, improving relationships, promoting positive appraisal for the self and the world, listening, empathy, structure, well-timed and dosed intervention, caring and respect, ethical guidance, and the encouragement of self-empowerment and mastery.

Specifically for PTSD, these same authors state that all the various therapies have at least two other things in common, their engagement in or operation along three metaphases of treatment and the extent to which they vary along a continuum of suppression or expression of the trauma. Here are the metaphases:

Phase 1: establishing safety, building the alliance, establishing trust, and relaxation training

Phase 2: disclosure, trauma narrative, trauma script, and imaginal exposures

Phase 3: reconnection, self-continuity and meaning, integration, and synthesis

Regarding the suppression or expression of trauma, Wilson et al. (2001) propose that some treatments are suppressive toward trauma and its sequelae, seeking to reduce or diminish symptom expression (e.g., medication), while others are more expressive (e.g., group therapy). Maintaining a balance between these two poles is a delicate act and is seen as critical to therapeutic change and movement.

Finally, Wilson et al. (2001) summarize quite nicely the mechanisms or modes of therapeutic action operative within some (but not all) of the major treatment approaches. These aspects make these treatments work.

Cognitive-behavioral therapies focus on intrusive phenomena with the goal to extinguish reactivity through reframing and desensitization, overcoming avoidance, and achieving physiological mastery.

Group therapy addresses alienation through peer acceptance, empathy, support, and adaptive suggestions. There is also an educational component and feedback about the interpersonal consequences of trauma and subsequent behavior. There is a focus on normalizing, and true empathy is facilitated because other group members have truly been there.

Constructivist self-development theories focus on boundaries as central to traumatic experience and the creation of new interpersonal and self-narratives.

Psychodynamic and analytic therapies focus on the internalization of the therapist's voice as transference, countertransference, and reenactments unfold and are played out, building toward mastery and a sense of healing. Interpretation, reflection, and empathy are critical tools that allow corrective experiences to develop.

Family and couples therapies are useful modes for discussing disruptions in intimacy and make use of existing alliances, empathy, and trust to facilitate processing and bypassing of defenses.

Psychopharmacological therapies focus on deactivation of physiological mechanisms involved in arousal and reactivity along with the development of mastery and the freeing up of resources in order to devote more energy to other problem areas and symptoms.

Summary

As one can see from the material in this chapter, the issues underlying treatment of PTSD in general are complex but also extremely important. At the heart of treatment for PTSD are the principles of empowerment, safety, and vitality. Posttraumatic Stress Disorder is a powerful disorder that can rock the very foundation that someone's reality and personality are built upon. Treatment should only proceed after a profound respect for the power of the trauma experience is established and only after thinking through the important issues mentioned in this chapter.

Quick Review

- Trauma treatment begins with a willingness to face squarely the profound human suffering and fear of trauma victims and survivors and to respond with empathy and courage.

- Treatment of PTSD is multidisciplinary and multimodal, addressing the various components of PTSD from a true biopsychosocial and even spiritual model.

- The following are three important treatment principles: (1) Process—help the client access traumatic material and be able to discuss it. (2) Integrate—help the client integrate his or her experience into a healthy and present- and future-oriented behavioral and emotional framework. (3) Deactivate—reduce or deactivate hyperactive stress response mechanisms.

- Wilson et al. (2001) introduce their *criteria for healing and recovery* as (1) maximizing stabilization of symptoms and functioning, (2) a return toward optimal functioning, (3) integration of the traumatic experience, and (4) reduction of the client's sense of fragmentation and experience of ego-alien states.

- Wilson et al. (2001) believe healing and recovery from trauma should be concerned with a patient's perception of trauma and its impact on his or her identity and personhood; the allostatic (regulatory) disruption of his or her lives in terms of affect regulation and capacity to reorganize and modify noneffective allostatic processes that perpetuate the syndrome; and restoration of a meaningful sense of self-sameness and self-continuity with warmth, dignity, wholeness, purpose, and vitality.

- Wilson et al. (2001) have introduced 30 principles to guide trauma treatment, with 80 specific target goals for the five core dimensions. The reader is directed to Chapter 3 in Wilson et al.'s book.

- Wilson et al. (2001) ask that we respect the *trauma membrane,* a protective skin of individual and social responses to posttraumatic dysfunction.

- Both general and PTSD-specific treatment planning issues are critical components to treatment.

- Treatment can be found within a community's mental health services community of professionals, including psychiatrists, psychologists, and clinical social workers.

- Posttraumatic Stress Disorder treatments have at least two things in common: their engagement in or operation along three metaphases of treatment and the extent to which they vary along a continuum of suppression or expression of the trauma.

References

Das, R., & Gorman, P. (1985). *How can I help?* New York: Alfred A. Knopf.

Prochaska, J. O., & Norcross, J. C. (1994). *Systems of psychotherapy: A transtheoretical analysis* (3rd ed.). Belmont, CA: Brooks/Cole.

Shalev, A., Friedman, M. J., Foa, E. B., & Keane, T. M. (2000). Integration and summary. In E. B. Foa, T. M. Keane, & M. J. Friedman (Eds.), *Effective treatments for PTSD: Practice guidelines from the International Society for Traumatic Stress Studies.* New York: Guilford.

Thomas, C. L. (1993). *Taber's cyclopedic medical dictionary.* Philadelphia: F. A. Davis.

Wilson, J. P., Friedman, M. J., & Lindy, J. D. (Eds). (2001). *Treating psychological trauma and PTSD.* New York: Guilford.

Wolberg, L. R. (1967). *The technique of psychotherapy* (2nd ed.). New York: Grune and Stratton.

CHAPTER 12

Cognitive and Behavioral Treatments

The histories of psychology and mental health treatment specifically have seen periods in which certain phenomena are treated as central to an understanding of human mental life and behavior, while others are neglected, ignored, or written off as unimportant. Psychoanalysis once dominated until the behaviorists came along and warned us to stay out of the *black box* of the mind. Biological models have come to prominence within the last 10 to 15 years or so. The mid-twentieth century ushered in an era in which the mind reemerged. This approach to mental life was a break from psychoanalysis and owed a great deal to developments in the field of cognitive science. This era is sometimes referred to as the *cognitive revolution*. The mind once again mattered, and there were fresh ways to approach it without reference to legions of Freud. The cognitive approach took root in both experimental psychology and eventually in the treatment of mental disorders and psychotherapy. With respect to psychotherapy, cognitive approaches were often combined with more behavioral approaches, yielding what is often referred to as *cognitive-behavioral therapy* (CBT). There are behavioral, cognitive, and cognitive-behavioral therapies for depression, Anxiety Disorders, phobias, and even psychosis. There are also a number of cognitive-behavioral approaches to the treatment of PTSD. Research and practice have shown that such treatments are effective. The National Center for Post-Traumatic Stress Disorder cites CBT for PTSD as a successful intervention in one of their public-information guides.

Before we go on, however, let's define some terms:

Behavior therapy. At its most basic level, behavior therapy consists of the application of learning theory, classical conditioning, operant conditioning, and social learning theory to the treatment of clinical disorders and abnormal behavior. Disorders are viewed as acquired or learned in the same way as nondisordered or normal behavior and, therefore, can be unacquired or unlearned in turn. The historical or developmental roots of disordered behavior are important only as histories of chains of operant behavior or associations. It does not matter, per se, why a disordered behavior exists or what caused it but, rather, what is maintaining it through positive reinforcement, negative reinforcement, or other learning principles.

Cognitive therapy. Aaron Beck and Marjorie E. Weishaar (1989) provide an excellent definition of *cognitive therapy:*

Cognitive therapy is based on a theory of personality which maintains that how one thinks largely determines how one feels and behaves. The therapy is a collaborative process of empirical investigation, reality testing, and problem solving between therapist and patient. The patient's maladaptive interpretations and conclusions are treated as testable hypotheses. Behavioral experiments and verbal procedures are used to examine alternative interpretations and to generate contradictory evidence that supports more adaptive beliefs and leads to therapeutic change. (Beck & Weishaar, 1989, p. 229)

Cognitive-behavioral therapy. For our purposes, CBT can be understood as any treatment that utilizes any combination of either behavior therapy or cognitive therapy. Most therapies from this perspective appear to be more CBT than either pure behavioral or cognitive.

Some pioneers and heavy hitters of behavior therapy include Joseph Wolpe, S. Rachman, E. Jacobson, Alan Kazdin, Ivar Lovaas, and Albert Bandura. From the cognitive therapy perspective, Albert Ellis, Aaron Beck, and Eric Byrne are important figures. Finally, big names in CBT include, again, Aaron Beck, but also Marsha Linehan, Christine Padesky, J. E. Young, and Arnold Lazarus. Two others require mentioning despite their eventual expansion and moving beyond CBT; they are Donald Meichenbaum and Mardi Horowitz.

Basic Principles of Behavior and Cognitive-Behavioral Therapy

Basic Behavioral Principles

Behavior therapy involves the application of the principles of learning and behavior. Classical conditioning is used to explain the acquisition of abnormal behaviors through contingency learning; in PTSD, this might account for the pairing of certain sounds (loud bangs or breaking glass) with arousal and escape or avoidance behavior. Operant conditioning, with its principles of positive reinforcement, negative reinforcement, and punishment accounts for behavior through an analysis of the conditions or consequences that follow it. In PTSD, negative reinforcement might account for maintaining the core symptoms of avoidance, for example. Extinction occurs when a behavior ceases to be reinforced and may be helpful in eliminating particular behaviors by the withholding or preventing of reinforcement. The principles of discrimination, stimulus control, and generalization are important in understanding how particular stimuli elicit particular responses and how these same responses may be generalized across a wider range of stimulus situations or how a particular behavior might be brought adaptively under more appropriate stimulus control. In PTSD, the principle of generalization is illustrated in the phenomenon of reacting to a loud sound as if it is a gunshot or explosion for example. July 4th celebrations can be particularly stressful for combat veterans because of this very principle.

Behavior Therapy Techniques

Behavior therapy emphasizes the unlearning of maladaptive or problem behavior and the acquisition of more adaptive and healthy behavior. Therapists attempt this with a number of techniques, including behavior modification, guided imagery, role-playing, self-monitoring, relaxation training, progressive relaxation, behavioral rehearsal, activity scheduling, and exposure techniques. There are a variety of exposure techniques, including imagery-based (e.g., guided imagery and systematic desensitization) versus direct-exposure techniques (e.g., graduated exposure and flooding). Behavior therapy works in many ways but often by removing reinforcement of a negative behavior; reinforcing the practice, occurrence, and utilization of healthy behavior; pairing learning conditions and situations for adaptation or adjustment; or increasing stimulus control and discrimination while reducing negative generalization and increasing positive generalization. Again, at the core of all behavior therapies is learning and unlearning.

Basic Cognitive Principles

Cognitive therapy is built on an information-processing model of psychology, viewing pathology as a consequence of systematic biases in the processing of information. (See Chapter 5 for more detail on cognitive models of PTSD.) In essence, the mediating role of thinking between stimulus and behavior is the critical point of change and alteration in cognitive therapy. Errors in thinking and the processing of information, be it environmental or more internal in nature, are the targets of therapy. Many different concepts and terms are used to characterize and describe thinking and dysfunctional cognitions in cognitive therapy, such as schemas, automatic thoughts, conditional assumptions, maladaptive cognitions, and cognitive distortions. Different classes of mental disorders are characterized by a specific type of cognitive errors. For example, depression is characterized by a negative view of self, the world, others, current experience, and the future. Panic Disorder is characterized by a catastrophic interpretation of body and mental experiences. Anxiety Disorders are characterized by thinking that maintains a sense of danger.

Cognitive distortions are systematic errors in thinking and are a central feature of cognitive therapy. Here are some examples of cognitive distortions (Beck & Weishaar, 1989):

Arbitrary inference: drawing a specific conclusion without evidence in the face of contradictory evidence

Selective abstraction: taking details out of context or ignoring pertinent information

Overgeneralization: abstracting a general rule from a few incidents

Magnification and minimization: imbuing more or less significance to a situation or event

Personalization: attributing events to oneself without evidence

Dichotomous thinking: categorizing events in either black and white terms

Basic Cognitive Techniques

Cognitive therapy is about examining thinking and changing the way one thinks and arrives at conclusions. This is embodied in the process of collaborative empiricism, in which therapist and patient engage in the empirical or experiential testing of the evidence that allegedly supports a patient's cognitive distortions. Socratic dialogue, a specific form of questioning that is designed to promote new learning (Beck & Young, 1985), is used. This is like asking a question to which you already know the answer. Other cognitive therapy techniques include guided discovery, reattribution, redefining, decentering, cognitive restructuring, reframing, hypothesis testing, and homework.

Cognitive-Behavioral Therapies for PTSD

The treatments covered in this section fall into one of the three (behavior, cognitive, or CBT) categories listed in the preceding section to one degree or another. However, most therapies are combined. In order to simplify things a bit, we will discuss the various treatments or therapies separately as behavior, cognitive, or CBT where appropriate and helpful. That is, if a therapy is primary behavioral, it will be discussed as a behavioral treatment, and so on.

Table 12.1 might help with classifying the various treatments.

Student Alert

In order to learn the actual nuts and bolts and step-by-step procedures for each therapy, please see the various treatment manuals that exist for each, the scope of which goes well beyond the space we have here.

TABLE 12.1

Components of Cognitive and Behavioral Therapies

Behavior Therapies	Cognitive Therapies	Cognitive-Behavioral Therapies
Direct exposure therapy	Cognitive therapy	Stress-inoculation training
Systematic desensitization	Thought stopping	Cognitive processing therapy
Breath control	Cognitive restructuring	Imagery-based exposure
Biofeedback	Guided self-dialogue	Assertiveness training
Relaxation training		Dialectical behavioral therapy
		Covert modeling
		Role play

Behavior Therapies

Conceptually, from a behavior therapy perspective, PTSD is viewed as a specific form of conditioned emotional (fear) reaction. The natural emotional reaction is paired with particular stimuli and other related stimuli, which ultimately serve to maintain the conditioned behavior and responses over time. Successful behavior therapies for PTSD work to break the conditioning between the traumatic event and the conditioned emotional responses through subsequent learning episodes or trials. They also seek to increase behaviors that are incompatible with the high levels of arousal in PTSD, such as teaching breath control.

Exposure Therapies

Exposure therapy involves a patient being exposed to trauma-inducing stimuli on purpose and for a significant period of time. It works on the principle of extinction. A patient is encouraged to essentially relive the traumatic experience and to reexperience the full arousal and related images associated with the trauma. As arousal and fear are maintained, they eventually remit as the patient learns that the original trauma is not going to happen and is not actually occurring despite the high arousal. It is as if the therapist is saying, "See, you are scared, but you are not going to die and therefore there is nothing to be afraid of!"

Zoellner, Fitzgibbons, and Foa (2001) address the therapeutic mechanism in exposure therapy. They cite that it has long been believed that emotional engagement with traumatic memories is a core feature of recovery. In turn, it is thought that avoidance of such engagement only serves to maintain symptoms. A critical component of exposure therapy is not engaging in escape and avoidance behavior or mechanisms. This is sometimes referred to as *escape prevention*. It plays a critical role in diminishing escape and avoidance behavior as escape and avoidance behaviors are thought to be negatively reinforcing in Anxiety Disorders and work to maintain symptoms. Zoellner et al. (2001) state that ultimately, "The beliefs that particular situations are unsafe and that escape is necessary for anxiety reduction are disconfirmed" (p. 170). Empirical support exists for exposure therapies (Rothbaum, Meadows, Resick, & Foy, 2000a, b).

Direct exposure is one of the therapies that is sometime more cognitive than behavioral in that the act of reexperiencing often involves imagining the traumatic event. However, a patient is often directly exposed to fear-inducing stimuli and triggers in the extinction process. Imaginal exposure will be discussed in the CBT section that follows.

Case Illustration: In Vivo Exposure

A patient's daughter was born premature and suffered severe complications during the birth process. The child nearly died but was saved by aggressive intervention by hospital staff. She was eventually discharged and scheduled for a follow-up appointment in a couple of weeks. The patient was unable to take the child to the appointment, and after several reschedules the treating pediatrician consulted with a psychologist. The mother agreed to see the psychologist and, after several sessions, was finally able to take her daughter to the hospital for her follow-up visits. Here is an excerpt from the treatment:

> *Therapist:* Your homework assignment is to put your daughter in the car and drive toward the hospital. Don't go all the way there; just go a few miles down the freeway toward the hospital, and then go home.
> *Client:* Don't worry; I won't go all the way. I can't go without my husband.
> *Therapist:* That's fine.
> *Client:* I think I can do that. But what if I start having a panic attack?
> *Therapist:* Just start using the breathing techniques we practiced, and pull off the road until you calm down. Then you can either proceed or head home for another trial the next day. I want you to do this three times before I see you again.

Systematic Desensitization

Joseph Wolpe developed systematic desensitization as a means to desensitize an individual to stimuli that is initially very arousing. It is a practice- or learning-based technique in which a desirable behavior that is incompatible with the undesired behavior is first established (Blake & Sonnenberg, 1998). Then, while engaged in the incompatible and positive behavior, typically a state of calm or relaxation, the patient is exposed to arousing or fear-inducing stimuli while attempting to remain calm and relaxed. Eventually, arousal in reaction to previously arousing stimuli will subside and be replaced by a relaxed state. A patient can then encounter arousing stimuli without the arousal reaction. Systematic desensitization is sometimes done with imagery exposure, making it more cognitive, but it is often used with real life stimuli, thus putting it in the behavioral camp. An anxiety hierarchy is developed in which a patient establishes how specific stimuli rank in terms of how much arousal they induce. Relaxation training is then undergone. Exposure then begins, moving through the hierarchy until all the stimuli on the list can be tolerated to the patient's satisfaction. Rothbaum et al. (2000a, b) cite that systematic desensitization has some research support of its effectiveness but is generally considered unsupported. They state that it has generally been replaced by exposure and relaxation techniques.

Breath Control and Retraining, Biofeedback, and Relaxation Training

Diaphragmatic breathing is sometimes taught as a means for patients to calm themselves down and maintain relaxation during exposure and desensitization procedures. Therapists train patients and encourage them to use this out of session as a means to manage their anxiety. Homework as practice is assigned, to be practiced several times a day. Biofeedback and relaxation training can also be utilized to help patients develop stress- and arousal-control skills in the face of trauma stimuli and everyday stressors as well. The focus of these techniques is the control of physiological arousal. Deep muscle relaxation, a technique used to relax all the major muscle groups, is also employed. As PTSD-specific treatments, Rothbaum et al. (2000a, b) indicate that these techniques have not been found to be effective in and of themselves. These treatments can be used as adjuncts, however.

Cognitive Therapies

From the cognitive perspective, PTSD treatment is approached from an information processing perspective. Emotional reactions and mood states are produced by how a stimulus, situation, or event is interpreted and not by the stimulus in and of itself. Such interpretations can be fraught with bias and distortion and are sometimes referred to as *automatic thoughts* or *maladaptive cognitions*. A patient is taught to overcome the influence of these systematic biases and distortions in the processing of information and thinking through exploration, examination, putting them to the empirical test and challenging them, and appropriately altering and changing them in order to produce more logical, more accurate and helpful ways of thinking. Other techniques, such as thought stopping, cognitive restructuring, and guided self-dialogue, are also used to bring automatic thoughts to a patient's attention and either stop them or alter them.

Traditional cognitive therapy was developed for treating depression, but adaptations for Anxiety Disorders and PTSD have been developed (Clark, 1986; Frank et al., 1988; Marks, Lovell, Noshirvani, Livanou, & Thrasher, 1998). Rothbaum et al. (2000a, b) report that cognitive therapy for PTSD has been shown to be effective for reducing posttraumatic symptoms in two well-controlled studies.

Cognitive therapies are combined with exposure therapy. Its unique contribution is to focus on the identification and modification of "target core dysfunctional cognitions" (Moore, Zoellner, & Bittinger, 2004, p. 132). These dysfunctional cognitions and cognitive processes include disruptions in Janoff-Bulman's (1992) "fundamental assumptions about a safe and meaningful world" (Moore, Zoellner, & Bittinger, 2004, p. 130). Disruptions in Epstein's four beliefs that the self is worthy, people are trustworthy, the world is benign, and the world is meaningful; and Foa and Rothbaum's (1998) dysfunctional cognitions that the world is a dangerous place, and the self is incompetent. Cognitive therapy through restructuring might also focus on the process identified by Ehlers and Clark (2000) in which an individual maintains the perception of current environmental threat by misinterpreting the physiological symptoms of PTSD, such as arousal and numbing, and taking them as threat signals. That is, a person might be keyed up or on edge because of the ongoing state of arousal of PTSD, yet they may interpret this as proof that there is, in fact, danger present. This is akin to the cognitive account of panic attacks and Panic Disorder.

Moore et al. (2004, p. 144) also propose that cognitive therapies should focus on dysfunctional information processing in PTSD, stating that PTSD is necessarily associated with "deficits in the automatic and strategic processing of information." These errors include the quick and unconscious processing of information seen with intrusive thoughts. They emphasize the therapeutic importance of helping patients develop an understanding of these automatic processes and helping them frame and contextualize the symptoms, rather than misinterpreting them.

Cognitive-Behavioral Therapies

Cognitive-behavioral therapies combine both behavioral and cognitive orientations, theoretical rationales, and techniques to produce some of the most effective treatments for PTSD.

Stress-Inoculation Training

Donald Meichenbaum developed stress-inoculation therapy (SIT) for the management of anxiety. Stress-inoculation therapy consists of helping patients identify stressors or stressful stimuli, learning adaptive coping while confronting it, and practicing the coping techniques while being faced with the stimuli. Coping techniques used while in the face of a stressor may include self-talk, deep breathing, or thought stopping. The goal is to reduce avoidance and reduce excessive arousal. In 1982, Kilpatrick, Veronen, and Resick modified SIT for treatment of rape trauma. Rothbaum et al. (2000a, b) cite that SIT has been found effective by at least two well-designed studies, but only for sexual assault victims. Kilpatrick et al.'s (1982) program and subsequent programs consist of education; the acquisition of coping skills; and the application of coping skills, including deep muscle relaxation, breathing control, communication skills and assertiveness training, covert modeling (imagery based modeling), thought stopping, and guided-self dialogue consisting of identifying one's internal dialogue and generating and substituting positive ones.

Cognitive Processing Therapy

Cognitive processing therapy was specifically designed for rape survivors. It is a combined approach using both cognitive therapy and exposure methods. Cognitive processing therapy combines cognitive therapy elements and exposure components. The cognitive aspects focus on self-blame and attempt to "mentally undo the event" and "overgeneralized beliefs emanating from the rape" (Rothbaum et al., 2000a, p. 65). The exposure component consists of writing an account of the rape and reading it to the therapist.

Cognitive-Behavioral Therapy–Exposure Treatments

Exposure therapies from a combined behavioral and cognitive perspective are considered one of the two most effective treatments for PTSD, next to pharmacological treatment with selective serotonin reuptake inhibitor (SSRI) medication. I use the word *therapies* in the plural deliberately because there is no single type or form of CBT–exposure-based therapy. Exposure therapies typically include an imaginal exposure component such as writing about or reading about the trauma (Taylor, 2004) and an in vivo or real-life exposure component to trauma reminders or classically conditioned trauma cues.

Imaginal or imagery-based exposure consists of various techniques in which exposure is achieved by imagination, within a role-play scenario, or some other form of non-real-life setting. Other techniques include telling the story of the trauma in a narrative format with the therapist, the therapist presenting a scene to the patient, or trying to imagine the event in all its detail in a manner akin to experiential therapy techniques.

Case Illustration: Imaginal Exposure

Therapist: I want you to tell me what happened, starting at the beginning.

Client: I can't, not without getting upset. But I'll try. I was in the park with my family, just barbecuing, having fun. It was sunny. I remember running and falling down, watching the guy with the gun approaching me.

Therapist: What are your tension and fear level ratings right now? Last time you told me the story, they were nine, and today they are a seven. That's improvement! Please continue.

Client: He just walked up and shot me in the face and chest. All I remember after that is waking in the middle of surgery, looking down and seeing my chest opened up and then feeling the most intense pain I have ever felt in my life. I knew I was going to die.

Therapist: What are your ratings now?

Client: They are a one hundred on a scale of ten, Doc!

Therapist: Okay. Let's stop for a minute.

Assertiveness Training

Assertiveness training is a skill-building intervention sometimes used in conjunction with other therapies. It is intended to be a coping skill that helps reduce arousal in tense or otherwise arousing situations that a PTSD sufferer may have otherwise avoided or overreacted to. It may also be viewed as a solid adjunct for helping a patient develop a stronger sense of self-efficacy and self-control. However, it is not considered a therapy or treatment in and of itself and is not considered a vital component of treatment overall (Rothbaum et al., 2000a, b).

Dialectical Behavioral Therapy

Marsha Linehan first developed dialectical behavior therapy (DBT) for Borderline Personality Disorder. Since then it has been developed for use with other disorders. However, its use with Borderline Personality Disorder may have, in fact, lent itself directly to a PTSD application, as some professionals believe that Borderline Personality Disorder is a form of complex PTSD in and of itself. Melia and Wagner (2000) state that DBT is a form of cognitive-behavioral therapy but different in two additional underlying, guiding theories: (1) the biosocial theory of emotional dysregulation and (2) the theory of dialectics and its inclusion of Eastern philosophy and mindfulness practices. Dialectical behavioral therapy is suggested as one possible approach to those patients who have difficulty engaging in the more common therapies and whose lives are characterized by instability, chronic crises, and living difficulties. Dialectical behavioral therapy may be particularly well suited for these particular clients because of its emphasis on and varied methods for dealing with early engagement and treatment compliance. Posttraumatic Stress Disorder is characterized as a form of emotional dysregulation and as such can benefit from the DBT methods for addressing such dysregulated emotion. Dialectical behavioral therapy is unique in its high degree of structure and systematic approach to symptoms and behavior problems, including suicidal behavior and self-harm, and in its use and integration of Eastern philosophy and its use of dialectics. An underlying worldview in which reality is seen as a dynamic of opposing forces that are constantly changing is used to bring dichotomous thinking and behavior into a more flexible, fluid, and less black-and-white perspective. This helps clients work through rigid behaviors and beliefs and reduces overreactions. The dialectic technique is employed as a form of persuasion that works hand in hand with this philosophy in which change occurs through the simultaneous consideration of opposing viewpoints (Melia & Wagner, 2000). However, DBT has yet to be empirically evaluated or validated as a specific treatment for PTSD.

Before we wrap up, it is important to mention that, despite the powerful and numerous treatments discussed in this chapter, many people continue to suffer from PTSD after having been treated with such methods. Personally, I can attest to this fact as I have evaluated numerous PTSD sufferers for disability who are still symptomatic and still having functional difficulties, despite having been through treatment. Steven Taylor (2004) suggests that for individuals in which exposure therapy, cognitive therapy, or a combination of both does not work, perhaps other related issues of significance need to be addressed. These include trauma-related anger, utilizing virtual reality exposure intervention, improving social support, or utilizing interoceptive exposure, a method of deliberately, inducing PTSD-symptoms. He cautions, however, that research still needs to be done before final, concrete suggestions are made, but his recommendations are well taken.

Summary

Although historians of psychology, psychiatry, and psychotherapy might disagree, the cognitive revolution may just in fact represent a paradigm for all mental health treatment. To paraphrase the philosopher Thomas Kuhn, a *paradigm* is an overarching explanatory framework that defines the subject matter and variables a particular discipline studies (i.e., the objects of study), the methods by which these objects are studied, and the methods by which these studies are evaluated for their accuracy in representing reality. Cognitivism and behaviorism in experimental psychology have found solid homes in clinical application. This has brought us to a point of wanted convergence between research and practice. Many solid cognitive and behavioral therapies have been developed. They are solid in both an empirical and practical sense, and clinicians are encouraged to employ the power of these varied approaches.

Quick Review

- Behavior therapy consists of the application of learning theory and its core principles (e.g., classical conditioning, operant conditioning, and extinction). Behavior therapy techniques include systematic desensitization, relaxation training, and in vivo exposure.

- Cognitive therapy is based on a theory of personality that maintains that how one thinks largely determines how one feels and behaves. The therapy is a collaborative process of empirical investigation, reality testing, and problem solving between therapist and patient. Cognitive therapy techniques include cognitive restructuring, reframing, and guided self-dialogue.

- Cognitive-behavioral therapy can be understood as any treatment that utilizes any combination of either behavior therapy or cognitive therapy. Most therapies from this perspective appear to be more CBT than either pure behavioral therapy or cognitive therapy.

- Successful behavior therapies for PTSD work to break the conditioning between the traumatic event and the conditioned emotional responses through subsequent learning episodes or trials. They also seek to increase behaviors that are incompatible with the high levels of arousal in PTSD. Specific therapies include in vivo exposure, systematic desensitization, breathing control, and relaxation training.

- From the cognitive perspective, PTSD treatment is approached from an information processing perspective in which systematic biases and distortions in the processing of information and thinking are altered through exploration, examination, putting them to the empirical test and challenging them, and appropriately altering and changing them in order to produce more logical and more accurate and helpful ways of thinking. Cognitive therapies techniques include cognitive therapy, imaginal exposure, and thought stopping.

- Most therapies from either the behavioral or cognitive perspective are, in fact, combined treatments utilizing components of both. Common CBT therapies include stress-inoculation training, CBT-exposure therapy, and cognitive processing therapy.

- Research has shown that CBT therapies that include combined cognitive and exposure techniques are among the two most effective treatments for PTSD alongside medication treatment with SSRIs. However, issues of medication discontinuance and treatment dropout rates seem superior with CBT.

- Despite its efficacy, not everyone benefits from CBT for PTSD. These cases require reanalysis for missed issues and symptoms and may require adding components to the treatment regimen.

References

Beck, A. T., & Weishaar, M. E. (1989). Cognitive therapy. In R. J. Corsini & D. Wedding (Eds.), *Current psychotherapies* (4th ed., pp. 285–320). Itasca, IL: F. E. Peacock.

Beck, A. T., & Young, J. E. (1985). Depression. In D. H. Barlow (Ed.), *Clinical handbook of psychological disorders: A step-by-step treatment manual* (pp. 206–244). New York: Guilford.

Blake, D. D., & Sonnenberg, R. T. (1998). Outcome research on behavioral and cognitive-behavioral treatments for trauma survivors. In V. M. Follette, J. I. Ruzek, & F. R. Abueg (Eds.), *Cognitive-behavioral therapies for trauma* (pp. 15–47). New York: Guilford.

Clark, D. M. (1986). A cognitive approach to panic. *Behaviour Research and Therapy, 24,* 461–470.

Ehlers, A., & Clark, D. M. (2000). A cognitive model of Posttraumatic Stress Disorder. *Behaviour Research and Therapy, 38,* 319–345.

Foa, E. B., & Rothbaum, B. O. (1998). *Treating the trauma of rape: Cognitive-behavioral therapy for PTSD*. New York: Guilford.

Frank, E., Anderson, B., Stewart, B. D., Dancu, C., et al. (1988). Efficacy of cognitive behavior therapy and systematic desensitization in the treatment of rape trauma. *Behavior Therapy, 19,* 403–420.

Janoff-Bulman, R. (1992). *Shattered assumptions: Towards a new psychology of trauma*. New York: Free Press.

Kilpatrick, D. G., Veronen, L. J., & Resick, P. A. (1982). Psychological sequelae to rape: Assessment and treatment strategies. In D. M. Dolays & R. L. Meredith (Eds.), *Behavioral medicine: Assessment and treatment strategies* (pp. 473–497). New York: Plenum Press.

Kuhn, T. (1996). *The structure of scientific revolutions*. Chicago, IL: University of Chicago Press.

Linehan, M. M. (1993). *Cognitive-behavioral treatment of borderline personality disorder*. New York: Guilford.

Mahrer, A. R. (1996). *The complete guide to experiential psychotherapy*. Oxford, England: Wiley.

Marks, I., Lovell, K., Noshirvani, H., Livanou, M., & Thrasher, S. (1998). Treatment of Posttraumatic Stress Disorder by exposure and/or cognitive restructuring: A controlled study. *Archives of General Psychiatry, 55,* 317–325.

Meichenbaum, D. (1977). *Cognitive-Behavioral Modification: An integrative approach*. New York: Plenum Press.

Melia, K., & Wagner, A. (2000). The application of dialectical behavior therapy to the treatment of Posttraumatic Stress Disorder. *National Center for PTSD Clinical Quarterly, 10*(1), 6–7, 10–12.

Moore, S. A., Zoellner, L. A., & Bittinger, J. N. (2004). Combining cognitive restructuring and exposure therapy: Toward an optimal integration. In S. Taylor (Ed.), *Advances in the treatment of Posttraumatic Stress Disorder: Cognitive-behavioral perspectives* (pp. 129–149). New York: Springer.

Rothbaum, B. O., Meadows, E. A., Resick, P., & Foy, D. W. (2000a). Cognitive-behavioral therapy. In E. B. Foa, T. M. Keane, & M. J. Friedman (Eds.), *Effective treatments for PTSD: Practice guidelines from the International Society for Traumatic Stress Studies* (pp. 60–83). New York: Guilford.

Rothbaum, B. O., Meadows, E. A., Resick, P., & Foy, D. W. (2000b). Cognitive-behavioral therapy. In E. B. Foa, T. M. Keane, & M. J. Friedman (Eds.), *Effective treatments for PTSD: Practice guidelines from the International Society for Traumatic Stress Studies* (pp. 320–325). New York: Guilford.

Taylor, S. (2004). Efficacy and outcome predictors for three PTSD treatments: Exposure therapy, EMDR, and relaxation training. In S. Taylor (Ed.), *Advances in the treatment of Posttraumatic Stress Disorder: Cognitive-behavioral perspectives* (pp. 13–37). New York: Springer.

Zoellner, L. A., Fitzgibbons, L. A., & Foa, E. B. (2001). Cognitive-behavioral approaches to PTSD. In J. P. Wilson, M. J. Friedman, & J. D. Lindy (Eds.), *Treating psychological trauma and PTSD* (pp. 159–182). New York: Guilford.

CHAPTER 13

Psychodynamic Treatments

What many people imagine when thinking about psychotherapy or psychological treatment is psychoanalytic or psychodynamic treatment—the aloof and distant *shrink* sitting back, taking notes, and making interpretations of the products of the analysand's (the person being "psychoanalyzed") mental productions, thoughts, images, dreams, and so on. In some ways, associating psychological treatment with psychoanalytic or psychodynamic treatment is fair because it was one of the first, if not the first, therapy modalities and continues to be widely used to this day. Before we go on, however, let me clarify the issue of *psychoanalytic* versus *psychodynamic* therapy. *Psychoanalytic* typically refers to treatment and therapy methods that originated with Sigmund Freud and those who developed his ideas after him but stayed close to home and more strict in their adherence to Freud's ideas. *Psychodynamic* is a broader term and includes psychoanalytic therapy that uses psychoanalytic theory and its countless permutations as both theoretical and practice bases, including object relations theory, attachment theory, the neo-Freudians, the British school of psychoanalysis, and so on. From this point on, we will use *psychodynamic* to refer to the treatments in this chapter.

Psychodynamic psychotherapy is a form of therapy that utilizes the relationship between the therapist and client to elucidate the unconscious workings of the mind as they manifest in client behaviors, thoughts, dreams, and relationships. Specific attention is paid to the relationship dynamics between therapist and client, with issues of transference and countertransference representing the center of this focus. The clinical tool of interpretation of client behaviors and thoughts in light of the client's history and experience is used to bring awareness to connections between unconscious processes and current issues. This insight is used to alter behaviors and break the hold of the unconscious on current behavior, thought, emotions, and interpersonal dynamics. In addition to insight, the process of *working through* is used as a means of exploring the continuing role of the unconscious in ongoing experience. More interpersonally oriented psychodynamic therapies focus on what is called the *corrective emotional experience*, a form of relational learning that occurs as a therapist helps a client relearn relationship dynamics and function more effectively. In many ways, psychodynamic therapy is a form of behavioral and cognitive analysis within the context of a real relationship, the data from which is used for change. The ultimate goals of psychodynamic therapy, generally speaking, include furthering the development and maturation of personality, helping a patient become more fully aware of conflicts and his or her contributions to current issues, helping a patient become more fully aware of defenses and adaptations and that he or she distorts reality, helping the patient develop more mature defenses, helping the patient develop healthier ways and means to express impulses; and helping the patient gain a general increase in ego strength (Cash, 2002; Kudler, Blank, & Krupnick, 2000a, b).

There are numerous schools of psychodynamic therapy, and it would be impossible to touch on the nuances of each in this space. However, each of them has the elements in common mentioned earlier. Psychodynamic therapies for PTSD are also diverse, but they all have a psychodynamic formulation of patient symptoms and functioning as their base or core. In psychodynamic theory and therapy, a posttraumatic symptom is an adaptive attempt to manage the trauma (Kudler et al. 2000a, b). (For more on the psychodynamic theory of PTSD, see Chapter 7.) Trauma overwhelms us, and in response we engage in psychic defensive action and eventually will return to a state of balance between psychological resources and environmental demands (a situation that traumatic stressors obviously strain). Kudler et al. (2000a) state:

> In PTSD, [mental] equilibrium has not been reestablished because the adaptive process, itself, has been overwhelmed. The defenses become entangled with the traumatic impressions against which they were meant to defend. The resulting complexes are symbolically represented as symptoms. (p. 181)

Specific psychodynamic psychotherapies have been developed, including the work of John Briere, Mardi Horowitz, and J. Lindy. Before we get into the specific therapies, Kudler et al. (2000a, b) make some recommendations before engaging in psychodynamic therapy in general and with PTSD sufferers specifically. They cite Gabbard's (1994) list of nine patient and situational characteristics indicating the possible use of psychodynamic therapy:

1. Strong motivation to understand oneself.
2. Suffering that sufficiently interferes with life.
3. The ability to regress and give up emotional control and then to come back from this and reflect.
4. Tolerance for frustration.
5. A capacity for insight and psychological mindedness.
6. Intact reality testing.

7. Meaningful and enduring object relations.

8. Reasonably good impulse control.

9. Ability to sustain employment.

Horowitz's Cognitive-Analytic Approach

Mardi Horowitz (1988, 1997, 1998, 2001) is widely recognized as a top name in PTSD research, theory, and practice. Although his treatment modality is somewhat of a hybrid in that he incorporates a fair amount of cognitive concepts into his work, the core of his work is typically considered psychodynamic. Horowitz himself refers to his treatment approach as *cognitive-dynamic*. He approaches PTSD as a disorder within a larger group of syndromes called *stress response syndromes*. He characterizes the pathology of stress response syndromes in the following way:

> Stress response syndromes include emotional flooding with intrusive images and ideas. To avoid dreaded states of mind, people automatically inhibit information processing. That leads to denial, numbing, and avoidance. Because of avoidance behavior, attention to defensive coping and resistances to treatment is important. Hence, this cognitive-dynamic approach addresses patterns of defensive coping, efforts to counteract dysfunctional beliefs, and disturbances in roles of self and others. (2001, p. 181)

Traumatized individuals will predictably go through a series of alternating phases between acknowledging the trauma and avoiding it. As this process goes on, the eventual goal should be a reformulation or reschematization of the event in relation to the person and the person in relation to him- or herself and others. This is sometimes referred to as *working through*, which was mentioned earlier. The goal of treatment is to "help the person work through the linkage between the self and the stressor events so that all such symptoms can be attenuated or terminated" (Horowitz, 2001, p. 182). The goal is to strike a balance between a state of emotional numbness and of being emotionally flooded or overwhelmed. There are also the general goals of helping the patient establish a sense of safety; develop decision-making skills and more adaptive coping; develop a realistic sense of self as stable, coherent, competent, and worthwhile; develop competence with family and community; and develop a rational preparation and resilience for future stressors. Horowitz (2001) also proposes that steps should be taken to help patients protect themselves from danger by improving their attention and reaction times, and by teaching them not to react to erroneous beliefs, social stigma and shame, demoralization, or impaired physiological functioning due to sleep deprivation or altered neurochemical functioning. Horowitz's treatment, as are so many for PTSD, is complex and very thorough.

There are six phases to his treatment: evaluation/diagnosis/formulation/treatment planning, support, exploration of meanings, improving coping, working through, and terminating. Initially, patients are diagnosed with a particular stress response disorder, such as PTSD or Complicated Grief Disorder. Next, the clinician should formulate the goals and issues to be addressed within treatment. Horowitz (2001) offers the *configurational analysis method* for this process. First, symptoms and problems are selected. Next, the states or situations in which intrusive symptoms and states of numbing and denial occur are determined. In the next step, unresolved stress-related topics and defensive control processes are addressed. The fourth step addresses self-other beliefs related to identity and relationship functioning. The fifth and final step of formulation is an integration of the previous steps into a treatment plan.

The second phase of treatment is the support phase. Because patients may be in states of unmodulated affect and experience and may be feeling they've lost their sense of control, they need support. For Horowitz (2001), this may include biological stabilization with medication, social support with time structuring and enlisting supportive efforts, and the establishment of a supportive therapeutic relationship and concrete plan. Adequate support needs to be in place before the next phase of treatment, exploration, is undertaken. This is necessary because of the possibility of intense affect in this next phase.

In the exploration phase, intense and powerful affective experiences are analyzed in dose-by-dose fashion, with the goal of coming to conclusions regarding the event's meaning to the self. Horowitz states that blocks may occur at this phase and addresses them in the following way:

> [the clinician] . . . may help the patient by clarifying the differences between realistic and fantasy-based beliefs. In doing so, the clinician allows the patient to learn by identification. The clinician is a person who is not overwhelmed by thinking about the implications of illness, injury, or loss. The presence of the clinician as a compassionate and empathic person, thinking logically, is reassuring. (2001, p. 192)

This is an important point when one considers the powerful experience the therapist may have in reaction to the discussion of traumatic material. (For more on issues of the impact of trauma work on therapists and countertransference issues, see Chapter 19.)

The next phase of treatment involves helping the patient improve his or her *future coping style*. These words are italicized because this treatment approach addresses the patients functioning in response to both current and anticipated stressors on the part of the patient—realistic or otherwise. It is explained that thoughts about the event or events are being inhibited and can be experienced in a dose-by-dose approach with "specific controls rather than global inhibitions" (Horowitz, 2001, p. 193) being utilized to cope. As defensive functioning is reduced, negative emotions will emerge but within the context of tolerable limits. If these experiences are too overwhelming, Horowitz (2001) suggests adding desensitization procedures for relaxation and self-control. Maladaptive defenses should give way to more consciously controlled and adaptive controls. Defensive operations such as inhibition of thought, suppression of emotion, distortion of reality, or dissociation need to be brought to the patient's attention and replaced. At this phase, Horowitz (2001) suggests the option of utilizing exposure techniques found in cognitive-behavioral therapy. (For more on cognitive-behavioral therapy, see Chapter 12.)

The working through phase is designed to help patients reschematize their identity and relationships. Patients analyze pretrauma personality beliefs about themselves and others. This may lead to specific themes being activated, such as fear of victimization, shame, feelings of incompetence, anger at the source of the trauma or a displacement figure, or guilt. An individual may also have a developmental history that leads to a lower threshold for tolerating despair and depression, which is then reactivated with trauma. Regardless of the various schematic and developmental material and issues that get activated, this phase of treatment involves helping the client differentiate between what comes from the past and what comes from the present. Attention to warded-off issues and trauma-specific struggles is intensified, and deeper interpretations are offered. These interpretations serve as a basis for a clearer sense of self and others within the context of the current trauma.

The final phase of treatment is termination. This is never a simple ending to therapy but a unique and important stage in and of itself. Emotions about separating from the therapist must be addressed. Also, therapeutic gains must be reinforced. Horowitz (2001) suggests making plans for practicing the newly acquired cognitive-analytic skills. He reminds us that the client's vulnerability is likely to resurface in this final phase and recommends terminating gradually over a series of sessions in an almost stress-inoculation manner. Finally, he recommends that the client be benevolently forewarned that these issues may crop up again but that this is expected and should be framed as a time to practice what has been learned.

The Self-Psychological Approach

Self-psychology is considered a descendent of Freudian psychoanalysis and was developed by, among others, Heinz Kohut. Richard Ulman and Doris Brothers (1988) present a treatment approach from the Kohutian self-psychology perspective. At the core of self-psychology is the notion that the structure of the self is created through relationships. Each of us possesses the psychic structure, the *self-object*, to refer to someone who is important in satisfying our basic, narcissistic-oriented needs. Self-objects are in the service of the self. The self is developed through the mirroring processes of the parents and primary caregivers. This sense of self develops and progresses from grandiosity and being the center of the world into a more healthy sense of self-esteem and ambition. Failures in mirroring result in an inadequate sense of self. In future relationships, the self-object is used to symbolize other people, and such people are expected to respond to you in a way that your self-object-mirroring experience has determined.

From the perspective of therapy, this self-object transference serves as a vehicle for working through the unconscious meanings of trauma. Similarly to
Horowitz and other psychodynamic thinkers, trauma will inevitably activate
unconscious material and will need to be differentiated from current issues in
order to facilitate adjustment. Kohut is cited as viewing the self-object transference as the "primary therapeutic medium within which to restore and transform
. . . archaic narcissistic fantasies" (Ulman & Brothers, 1988, p. 216). Therapy helps
bring to consciousness the existence and action of "shattered and faultily restored
archaic narcissistic fantasies" (Ulman & Brothers, 1988, p. 218), and eventually
working through these helps further the patient's psychic growth. These shattered
experiences must be transformed in order to restore a sense of safe centrality in
the patient. Each patient will be reenacting and playing out the script of fantasies
around which they have organized their psychological functioning. These may be
grandiose fantasies, idealization, merger, or numerous others. The important
thing to note here is that the therapist must be aware of the action of these within
the context of the therapeutic relationship and interaction.

Ulman and Brothers (1988) organize treatment into three phases: initial, recon-
structive, and working through. They provide a very good summary as follows:

> The initial phase of treatments focuses on the vacillations between resistance to
> and establishment of self-object transference fantasies. . . . The reconstructive phase
> centers on the analysis of resistances to self-object transference fantasies as well as
> both traumatic and genetic reconstruction. Finally, the working through phase
> involves the consolidation and analysis of self-object transference fantasies. The
> therapeutic transformation of these fantasies as part of the resolution of a trau-
> matic transference-neurosis leads to further psychic structuralization of the
> patient's subject world and to increased introspection or insight into the uncon-
> scious meanings of trauma. (p. 223)

Ulman and Brothers (1988) point out several important issues for the initial
phase of treatment. They warn that it is important not to push too hard for the
establishment of a self-object transference too soon as this may further fragment
and disorganize the patient. Further, the clinician wants to be careful not to create a false transference based on a fantasy bond between patient and therapist.
Resistance to the establishing of a transference fantasy of self in relation to a
positive mirroring and idealizing object may occur as well. This resistance needs
to be analyzed. Kohut cites two types of resistance that the therapist might
encounter: *nonspecific narcissistic resistance,* in which the patient resists loss of independence and autonomy by the act of coming to someone else for help, and *specific narcissistic resistance,* which is related to the patient's disturbed self and
unconscious fear of disintegration. A focus on symptoms and the more technical aspects of PTSD help focus the patient without too much stimulation. There
may also be projections of inadequacy and incompetence upon the therapist.

The reconstruction phase involves reviving the self-object transference that
imbues the current trauma with unconscious meaning. It is important to pay

attention to the organizing fantasies of self at this stage, as they will shape the nature of patient defenses and the nature of the therapeutic interaction within the context of the relationship. Ulman and Brothers (1988) state, "the therapeutic objective of reconstruction is to arrive at valid empathic inferences about the unconscious meaning of trauma" (Ulman & Brothers, 1988, p. 225). In this phase of treatment, the therapist should monitor the patient's attempts to recapitulate the faulty fantasies. Nightmares are important symptoms of PTSD that play an important role in this form of treatment. Nightmares present an opportunity for interpretation of the patient's shattered narcissistic fantasies. As treatment progresses, nightmares that depict victimization might turn into dreams of triumph, signaling the transformation of the shattered fantasies to healthier organized fantasies. Also, narcissistic rage might emerge that can be directed at either the therapist or the patient him- or herself as the patient becomes more aware. This rage can be a reaction to the experience of the environment having failed to provide support, or it may be a reaction to a failure of the self to live up to grandiose expectations of "omnipotent control of basic mental and physical processes" (Ulman & Brothers, 1988, p. 222), or even a reaction to the self failing to, or not being able to, enlist environmental support.

The final phase, working through, is divided into three subphases: consolidating a selfobject transference fantasy in order to restore damaged archaic narcissistic fantasies, increasing insight into the unconscious meaning of psychic trauma as "encoded in PTSD symptoms," and analyzing the transference and advancing development toward a more mature sense of self.

Other Psychodynamic Approaches and Techniques

Judith Chertoff (1998) proposes treatment of PTSD from an ego psychology perspective. She defines the *ego* as "a complex dynamic system of internal, and often unconscious, defenses and function that mediate between the physiological and emotional needs of the self, such as food, nurturing, or erotic gratification, and the demands of the external world" (p. 37). Practitioners from the ego psychology perspective work from a foundation in Freud's structural model (ego, id, and superego) and view trauma as an external event that overwhelms the ego's defenses and results in regression.

Treatment begins with a specific psychodynamic-oriented assessment that examines current functioning, past treatment, early development, relationships, and ego functioning. This may take several sessions. Early on, the therapist attempts to understand the meaning of the trauma for the patient, with specific reference to his or her developmental history. Treatment then focuses on helping the patient see the unconscious meaning of the trauma while taking care not to overwhelm his or her current ego defenses. The tact, dosage, and timing of interpretations are critical issues when attempting to uncover the unconscious without overwhelming the patient.

Marshall, Yehuda, and Bone (2000) suggest that psychodynamic treatment of PTSD should focus on facilitating the resumption of the patient's stalled attempt at processing the event. They state that psychodynamic therapy helps,

> . . . by constructing a verbal narrative of the experience and exploring its associated meaning. Psychotherapy consists of reconstructing the event, exploring the patient's associations, and encouraging him or her to identify and express the patient's associations, and encouraging him or her to identify and express these beliefs and emotions. (p. 356)

In a model from Jacob Lindy (1996), trauma treatment focuses on interpretation of symptoms, memory reconstruction, and insight. He provides a summary of the technical principles of his approach as follows:

1. Trauma reconstructions should occur when intrusive rather than numbing aspects of PTSD are present.

2. Under ideal circumstances, the alliance should be strong and the general transference positive; the intrusion should be limited and should be occurring within the context of a generally improving clinical condition.

3. However, when the therapist is faced with a rapidly deteriorating clinical situation in which there is a significant negative component to the transference, reconstruction of trauma can provide a new temporary structure around which ego functions can be consolidated rather than fragmented and an alliance has the opportunity to develop.

Empirical Status of Psychodynamic Treatment for PTSD

According to the practice guidelines from the International Society of Traumatic Stress, "only a few empirical investigations with randomized designs, controlled variables, and validated outcome measures have been reported" (Kudler et al., 2000b, p. 339). However, numerous case studies have been published that establish the utility of psychodynamic treatment methods. It is suggested that before considering the use psychodynamic-oriented psychotherapy for PTSD, certain patient characteristics should be taken into consideration, including frustration tolerance, tolerance for strong emotions, psychological mindedness, intact reality testing, an ability to form and maintain relationships, impulse control, and an ability to sustain employment.

Summary

The psychological and interpersonal complexity of PTSD sometimes requires a psychodynamic approach to treatment. The idiosyncratic meaning of a particular traumatic event can be a powerful influence on a patient's ability to acknowledge, process, work through, integrate, and move on from a trauma. Psychodynamic therapies, with their focus on uncovering the unconscious meanings of trauma for an individual and the use of the therapeutic relationship to facilitate this process, as well as growth are particularly suited for such a challenge.

Quick Review

- Psychodynamic psychotherapy utilizes the therapeutic relationship to explore the unconscious meaning of trauma.

- Important aspects of psychodynamic therapy are the relationship dynamics between therapist and client with issues of transference and countertransference.

- Gabbard (1994) lists nine patient and situational characteristics indicating the possible use of psychodynamic therapy, including a strong motivation to understand oneself, suffering that sufficiently interferes with life, the ability to regress and give up emotional control and then to come back from this and reflect, and tolerance for frustration

- Mardi Horowitz developed a cognitive-analytic approach to treatment in which the purpose of therapy is to help the patient reformulate or reschematizate the event in relation to the person and the person in relation to him- or herself and others.

- The self-psychology approach to treatment focuses on uncovered unconscious meanings and facilitates a corrective transference in which a basic sense of safety can be reestablished in the patient.

- Care should be taken to not overwhelm a patient's ego defenses when attempting to uncover unconscious meanings, making interpretations, or helping the patient construct a coherent narrative of the trauma.

- In the strictest sense, psychodynamic therapy for PTSD has not been put to rigorous empirical test. However, a large body of clinical experience supports its use with patients who are good candidates.

References

Cash, A. (2002). *Psychology for dummies.* New York: Hungry Minds.

Chertoff, J. (1998). Psychodynamic assessment and treatment of traumatized patients. *Journal of Psychotherapy Practice & Research, 7,* 35–46.

Gabbard, G. O. (1994). Psychodynamic psychiatry in clinical practice: The *DSM-IV* edition. Washington, DC: American Psychiatric Association.

Horowitz, M. J. (1988). *Introduction to psychodynamics: A new synthesis.* New York: Basic Books.

Horowitz, M. J. (1997). *Stress response syndromes: PTSD, grief, and Adjustment Disorders* (3rd ed.). Lanham, MD: Jason Aronson.

Horowitz, M. J. (1998). *Cognitive psychodynamics: From conflict to character.* Hoboken, NJ: Wiley.

Horowitz, M. J. (2001). *Stress response syndromes: Personality styles and interventions* (4th ed.). Northvale, NJ: Jason Aronson.

Kohut, H., & Ornstein, P. H. (Eds.). (1990). *The search for the self: Selected writings of Heinz Kohut: 1978–1981* (Vol. 3). Madison, CT: International Universities Press.

Kohut, H., & Ornstein, P. H. (Eds.). (1991). *The search for the self: Selected writings of Heinz Kohut: 1978–1981* (Vol. 4). Madison, CT: International Universities Press.

Kudler, H. S., Blank, A. S., Jr., & Krupnick, J. L. (2000a). Psychodynamic therapy. In E. B. Foa, T. M. Keane, & M. J. Friedman (Eds.), *Effective treatments for PTSD: Practice guidelines from the International Society for Traumatic Stress Studies* (pp. 176–198). New York: Guilford.

Kudler, H. S., Blank, A. S., Jr., & Krupnick, J. L. (2000b). Psychodynamic therapy. In E. B. Foa, T. M. Keane, & M. J. Friedman (Eds.), *Effective treatments for PTSD: Practice guidelines from the International Society for Traumatic Stress Studies* (pp. 339–341). New York: Guilford.

Lindy, J. D. (1996). Psychoanalytic psychotherapy of Posttraumatic Stress Disorder: The nature of the therapeutic relationship. In B. A. van der Kolk, A. C. McFarlane, & L. Weisaeth (Eds.), *Traumatic stress: The effects of overwhelming experience on mind, body, and society* (pp. 525–536). New York: Guilford.

Marshall, R. D., Yehuda, R., & Bone, S. (2000). Trauma-focused psychodynamic psychotherapy for individuals with posttraumatic stress symptoms. In A. Y. Shalev, R. Yehuda, & A. C. McFarlane (Eds.), *International handbook of human response to trauma* (pp. 347–361). Dordrecht, Netherlands: Kluwer Academic.

Ulman, R. B., & Brothers, D. (1988). *The shattered self: A psychoanalytic study of trauma.* Hillsdale, NJ: Analytic Press.

CHAPTER 14

Psychopharmacological Treatments

Psychopharmacological treatment of PTSD focuses on medications and their efficacy in alleviating symptoms and restoring stability to the biological systems and processes that underlie the disorder. Logically, psychopharmacological treatments are intrinsically tied to the brain systems and neurochemical processes that produce symptoms. Many authors have cited that psychopharmacological treatment of PTSD is relatively underdeveloped compared to other disorders and the casual observer might agree, particularly when compared to the medication treatment of Schizophrenia and depression. However, there has been considerable progress over the years for both specific symptoms and the syndrome as a whole. Throughout this chapter, the reader is encouraged to stay focused on three main areas of PTSD that are *metatargets* for pharmacological treatment: deactivation, restoration, and stability. Medications are used to deactivate the hyperaroused and reactive brain systems, help facilitate restoration of more normal levels of arousal and responsiveness, and promote biological stability over time. Before we get into the specifics of PTSD treatment, however, let's embark on a quick review of basic pharmacological principles and practices in order to form a foundation for understanding the more complex issues specific to PTSD treatment.

Psychopharmacology 101

Psychopharmacological treatment of mental disorders is the direct outgrowth of the medical model within psychiatry, the biological revolution in psychiatry, and the biological and brain-based focus of psychology and the mental health fields. Psychiatry, for many years, was dominated by psychoanalytic formulations of mental disorders stemming to a large degree from Sigmund Freud and his follow-ers. This is not to say that the biological and medical foundations of mental disor-ders were completely neglected during this era as is demonstrated by the influence of Kraeplin and Schneider. However, psychoanalysis was central to the treatment of mental disorders. About mid-twentieth century however, some findings with and applications of dopaminergic drugs in the treatment of psychotic symptoms in Schizophrenia ushered in what some historians of psychiatry call the *biological rev-olution*. This revolution saw the medical model brought to prominence in the understanding and treatment of mental disorders in psychiatry. Eventually, advances in neuropsychology, techniques in biological research in psychology, and imaging techniques and other related advances broadened this focus from mental disorder to psychology and human behavior and mental processes as a whole. This was reflected in the National Institute of Mental Health's (NIMH) research pro-gram of the 1990s, which was dubbed the *decade of the brain*.

Psychopharmacological treatment is based on the medical or biological model of mental disorders, with two primary assumptions (Gitlin, 1996): (1) mental dis-orders can be reliably classified according to diagnostic methods used in medi-cine before the introduction of laboratory tests and, (2) medications are effective in treating a variety of psychiatric disorders. I would add that both of these are built upon the assumption that mental disorders are, at their core, biological dis-orders and therefore alteration of the biological underpinnings constitutes treat-ment. This assumption is predicated on a monist view of the mind-body or mind-brain relationship. However, an alternative view of psychopharmacological treatment can be taken. That is, medications that successfully alleviate the symp-toms of a mental disorder may not directly address underlying biological abnor-malities but may instead influence the expression of symptoms or related systems that subsequently impact underlying biological abnormalities. For instance, I would suggest that medications used to treat seizures that are based on increas-ing the role and functioning of GABA in the brain do not indicate that seizures are a direct result of GABA dysfunction per se but, rather, are influential some-where along the line of biological processes involved in the expression of neural dysfunction. More bluntly, if drinking alcohol helps me relax, this does not sug-gest that I have an alcohol deficiency disorder in my brain. This is important because as biological treatments are created and found to be helpful, we must not make the mistake of drawing causality from correlation!

General Goals of Pharmacotherapy

Psychiatrist Michael Gitlin (1996) identifies three general goals for pharma-cotherapy. Medications may be prescribed for the following reasons:

1. To treat an acute disorder and alleviate symptoms of an active disorder.

2. Prevent a relapse after clinical improvement.

3. Prevent future episodes, sometimes referred to as *maintenance treatment.*

Friedman, Davidson, Mellman, and Southwick (2000a) identify four major techniques used in pharmacotherapy: (1) selecting a drug to normalize the psychobiological abnormalities associated with a disorder, (2) choosing the most appropriate drug with efficacy for particular symptoms or a comorbid disorder, (3) monitoring and readjusting the dosage in order to optimize efficacy and minimize side effects, and (4) recognizing an adequate therapeutic trial of a given drug in order to supplement with an additional drug or switch to a different drug.

It might be helpful to address just when someone, a friend, family member, client, or patient, might need a medication consultation with a medical doctor or prescribing psychologist. Gitlin (1996) outlines six factors or circumstances for such:

1. Significant psychiatric symptoms exist, such as sleep or appetite disturbance; fatigue; panic attacks; ritualistic behavior; cognitive symptoms, such as poor memory, concentration problems, and confusion; or psychotic symptoms, such as delusions and hallucinations.

2. Prominent physical symptoms or the presence of significant medical disorder such as headaches, abdominal pain, or clumsiness. A differential diagnosis may be in order!

3. Significant suicidality exists. In fact, any significant risk factor or issue such as danger to oneself (e.g., suicidality or self-mutilation), danger to others (aggression, violence, homicidal ideation, and even significant paranoia), and dysfunction in self-care, hygiene, and availing oneself of food, clothing, or shelter. This last one might also be particularly salient in situations where children are involved and their well-being is compromised as a result of mental disorder. A restoration or functioning is critical in such a situation.

4. Family history of a major psychiatric disorder exists.

5. Marked mood lability exists, especially in response to environmental events, with rage or depression. I would add irritability and even significant fear-reactions as is seen with PTSD to this factor.

6. There is nonresponse to psychotherapy. I would add to this factor those situations in which psychotherapy is either unavailable for any number of reasons or is very limited in scope and practice. Such is often the case for individuals with limited financial and health-insurance resources and in situations that have logistic challenges, such as rural settings, war zones, or even correctional or jail settings in which access to mental health services may be limited to contact with a psychiatrist, and psychotherapy is not feasible.

General Biological Bases of Psychopharmacology

As was discussed in Chapter 6, ultimately, what happens at the level of the neuron and, more specifically, at the level of the synapse, is critical in the biology of any mental process or behavior. One could take the ultimate reductionist approach and state that mental life and behavior is synonymous with synaptic functioning and its molecular biology. In either case, pharmacological treatment focuses on neural and synaptic functioning as the locus for action and effect. Medications used in the treatment of mental disorders work in at least one of the following ways: (1) mimicking a neurotransmitter and binding to a receptor site with subsequent stimulation of the receptor site, referred to as an *agonist* drug,

TABLE 14.1

Major Drug Classes for Mood and Anxiety

Antidepressants and anxiolytics	Common names	Neurochemical effects
Tricyclic and Tetracyclic drugs	Elavil Sinequan Tofranil	Serotonin reuptake blocking and norepinephrine reuptake blocking
Fluoxetine	Prozac	Serotonin reuptake blocking
Sertraline	Zoloft	Serotonin reuptake blocking
Paroxetine	Paxil	Serotonin reuptake blocking
Fluvoxamine	Luvox	Serotonin reuptake blocking
Monoamine Oxidase Inhibitors	Phenelzine	Enzyme production inhibition
Trazadone	Desyrel	Serotonin reuptake blocking
Nefazodone	Serzone	Serotonin reuptake blocking and norepinephrine reuptake blocking
Bupropion	Wellbutrin	Largely undetermined, possible noradrenergic and dopaminergic effects
Venlafaxine	Effexor	Serotonin reuptake blocking and norepinephrine reuptake blocking
Duloxetine and Milnacipran	Cymbalta & Ixel	Serotonin reuptake blocking and norepinephrine reuptake blocking
Benzodiazepines	Xanax Klonopin Ativan	GABA-benzodiazepine receptor complex
Buspirone	Buspar	Serotonin effects, varied and complex
Sedative-Hypnotics	Ambien	Benzodiazepine effects

(2) mimicking a neurotransmitter and binding to a receptor site with subsequent lack of or blocking of stimulation, referred to as an *antagonist* drug, (3) having a presynaptic effect leading to the increased release of a particular neurotransmitter, (4) having a partial agonist effect, causing the same effect but less so than the endogenous neurotransmitter, (5) blocking neurotransmitter reuptake back into the presynaptic neuron having the functional effect of increasing the level of a neurotransmitter's effects and enhancing the excitability of the postsynaptic neuron, (6) decreasing or increasing the sensitivity of receptors on postsynaptic neurons or the number of receptor sites, (7) altering the metabolism of a particular neurotransmitter, altering its availability within the system, and, finally, (8) altering the availability of a neurotransmitter by altering the availability of its precursor elements utilized in synthesis.

The classes of drugs used in psychopharmacological treatment are defined dually by the disorder and symptoms they are used for and targeting the underlying neurobiological effects and mechanisms. Table 14.1 summarizes the major classes of drugs used primarily in the treatment of depression and Anxiety Disorders including PTSD, with some examples and their underlying target neurochemical processes.

Psychopharmacological Therapy for PTSD

There appears to be professional consensus that pharmacotherapy in PTSD is a critical and important treatment component for PTSD (Friedman et al., 2000a) for a number of reasons: research supported biological abnormalities in PTSD; overlap with other disorders that are very responsive to drug treatment, such as depression and Panic Disorder; and its general acceptance by patients despite side effects and often prohibitive costs. The National Center for Post-Traumatic Stress Disorder proposes the use of pharmacological treatment for individuals who have already been through debriefing or brief crisis-oriented psychotherapy.

Without being facetious, alcohol is probably the oldest form of medicinal treatment for PTSD. Heroin abuse and dependence was not uncommon in Vietnam and in those who returned home with addictions. In essence, any medicine, drug, or substance that could calm one's nerves might be sought out as a medicinal remedy to the distress of PTSD. Barbiturates, powerful central nervous system depressants, have been used in the past, but their strong addictive properties and drugging effects have resulted in their falling out of favor. As medicine and pharmacology progressed in both research and practice, newer, more efficacious drugs that could produce the desired effects without the undesired consequences of side effects and nontarget effects came into use. The pharmacological treatment of PTSD involves the use of the following classes of drugs: anxiolytics, antidepressants, anticonvulsants, antiadrenergic drugs, antipsychotic agents, and various other, more atypical drugs.

Goals of Pharmacotherapy in PTSD

Pharmacotherapy of PTSD should logically focus on reducing the core symptoms of the disorder of reexperiencing, avoidance and numbing, and hyperarousal. Also, increased resilience and coping, improved quality of life, reducing comorbidity, and limiting the degree of disability are important target goals for treatment (Davidson & Connor, 1999). Foa, Keane, and Friedman (2000) suggest that the course of drug treatment for PTSD carry on for 8 to 12 weeks, keeping in mind, however, that symptom reduction has been observed as soon as within 2 to 5 weeks.

Friedman (2001) recommends working from an allostatic load perspective in the pharmacological treatment of PTSD. From this perspective, it is important to keep in mind that "a system can overshoot, undershoot, fail to recover, or become otherwise dysregulated because it is incapable of accurately titrating its adaptive repertoire to environmental demands" (Friedman, 2001, p. 94). This implies that there is a broad range of psychobiological processes implicated in the disorder and, as such, each component of the disorder may respond to a different medication or a different form of treatment. I think the lesson Friedman is teaching us is that although it is prudent to be flexible and open-minded in all treatment, it may be absolutely essential with PTSD.

Anxiolytics and PTSD

Anxiolytics are the large class of drugs used to treat anxiety. Gitlin (1996) cites that *anxiolytic* literally means "loosening of anxiety" (p. 349). Early treatments of Anxiety Disorders as a broad class were dominated by sedating hypnotic drugs and barbiturates. These, however, had significant complications, such as interfering with someone's ability to think clearly, physical responsiveness, and sleepiness, which interfered with everyday functioning and even contributed to dangerousness. These drugs and agents were also highly addictive. Gitlin (1996) identifies that there has been a progressive search to find the perfect tranquilizer. Eventually, benzodiazepines replaced these drugs and were more widely used. Librium and Valium made their way onto the scene in 1960 and 1963, respectively.

Benzodiazepines work primarily by enhancing GABA-induced inhibition in the brain, inhibiting glutamate's ability to produce postsynaptic excitation in select and implicated brain areas. Benzodiazepines achieve their effect by functionally increasing the firing threshold of the amygdala in response to either external or internal stimuli by affecting GABA cells. Ultimately, benzodiazepines work to reduce arousal and reactivity by increasing inhibition. Fear is suppressed by setting the system at a higher threshold for responding and inhibiting subsequent reactions.

Research and practice guidelines suggest that benzodiazepines be used as an adjunctive treatment in PTSD for treating sleep difficulties and for quick relief of global anxiety and immediate treatment of impending panic attacks. It is not recommended as a monotherapy.

Antidepressants and PTSD

Selective Serotonin Reuptake Inhibitors, Tricyclic Antidepressants, and Monoamine Oxidase Inhibitors

Selective serotonin reuptake inhibitors (SSRIs) are currently considered first-line therapies for PTSD and are considered a treatment of choice (Friedman, 2004). Treatment guidelines from the International Society for the Treatment of Traumatic Stress (ISTSS) state that SSRIs are the most effective medication for PTSD. Improvement and symptom reduction has been shown as early as 1 to 2 weeks after the drugs are first administered. Remission has been associated with treatment lasting at least 15 months. Fluoxetine has been found to significantly reduce overall PTSD symptoms, including intrusive symptoms and arousal. Sertraline has been found efficacious in both short-term and long-term therapy and has shown specific effects on anger and irritability. Further, the United States Food and Drug Administration recently designated sertraline as a specific treatment for PTSD. This finding is of note according to Friedman (2001) because the effectiveness of sertraline for PTSD appears to be unrelated to its efficacy as an antidepressant as research has revealed that when subjects with PTSD and a history of Major Depressive Disorder were compared to subjects with just PTSD, there was no difference. Paroxetine and flovoxamine both have been effective as well. A bonus feature of this class of drugs is that SSRIs are also very effective in treating common comorbid conditions, such as depression, Panic Disorder, and Social Phobia.

The effectiveness of SSRIs for treatment of PTSD is not a completed picture, however, with no questions remaining. For instance, research has shown that fluoxetine may be less effective with Vietnam veterans, perhaps due to the severity and chronicity of their symptoms (van der Kolk et al., 1994; Friedman, 1997).

Tricyclic antidepressants (TCAs) have been found effective for short-term treatment of PTSD. Perhaps the most commonly used and most popular TCA is imipramine, which first made its way onto the scene for treatment of depression in the late 1950s. Tricyclic antidepressants have been used as effective treatments for depression and were considered first-line treatments until the advent of the SSRIs. Tricyclic antidepressants have both serotonergic and noradrenergic effects, essentially leading to blocking of reuptake of serotonin and norepinephrine. After initial reuptake is blocked, serotonin levels rise in response to feedback from the hence inhibited presynaptic neuron. Ultimately, serotonin transmission is enhanced, and postsynaptic reception and sensitivity of serotonin is increased. Noradrenergic functioning is altered by inhibiting reuptake as well. Although TCAs have been shown to be effective in treating both depression and PTSD to some extent, once the SSRIs came along, they fell out of favor as comparatively they are more difficult to use, have more side effects, are slightly less effective for the same range of disorders, have a narrower range of disorders for which they are effective, and are less preferred by patients. However, Gitlin (1996) cites that imipramine is still the standard by which all newer antidepressants are held up against in the treatment of depression. He states, "after thirty-five years of research, we still do not have an antidepressant that treats major depression more successfully than imipramine" (p. 279).

Research on the use of monoamine oxidase inhibitors (MAOIs) in the treatment of PTSD has shown some effectiveness, but few studies have been done. Three controlled studies reviewed by Davidson and Connor (1999) demonstrated improvement in intrusion and, to a lesser degree, in avoidance or numbing as well as global or generalized improvement. Monoamine oxidase inhibitors work by inhibiting an enzyme that metabolizes serotonin, norepinephrine, and a number of other neurotransmitters. This has the functional effect of increasing their levels within the synapse. Monoamine oxidase inhibitors are considered third-line antidepressants due at least in part to dietary restrictions for individuals taking MAOIs and with interaction complications with other drugs. It must be stated, however, that research and practice have shown that they are considered just as effective in treating Major Depressive Disorder and may even be more effective than the TCAs in treating atypical depression. Their use with PTSD, however, remains to be fully supported by research and ongoing practice.

What is the mechanism of the antidepressant drugs in PTSD pathophysiology? More research needs to be done, but a gross understanding reveals that this class of antidepressant drugs has the effect of functionally increasing the levels of serotonin available within particular brain systems, and, as was discussed in Chapter 6, serotonin is implicated in the human stress response and in fear responding. Increased levels of serotonin may have the effect of keeping the amygdala in check, for example.

Although more research and clinical experience is needed, a few other antidepressant drugs have been implicated for use with PTSD. Nefazadone both blocks serotonin reuptake and engages in postsynaptic blockade. Practitioners have endorsed it as a second-choice drug after SSRIs despite a lack of research (Friedman, 2004). Trazadone is a similar drug to nefazadone and has been shown to be modestly effective in one small study (Hertzberg, Feldman, Beckham, & Davidson, 1996).

Other Drugs

Although SSRIs are leading the proverbial way in pharmacological treatment for PTSD, still other drugs have been used, are still used, and have shown effectiveness. The anticonvulsant carbamazepine has been effective in treating intrusion and arousal symptoms and another, valproate, has been shown to reduce avoidant or numbing and arousal symptoms. Antiadrenergic drugs such as clonidine and propranolol have shown to be effective in reducing arousal, reexperiencing, and dissociative symptoms (Friedman, 2001). Finally, a note about antipsychotic drugs needs to be made. Certainly, individuals with PTSD may suffer from comorbid psychotic disorders and have flashbacks of a severe nature that may warrant separate clinical attention. However, research and clinical practice have yet to yield suggestions or recommendations for use of antipsychotic medication, although Friedman (2001) acknowledges they are currently being used despite adequate guidelines or empirical support for such.

Treatment of Comorbid Disorders and Associated Symptoms

More often than not, PTSD sufferers are plagued by comorbid or other association symptoms and conditions. Matthew Friedman states, "people with PTSD exhibit abnormalities in almost every psychobiological system" (p. 95). Kessler et al. (1995) estimate that more than 80 percent of individuals with PTSD have a comorbid psychiatric condition. Such disorders and related conditions as depression, Generalized Anxiety Disorder, Panic Disorder, psychosis, substance abuse, and irritability and anger should be addressed with their respective and indicated medications, with proper attention paid to interaction effects and how the treatment of these issues ties into the overall clinical picture. Selective serotonin reuptake inhibitors are implicated for treatment of depression and Anxiety Disorders as well. Effective medications for psychotic symptoms include Zyprexa and Seroquel. Methadone has been effectively used in the treatment of Opioid Dependence. Fluoxetine has been used successfully in the treatment of anger and hostility.

Psychopharmacological Prevention of PTSD

Part of effective treatment of PTSD involves prevention of full-blown PTSD from developing by intervening as immediately posttrauma as one can with debriefing, crisis intervention, and psychological first aid. This is particularly true in cases of Acute Stress Disorder. Interventions that can reduce immediate and acute posttrauma levels of arousal, such as relaxation training and utilizing social supports, are often effective. Can pharmacological treatment play a role in prevention or early intervention? Stahl (2005) suggests that medications can be given to disrupt the psychobiological processes that lead to PTSD, ideally preventing the disorder but conservatively attenuating its severity. Two studies suggest that administration of propranolol may be effective as its effects on suppressing epinephrine may interfere with the formation of strong traumatic memories. Still other research is suggesting that early use of benzodiazepines and SSRIs, too, may be helpful. More research needs to be conducted, however.

The Psychodynamics of Pharmacotherapy

Although we live in a "*Prozac Nation*" and it sometimes appears that everyone is on a psychotropic medication of one sort or another, the issue of taking medication is sometimes quite complicated. Patients and family members alike have multiple concerns that may affect whether he or she is willing to engage in pharmacotherapy at all or whether he or she is going to be compliant.

Specific issues for the treating therapist might arise when medication is brought into treatment or a medication consultation is sought. A patient might feel rejected as too sick for just plain psychotherapy. He or she might feel that they are "too much" for the clinician to handle. The possibility of narcissistic injury exists as well. A patient might think he let his therapist down. He might think the therapist disapproves of him.

Transference issues toward the prescribing physician or prescribing psychologist might occur, particularly around issues of parental authority. Such a transference might be positive or negative in nature. Medication might be viewed as a form of external or social control, inducing suspicion, rage, or helpless feelings. Taking medications might be seen as giving in or as a crutch. This may be particularly the case with patients who are involved in recovery from substance dependence who might view taking medications as continuing to take drugs. Fantasies and expectations might develop such as an expectation of cure, personal transformation, or even negative fantasies or ruminations of passivity, perhaps stimulating issues and experiences related to the traumatic event or secondary traumatization.

Professional Alert

Keep in mind that these perceptions on the patient's part might be accurate reflections of countertransference issues occurring within the treatment relationship and should be addressed subsequently.

Noncompliance is a critical issue that must be addressed. Gitlin (1996) states that up to 50 percent of all patients may be noncompliant to one degree or another. They might simply miss doses here and there, or they might refuse to take their medication altogether. There are several patient factors that may contribute to noncompliance: symptoms such as paranoia, denial, or cognitive impairment, such as memory dysfunction; character pathology involving issues with authority; fears of addiction; beliefs that taking medications means someone is crazy; sensitivity to feeling as if one is not in control; and secondary gain, factitious issues, or Somatization Disorder issues.

Other nonpatient issues may contribute to noncompliance as well. Poor service delivery systems in which continuity of care is jeopardized might be at play. A patient may not have the financial resources to afford the medications and yet may out of pride or embarrassment not inform the clinician. There might be poor follow up on the part of the clinician as well. Finally, sociocultural issues such as trust, fears of racism, religious beliefs, and even family chaos can all play a role.

Gitlin (1996) provides the following recommendations for improving medication treatment compliance:

1. Increased active participation by the patient in which he or she feels engaged and is actively participating in the control and direction of treatment.

2. Congruent expectations between patient and prescribing professional and finding a sufficient explanatory model for the patient to justify the taking of the medications.

3. Good communication.

4. Creating a tone of understanding, caring, empathy, and respect.

Summary

Psychopharmacological treatment of PTSD is considered a critical component in PTSD treatment. It should proceed with a careful and well-thought-out plan. Treatments should be selected based on myriad factors, including presenting symptoms, comorbid conditions, and logistic and economic factors. A variety of medications have been found useful, but the SSRIs appear to be the mainstay of pharmacotherapy of PTSD at this point in time. Ultimately, as with other treatments, a sound clinical approach and the establishment of a solid therapeutic relationship are key elements in treatment success.

Quick Review

- Psychopharmacological treatments are intrinsically tied to the brain systems and neurochemical processes that produce symptoms.

- Three general goals for pharmacotherapy are to treat an acute disorder and alleviate symptoms of an active disorder; prevent a relapse after clinical improvement, sometimes referred to as *continuation treatment;* and to prevent future episodes, sometimes referred to as *maintenance treatment.*

- Six reasons to seek a medication consultation are significant psychiatric symptoms, prominent physical symptoms or the presence of a significant medical disorder, significant suicidality, violence risk or grave disability, family history of major psychiatric disorder, marked mood lability, and nonresponse to psychotherapy.

- The goals of pharmacotherapy of PTSD are reducing the core symptoms of the disorder, reexperiencing, avoidance and numbing, and hyperarousal; increasing resilience and coping; improving quality of life; reducing comorbidity; and limiting the degree of disability.

- Anxiolytic drugs, particularly benzodiazepines, are suggested as adjunctive treatments for sleep disturbance and acute treatment of panic attacks.

- The broad class of antidepressant drugs has been found to be effective treatments for the symptoms of PTSD. Selective serotonin reuptake inhibitors, in particular, are considered first-line treatments, with sertraline being specifically designated as a treatment for PTSD.

- Other drugs used in PTSD treatment include anticonvulsants and antiadrenergic drugs.

- Comorbid conditions should be addressed accordingly in a manner that is consistent and contributory to the PTSD treatment regimen.

- Psychopharmacological prevention of PTSD holds promise with the administration of propranolol and some benzodiazepines.

- Issues of treatment compliance and the psychodynamic issues of pharmacotherapy must be addressed as they arise in order to assure effective treatment.

References

Davidson, J. R. T., & Connor, K. M. (1999). Management of Posttraumatic Stress Disorder: Diagnostic and therapeutic issues. *Journal of Clinical Psychiatry, 60,* 33–38.

Foa, E. B., Keane, T. M., & Friedman, M. J. (Eds.). (2000). *Effective treatments for PTSD: Practice guidelines from the International Society for Traumatic Stress Studies.* New York: Guilford.

Friedman, M. J. (1997) Drug treatment for PTSD: Answers and questions. *Annals of the New York Academy of Sciences, 821,* 359–468.

Friedman, M. J. (2001). Allostatic versus empirical perspectives on pharmacotherapy for PTSD. In J. P. Wilson, M. J. Friedman, & J. D. Lindy (Eds.), *Treating psychological trauma and PTSD* (pp. 94–124). New York: Guilford.

Friedman, M. J., Davidson, J. R. T., Mellman, T. A., & Southwick, S. M. (2000a). Pharmacotherapy. In E. B. Foa, T. M. Keane, & M. J. Friedman (Eds.), *Effective treatments for PTSD: Practice guidelines from the International Society for Traumatic Stress Studies* (pp. 84–105). New York: Guilford.

Friedman, M. J., Davidson, J. R. T., Mellman, T. A., & Southwick, S. M. (2000b). Pharmacotherapy. In E. B. Foa, T. M. Keane, & M. J. Friedman (Eds.), *Effective treatments for PTSD: Practice guidelines from the International Society for Traumatic Stress Studies* (pp. 326–329). New York: Guilford.

Gitlin, M. J. (1996). *The psychotherapist's guide to psychopharmacology* (2nd ed.). New York: Free Press.

Hertzberg, M. A., Feldman, M. E., Beckham, J. C., & Davidson, J. R. T. (1996). Trial of trazodone for Posttraumatic Stress Disorder using a multiple baseline group design. *Journal of Clinical Psychopharmacology, 16,* 294–298.

Kessler, R. C., Sonnega, A., Bromet, E., Hughes, M., et al. (1995). Posttraumatic Stress Disorder in the National Comorbidity Survey. *Archives of General Psychiatry, 52,* 1048–1060.

Stahl, S. M. (2005). Is psychopharmacologic "inoculation" effective in preventing Posttraumatic Stress Disorder? *Journal of Clinical Psychiatry, 66,* 5–6.

van der Kolk, B. A., Dreyfuss, D., Michaels, M., Shera, D., et al. (1994). Fluoxetine in Posttraumatic Stress Disorder. *Journal of Clinical Psychiatry, 55,* 517–522.

CHAPTER 15

Integrated and Other Treatment Approaches

The developmental history of mental health treatments parallels the development of any scientific endeavor, including the development of the various health and clinical sciences. The objects of study change with paradigm shifts, technological advances, and social forces that any particular practice exists among and within. The treatments discussed in the previous chapters (Chapters 12, 13, and 14) in some respects represent the more stereotypical forms of treatment for mental disorders in general and PTSD specifically. The treatments to be covered here are less mainstream in some ways and less rooted in the historical tradition of mental health treatment. However, this is not to imply they are lacking in efficacy, sophistication, or rigor for these reasons. Just as the history of psychology, for instance, moves from paradigm to paradigm, from psychoanalysis to behaviorism to cognitivism, so, too, do these shifts occur in the development of clinical science and practice.

The main difference between the treatments to be covered in this chapter is their focus on clinical variables and phenomenon the treatments in the previous chapters did not. Of course, there is considerable overlap between the underlying biopsychosocial foundations of these treatments with the previous ones, but these treatments are different in important ways and deserve discussion in their own right. Further, an inevitable outcome of the existence of these various treatments and both the theoretical and empirical exploration of their efficacies is the bringing together of the various effective treatments and helpful elements into comprehensive and integrated models of treatment. As researchers, theorists, and practitioners explore these various treatments, someone eventually sees a way to bring them together into a complete clinical picture. Some of these integrated models will also be introduced and discussed here.

Group Therapy

Human beings are undeniably social beings. This holds true for the vast majority of us at least. There is intuitive and evolutionary wisdom regarding the power of gathering in groups. We find protection in groups. In groups, we gain the ability to accomplish that which we cannot accomplish alone. Our very being and identities are tied to our relationships with other people. This natural wisdom and the healing power of groups was likely behind the formation (be it explicitly or implicitly) of the early group-type treatments called *rap groups* for Vietnam veterans in which they discussed their experiences, bonded, and supported each other. Group therapy for PTSD has become a very involved specialty of treatment.

Group therapy is not simply individual therapy with more than one person at the same time. There are, of course, many different types of group therapy, each with its own theoretical basis and explanation for curative or helpful mechanisms. The study of group dynamics and systems is quite involved, a discussion of which fills numerous books and journal pages. There are dozens of group therapy techniques derived from the various schools of psychology, including psychoanalytic group therapy, interpersonal group therapy, cognitive-behavioral group therapy, psychodrama, and Gestalt group therapy, to name just a few.

With respect to trauma and PTSD, there are also many different group therapy approaches, each with their own unique and specific techniques. Each of these, however, derives at least some of the effectiveness from general principles of group therapy relevant to PTSD. Bessel van der Kolk (1993) states:

> Regardless of the nature of the trauma or the structure of the group, the aim of group therapy is to help people actively attend to requirements of the moment, without undue intrusions from past perceptions and experiences. By actively attending to their own and other people's histories and associated emotions, patients in group psychotherapy can learn to manage the aftermath of trauma through transformation rather than reenactment of the bewilderment, isolation, disbelief, helplessness, submission, hate, and pain associated with the trauma. (p. 294)

van der Kolk (1993) and Foy, Eriksson, and Trice (2001) identify the following common goals for all trauma groups:

1. Stabilize psychological and physiological reactions to the trauma.
2. Explore and validate perceptions and emotions.
3. Retrieve memories.
4. Understand the effects of past experiences on current affects and behaviors.
5. Learn new ways of coping with interpersonal distress.
6. Validation of behaviors required for survival during the trauma.
7. Challenge the idea that the nontraumatized therapist cannot be helpful through the presence of the fellow survivors.

Clinician Alert: Individual versus Group Therapy?

Before we explore some specific group approaches to PTSD, the issue of treatment selection needs to be addressed. As with all patients, deciding whether to place or refer a patient to group therapy versus individual therapy is a complex issue that depends on a host of factors. Of course, nothing precludes a patient from being involved in both if deemed appropriate. However, the existence of group therapy begs the question of appropriateness for group therapy for certain patients. van der Kolk (1993) proposes that group therapy for trauma has some distinct advantages over individual therapy. For instance, he identifies an *inherent limitation* of individual therapy to help people overcome their hopelessness and experience of lack of efficacy by sometimes perpetuating a "position of submission and passivity" because the therapeutic relationship is set up to communicate that "the therapist implicitly has all the answers and is not helpless, and the patient needs help and needs to accept some degree of passivity, dependence, and lack of control" (p. 294). van der Kolk also cites that group therapy helps facilitate a patient's sense of usefulness toward others by giving them an opportunity to share what they have learned or accomplished. Foy et al. (2000) identify several characteristics and factors that make someone either a good candidate or not for group therapy. Examples of what makes someone a good candidate include having flexibility in personal schedule in order to accommodate the other group members, not being actively suicidal or homicidal, having the ability to share similar traumatic experiences with others, not being severely paranoid or psychopathic, and being willing to abide by the rules of the group. Factors that might preclude someone from group therapy include active psychosis, including paranoia, limited cognitive capacity, and pending or looming legal litigation or being a compensation-seeking individual. The important thing to remember is that a decision to place someone in group therapy should be based on sound clinical judgment and forethought and not done carelessly or out of simple convenience.

Foy et al. (2001) propose that group therapies for PTSD fall into one of three categories: (1) supportive, (2) psychodynamic, or (3) cognitive-behavioral. The key features of each will be discussed in the following.

Supportive group therapy for PTSD consists of an open format, with new members being allowed to join at any point along the way. Empirical evidence suggests that supportive group therapy for PTSD is helpful in reducing depression and overall anxiety and in increasing self-esteem. It can be used as an adjunct to individual therapy or as a primary approach in and of itself. The groups typically meet once a week for anywhere from 10 to 15 weeks. Supportive groups focus on issues of current coping and activities of daily living and how the symptoms of PTSD interfere with these. Foy and colleagues (2001) state that little attention is directed to the details of the event and instead there is a primary focus on group validation of the experience, exploration of affects such as anger or disappointment, and the development of supportive relationships.

Relationship dynamic issues such as transference are not emphasized, while a supportive and comforting atmosphere is maintained. This has been cited as particularly helpful in "diffusing extreme affects" (Foy et al., 2001, p. 247) such as terror and rage.

Psychodynamic group therapy for PTSD works along the same theoretical lines as individual psychodynamic therapy by focusing on the uncovering of the unconscious meanings of the traumatic event. Issues of self-representation with respect to interpersonal dynamics and attachment issues get explored. Foy and colleagues (2001) state:

> During the retelling of their trauma stories, members may experience affective reactions that move from anxiety about disclosure, to fear and intense hurt during the description of the trauma event, to a later sense of relief or calm as they safety of telling the story in the group is internalized. (p. 248)

The group functions as a transferential object much the same way that the individual therapist does in individual therapy. The participant's thoughts and beliefs about themselves in relation to others with respect to the trauma gets made explicit and is corrected by a working through process between group members and a reworking of the relationships between the trauma, the self, and others is achieved. As with supportive therapy, psychodynamic group therapy for PTSD has enjoyed some empirical support for bringing about general improvement, reduced anxiety, and reduced depression.

Cognitive-behavioral group therapy for PTSD makes use of prolonged exposure procedures en masse. The operative mechanism for this form of group therapy is really quite simple and elegant. Each individual within the group is granted the opportunity to tell his or her story while the other group members listen. This is thought to have the effects of both being heard for the storyteller and providing an exposure for the group members. As each member tells their story, they are exposing themselves through telling and coexposing their cohorts. There is also a psychoeducational component in which information about coping skills and relapse prevention is discussed. Cognitive-behavioral group therapy for PTSD has been found effective in bringing about general improvement but has also shown promise for reducing PTSD symptoms specifically.

Constructivist Narrative Treatment

From Chapter 7, from the constructivist narrative perspective, traumatic events challenge or damage our personally constructed narrative representation of reality and the goal of treatment is thus constructing a new narrative and assumptive world that assimilates the traumatic experience is crucial to recovery. As Donald Meichenbaum (2000) states, "People are story-tellers. . . . They offer accounts that are designed to make sense out of the world and their places in it. . . . Now, consider what happens to people's stories when really bad things (traumatic events) are experienced" (p. 55).

Characteristics of individuals with ongoing PTSD symptomology include an inability to integrate their trauma stories, continued searching for an explanation and failures to find satisfactory answers to the *why* questions, constant engagement in counterfactual and *what if* thinking, and continual comparisons between life as it is and life as is could have been. Meichenbaum characterizes this narrative process as consisting of metaphors and language of damage, hopelessness, and fear.

Therapy from the constructivist narrative perspective is characterized as a "collaborative co-constructive approach" (Meichenbaum, 2000, p. 58). The patient sets out to rewrite his or her trauma narrative through engaging in a set of 10 core therapeutic tasks outlined as follows:

1. Establish a therapeutic alliance with empathy and support.
2. Provide education about PTSD through dialogue and discovery, not lecturing.
3. Increase patient's coping skills and enhance self-care activities.
4. Nurture hope by focusing on what the patient has accomplished and signs of resilience.
5. Help the patient do "memory work of trauma resolution and reintegration" (p. 59).
6. Help the patient find meaning with emphasis on mastery, control, competence, and self-acceptance.
7. Encourage and ensure social connections.
8. Encourage the patient to take credit for any change.
9. Help develop skills to avoid revictimization.
10. Address relapse prevention.

Meichenbaum (2000) reminds us that the construction of narratives comes from actually living our lives. He states that "the construction of a new narrative emerges out of the actions that patients take to refashion their lives" (p. 59). In essence, in practicing and living differently, we tell a different story.

Integrated Approaches

Eye Movement Desensitization and Reprocessing (EMDR)

Eye movement desensitization and reprocessing emerged as a trauma treatment from the astute observations of Dr. Francine Shapiro in the late 1980s. It has been used since and has enjoyed empirical support as an effective treatment for PTSD. It is considered an integrated treatment because it combines cognitive, behavioral, neurophysiological, and information-processing elements. Eye movement desensitization and reprocessing has gone from being a heavily doubted and suspiciously acknowledged therapy to being more widely used in the years since its introduction and being used with a wide range of clinical populations. Some consider it a significant breakthrough and substantial advancement in the treatment of PTSD (Parnell, 1997).

Rationale and Theoretical Basis

Although EMDR has enjoyed both clinical and empirical success as an effective treatment, the underlying mechanisms by which it works are still unclear. Smith and Yule (1999) warn that the theoretical understanding of how EMDR works lags behind its clinical practice. They summarize the current theoretical understanding:

> At the heart of EMDR is the notion that accelerated processing of disturbing material can be directly facilitated at a neurophysiological level using a variety of dual attention tasks. Accordingly, a by-product of resolution at the neurophysiological level is cognitive and emotional well-being. (p. 267)

The origins of EMDR seem part of a clinical myth of sorts told by the EMDR creator, Francine Shapiro. Dr. Shapiro states that essentially by accident, while walking through the woods one day, she discovered that some disturbing thoughts she had been having disappeared in conjunction with the rapid backward, forward, and upwardly diagonal movements of her eyes. From this discovery, EMDR was born. Shapiro (1995) proposes that the directed eye movements utilized in her treatment have a direct effect on the neurophysiological status of trauma material, resulting in desensitization and cognitive restructuring. Eye movement desensitization and reprocessing, to some, is viewed as another form of cognitive-behavioral therapy with a more direct physiological interface. Consider that food might be thought of as a form of chemotherapy (albeit slower) for cancer. Cognitive-behavioral therapy might be likened to food as chemotherapy, while EMDR might be considered the chemotherapy of trauma, simply a more direct form of mental change.

Lipke (1992) has proposed that EMDR elicits an orienting reflex that alters neurophysiological functioning by disrupting the configuration of the traumatic memory network, thus allowing proper information processing to resume. Marquis (1991) proposes that rapid eye movements (REMs) interrupt the neural connections between the frontal lobes, hypothalamus, and hippocampus and break the stimulus-response relationships produced by the symptoms. Shapiro herself in 1992 proposed that the eye movement procedure results in synaptic changes in mood-memory networks, lowering the bioelectrical valences within the network and allowing for more thorough processing. Smith and Yule (1999, p. 277) state, "The notion is that any shaking up of the neurophysiological system will automatically lead towards a more adaptive resolution." In some ways, then, EMDR might be related to the causal therapeutic mechanisms of electroconvulsive therapy (ECT), but this is solely conjecture at this point.

Work by Ross, Ball, Sullivan, and Caroff (1989), Winson (1993), and Nicosia (1994) suggest that EMDR's induction of alternating attention may have the same effects as REM sleep on the consolidation of memories. Shapiro (1989a) and Nicosia (1994) propose that EMDR creates alterations in brainwave activity between cerebral hemispheres that allow for consolidation and interhemispheric communication. (For more on the biology of PTSD, see Chapter 6.) In 1995, Shapiro proposed an overall theory for EMDR coined the *accelerated information-processing model* in which distorted memory processes are integrated through EMDR's activation of a self-healing process of memory consolidation. Regardless of the findings, a fully empirically supported model of EMDR is yet to emerge; this should not, however, suggest that it is any less clinically effective.

The EMDR Process
Chemtob, Tolin, van der Kolk, and Pitman (2000a) outline the EMDR process in an eight-step process. Step one includes taking a patient's history, and, in addition to traditional clinical assessment, the EMDR clinician identifies trauma memories considered suitable targets for treatment. In the next stage, preparation, information about EMDR is provided, along with the teaching of coping skills for general functioning, for dealing with emergent traumatic material, and for keeping perspective when the trauma is reactivated. Following the preparation stage, in the assessment stage, the patient is asked to "bring together the components of the traumatic memory in a structured manner" (p. 141), including identifying distressing images, negative thoughts, and alternative positive thoughts; rating the validity of the positive thoughts; rating the subjective level of distress; and identifying physical sensations as they occur.

The fourth stage of the procedure is identified as *desensitization and reprocessing*. The patient is instructed to hold the disturbing image, negative thoughts, and physical sensations in the mind. While doing this, the clinician moves his or her fingers back and forth about 12 inches in front of the patient's eyes while the patient is instructed to follow the fingers. After 20 or so back-and-forth movements, the clinician stops and instructs the patient to "let go of the memory, take a deep breath, and provide feedback" (p. 142) about any experienced changes, such as new memories, sensations, or thoughts.

The fifth stage involves instructing the patient to think of his or her earlier generated positive thoughts while focusing on the target image. While doing this, another eye movement session is performed, followed by an assessment of the validity of the positive thought. This process is repeated until the positive thought is eventually rated as high on the validity scale as possible. Similarly, in the sixth stage, this process is undergone with focus on the physical sensations, tension, and discomfort until subjective distress is substantially reduced.

The final two stages involve closure and reevaluation. In stage seven, the patient is instructed on how to use a variety of relaxation techniques to maintain calm between sessions. Journaling is also encouraged. Finally, stage eight involves an assessment of whether treatment goals have been reached, and additional sessions are planned and arranged to address what remains and what has emerged between previous sessions.

Feminist Therapy for Trauma

Feminist therapy is about many things, but its core is designed to bring about healing through the development of *feminist consciousness,* defined as "awareness that one's own suffering arises not from individual deficits but rather from the ways in which one has been systematically invalidated, excluded, and silenced because of one's status as a member of a nondominant group in the culture" (Brown, 2004, p. 464). Many people understand feminist therapy in general and for trauma specifically as more of a philosophy of treatment than a specific treatment per se. Although it is the case that the role of the overarching philosophy within treatment is a critical guiding point in feminist therapy, there are specific treatment techniques and approaches as well.

Feminist therapy is considered an integrated treatment primarily because of a therapist's ability to utilize any therapeutic technique or method that furthers the overarching feminist goal. Interpretations, behavioral techniques, exposure, relaxation training, and numerous others are all possibilities. As long as a technique helps the client move toward empowerment and an increase in self-care capacities, it can be used. Let's break down the goal of developing feminist consciousness into more practical terms. In essence, the development of feminist consciousness in practical therapy-goal terms involves more than simply the alleviation or elimination of PTSD symptoms. Brown (2004) states:

> For many treatment models, once symptoms have diminished, treatment is deemed complete. However, in feminist trauma treatment, the therapist will return to some of the themes that derive from the client's context as they resonate within the "why me" questions that are so common for trauma survivors. Many of the responses to "why me" that clients develop on their own reflect internalized oppression. Self-blame, while a coping strategy that appears to be an attempt to insert a sense of control into an otherwise out-of-control experience, frequently contains the themes of sexism, racism, heterosexism, and so on. Feminist trauma treatment will address the need for a reassertion of control and work with clients to make meaning out of their experiences without further adding to preexisting patterns of internalized oppression. The simple absence of symptoms is not the goal of feminist trauma treatment. Consciousness of one's kinship with other trauma survivors and the creation of nonblaming means of asserting one's sense of control are construed as equally important to symptom remission. (p. 469)

What exists at the heart of feminist therapy appears to be the belief that specific interpretations of traumatic experiences and the posttrauma behavior of both the survivor and those around him or her in terms of sociopolitical feminist terms are therapeutic in and of itself. As Brown (2004) states, "feminist strategies create powerful validation of clients' hunches that their victimization is indeed inextricably linked to their position in the social hierarchy of value" (p. 469). Specific techniques for accomplishing this include the believing game (Clinchy, 1996), in which the therapist adopts a position of believing the client's account of the trauma while avoiding the risk of reacting in a judgmental, invalidating, and unbelieving manner, and Comas-Diaz's (2000) ethnopolitical approach.

Judith Herman's Integrated Approach

Dr. Herman (1992), while employing to a large degree the preceding feminist approaches, has provided a very comprehensive and widely respected form of psychotherapy and treatment for PTSD as well as for complex-PTSD that incorporates components of other modalities, such as cognitive-behavioral therapy and psychodynamic approaches. Herman characterizes treatment within the context of stages of recovery and a healing relationship. She states:

> The core experience of psychological trauma is disempowerment and disconnection from others. Recovery, therefore, is based upon the empowerment of the survivor and the creation of new connections. . . within the context of relationships, it cannot occur in isolation. (p. 134)

Throughout the course of treatment, basic faculties that are damaged by the trauma and its aftermath are redeveloped. These include the ability to trust, a sense of competence, and a solid sense of identity. The survivor must be empowered and encouraged to be in charge of his or her own recovery. Herman cautions against trying to control the patient. Instead of external control, the therapist must facilitate the learning of self-control. The feeling of having a choice should be an integral part of the treatment. The therapeutic relationship is a critical component in this process. Herman identifies several unique aspects of the therapeutic relationship from her perspective:

- Its only purpose is to promote recovery for the patient.
- The therapist is a skilled ally.
- There must be respect for autonomy.
- The therapist does not attempt to gratify his or her own personal needs and should not advance a personal agenda.
- The therapist should not take sides in "inner conflicts or try to direct the patient's life decisions" (p. 135).
- The relationship is both intellectual and relational, with the therapist serving as a protective parent of sorts.

To the extent that Herman's treatment is feminist, she states in her own words quite eloquently:

> Therapy requires a collaborative working relationship in which both partners act on the basis of their implicit confidence in the value and efficacy of persuasion rather than coercion, ideas rather [than] force, mutuality rather than authoritarian control. These are precisely the beliefs that have been shattered by the traumatic experience. (p. 136)

Herman's (1992) model of treatment consists of three stages of recovery: (1) establishing safety, (2) remembrance and mourning, and (3) reconnecting. The focus of the first stage involves restoring a sense of safety, and, for Herman, this task takes precedent over all others. This is accomplished by helping the patient regain his or her sense of control over his or her thoughts, emotions, relationships, and bodies. Medication and relaxation training can help the patient begin to establish a sense of control in the early goings. Confusion from the disorder and its symptoms can be addressed by self-guided monitoring, daily logs of symptoms, and concrete safety plans. The focus on control begins with the body and then progresses to the environment. Body issues include sleep, eating, exercise, symptom management, and control of self-destructive behaviors such as suicide and self-mutilation.

In the second stage of recovery, remembrance and mourning, the survivor retells his or her story and reconstructs the event in minute detail. The therapist serves as a supportive ally in bearing witness to the event and facilitates the emergence of a coherent narrative from the often-encountered fragmented pieces of trauma narrative that first emerge. Once the trauma story has become clearer, the next step within this stage is to facilitate the mourning of any loss the survivor attaches to the trauma. This may include a loss of relationships, a loss of naïveté, a loss of bodily integrity, or a loss of a sense of identity.

In the final stage of Herman's (1992) approach, the task becomes the development of a new self, new relationships, and new beliefs. Part of this process involves the patient learning to face danger while being cognizant of their exaggerated sense of danger. The issue of whether to face danger becomes a matter of conscious choice. Herman characterizes this step as *learning to fight*. The process of creating a new self involves the survivor learning to value, utilize, and emphasize those aspects of him- or herself prior to the trauma, during the trauma, and during the recovery period. Relationships are approached with a sense of competence, trust, and intimacy but also from a position of autonomy. Finally, Herman states that at some point, although resolution and recovery are probably never complete, the survivor learns to turn his or her focus away from the trauma and toward ordinary life. Herman states:

> The survivor who has accomplished her recovery faces life with few illusions but often with gratitude. Her view of life may be tragic, but for that very reason she has learned to cherish laughter. She has a clear sense of what is important and what is not. Having encountered evil, she knows how to cling to what is good. Having encountered the fear of death, she knows how to celebrate life. (p. 213)

Summary

Different conceptualizations of trauma and emphasis on its various components have necessarily given rise to related treatments and therapies. Whether the focus is on the role of relationships in creating a sense of safety, reauthoring one's trauma story, or becoming empowered in the face of fear, the therapies in this chapter remind us that an understanding of PTSD and its alleviation is far from straightforward and can be successfully approached from many perspectives.

Quick Review

- Group therapy for PTSD is a successful form of therapy with three main forms: supportive, psychodynamic, or cognitive-behavioral.

- Constructivist narrative therapy addresses the important issue of how people tell stories that perpetuate symptomology and dysfunction versus stories that allow for competence and healing.

- Eye movement desensitization and reprocessing is a relatively newer integrated approach that makes use of information-processing and psychophysiological principles.

- Feminist therapy for trauma approaches treatment from a more philosophical and political perspective with its goals being empowerment and avoidance of perpetrating oppressive societal dynamics.

- Judith Herman's (1992) comprehensive model is considered a seminal work in the field and aims to empower individuals by helping them reconnect to damaged aspects of themselves and their lives and by constructing a courageous approach to the future.

References

Brown, L. S. (2004). Feminist paradigms of trauma treatment. *Psychotherapy: Theory, Research, Practice, Training, 41*, 464–471.

Chemtob, C. M., Tolin, D. F., van der Kolk, B. A., & Pitman, R. K. (2000a). Eye movement desensitization and reprocessing. In E. B. Foa, T. M. Keane, & M. J. Friedman (Eds.), *Effective treatments for PTSD: Practice guidelines from the International Society for Traumatic Stress Studies* (pp. 139–154). New York: Guilford.

Chemtob, C. M., Tolin, D. F., van der Kolk, B. A., & Pitman, R. K. (2000b). Eye movement desensitization and reprocessing. In E. B. Foa, T. M. Keane, & M. J. Friedman (Eds.), *Effective treatments for PTSD: Practice guidelines from the International Society for Traumatic Stress Studies* (pp. 333–335). New York: Guilford.

Clinchy, B. M. (1996). Connected and separate knowing: Toward a marriage of two minds. In N. Goldberger, J. M. Tarule, B. M. Clinchy, & M. F. Belenky (Eds.), *Knowledge, difference and power: Essays inspired by women's ways of knowing* (pp. 205–247). New York: Basic Books.

Comas-Diaz, L. (2000). An ethnopolitical approach to working with people of color. American Psychologist, 55, 1319–1325.

Foy, D. W., Eriksson, C. B., & Trice, G. A. (2001). Introduction to group interventions for trauma survivors. *Group Dynamics: Theory, Research, and Practice, 5*, 246–251.

Foy, D. W., Glynn, S. M., Schnurr, P. P., Jankowski, M. K., Wattenberg, M. S., Weiss, D. S., et al. (2000a). Group therapy. In E. B. Foa, T. M. Keane, & M. J. Friedman (Eds.), *Effective treatments for PTSD: Practice guidelines from the International Society for Traumatic Stress Studies* (pp. 155–175). New York: Guilford.

Foy, D. W., Glynn, S. M., Schnurr, P. P., Jankowski, M. K., Wattenberg, M. S., Weiss, D. S., et al. (2000b). Group therapy. In E. B. Foa, T. M. Keane, & M. J. Friedman (Eds.), *Effective treatments for PTSD: Practice guidelines from the International Society for Traumatic Stress Studies* (pp. 336–338). New York: Guilford.

Herman, J. L. (1992). *Trauma and recovery.* New York: Basic Books.

Lipke, H. (1992). *Manual for teaching of Shapiro's EMDR in the treatment of combat-related PTSD.* Pacific Grove, CA: EMDR Network.

Marquis, J. N. (1991). A report on seventy-eight cases treated by eye movement desensitization. *Journal of Behavior Therapy and Experimental Psychiatry, 22,* 187–192.

Meichenbaum, D. (2000). Treating patients with PTSD: A constructive narrative approach. *Center for PTSD Clinical Quarterly, 9*(4), 55, 58–59.

Nicosia, G. (1994, March). *A mechanism for dissociation suggested by the quantitative analysis of electroencephalography.* Paper presented at the International EMDR annual conference, Sunnyvale, CA.

Parnell, L. (1997). *Transforming trauma: EMDR: The revolutionary new therapy for freeing the mind, clearing the body, and opening the heart.* New York: W. W. Norton.

Ross, R. J., Ball, W. A., Sullivan, K. A., & Caroff, S. N. (1989). Sleep disturbance as the hallmark of Posttraumatic Stress Disorder. *American Journal of Psychiatry, 146,* 697–707.

Shapiro, F. (1989a). Efficacy of the eye movement desensitization procedure in the treatment of traumatic memories. *Journal of Traumatic Stress, 2,* 199–223.

Shapiro, F. (1989b). Eye movement desensitization: A new treatment for Post-Traumatic Stress Disorder. *Journal of Behavior Therapy and Experimental Psychiatry, 20,* 211–217.

Shapiro, F. (1992). Dr. Francine Shapiro responds. *Behavior Therapist, 15,* 111–114.

Shapiro, F. (1995). *Eye movement desensitization and reprocessing: Basic principles, protocols, and procedures.* New York: Guilford.

Smith, P., & Yule, W. (1999). Eye movement desensitization and reprocessing. In W. Yule (Ed.), *Post-Traumatic Stress Disorders: Concepts and therapy* (pp. 267–284). New York: Wiley.

van der Kolk, B. A. (1993). Group for patients with histories of catastrophic trauma. In A. Alonso & H. I. Swiller (Eds.), *Group therapy in clinical practice* (pp. 289–305). Washington, DC: American Psychiatric Press.

Winson, J. (1993). The biology and function of rapid eye movement sleep. *Current Opinion in Neurobiology, 3,* 243–248.

Crisis Intervention, Debriefing, and Prevention of Posttraumatic Stress Disorder

S
o much of the mental health field deals with disorder and dysfunction after the fact. Medicine, too, spends the vast majority of its resources responding to illness once it has taken hold and begins to cause problems. Of course no one advocates for not treating illness or disorder once it develops, but professionals have increasingly focused on prevention as a form of mental health treatment in and of itself. I'm not sure how far back the concept of treatment goes in the history of health care, but the maxim "an ounce of prevention" has an age-old ring to it. Health professionals are not the only ones concerned with preventing illness or disorder, particularly when it comes to the pathological consequences of exposure to traumatic stress. The very concept of *safety* is predicated on the notion that being safe prevents accident, injury, and death, no matter what the activity, be it recreation (e.g., dirt bike riding), around the house (e.g., baby-proofing your home), or on the job (e.g., fire evacuation drills). In essence, the best way to prevent PTSD is to prevent the occurrence of traumatic events. This would be nice, but I fear it is probably impossible, particularly in this day and age of fast-paced living and exposure to bigger, faster, and more powerful technologies. Unfortunately, as the Greeks seemed to know thousands of years ago, trauma and tragedy seem permanent fixtures of the human experience.

Does this mean then that as mental health professionals we are left picking up the pieces in the aftermath? Hardly. This is where the concept and practice of *prevention* comes into play. Prevention in mental health exists in three forms: *primary prevention, secondary prevention,* and *tertiary prevention*. Primary prevention efforts and interventions involve efforts to reduce the occurrence of mental disorders. These include efforts such as public education, public policy efforts, skill development, and arranging for environmental safety. An example of a primary prevention for adolescent substance abuse, for example, might involve arranging for after-school and weekend activities, programs, and events to provide teens with a safe, supervised setting in which to have fun. Slaikeu (1990) states, "primary prevention takes place well before crisis events actually occur. True prevention literally means keeping some events from happening in the first place. . . " (p. 12).

Secondary prevention refers to intervening in the immediate wake of an event in order to prevent and head off the development of pathological responses and potentially impending disorders. It typically occurs right after an event has occurred. An example of secondary prevention is provision of grief counseling to families who have recently lost a loved one to cancer. The third form of prevention, tertiary prevention, involves repairing or preventing further disorder from developing after an initial disorder or illness has developed. Forms of tertiary prevention include long-term psychotherapy, medication, or rehabilitation efforts. It is typically synonymous with *treatment* in the classic sense. Again, Slaikeu (1990) states, "Treatment or tertiary prevention includes strategies whose aim is to reduce impairment and emotional disorders that result from poor resolution of life crises. Its goal is to repair damage already done to patients who are psychiatric casualties of life stress" (p. 12).

Prevention efforts with respect to PTSD are often characterized as acute prevention or treatment efforts that occur within a short time (usually within 48 hours or so) following a traumatic stressor. This would classify acute PTSD interventions as either secondary or tertiary forms of prevention, with the majority of those being secondary forms. Some have cited that among the varied responses to witnessing or hearing about trauma is a sometimes powerful desire by others to come to the aid of victims and help ease victims' suffering (Bisson, McFarlane, & Rose, 2000a,b). I would add that oftentimes I am moved by the humane and caring response of many people in the immediate aftermath of traumatic events. In the wake of Hurricane Katrina in late summer of 2005, the public response was massive and intense, for example. Raphael and Dobson (2001), in discussing the various acute interventions that exist, state, "They [the interventions], are motivated as well by a powerful and altruistic human need to assist those who have been 'hurt' and to undo what has happened" (p. 139).

Bisson and colleagues (2000a) state that the implementation of acute interventions for PTSD is dependent on a "broad acceptance of a notion of collective responsibility and the value of group survival and care for individuals" (p. 40) and not particularly from a sound research, clinical, or theoretical foundation. This has led to, in some people's opinion, many well-meaning but misguided and ineffective attempts at acute intervention. However, according to Bisson and colleagues, the history of acute interventions reveals the existence of some coherent theoretical rationale. A model called the *PIE model* (proximity, immediacy, and expectancy), which was created and implemented in military and combat settings, is based on the theoretical premise that the sooner a soldier is treated for combat stress, the sooner he or she can be returned to the battlefield.

Other than our deep human need to respond to the traumatized, it is generally accepted that early or acute intervention is a necessary component of the continuum of mental health care because the pathological, long-term outcomes of PTSD are "pernicious and disabling across the lifespan" (Litz & Gray, 2004, p. 93). The interpersonal, familial, cultural, and societal costs are too high to rely solely on an after the fact, tertiary philosophy and approach to care.

An understanding of the issue of the timing of acute interventions is an important concept when considering offering help to those recently exposed to traumatic stress. When should someone offer help exactly? Neria and Solomon (1999) discuss the temporal aspects of posttrauma reactions, breaking the various reactions down into two large temporal groupings: *immediate* and *long-term*. At this point it is important to mention that we should always keep in mind that there are normal and expectable reactions to traumatic events that should not be considered pathological. The time frames for diagnoses are critical in making the distinction between normal responses and pathological ones. Immediate responses can include no response, no severe distress, manageable distress, Acute Stress Disorder, or a variety of subclinical manifestations of various symptoms and adjustment challenges. Long-term responses can include PTSD and the same range of responses seen in the immediate phase. These time frames are not only crucial in determining when to intervene but also serve to define the very purpose of acute intervention, which is to *prevent long-term disorder*. Each specific intervention method, technique, or program has goals within its system that are designed to accomplish this overarching goal.

Litz and Gray (2004) suggest that the timing of an intervention be dependent on the readiness and openness of the potential participant(s). They distinguish between an *immediate impact phase*, which involves acute arousal and distress and coping efforts, and an *acute phase*, which follows the immediate phase and is recommended as a better time for secondary prevention interventions. Survivors are simply not in a state to listen, learn, and engage during the immediate impact phase. Litz and Gray (2004, p. 94) determine the time frame for the immediate impact phase "to be from the time the person is objectively safe to two days posttrauma." They cite, consistent with recommendations from the American Red Cross, that mental health interventions be secondary to safety, security, and basic-needs provision and acquisition.

In keeping with the concept of appropriateness of intervention, Raphael and Dobson (2001) suggest the would-be helper consider the following issues before engaging in the acute-phase helping process:

1. Maintain respect for the trauma membrane that typically develops as a protective measure. Be careful not to puncture it and risk overwhelming the survivor.

2. Be aware of the dosing of affect and avoid pushing the survivor too hard, leading to decompensation.

3. Be sure to differentiate between trauma and grief issues.

4. Consider the option of forgetting and that "People must be allowed to handle things in their own way, at their own pace, in their own time, natural 'forgetting' may be the most normal of adaptations, even though all is not really forgotten, but rather set aside and moved on from" (p. 151).

5. Be aware of victim dynamics, and be careful not to reinforce this as the "most valued and sought after part of the individual" (p. 151).

6. Avoid focusing on the wrong trauma by determining through careful assessment and evaluation the role of the past and concurrent traumas and struggles with respect to the current trauma.

7. Be attentive to the issue of unmeetable needs that can arise or be reactivated by the current trauma. Consider the possibility that the current trauma may "open into [the] devastating emptiness or unmet needs, early deprivations, and few psychological resources" (p. 152). Be careful about what is discussed, uncovered, explored, and opened up.

8. Be cognizant of therapist issues of vicarious trauma and indulgence by respecting boundaries and maintaining awareness of countertransference issues.

Finally, before we get into discussing some of the specific acute intervention methods, the issue of *formal* versus *informal* acute intervention should be discussed. The very existence of acute interventions begs the question of their necessity. After witnessing or being made aware of traumatic events in my own personal life, I've often wondered what naturalistic or informal processes exist in the immediate aftermath of a traumatic event. After all, trauma workers haven't always been a part of our health care system, and there are certainly communities all over the world who have no idea of or access to trauma workers at any phase of the intervention process—acute, tertiary, or otherwise. In a small village in the Middle East, for example, what did the people say to or do for each other in the immediate aftermath of four young men falling victim to a suicide bomber's indiscriminant attack? The community response included dysfunction, numbing, solidarity, artistic memorial, increased political involvement, and increased participation in religious activities. Ursano, Fullerton, Vance, and Wang (2000) discuss the concept of *natural debriefing*, consisting of natural interpersonal exchanges between victims and significant others and connecting to their experiences with trauma. They identify several potential advantages of natural debriefing over formal debriefing, for example, saving of resources such as money and personnel, and state that it is often more readily available and continuous.

Lay Person Alert

Many people have asked me in casual settings what they should say or do for a trauma survivor in the immediate aftermath. Litz and Gray (2004) provide the following response to the question, "How should we respond?"

We would ask the person what he or she needed and empower that person to decide the kind of help he or she wanted. We would provide soothing comfort, respectful and well-timed physical touch (e.g., handholding, a hug), and we would do our best to remain calm. We would accurately convey the person's experiences and we would be extremely accepting and validating. We would emphasize that the person is not alone and that we are there to help him or her. We would provide information relevant to recovery, assist with problem solving, and seek professional assistance when necessary. We would work toward reducing stigma and shame. We would not be intrusive and we would not pressure the person to disclose what happened unless he or she felt the need to. At the other end of the continuum are recovery environments that are impoverished, punitive, blaming, demanding, anxious, and invalidating; features that create risk for chronic PTSD. (p. 95)

Crisis Intervention and Psychological First Aid

The period immediately following exposure to a traumatic stressor will sometimes constitute a crisis. A *crisis* consists of a state of temporary disorganization and a breakdown in an individual's ability to cope with customary needs. There can be a breakdown in adequate practical problem solving and difficulty perceiving and processing new information. There is a state of emotional disequilibrium.

Case Study—An Emotional Crisis

Tom, a 24-year-old man, called a friend of his at work and needed to meet him for lunch. There was an intense urgency in Tom's voice. He really needed to get together with his friend. Tom was on the verge of tears when he told his friend that he was in a car accident a few hours earlier after he left work. He left work because he was fired. Tom told his friend that he didn't take the news well and tore up some things in the office and stormed out of the building. He got into his car, and before he knew it, the only thing he was aware of was broadsiding another car at the traffic signal down the street. Tom was told by the responding police officer that he ran the red light. Tom was cited and let go. He called his friend.

This vignette demonstrates some of the key points of a crisis. A crisis can be precipitated by an experience of threat, loss, or overwhelming challenge. Reactions can range from disorganization to disequilibrium with feelings of being overwhelmed, ineffective, confused and thoughts fraught with catastrophizing. Feelings can range from rage to intense fear and panic. Our bodies can be severely tense or even fatigued, and we have an overall sense of being vulnerable. G. Caplan (1964) outlines the developmental process of an unfolding crisis in the following steps:

1. Rise in tension.

2. Activation of typical problem solving.

3. Failure of typical problem solving with continued impact of tension and stressor.

4. Feelings of ineffectuality.

5. More problem solving with either an averted crisis through the reduction of the threat, the application of new problem solving strategies, redefinition of the problem, or altering one's goals.

6. Breaking point and disorganization.

Mardi Horowitz (1976) provides a descriptive model of crisis resolution:

1. *Outcry* refers to the initial reactions at the time of the event.

2. *Denial* refers to the blocking of the impact of the event, including emotional numbing, not thinking about what happened, or structuring the event as if it did not occur.

3. *Intrusiveness* refers to an involuntary flooding of thoughts and feelings about the event.

4. *Working through* refers to the identification, expression, and airing of thoughts, feelings, and images.

5. *Completion* refers to the integration of the experience into one's life.

There are two levels of crisis intervention: *first order* and *second order*. First-order crisis intervention typically takes the form of *psychological first aid*, while second-order crisis intervention typically takes the form of crisis therapy. Crisis therapy is more long term and falls outside our focus on acute interventions for purposes of this chapter. Let's take a closer look at psychological first-aid.

Psychological first aid involves the provision of immediate assistance, usually within the immediate impact phase of a traumatic event, which includes providing support, reducing lethality or threat to life, and linking victims to helping resources. It is intended to be given by persons who first come in contact with a victim or survivor and usually in the physical place or location in which the problems first arise. The goal of providing support is important because it is better for people not to be alone when in crisis. The helper shares some of the burden, allows the person to talk, and allows feelings to be expressed without judgment.

The goal of reducing lethality aims at saving lives and preventing physical injury during a crisis. This may involve removing means to suicide, such as removing weapons. This may also involve arranging for the victim to spend time with a friend or significant other or even to initiate emergency hospitalization. Linking victims to helping resources involves pinpointing the critical needs of the victim and making appropriate referrals to some other helping agency or person. This can sometimes be a mental health provider or a more logistic-issue-oriented agency, such as the person's insurance company. These linkages can help a person begin to take concrete steps toward resolving their crisis for themselves. The overarching goals of psychological first aid are to facilitate the induction of a state of calm, organize and orient the victim, and stimulate the eventual self-directed problem-solving process. Successful psychological first aid helps get someone back on track before they get too far off the track. It is designed to facilitate the experience of empowerment.

Slaikeu (1990) identifies five steps in psychological first aid:

1. *Making psychological contact.* Allow the victim to feel heard, accepted, understood, and supported. This can be accomplished by inviting the person to talk, listening for facts and feelings, summarizing those facts and feelings and stating them back to the person, making empathic statements, and by remaining calm.

2. *Exploring the dimensions of the problem.* Gather information regarding his or her behavior, affects, bodily sensations, interpersonal functioning, thinking: the *who, what, where, when,* and *how* of the event(s). Inquire about resources, both internal and external, and assess for issues of lethality. It is also helpful to help the victim rank order his or her needs.

3. *Examine possible solutions.* Identify a range of alternative solutions and facilitate a sense of self-direction. Inquire about what he or she has planned to do or have done thus far. What can he or she do now? What are the alternatives available to the victim?

4. *Assist in taking concrete action.* Facilitate the taking of the next best step, being increasingly more directive as the situation requires but respecting the need for the individual to take charge of the situation for him- or herself. In situations of high lethality, direct control may need to be seized in order to prevent injury or the loss of life.

5. *Following-up with the victim.* This final step involves setting up a follow-up contact after the solutions have been attempted or enacted and inquire about the victim's experience of the aid provided to him or her. Did the victim feel heard and connected? Was lethality reduced? Was linkage achieved?

The empirical status of psychological first aid as an acute intervention for post-traumatic stress is not well established at this point in time. Bisson et al. (2000a, b) state that there is no existing evidence that psychological first aid specifically or crisis intervention more generally actually prevents PTSD. They do suggest, however, that these techniques are generally well received and have benefits in their own right in terms of reducing overall distress in the immediate aftermath of an event and are useful for "screening, education, and support" (p. 318).

Critical Incident Stress Debriefing (CISD)

There is an almost intuitive understanding amongst people that telling or talking about what happened in a traumatic event has healing power and qualities. This may very well be part of our natural response systems to traumatic stress that allow for the majority of us to never develop PTSD. The formal process of being allowed to do this, to be able to review what happened and attempt to make sense of an event or events, has come to be known as *psychological debriefing*. Raphael and Wilson (2000) state that debriefing is an attempt to facilitate this type of review.

Psychological debriefing as a formal mental health practice began as an intervention targeting emergency workers and military personnel. The impact on emergency personnel of working with trauma survivors and amidst the aftermath of a trauma, such as a natural disaster, fire, or airline crash, became a focus for the agencies these workers worked for and mental health professionals alike.

There are numerous forms of psychological debriefing, some with a focus on psychoeducation and others focused on catharsis. The most well-developed, researched, and widely used form of psychological debriefing was developed by Mitchell and Everly (2000) and is called *critical incident stress debriefing* (*CISD*). According to Litz and Gray (2004), CISD is so popular that the American Red Cross mandates its use when services are offered on the ground. Critical incident stress debriefing is considered only one component, however, of a larger systematic prevention program for emergency workers and personnel called *critical incident stress management* (*CISM*). Critical incident stress management includes CISD but also involves the prebriefing or psychological preparation before entering dangerous work, consultation, and longer-term facilitation of treatment and crisis management. Mitchell and Everly (2000) identify three main categories of CISM: (1) interventions for the individual (e.g., stress management education, on-scene support, and referrals for psychotherapy), (2) interventions for groups (e.g., preincident education and follow-up meetings), and (3) interventions for the environment (e.g., support for families, community outreach, and community education).

Mitchell's model of CISD has been adapted to specific groups and altered by many different practitioners, but at the core, each of these share the same common goals. Bisson et al. (2000a, b) and Mitchell and Everly (2000) identify the following goals and components of CISD:

Reduce initial distress.

Prevent the development of later psychological sequelae (e.g., PTSD).

Promote emotional processing through ventilation and normalization of reactions.

Prepare for future experiences.

Identify individuals who may need further treatment.

Avoid psychiatric labeling and emphasis on normalization.

Educate individuals about stress reactions and ways of coping adaptively with them.

Provide information and opportunities for further treatment.

Mitchell outlines CISD as consisting of a seven-phase model. It is usually offered to individuals and groups within 24 to 72 hours of a traumatic event (Mitchell & Everly, 2000). As was mentioned earlier, many adaptations have been made of the original Mitchell model. The following description of the seven-phase-model is based on an adaptation by Dyregrov (1989), as discussed in Bisson et al. (2000a, b).

1. *Introduction.* The purpose of the meeting is made explicit, it is to review and discuss the participants' reactions and come up with ways to adaptively cope with these. The debriefer establishes him- or herself as competent, and three rules are stated: (1) There is no obligation to talk about anything other than why they are there and what their role was in the event, (2) confidentiality is emphasized, and (3) the focus is on the impact and reactions to the event.

2. *Expectations and facts.* The details of the event are discussed without focusing on thoughts, feelings, or impressions. Participants are asked to discuss their expectations at this point.

3. *Thought and impressions.* Thoughts and impressions are then elicited with targeted questions with the goals of constructing a picture of the event, placing reactions into perspective or context, and facilitating the integration process. Focusing on the five senses is encouraged.

4. *Emotional reactions.* There is an attempt by the debriefer to facilitate the catharsis and emotional release process by asking questions about fear, helplessness, frustration, anger, or depression. Emotions felt since the event are also discussed.

5. *Normalization.* The survivor's reactions are normalized by the debriefer by stating that these are understandable, common, and normal reactions. The debriefer also educates about potential future symptoms and experiences, such as avoidance reactions, detachment, anhedonia, irritability, nightmares, or hypervigilance.

6. *Future planning and coping.* Methods and techniques for managing symptoms and difficulties are discussed with an emphasis on talking to supportive others and loved ones.

7. *Disengagement.* Suggestions are made if further help is needed, and participants are advised to consider getting more help if their symptoms persist for 4 to 6 weeks, if they increase, if there is disruption in family and occupational functioning, or if others comment on marked personality changes.

Although the steps outlined in the preceding appear to be straightforward and perhaps rather simple, CISD is a technical intervention, and it is recommended that those who wish to provide it be specifically trained and even certified in CISD provision. Also, as is the case with psychological first aid, ultimately, CISD and other forms of psychological debriefing have not been found to prevent PTSD in well-designed empirical studies. However, it is still considered a very beneficial program in helping reduce overall levels of distress and in education, screening, and support (Bisson et al., 2000a, b).

Summary

The prevention of PTSD is a noble and worthwhile pursuit. To date, no hard evidence exists that the current forms of formal intervention have lived up to the prevention challenge. However, these interventions are unarguably useful in their own right, and many trauma survivors welcome the help with varying degrees of enthusiasm. Some would prefer more naturalistic methods, and still others highly value the more formal ones. Ultimately, we may only be able to prevent PTSD by preventing traumatic events from happening. This makes civic involvement evermore important. This prediction, however, should not prevent us from seeking to ascertain and understand the critical components of what might constitute a real PTSD prevention intervention and improving the state of acute interventions based on such an understanding.

Quick Review

- Prevention in mental health exists in three forms: primary prevention, secondary prevention, and tertiary prevention.

- Prevention efforts with respect to PTSD are often characterized as acute prevention or treatment efforts that occur within a short time (usually within 48 hours or so) following a traumatic stressor.

- The desire by others to step in and respond to trauma survivors in the immediate aftermath is very common and seems to be part of a deeply humane social instinct.

- The purpose of acute interventions is to prevent long-term disorder.

- Acute interventions should occur within a window of opportunity that is not too early for the survivor to appreciate or benefit from but not too late that the disorder has emerged.

- Many, if not all, social systems have inherent, naturalistic mechanisms for responding to traumatized individuals in both the acute and long-term aftermath of a traumatic event.

- Crisis intervention and psychological first aid can be used to help restore equilibrium to an out-of-balance survivor and get them back on a self-directed track of coping.

- Critical incident stress debriefing is a useful and formalized acute intervention that focuses on helping survivors express themselves, normalizing survivor reactions, and facilitating connections to further help if necessary.

References

Bisson, J. I., McFarlane, A. C., & Rose, S. (2000a). Psychological debriefing. In E. B. Foa, T. M. Keane, & M. J. Friedman (Eds.), *Effective treatments for PTSD: Practice guidelines from the International Society for Traumatic Stress Studies* (pp. 39–59). New York: Guilford.

Bisson, J. I., McFarlane, A. C., & Rose, S. (2000b). Psychological debriefing. In E. B. Foa, T. M. Keane, & M. J. Friedman (Eds.), *Effective treatments for PTSD: Practice guidelines from the International Society for Traumatic Stress Studies* (pp. 317–319). New York: Guilford.

Caplan, G. (1964). *Principles of preventive psychiatry.* New York: Basic Books.

Dyregrov, A. (1989). Caring for helpers in disaster situations: Psychological debriefing. *Disaster Management, 2,* 25–30.

Horowitz, M. J. (1976). Diagnosis and treatment of stress response syndromes: General principles. In H. J. Parad, H. L. P. Resnik, & L. G. Parad (Eds.), *Emergency and disaster management.* (pp. 259–269). Bowie, MD: Charles Press.

Litz, B. T., & Gray, M. J. (2004). Early intervention for trauma in adults: A framework for first aid and secondary prevention. In B. T. Litz (Ed.), *Early intervention for trauma and traumatic loss* (pp. 87–111). New York: Guilford.

Mitchell, J. T., & Everly, G. S., Jr. (2000). Critical incident stress management and critical incident stress debriefings: Evolutions, effects and outcomes. In B. Raphael & J. P. Wilson (Eds.), *Psychological debriefing: Theory, practice and evidence* (pp. 71–90). New York: Cambridge University Press.

Neria, Y., & Solomon, Z. (1999). Prevention of posttraumatic reactions: Debriefing and frontline treatment. In P. A. Saigh & J. D. Bremner (Eds.), *Posttraumatic Stress Disorder: A comprehensive text* (pp. 309–326). Needham Heights, MA: Allyn & Bacon.

Raphael, B., & Dobson, M. (2001). Acute posttraumatic interventions. In J. P. Wilson, M. J. Friedman, & J. D. Lindy (Eds.), *Treating psychological trauma and PTSD* (pp. 139–158). New York: Guilford.

Raphael, B., & Wilson, J. P. (Eds.). (2000). *Psychological debriefing: Theory, practice and evidence.* New York: Cambridge University Press.

Slaikeu, K. A. (1990). *Crisis intervention: A handbook for practice and research* (2nd ed.). Needham Heights, MA: Allyn & Bacon.

Ursano, R. J., Fullerton, C. S., Vance, K., & Wang, L. (2000). Debriefing: Its role in the spectrum of prevention and acute management of psychological trauma. In B. Raphael & J. P. Wilson (Eds.), *Psychological debriefing: Theory, practice and evidence* (pp. 32–42). New York: Cambridge University Press.

CHAPTER 17

Specific Therapies for Specific Traumas and Adjunctive Treatments

M uch of the treatment discussed in previous chapters has been rather generic and relevant to the treatment of PTSD in general. But are all traumas and traumatic stressors created equal? To answer this question, one needs only to ask yet another question, "Are all patient's the same?" Certainly not. The development and use of specific treatments for specific types of trauma (e.g., sexual assault, disasters, or combat-PTSD) is the product of at least two phenomena, basic pragmatics of clinical theory and research and the expanding sophistication of clinical science in the mental health field. In order to develop a sound study to test the effectiveness of a particular treatment, the more specific and targeted the population and sample, the better a study will be on methodological and statistical grounds. It is easier to develop a model and a treatment protocol for a small, more circumscribed treatment sample than for an entire population. Further, once such a study is developed and (hopefully) validated, the issue of generalizability comes into play. For example, if I want to develop and test a treatment for test taking anxiety, I might begin by focusing on just prospective college students taking the SAT. If the intervention is effective, I must test the protocol with different samples before I can claim it is relevant to the entire test-taker population. So specific therapies for specific trauma groups are a matter of methodological pragmatics.

Another reason that specific therapies for specific traumas are utilized is the growing scientific sophistication of both clinical research and clinical practice. Many professionals advocate the use of empirically supported treatments as the only way to practice ethically and effectively. As was just discussed, this is going to result in clinicians' having to use more circumscribed treatments for more specific populations, and clinical phenomena as these are the treatments being

Student Alert

Looking back on my training as a psychologist, I realize that one area that was sorely lacking was specific training in clinical method. Sure, we all got training in how to conduct a clinical intake, how to do a history, how to administer and interpret psychological testing, how to diagnose, and even how to treat. "What more is there?," you might ask. Clinical method refers to your specific approach to clinical problem solving and the management of clinical issues beyond the disorder you are treating. Clinical problem solving is sometimes referred to as clinical cognition or expert cognition. Management of clinical issues includes managing such things as informed consent, how to write a child custody report, when to intervene in an emergency, when *not* to treat, and so on. These nuances of clinical practice get learned over the years through experience. I only mention these here because as students, we often seek this kind of guidance only to find we have to learn it on our own. Don't lose faith, though. An important remedy to this problem is to find a good professional mentor or two and study their every move. Don't be afraid to ask stupid questions. Eventually, you'll develop a clinical method and approach that works best for you.

---

put to the empirical test. I also believe, however, that as our clinical science evolves, our ability to utilize prescriptive treatments will grow. I see the one-size-fits-all approach to psychotherapy, for example, as clinical science in a less-developed and earlier stage of professional and paradigmatic development. Theoretically, at least, as we become more sophisticated diagnostically, in research, and in application, we can't help but be more specific in our treatment approaches. This is not to say that there is not a place for more broad and generic approaches to treatment. In fact, I believe it is possible that treatment research will show these one-size-fits-all treatments to be as effective or more so than more prescriptive treatments. However, in the words of one of my favorite professors, "That is an empirical question," and only time will tell.

As far as adjunct treatments are concerned, most clinicians know from experience that client difficulties are often so multifaceted and layered that the use of adjunctive treatments is an absolute necessity. It is just good clinical practice.

Child Abuse

Working with children with PTSD as a consequence of physical or sexual abuse is extremely challenging from a number of perspectives, including technical, emotional, ethical, and moral. It is certainly a test of a clinician's level of knowledge and skill. Working with children is a specialty in and of itself, and working with abused children with posttraumatic syndromes is certainly a subspecialty.

William Friedrich (1996) proposes an integrated treatment model for abused children with a focus on three biopsychosocial domains: attachment, behavioral and emotional regulation, and self-concept, each representing a different component and focus in treatment. This model includes trauma theory and PTSD as foundational constructs used to explain symptoms but is also attentive to contextual, developmental, and familial factors in a child's pathology. A quick note about the concept of *abuse;* this section will refer to abuse as either physical or sexual and not to psychological abuse, emotional abuse, or neglect.

Research has substantiated that child abuse can result in impaired attachment in children as manifested by boundary problems in relationships, poor social skills, recapitulation of victim or victimizer behavior in relationships, distrust of others, and the sexualizing of relationships (Friedrich, 1996). From this integrated approach, treatment of attachment issues within this context requires the formation of a solid therapeutic alliance. Different children's attachment histories will manifest and play out differently within the context of the therapist-child relationship and require different responses from the therapist. For example, children with a disorganized attachment requires clear and firm boundaries on the part of the therapist in order to tolerate, absorb or contain, and redirect such children's dependency and "physical proximity-seeking" (Friedrich, 1996, p. 108). It is crucial to help establish a secure-base as trauma in this population is partially understood as either a failure to properly develop or destruction or violation of a child's secure base. Groups and family interventions are also suggested for attachment-related dysfunction.

Interventions for the second component, behavioral and emotional regulation and dysregulation, begin with a characterization of the child's abilities in this area. Katz and Gottman (1991) outline four important behavior and emotion regulation skills:

1. The ability to inhibit inappropriate behaviors related to strong negative or positive affects.

2. The ability to self-soothe and reduce physiological arousal related to strong affects.

3. The ability to focus attention.

4. The ability to organize behavior and psychological functions for coordinated action in the service of an external goal.

Common symptoms of emotional dysregulation include anxiety, sleep difficulties, regression, and inattentiveness. Treatment for dysregulation deficits generally involves predictability and structure. Friedrich (1996) makes the creative suggestions that therapists and children can schedule when they talk about specific victimization experiences or they may develop a code word or phrase of sorts to discuss the abuse that is easier to use. Psychoeducation can be helpful and is considered of sufficiently low-intensity and is nonarousing, per se. Another unique technique suggested by Friedrich is to use the *as-if approach* in which the child talks to the therapist as if the trauma happened to someone else or as if they were offering advice on how to help another child. Anxiety reduction techniques such as autogenic training can be taught as well.

Finally, alterations in self-concept or self-perception require treatment to focus on techniques that "help children connect to immature and inaccurate self-perceptions that they hold" (Friedrich, 1996, p. 113). Initially, the focus may be on identifying and understanding feelings and emotions followed by activities and techniques designed to boost self-efficacy and a sense of competency, sometimes referred to as *mastery tasks*. Michael White suggests a technique called *externalizing the problem* in which the child learns to talk *about* him- or herself instead of *as* him- or herself. Finally, various cognitive techniques are used to address distorted cognitions.

Rape and Sexual Assault

Edna Foa and Barbara Olasov Rothbaum (1988) outline a comprehensive cognitive-behavioral treatment (CBT) approach to PTSD from rape and sexual assault. Earlier analyses of posttraumatic reactions to rape have been referred to as *rape trauma syndrome* (Burgess & Holmstrom, 1974). Foa and Rothbaum outline these common affective and functional sequelae to rape in addition to PTSD core symptoms:

Anxiety: intense fears of rape-related situations and generalized anxiety

Depression: may be more common than in victims of other forms of crime

Anger

Dissociation

Social problems: restricted social life, activities, marital problems, and family problems

Sexual problems: considered common: decreased sexual satisfaction, decreased arousal and desire, and sometimes total avoidance of sex

Foa and Rothbaum (1998) suggest the use of general CBT techniques, including imaginal exposure, in vivo exposure, breathing retraining, cognitive restructuring, thought stopping, guided self-dialogue, deep muscle differential relaxation, and covert modeling and role playing. They mention some important treatment considerations for rape trauma victims that are critical to address. They begin by warning that rape victims are particularly and extremely avoidant, and if this issue is left unaddressed, it may significantly interfere with treatment. Suggestions for dealing with these high levels of avoidance include validation of the client's feelings, perhaps allowing for more cancellations and support clients when they do avoid treatment as a way to get them to come in for treatment. A supportive attitude and understanding is critical. Another complicating factor is that unlike with Panic Disorder and many other phobias, the fears and anxieties that a rape victim often feels are "strongly rooted in reality" (Foa & Rothbaum, 1998, p. 95).

Clinician Alert

Foa and Rothbaum (1998) suggest the following therapeutic do's (as opposed to don'ts):

- Do be active and directive in encouraging the client to attend to sensations, comply with therapeutic instructions, learn new skills, and practice them during homework.

- Do be supportive and sensitive when your client confronts assault-related memories, feelings, and thoughts about her assault.

- Do remember that the treatments programs are time limited. However, if a client needs further help, it is important that you help her to find appropriate resources or continue to work with her yourself.

It is important to assess the reality of a patient's fears when constructing the in vivo hierarchy. However, it is also important to not get into the crystal ball game and try to determine which situations may be potentially safe versus dangerous in an absolute sense, but, instead, determinations should be based on the concept of an "acceptable level of risk" (p. 96) for the client's anxiety tolerance. Foa and Rothbaum warn that it can be difficult to use cognitive techniques for distorted cognitions regarding danger when they are connected to actual events. Some situations are clearly safe, and others are more ambiguous. The clinician should engage in open and frequent discussions about this issue.

Three treatment schedules are outlined for rape trauma treatment: (1) a prolonged exposure (PE) protocol, (2) a PE protocol with cognitive restructuring, and (3) a PE protocol with stress-inoculation training (SIT). Each of these are similar in structure and form to prolonged exposure, cognitive restructuring, and SIT used with other disorders with some specific alterations and additions relative to rape and sexual assault. For example, in all of the schedules, pretreatment assessment should proceed with the assault information and history interview in order to obtain specifics relevant to structuring treatment. Handouts are typically used in CBT treatment. Foa and Rothbaum (1998) recommend using the handout or information pamphlet *Common Reactions to Assault* as part of the patient education materials.

The PE alone schedule is recommended as a first-line approach, particularly for uncomplicated PTSD as opposed to complex PTSD. The PE plus cognitive restructuring schedule is suggested for patients who have both anxiety and a significant amount of guilt, shame, and debilitating anger. Dealing with negative automatic thoughts, dysfunctional beliefs, and cognitive distortions is an integral part of this approach, and Foa and Rothbaum (1998) suggest the use of a client–self-report daily diary as a means to record cognitive components. This provides a ready list of specific cognitions that are particularly relevant to the

Professional, Student, and Lay-Person Alert

I believe that this issue of generic cognitive distortions is extremely important when approaching treatment from a CBT perspective. In my experience, some potential therapy clients have a negative reaction to what they feel is a cookbook form of therapy in CBT. Of course, this is an arguable point, but the empirical validity and efficacy of CBT is well established in the literature. However, whether it is an effective treatment is often not the point for prospective patients or patients in the early stages of treatment. Posttraumatic Stress Disorder patients may be sensitive to feeling dehumanized, and these potential reactions must be factored in and discussed early on in treatment if they become apparent. Some professionals, too, have this reaction to CBT techniques as it seems to violate some of their schemas and scripts for what therapy or treatment should look like and feel like. Cognitive-behavioral therapy works; however, getting it into place and getting patients to buy in can be extremely difficult. I have seen effective practitioners of CBT who were as warm and nondehumanizing as anyone in the field. But it is important to keep in mind that a professional can be extremely warm and accepting but be using an ineffective treatment approach. It is also important to not fall into a cognitive distortion of our own when thinking about CBT. It is effective, and many well-trained, supportive, and empathic professionals have been able to help patients get better and feel better using this approach. As patients and consumers, we must not make the mistake of confusing the order and structure of CBT with coldness and lack of empathy. As professionals, we must not let the order and structure of CBT overshadow the basic clinical skills of empathy and support and get caught hiding behind technique.

client and not just generic cognitive distortions. Finally, Roa and Rothbaum suggest the PE and SIT combined approach for patients who are dealing with very high levels of arousal, feelings of being out of control, and who are extremely hesitant to engage in exposure. Stress-inoculation therapy is suggested as a means to help the patient gain a sense of control before exposure proceeds.

Motor Vehicle Accidents

For those people who have ever been involved in a motor vehicle accident, you know what I mean when I say the sounds of twisting metal, shattering glass, and screeching tires and brakes are like no others. Together they form a perceptual conglomerate that can be firmly stamped into our memories and difficult to get out. They represent a soundtrack of trauma for those persons traumatized from being in an automobile accident, the way explosions, screams, and gunshots may represent the soundtrack for combat trauma. Even as I write this, I have images, though not intrusive, per se, of my own car accidents; shamefully, there have been a few too many. Posttraumatic Stress Disorder can develop in a certain percentage of car accident victims. Laurence Miller (1998) depicts the posttraumatic experience for car accident survivors quite well in the following description:

> [A] survivor of a serious motor vehicle accident may be afraid to ride in cars or may be such a jittery passenger that she becomes a pest to drive around with. She may develop a paralyzing preoccupation with physical symptoms or injuries result-ing from the accident. She may suffer headaches and other aches and pain, even when no physical injury has occurred. Anxieties, irritability, and depression are common. She may be unable to read or watch stories of traffic accidents, hear traffic reports on the radio, or even tolerate automobile commercials on TV. Phobias to particular mod-els of cars involved in the accident may develop, even to colors that remind her of the vehicles. Some patients develop a curious perceptual distortion in which cars or street corners appear closer then they actually are. The usual posttraumatic stress reac-tions of intrusive recollection and emotional numbing are typically seen. (p. 122)

Miller (1998, p. 122) cites that some estimates are as high as one-third of car drivers who have been involved in an accident with a fatality suffer "persistent psychological aftereffects," including PTSD. One study showed that nearly 50 percent of car accident victims who sought medical treatment met criteria for PTSD (Blanchard et al., 1994). An important caveat to this is that these same individuals were found to have a history of prior trauma and a significant per-centage of PTSD diagnoses from prior trauma. This group also had higher rates of prior depression. Blanchard et al. (1994) found that for some victims, avoid-ance and numbing symptoms fade after a 6-month period, but hyperarousal is more persistent.

Most, if not all, of us depend on cars and automobiles in one form or another to get to work, pick up our children, and go to the grocery store. Few of us rely on trains or other nonautomobile forms of transportation to the extent that we rely on cars, buses, and trucks. The fact is, the economy of the United States, and the world for that matter, depends heavily on automobiles. Being able to drive or ride in a car is a near absolute requirement for modern survival. If someone cannot, they cannot function. I don't believe that it is being dramatic to state that with so much riding (pardon the pun) on being able to travel in an automo-bile, treatment of motor vehicle accident–related PTSD (MVA-PTSD) is of vital importance.

Miller (1998) discusses various treatment approaches to MVA-PTSD. Therapy may vary in length from a few sessions to months. Miller cites the work of Best and Ribbe (1995), who recommend that treatment should begin with patient edu-cation, followed by a treatment phase that focuses on physical symptoms, then cognitive symptoms, then behavioral symptoms. Best and Ribbe make several general treatment recommendations for MVA-PTSD sufferers. During evaluation and assessment, it may be important to simply and in a straightforward manner ask the patient if they believed they might have died. They also suggest that in addition to structured and directive treatment, simply letting the patient tell his or her story has vital assessment and therapeutic value.

Miller (1998) outlines three areas for treatment: (1) reducing arousal, (2) cognitive-behavioral therapy, and (3) exposure therapy. Deep muscle relaxation, systematic desensitization, and cure-controlled breathing are common and useful techniques. Among the cognitive-behavioral modalities, Albert Ellis's rational-emotive therapy is considered specifically useful for accident survivors (Best & Ribbe, 1995) because of its focus on cognitions of fairness, causality, and control. Other more specific CBT techniques, including cognitive restructuring, thought stopping, and role playing, are also suggested. Finally, exposure therapy using in vivo exposure procedures have been found to be especially helpful for MVA-PTSD. If patients are particularly fixed on fears of injury, imaginal flooding may be used to augment in vivo procedures. Kuch (1989) suggests that when the victim is particularly avoidant of driving, exposure techniques as a passenger may have to be done first. Kuch also recommends beginning the exposure hierarchy with practicing in empty parking lots, on deserted or country roads, or even in an idling car and then moving on to more intense and involved driving experiences.

Anger and Trauma

I don't believe it is overstating to say that *anger* is a relatively neglected concept in mental health research and practice. Consider the existence of literally hundreds of professional books on depression and only a handful on anger. Two classes of emotional disorders occupy a large portion of the *DSM-IV-TR*, depression (sadness) and anxiety (fear), but where are the anger disorders? They're not in there! I find the seeming lack of recognition of anger as a clinical issue odd, given that crimes related to anger, such as murder and assault, are quite common, some may say of epidemic proportions in our society. Anger in and of itself is not problematic; after all, it is just an emotion. This is true to some degree. Anger can have negative health consequences if it persists and is consuming in an individual's life. Anger in action can lead to aggressive behavior and violence.

Anger can come from many sources, one such source is being severely hurt or injured by another person, in other words, from trauma. Discussions of anger and its amelioration relative to PTSD are as few and far between as their relative invisibility in the clinical literature at large. However, anger can be an integral part of an individual's PTSD presentation and should, therefore, be an integral part of treatment as well.

According the Novaco and Chemtob (1998), anger in PTSD is part of the arousal symptom cluster in the *DSM-IV-TR* criteria. Anger can manifest in patients in the following ways:

Hostility in relationships

Explosive irritability and rage

Becoming easily aroused to anger (Kardiner & Spiegel, 1947)

Verbal altercations

Physical fights and reactive aggression

Violent and revengeful fantasies and dreams

Distrust of authority figures

Few close friends

Estrangement from society

Estrangement from family

Rage at the source and rage at those exempt (Krupnick & Horowitz, 1981)

Novaco and Chemtob (1998, p. 167) provide a model for anger that serves as the foundation for treatment. From their perspective, anger can be adaptive in mobilizing corrective action in coping with threat, adversity, and situations requiring "perseverance in overcoming obstacles." Anger control is important in preventing aggressive action. Anger control is also important for sound decision making because anger can oftentimes interfere with information processing. There is no one-to-one correspondence between anger and aggression because the expression of aggressive behavior is multiply determined, by both internal (biological and psychological) and external forces. Important control factors include external restraints, expectations of punishment, or empathy. However, inhibitory factors can be overridden by heightened arousal, aggressive modeling, lowered probability of punishment, biochemical agents (e.g., drugs or alcohol), and environmental cues (Novaco & Chemtob, 1998). Ultimately, reducing anger arousal specifically and arousal in general is likely to reduce aggression. Novaco and Chemtob cite the work of Albert Bandura, who "asserts that anger can be self-generated by provocative thoughts, it can be inferred that changes in cognitive meaning systems and in rumination would be expected to have a regulatory effect on anger" (Novaco & Chemtob, 1998, p. 168).

Anger in PTSD is considered part of the dyscontrol syndrome of PTSD and part of the "context-inappropriate activation of 'survival mode' functioning" in PTSD. That is, in PTSD, this survival mode functioning is inappropriately and sometimes indiscriminately active, which leads to overarousal in multiple emotional systems, particularly fear and anger, because of the relevance of these two emotions to survival and engaging and coping with threat.

According to Novaco and Chemtob (1998), angry patients can present a problem in a number of ways. They can be resistant to treatment and hostile to staff and the therapist. They may also represent potential dangers to the therapist. Certain precautions may have to be undertaken if this is the case. Angry clients may also have very low levels of frustration tolerance. This can make progress through an exposure hierarchy particularly problematic.

Adjunctive treatment of anger in PTSD can be approached from a cognitive-behavioral perspective (Novaco & Chemtob, 1998). The features of that treatment are as follows:

1. Client education about anger, stress, and aggression.

2. Self-monitoring of anger frequency, intensity, and situational triggers.

3. Construction of a personal anger provocation hierarchy, created from the self-monitoring data and used for the practice and testing of coping skills.

4. Arousal reduction techniques of progressive muscle relaxation, breathing-focused relaxation, and guided imagery training.

5. Cognitive restructuring by altering attentional focus, modifying appraisals, and using self-instruction.

6. Training behavioral coping in communication and respectful assertiveness as modeled and rehearsed with the therapist.

7. Practicing the cognitive, arousal regulatory, and behavioral coping skills while visualizing and role playing progressively more intense, anger-arousing scenes from the personal hierarchies.

A final and important note on the provocation component of this treatment program needs to quickly be made. Novaco and Chemtob (1998) state that provocation exposure should be done in an imaginal format, or perhaps in a role-play format, for safety reasons. We can't have our patients picking fights with people for therapeutic purposes after all.

Medical Traumatic Stress

Trauma researchers and practitioners, within the last few years, are more widely acknowledging the concept of *medical traumatic stress*, defined as the development of PTSD symptoms in relation to life-threatening illness, injury, or medical procedures, treatment, or intervention. Most of the work has been done with children, with focus on very serious medical procedures and illnesses, such as organ transplants and cancer. This is in part because of their life-threatening potential. The remainder of this section will focus on pediatric or child medical traumatic stress (M-PTSD).

Some risk factors for developing M-PTSD include perception of threat to life and the intensity of a particular treatment or intervention. The more invasive and dangerous a procedure is, the more potential there is for M-PTSD. Burn injury has been associated with an increased risk of M-PTSD (Stoddard, Norman, Murphy, & Beardslee, 1989), in part because of the often horrendous pain involved. Laurence Miller talks about the concept of *traumatic pain*, for instance. Pollin (1995) and Koocher and Pollin (1995) discuss the use of the *medical crisis counseling model* in addressing the emotional complications in children and families secondary to traumatic injury or illness. They suggest focusing on eight critical issues that arise for children and families for intervention: loss of control, loss of self-image, dependency, stigma, abandonment, fear of expressing anger, isolation, and fear of death.

Bronfman, Biron, Campis, and Koocher (1998) focus on event-related traumatic injury treatment. Initially, the focus should be on helping the child (and families) review what happened and tell the story. It is important to facilitate a recounting of what led up to injury and afterward. These authors warn to be careful not to communicate to the child not to talk about it and to be sensitive to the child's ability to tolerate arousal and emotion. Be careful not to push too hard, but also be supportive enough to push just enough. The next step in treatment involves helping the child explore his or her physical sensations and perceptions of the event (what did they see, hear, smell, etc.). This can help elicit a more complete and vivid recounting and assist in deeper processing and integration of oftentimes fragmented percepts. Next, therapist and child should engage in exploration of his or her trauma related beliefs. Bronfman and colleagues suggest the clinician "support the children's efforts to make sense of what happened to them, including their frequent attempts to formulate a plan that would have, or could in the future, prevent such an event from recurring" (p. 4).

The fourth step involves the use of drawing and play therapy as methods to help organize a child's experience, which can be less threatening than talking. The fifth step is to explain the medical interventions in sufficient detail and to reassure the child about his or her ability to cope with any procedure, reinforcing that the purpose of any procedure is to help and not to punish, a belief that some children may hold. Provide clear and accurate information in a developmentally appropriate language and format. Finally, Bronfman and colleagues (1998) suggest the clinician assist parents in managing their own affect related to the event and subsequent injury as some parents may neglect themselves and focus exclusively on the child. This can be detrimental as parents may lose sight of their own well-being and serve as poor models for courage, self-care, and confidence. It is important to help parents avoid overwhelming the children with their own fears.

Summary

As clinical science in mental health becomes more sophisticated, specific treatments are developed for more targeted populations, problems, and disorders. Although clinical research often shows that broad-based therapies in general, such as CBT or interpersonal psychotherapy, are effective in a wide range of applications, it is important to pursue the development of specific therapies for specific clinical problems. Adjunctive therapies, too, are a vital part of many effective treatment regimens. Ultimately, as empirically based practice guides professional work, knowledge of specific treatments becomes more and more important.

Quick Review

- Friedrich (1996) proposes an integrated model of treatment for trauma in physically and sexually abused children, including focusing on attachment, behavioral and emotional dysregulation, and disturbances in self-concept.

- Foa and Rothbaum (1998) developed a comprehensive CBT-based treatment for rape survivors that includes imaginal exposure, in vivo exposure, breathing retraining, cognitive restructuring, thought stopping, guided self-dialogue, deep muscle differential relaxation, and covert modeling and role playing.

- Miller (1998) outlines three areas for treatment of motor vehicle related trauma: (1) reducing arousal, (2) cognitive-behavioral therapy, and (3) exposure therapy.

- Adjunctive treatment of anger in PTSD can be approached from a cognitive-behavioral perspective. Novaco and Chemtob (1998) propose a CBT model for treatment of anger in PTSD that includes education, self-monitoring, provocation exposure, and cognitive restructuring components.

- Bronfman, Biron, Campis, and Koocher (1998) focus on event-related traumatic injury treatment in cases of medical traumatic stress, with a six-step model, including reviewing the episode, processing sensations, exploring beliefs, drawing and playing, educating, and assisting parents.

References

Best, C. L., & Ribbe, D. P. (1995). Accidental injury: Approaches to assessment and treatment. In J. R. Freedy & S. E. Hobfoll (Eds.), *Traumatic stress: From theory to practice* (pp. 315–337). New York: Plenum Press.

Blanchard, E. B., Hickling, E. J., Taylor, A. E., Loos, W. R., et al. (1994). Psychological morbidity associated with motor vehicle accidents. *Behaviour Research and Therapy, 32,* 283–290.

Bronfman, E. T., Biron Campis, L., & Koocher, G. P. (1998). Helping children to cope: Clinical issues for acutely injured and medically traumatized children. *Professional Psychology: Research and Practice, 29,* 574–581.

Burgess, A. W., & Holmstrom, L. L. (1974). Rape trauma syndrome. *American Journal of Psychiatry, 131,* 981–986.

Foa, E. B., & Rothbaum, B. O. (1998). *Treating the trauma of rape: Cognitive-behavioral therapy for PTSD.* New York: Guilford.

Friedrich, W. N. (1996). An integrated model of psychotherapy for abused children. In J. Briere, L. Berliner, J. A. Bulkley, C. Jenny, & T. Reid (Eds.), *The APSAC handbook on child maltreatment* (pp. 104–118). Thousand Oaks, CA: Sage.

Kardiner, A,. & Spiegel, H. (1947). *War stress and neurotic illness.* New York: Paul B. Hoeber.

Katz, L. F., & Gottman, J. M. (1991). Marital discord and child outcomes: A social psychophysiological approach. In J. Garber & K. A. Dodge (Eds.), *The development of emotion regulation and dysregulation* (pp. 129–155). New York: Cambridge University Press.

Koocher, G. P., & & Pollin, I. (1995). Medical crisis counseling: A new service delivery model. *Journal of Clinical Psychology in Medical Settings, 1,* 292–299.

Krupnick, J. L., & Horowitz, M. J. (1981). Stress response syndromes: Recurrent themes. *Archives of General Psychiatry, 38,* 428–435.

Kuch, K. (1989). Treatment of post-traumatic phobias and PTSD after car accidents. In P. A. Keller & S. R. Heyman (Eds.), *Innovations in clinical practice: A source book* (Vol. 8., pp. 263–270). Sarasota, FL: Professional Resource Exchange.

Miller, L. (1998). *Psychotherapy of traumatic disability syndromes—Shocks to the system.* New York: W. W. Norton.

Novaco, R. W., & Chemtob, C. M. (1998). Anger and trauma: Conceptualization, assessment, and treatment. In V. M. Follette, J. I. Ruzek, & F. R. Abueg (Eds.), *Cognitive-behavioral therapies for trauma* (pp. 162–190). New York: Guilford.

Pollin, I. (1995). *Medical crisis counseling: Short-term therapy for long-term illness.* New York: W. W. Norton.

Stoddard, F. J., Norman, D. K., Murphy, J. M., & Beardslee, W. R. (1989). Psychiatric outcome of burned children and adolescents. *Journal of the American Academy of Child & Adolescent Psychiatry, 28,* 589–595.

White, M. (1989). The externalizing of the problem and the re-authoring of lives and relationships. *Dulwich Centre Newsletter,* Summer, 3–20.

Special Sections

THE WILEY
CONCISE GUIDES
TO MENTAL HEALTH

Posttraumatic Stress Disorder

CHAPTER 18

Future Research Directions and the Cutting Edge

A t the end of virtually every research article in psychology and psychiatry is a section named, "Issues in Need of Further Investigation" or "Future Directions." It is intended to outline what the study or article failed to do to the author's satisfaction and leaves room for what particulars need to be addressed further. One of the main features of science is that it progresses, with scientists building on and adding to the findings of those who came before them. Although it appears to take steps backward, science keeps moving forward. The fields of traumatology and PTSD theory and research are no exception to this ever-moving force within science. The history of PTSD reflects an evermore sophisticated, complex, and widening breadth of understanding of the etiology, assessment, and treatment of traumatic stress disorders and syndromes. The majority of this book has been about the current state of affairs in the field of PTSD studies. Let's take a look at where we've been heading and what the future might bring.

Understanding and Mining the Trends

In setting out to develop this chapter, I had to engage in a little bit of a crystal ball exercise of sorts. Well, that might sound a little too unscientific or systematic. How exactly can the trends and future of PTSD studies be spotted? I will confess that I make no claim to being a visionary. In fact, my method for trying to figure out where the field is going was quite simple and tedious. It was also systematic, however.

The methodology used to develop the details of this chapter involved a comprehensive search of the mental health literature in basic research, clinical practice, and developing theory. Some refer to this method as *bibliometric*. The following is a list of data sources used:

- PsycINFO database from the American Psychological Association
- PILOTS database from the National Center for Post-traumatic Stress Disorder
- *National Center for PTSD Research Quarterly* from the National Center for Post-Traumatic Stress Disorder
- *National Center for PTSD Clinical Quarterly* from the National Center for Post-Traumatic Stress Disorder
- Publications of the American Psychiatric Association
- Internet search using Google search engine

Each of the relevant databases was examined between the years 2003 and 2005 in order to represent the most recent state of the field. Also, rather than simply list or present the various articles, I have attempted to glean the general trend from each and attempted to group various studies into such trends and directions.

Important General Societal Trends

There are several prominent trends in the mental health field that in many ways reflect trends in society, culture, and the world in general. These include globalization, increasing diversity, advances in technology and information science, changes in social arrangements and communication, and interdisciplinary and integrated approaches in the advancement of knowledge (including science, humanities, and business).

The globalization of the planet is a direction that mental health researchers and professionals must inevitably contend with. The world is becoming smaller through advanced technology in travel and communication. National and ethnic identities are seemingly in flux and are becoming more and more salient. The diversity of the planet is modeled on a microlevel in ways that history has never quite seen. Cultural and ethnic diversity forces scientists to address the cultural boundedness of their work. After all, if a particular theory or finding is not applicable across groups, its universality is certainly suspect.

Although not a topic most people like to think about when looking forward into the future, the issue of health insurance and access to health care, particularly mental health care, is a critical feature of our future. Although the economies of the world and the United States continue to grow and the material wealth of many millions around the world is unprecedented, there still remain millions and millions of people across the planet who do not have adequate access to health care, and, if they do have access, it can be severely limited by one's ability to pay for it. It is a particular shame for the mental health field to continue to develop better and better treatments only to have them available to a select few people. Certainly, the future of mental health care must include a solution to this growing problem.

There is exponential growth in the development and dissemination of knowledge. This is due in no small part to the Internet and the World Wide Web. Make no mistake about it, ignoring the massive growth in knowledge through the proliferation of information technology and information science would place future knowledge seekers in the Stone Age. The digital age and its high-speed, high-volume production of knowledge is the future. However, I feel I must make one editorial point about this fact. I have great concerns regarding this massive growth of information with regard to its actual availability to the masses, how it is critically analyzed, and the extent to which it serves a pragmatic purpose. The practitioner in me is always looking for the application and usefulness of the information being produced. The skeptic in me is always looking for how this information can either harm or benefit people in general.

A final trend worth mentioning is an informal but definite movement across the various sciences that can be referred to as a movement toward *unification in science*. The trend in many disciplines is to cross disciplinary lines and work from any number of approaches to address common problems. The field of PTSD research and practice, in fact, represents this trend quite well. Work on PTSD includes players from medicine, neuroscience, psychobiology, biology, psychology, social work, and even political science. This is an exciting trend in many ways as one might imagine that the academic institution of 10 to 20 years from now might have very different majors than it does now (e.g., neurophilosophy, computer psychology, or cyborg robotics).

Before we go into some specific trends with PTSD, the following quick list of hot and emergent topics in mental health, psychiatry, and psychology might be of interest:

- Ethnopsychology, ethnopsychiatry, ethnobiology, and ethnopharmacology
- Service delivery methods, such as the Internet and Telehealth
- Increasing focus on prevention and public education and public policy
- Increasing prominence of neuroscience in research and treatment
- Increasing prominence of genetics in research
- Increasing awareness of developmental progression and related issues
- Addressing religion and spirituality
- Alternative treatments
- Focus on special populations, such as children, the elderly, and differing sexual orientations
- Disparities in care
- Culture-bound syndromes

- International collaboration and proliferation of knowledge
- Culturally relevant and fair assessment, diagnosis, and treatment
- Contextual and interpretive psychology (e.g., postmodernism)
- New statistical techniques and publication of negative findings
- Terrorism and violence
- Forensic and legal applications
- Positive psychology and the psychology of human strengths and virtues
- Use of technology in practice

Future Directions with PTSD

In reviewing the database PsycINFO just for the last 2 years, I found that well over 1,200 journal publications were found. In just 2005, well over 300 publications were found. These numbers represent a staggering amount of work being done on PTSD. If one was to predict the next big thing in the field, it might be reading and consuming the massive amounts of information being produced. Emerging trends and current research directions ascertained from PsycINFO for the year 2005 include the following:

- Focus on the elderly
- Development of more broad-based, eclectic, and integrated therapies
- Exploration of the relationship between PTSD and various health problems, including fibromyalgia, human immunodeficiency virus (HIV) or acquired immunodeficiency syndrome (AIDS), and severe acute respiratory syndrome (SARS)
- Terrorism and PTSD
- Alternative therapies, such as mindfulness and acceptance and commitment therapy
- Telehealth
- Issues of treatment adherence
- Neurofeedback treatment of PTSD

The American Psychiatric Association is in the process of developing the newest version of their *Diagnostic and Statistical Manual of Mental Disorders* (*DSM*), the *Diagnostic and Statistical Manual of Mental Disorders,* fifth edition (*DSM-V*). The process has begun with the development of several white papers outlining the research agenda for the various teams or workgroups that will eventually come together to decide what the *DSM-V* should consist of. Part of this process has included the development of diagnosis-related research conferences, one of which is the Stress-Induced and Fear Circuitry Disorder Conference. The following is a list of directions and relevant issues produced by the participants that are not redundant with the preceding PsycINFO list:

- Addressing the inclusiveness or exclusiveness of the PTSD diagnostic criteria
- Subsyndromal PTSD
- Complex PTSD
- Cross-cultural variability of PTSD
- The importance or nonimportance of structural brain abnormalities
- Focus on resilience and vulnerability factors
- The connection between childhood Anxiety Disorder and later adult manifestations
- Genetic issues
- Classification of the disorder by neurological or cognitive symptoms rather than in a descriptive fashion
- Comorbidity issues in diagnosis and treatment
- Role of cognition in development of PTSD
- Psychosocial factors in the development of PTSD
- Neuroendocrinological factors in etiology and maintenance of PTSD
- Neuroimaging methods in research
- Posttraumatic Stress Disorder and Substance Abuse or Dependence

A final list of future directions consists of research and practice issues discussed in two quarterly journals put out by the National Center for Post-Traumatic Stress Disorder, a division of the Veteran's Administration and Department of Defense. Beginning with 2003 and covering until the winter of 2005 issue, the following topics have emerged (again, only those that are different than those found in the previous two lists are listed):

- Sexual revictimization
- Iraq war veterans, PTSD, and Gulf War syndrome
- Posttraumatic Stress Disorder and sleep
- Posttraumatic Stress Disorder and 9/11

Specific Technological Innovations

Three innovations and trends in PTSD treatment deserve specific attention: Internet-based assessment and treatment, virtual-reality therapy, and transcranial magnetic stimulation. Each of these is making use of exciting new technologies or social trends and forces that are unarguably the wave of the future in mental health research and practice.

Internet-Based Assessment and Treatment of PTSD

European researchers Lange, Rietdijk, Hudcovicova, van de Ven, Schrieken, and Emmelkamp (2003) developed and tested an Internet-based treatment for PTSD. Internet-based therapy, although new and with many ethical and practical issues yet to be worked out, is a promising line of inquiry and practice. In contrast to simple computer-based therapy or even workbook-based therapy, Internet-based therapy provides direct feedback to the patient or participant via computer and the Internet. Internet-based therapy is promising for many reasons. Patients who live in remote areas, those with mobility or transportation problems, and those who have difficulty leaving their home because of psychological or symptomatic reasons might benefit from the access provided via the Internet.

Lange and colleagues (2003) developed a form of Internet-based therapy they call *Interapy*, which consists of structured writing assignments with three phases, "self-confrontation, cognitive reappraisal, and social sharing" (pp. 1–2). Treatment consists of a ten 45-minute writing sessions over a 5-week period. Patients must log in to the treatment system on the Internet. In the middle of each of the three phases, the therapist provides feedback about what has been written about thus far and how to continue. The self-confrontation phase is essentially an exposure phase of treatment with instructions to describe the traumatic event and to write about emotions and thoughts the patient has. Patients must write in the first person and use substantial detail, and no emphasis is placed on the mechanics of writing, such as punctuation or spelling. The second phase of the treatment consists of cognitive reappraisal in which the patient receives some psychoeducation about cognitive reappraisal and instructions to formulate advice for a hypothetical friend who suffered the same trauma. The third phase consists of psychoeducation about sharing with others and instructions for patients to write about developing a new focus in life, with less focus on the trauma. Ultimately, Lange and colleagues found that more than 50 percent of participants "showed reliable change and clinically significant improvement, with the highest percentages being found for depression and avoidance" (p. 1).

Virtual-Reality Treatment of PTSD

Researchers have developed and tested an immersive virtual-reality (VR) therapy treatment for PTSD with various populations, including combat veterans and 9/11 victims (Difede & Hoffman, 2002; Hodges et al., 1999; Rothbaum, Hodges, Ready, Graap, & Alarcon, 2001). The necessary technology is much cheaper and more sophisticated than in years past. The power of VR therapy is explained by Glantz, Durlach, Barnett, and Aviles (1996):

> The power to "immerse" the user in a simulated, multimodal world–derives not so much from the realism of the displays, as from the fact that perception and

action are integrated, just as they are in the real world.... The user of VR is a doer, and since, as is well known, doing has a more powerful effect than passive participation, the probability that learning will be transferred from the therapy setting to the real world is increased. (p. 464)

Glantz, Rizzo, and Graap (2003) identify four strengths of VR therapy: (1) the potential to precisely control what is presented to the patient, (2) the ability to tailor treatment environments to the needs of each individual, (3) the ability to expose the client to a range of conditions that would be impractical or unsafe in the real world, and (4) the ability to improve confidentiality by substituting for group treatment or in vivo desensitization.

Virtual-reality treatments for PTSD utilize cognitive-behavioral principles, primarily brief or prolonged exposure. Virtual exposure environments are constructed based on the specific traumatic event, such as combat or war. Although VR is promising for many reasons, technological issues, cost, and people's attitudes and resistances to technology can be complicating factors. Nonetheless, VR therapy for PTSD as well as other disorders holds much promise for the future.

Transcranial Magnetic Stimulation and PTSD

Several studies have been conducted that investigate the use of magnetic brain stimulation on PTSD with some promise (Cohen et al., 2004; Grisaru, Amir, Cohen, & Kaplan, 1998; McCann et al., 1998; Rosenberg et al., 2002). The technology and technique is called *transcranial magnetic stimulation* (TMS) and has been used with other disorders as well, including depression and Schizophrenia. Transcranial magnetic stimulation is primarily an investigation tool for neuroscience research. An electromagnetic coil is placed on the head, and a series of high-intensity currents is turned on and off within the coil, thus producing an altered magnetic field around and amongst the brain. This results in the flow of electrical current throughout the brain and the depolarization of neural membranes. This can be done in a single episode or in repeated trials. Mantovani and Lisanby (2004) explain:

> The ability to focally alter cortical excitability opens up the potential to modulate cortical circuitry for potential therapeutic benefit. The focality of the effects also presents a challenge to clinical application, because it is necessary to know the circuitry of the underlying disorder to guide where and how to stimulate to ameliorate symptoms.

With respect to PTSD, as interpreted by McCann et al. (1998), TMS is considered to have an effect on the altered-baseline levels of cerebral metabolism. Grisaru et al. (1998) proposed that the possible active-change mechanism is a reduction in overall cerebral excitability and hyperarousal. This treatment is still in its infancy and is not approved by the U.S. Food and Drug Administration (FDA). Nonetheless, it holds promise in its short-duration, not requiring months and months of treatment, and in its ability to further research while also serving as a treatment.

Summary

My hopes for this chapter were to expose the reader to the future of PTSD. I am aware that I have only scratched the surface. As our knowledge increases at an unprecedented rate, it becomes extremely difficult to be comprehensive in even the simplest sense of the word. The task of staying on top of the field is a lifelong endeavor; consider this chapter a first step on that path.

Quick Review

- The booming human population of this planet poses a challenge to the future of all mental health.

- Technology is an integral part of human life and must be part of the future of mental health.

- Posttraumatic Stress Disorder research and treatment continues to understand the disorder from a neuroscience perspective.

- Posttraumatic Stress Disorder as a construct must be reevaluated from an ethnocultural perspective.

- Posttraumatic Stress Disorder treatments will continue to be more integrated and broad based.

- Technology comprises a big part of the future of PTSD treatment.

References

Cohen, H., Kaplan, Z., Kotler, M., Kouperman, I., Moisa, R., & Grisaru, N. (2004). Repetitive transcranial magnetic stimulation of the right dorsolateral prefrontal cortex in Posttraumatic Stress Disorder: A double-blind, placebo-controlled study. *American Journal of Psychiatry, 161,* 515–524.

Difede, J., & Hoffman, H. G. (2002). Virtual reality exposure therapy for World Trade Center Post-Traumatic Stress Disorder: A case report. *CyberPsychology & Behavior, 5,* 529–535.

Glantz, K., Durlach, N. I., Barnett, R. C., & Aviles, W. A. (1996). Virtual reality (VR) for psychotherapy: From the physical to the social environment. *Psychotherapy: Theory, Research, Practice, Training, 33,* 464–473.

Glantz, K., Rizzo, A., & Graap, K. (2003). Virtual reality for psychotherapy: Current reality and future possibilities. *Psychotherapy: Theory, Research, Practice, Training, 40,* 55–67.

Grisaru, N., Amir, M., Cohen, H., & Kaplan, Z. (1998). Effect of transcranial magnetic stimulation in Posttraumatic Stress Disorder: A preliminary study. *Biological Psychiatry, 44,* 52–55.

Hodges, L. F., Rothbaum, B. O., Alarcon, R., Ready, D., Shahar, F., Graap, K., et al. (1999). A virtual environment for the treatment of chronic combat-related Post-Traumatic Stress Disorder. *CyberPsychology & Behavior, 2,* 7–14.

Lange, A., Rietdijk, D., Hudcovicova, M., van de Ven, J., Schrieken, B., & Emmelkamp, P. M. G. (2003). Interapy: A controlled randomized trial of the standardized treatment of posttraumatic stress through the internet. *Journal of Consulting and Clinical Psychology, 71,* 901–909.

Mantovani, A, & Lisanby, S. H. (2004). Applications of transcranial magnetic stimulation to therapy in psychiatry. *Psychiatric Times, XXI, Issue 9.* Retrieved September 30, 2005, from http://www.psychiatrictimes.com/p040856.html.

McCann, U. D., Kimbrell, T. A., Morgan, C. M., Anderson, T., Geraci, M., Benson, B. E., et al. (1998). Repetitive transcranial magnetic stimulation for Posttraumatic Stress Disorder. *Archives of General Psychiatry, 55,* 276–279.

Rosenberg, P. B., Mehndiratta, R. B., Mehndiratta, Y. P., Wamer, A., Rosse, R. B., & Balish, M. (2002). Repetitive transcranial magnetic stimulation treatment of comorbid Posttraumatic Stress Disorder and major depression. *Journal of Neuropsychiatry & Clinical Neurosciences, 14,* 270–276.

Rothbaum, B. O., Hodges, L. F., Ready, D., Graap, K., & Alarcon, R. D. (2001). Virtual reality exposure therapy for Vietnam veterans with Posttraumatic Stress Disorder. *Journal of Clinical Psychiatry, 62,* 617–622.

CHAPTER 19

Professional Issues: Ethics, Risk Management, and Self-Care

T
here are at least two sides to every story. Much of this book is about the sufferers and survivors of PTSD. But sitting across from the traumatized are
the professionals, clinicians, and therapists who hear their stories, bear witness to their pain, and attempt to assist them in their journeys back from fear
and the persistence of painful memories. Whether a client or patient is suffering
from the afflictions of a mental disorder, a subclinical syndrome, or a "problem
in living," à la Thomas Szasz (1974), the mental health professional working with
them is being asked by the patient, society, their profession, and by him- or herself a basic question, can you help this person? I remember when I told some
friends of mine that I was going to become a psychologist and go to graduate
school. Although I am embarrassed to admit this, some of them reacted with a
question of their own, who are you to think you can help people? This question
was not so much about whether I thought I had all the answers but, rather, about
whether I was healthy enough myself to help those struggling with their own
mental health. This is a fair question and one that must be asked and answered
by all clinicians. The issue of clinician mental health is critical in dealing with
trauma survivors. This is not just clinical lore; research has substantiated the
potential risk facing trauma clinicians. Fortunately, the mental health field has
made attempts to face these issues in more general ways through addressing and
establishing ethical guidelines designed to maintain the integrity of the profession, professional, and patient alike and through more specific explorations of
clinician mental health and therapist-related issues that arise in treatment.

Ethical Considerations and Risk Management

In an attempt to preempt a negative answer to the question, who do we think we are? The various professional organizations involved in mental health treatment each have a set of ethics guidelines (e.g., the American Psychological Association and the American Psychiatric Association). These guidelines are designed to help clinicians avoid, or at least manage, serious problems with patients and to practice in a manner that ensures the utmost professionalism. Ethical practice is good practice. Ethical practice is safer practice. Regarding the issue of clinician mental health, healthy practice begins with ethical practice.

Ethical practice begins with knowledge of ethics guidelines and principles. A clinician must also know who his or her client is and the parameters under which they work, whether it is in private practice, an institution, a government agency, and so on. Sometimes ethics and law collide or contradict each other. Ethical and safe practice must also include a working knowledge of the specific risks for working with specific clinical issues and populations. For example, I learned early on in my training that if you are going to work with children, you are going to face a child abuse–reporting situation eventually and sometimes often. Various populations bring their own risks. Working with Personality Disorders may involve constantly managing suicidal or self-destructive crises. When working with PTSD patients, risks may include strong countertransference reactions, burnout risk, emotional contagion, being involved in litigation and legal proceedings, addressing repressed memories, and mandatory reporting issues. There may also be particular risks for finding oneself involved in political issues and causes related to war, torture, and human rights. In the spirit of Judith Herman, sometimes with trauma, it is hard to remain neutral. She states, "It is morally impossible to remain neutral in this conflict. The bystander is forced to take sides" (p. 7). (For more on this topic, see the section on therapist neutrality later in this chapter.)

Although not specific to PTSD, Thomas Plante (1999) provides 10 strategies to avoid "ethical and legal perils" (p. 1):

1. Always obtain informed consent. This includes information on the parameters of the services provided, the nature of the professional relationship, potential risks and benefits, limits to confidentiality, and relevant financial issues.

2. Get arms-length consultation. This is consultation with a professional who has objective distance from the situation.

3. Maintain professional competence. Plante identifies this as fundamental.

4. Know the law and ethics code.

5. Avoid or plan for high-risk patients and situations. Certain populations are more likely to generate ethical or legal complaints such as divorce or

child-custody evaluations, repressed memory, Dissociative Disorders, and Borderline Personality Disorders.

6. Do not use collection agencies.

7. Keep good written records. Minimally, these should contain identifying information, assessment results, consultation and summary reports, diagnoses, treatment plans, progress notes, dates and types of services, fees, release of information, and detailed information about suicide or violence risk.

8. Maintain confidentiality.

9. Be extra careful with managed care and insurance companies.

10. Get help when needed. This includes informal consultation, formal consultation, and legal consultation if necessary.

Now let's turn to issues specific to working with PTSD sufferers.

Professional Self-Care

As B. Hudnall Stamm (1995) states in the preface of *Secondary Traumatic Stress: Self-Care Issues for Clinicians, Researchers, and Educators*, trauma professionals are always at risk for being "wounded by the work" (p. ix). Professionals who work with the traumatized and PTSD sufferers are potentially at risk for developing a condition known as *compassion fatigue* or *secondary traumatic stress disorder* (STSD; Figley, 1995; Miller, 1998). *Secondary traumatic stress disorder* is defined by Figley as:

> the natural, consequent behaviors and emotions resulting from knowledge about a traumatizing event experience by a significant other. It is the stress resulting from helping or wanting to help a traumatized or suffering person. (p. 7)

Secondary traumatic stress disorder and PTSD are virtually the same, with the difference being between direct exposure versus vicarious exposure. Figley (1995) considers *compassion fatigue, compassion stress,* and *secondary traumatic stress disorder* as synonymous. It is also sometimes referred to as *burnout, emotional contagion, secondary victimization, covictimization,* or *secondary survivor syndrome.* Figley (1995) has even developed an instrument to measure compassion fatigue in professionals called the *Compassion Fatigue Self-Test for Psychotherapists.*

Although it may seem obvious to some, why should STSD even be of concern? As Shay (1995) states, "what is the ethical standing of the needs of the trauma therapist?" (p. 253). When does the care of the caregiver become an important issue or an even more important issue than the care of the patient? Shay shies away from taking a firm stance on this question, but I would propose that the answer to this question is that both parties involved have equal right to self-care, and, in fact, a professional who neglects his or her self-care regarding work with trauma sufferers is serving the best interest of no one. The simplest approach to take here is that an impaired professional is less likely to provide effective treatment and help.

Symptoms of STSD include intrusive imagery related to a client's trauma, avoidance, arousal, somatic complaints, distressing emotions, addictive behaviors, compulsive behaviors, and problems in functioning. Chrestman (1995) conducted a survey of therapists and found an association between STSD and secondary trauma exposure. Intrusion and avoidance symptoms were found. However, the mean levels of these symptoms were not in the clinical or diagnosable range despite the levels being higher than in professionals not secondarily exposed to trauma. This finding can be misleading, however. Although the mean levels for these subjects were not clinical, there was a percentage of the sample that did, in fact, experience clinical levels. In this study, there was a relationship between the amount of time therapists spent with trauma sufferers and certain changes in behavior, including decreasing the therapist's children's activities away from home, decreased so-called risky behavior, feeling less comfortable seeing clients when alone in the office, increased checking of doors, and increased listening for noises. Also, therapists with a higher percentage of trauma clients on their caseloads talk less to family and friends and attend more professional conferences. This study also cited that as professional experience, income, and postgraduate training increased, reported symptom levels went down.

Secondary traumatic stress disorder can develop from either a one-time exposure, as might be the case with a crisis worker with ongoing exposure with treatment cases, or in some other setting. For example, a pediatric neuropsychologist who works for an attorney assessing obstetrician malpractice claimants might develop STSD or compassion fatigue from assessing hundreds of young children and toddlers with neuropsychological deficits secondary to medical trauma at birth. Such an individual is exposed to the trauma of the child and the parents alike, not to mention the powerful effects of repeated exposure to heart-wrenching stories, dashed hopes, struggles to make sense in the family and by the parents, and actual disabling deficits. Danieli (1985) makes the important observation that a professional's exposure to traumatic stories serves as a powerful reminder of the reality of such events and of one's potential vulnerability. Certainly, being reminded on a regular basis of one's vulnerability can take its toll. Dutton and Rubinstein (1995) remind us that repeated exposure in long-term treatment is the rule. That is, with long-term treatment, a therapist will have to hear about a traumatic event again and again. These authors also remind us that therapists are also privy to graphic details and information that typically only a sufferer, a victim, or a perpetrator (in the case of violent trauma) would know. Other factors play a role in determining STSD reactions, including level of predictability of the event; source of information about the trauma (e.g., verbal recall versus photographs, etc.); relationship with a perpetrator; the extent to which the event violates vital assumptions about the world and people; level or degree of threat to life; level of professional development; whether there is a current threat; presence of mind control or mind-games, such as manipulation, on the part of the client; solo practice versus group versus institution; whether the therapist has knowledge of other traumas in other cases or was a survivor him- or herself; and level of intimacy in the traumatic event, such as an incest case (Dutton & Rubinstein, 1995).

Individual-Level Prevention of Compassion Fatigue

Protective factors for not developing STSD include more experience; training; increased social and professional support; engaging in more than just clinical work with trauma victims, such as teaching; and reduced stressors in other areas of the clinician's life (Chrestman, 1995). Other protective factors include recreation in addition to work, having a network of emotionally supportive relationships, self-exploration, taking care of personal needs, personal therapy, supervision, and diversifying clients (Dutton & Rubinstein, 1995). Still other important issues include obtaining training and information about STSD in the spirit of stress inoculation. Such training should include learning how to identify signs, make adjustments when necessary, and seek help when necessary. Trauma clinicians with a personal history of trauma should be well aware of the potential for their own issues to become salient in their professional work. This need not be a negative indicator, however, in that it can sometimes be positive by leading to potentially more empathy for clients. Finally, Janet Yassen (1995) provides a good list of individual-oriented prevention tools:

1. Maintaining physical health, including getting adequate sleep and nutrition.
2. Having a balanced life between work, play, and other activities.
3. Relaxation.
4. Contact with nature.
5. Creative expression.
6. Skill development.
7. Meditation or spiritual practice.
8. Self-awareness.
9. Humor.
10. Social support.
11. Professional help.
12. Social activism.
13. Professional balance.
14. Good professional boundaries and limits.
15. Not overworking.
16. Professional support by peers and in supervision and consultation.
17. Having a mentor or role model.
18. Commitment to the job.
19. Continuing to grow as a professional.

Vulnerability

One more important issue needs to be addressed before moving on to treatment. That is the issue of vulnerability. Are some of us more vulnerable to developing STSD than others? Certainly, professionals exposed to trauma versus those who are not are more at risk. But are there other factors? Williams and Sommer (1995) provide the following list of potential vulnerabilities in professionals:

1. Not having strongly formed ethical beliefs and values consistent with the profession and type of work.

2. Lacking a strong foundation in trauma theory.

3. Nonresolution and examination of your one's trauma history.

4. Lack of treatment skill, competence, available strategies, and techniques.

5. Lack of awareness for the potential of STSD and how one would cope with its onset.

Treatment of Compassion Fatigue

Pearlman and Saakvitne (1995) group treatments for STSD into three categories: personal, professional, and organizational. Personal treatment should involve identifying and analyzing disrupted schemas that arise from working with a particular trauma victim or victims. Schemas that are particularly related to safety, trust, self-esteem, intimacy, and control should be focused on. Also, trauma clinicians should have personal lives outside of work. They should also engage in healing activities such as art, music, spending time with loved ones, or even community services. This will vary for every individual, of course. Finally, one should attend to his or her spiritual needs.

Professional strategies discussed by Pearlman and Saakvitne (1995) should include arranging for and utilizing supervision. It is also important to develop professional connections. Similar to having a personal life outside of work, one should have a balanced work life with varied activities, not all trauma work, for instance. Clinicians should remain aware of their goals of being mental health practitioners, reminding themselves from time to time why they got into to the business to begin with. Also, continue to develop professionally in the form of continuing education and training.

Finally, certain organizational strategies are helpful in ameliorating the effects of STSD. The physical setting is important in trauma work. A safe, private, and comfortable space is vital. Organizations should also provide adequate training and warnings of the potential for STSD in working with particular populations. Adequate professional resources should be available, such as supervision and consultation. An atmosphere that encourages professional development and activities is also very important. The atmosphere should also be one of respect. Adjunctive services such as professional self-help groups, newsletters, books, and other supportive material are helpful.

Of course, if none of these work or if more help is needed, a professional should never hesitate to get professional help for him- or herself in the form of therapy, medication, or both.

Countertransference and Relationship Dynamics Issues

van der Kolk and McFarlane warn us that we must understand our own reactions to trauma and our patients in order to optimally help them. Often a misunderstood concept, but one that is present in all therapeutic relationships, is countertransference. Countertransference can be understood as the therapist's or clinician's biopsychosocial reactions to the patient's narrative and behavior (Wilson & Lindy, 1994).

There are different types of countertransference in general and some that are specific to trauma work. Sometimes countertransference reactions come from the clinician's own psychological issues, dynamics, and history that are activated by work with a particular client or clients. Other times, the reaction can be a more here-and-now type of reaction that is a response to the client-therapist dynamic of the moment. That is, countertransference need not always be about the therapist's issues. Both broad types of countertransference reactions are possible in PTSD treatment.

Countertransference often has a negative connotation. However, some professionals see it in the more pathological light, and others see it as an inevitable part of therapy: Sometimes there are negative countertransferences, some are positive, and some are rather understandable and predictable reactions to the relationship dynamics that can develop in therapy. For instance, it is not uncommon for a trauma therapist to feel that he or she needs to be strong, safe, or secure for a patient. Also, patient struggles with trust can lead to feelings of powerlessness and incompetence on the part of the therapist. I believe the point is not to develop countertransference reactions but instead to accept them as part of the process, address them with oneself and openly with the client if necessary and therapeutic, and utilize them in a manner that furthers treatment. van der Kolk and McFarlane remind us that trauma work requires patience, an ability to tolerate ambivalence and ambiguity, and resisting the urge to take care of patients rather than helping them take care of themselves. It is important to keep in mind that our reactions, whether you label them as *countertransference* can either help or hinder treatment (Wilson & Lindy, 1994). Treatment can be affected in many ways, including premature termination or dropouts, stagnation in treatment, increased trauma-related transference regarding safety or fear of abandonment issues, acting out, dissociation, or patient regression (Wilson & Thomas, 2004).

Wilson and Thomas (2004) identify four factors that influence the manifestation of countertransference reactions in trauma work:

1. The nature of the trauma story and description of intense traumatic experiences involving death, injury, dying, exposure to the grotesque, horror, catastrophic disaster, or chaos.

2. The therapist's personal characteristics, including their trauma history, personality style, defensive structure, capacity for affect modulation, and high versus low empathy position.

3. Institutional or organizational factors, such as adequacy of resources.

4. Specific demographic and characterological features of the client's trauma experience.

These authors propose that countertransference in trauma work takes two forms, Type I countertransference and Type II countertransference, both existing on a continuum that is characterized by the degree to which a clinician is responsive to a client's suffering.

Type I countertransference is characterized by a clinician moving away from a client and his or her story. It is often associated with compassion fatigue or STSD and perceived overwhelming dysregulated affect in the client on the part of the therapist. There are six subtypes of Type I countertransference:

1. *Denial:* includes denial of PTSD diagnosis in specific clients or the presence of trauma.

2. *Minimization:* failure to see PTSD, a medication only treatment, minimizing impact of trauma, or an overfocus on Axis II etiology of symptoms and problems.

3. *Distortion:* involves misperceiving dynamic issues in treatment, not dealing with countertransference as it arises, confusion, or even resentment of the client.

4. *Avoidance:* overutilizing the so-called blank-screen, overreliance on technique, canceling sessions, or avoiding talking about trauma histories.

5. *Detachment:* emotional distance, overintellectualization, dislike of client, or boredom.

6. *Withdrawal:* referral out, seeing the patient as untreatable, overuse of medication, overuse of Axis II diagnoses and etiologies.

Type II countertransference is on the opposite end of the continuum, and instead of being characterized as moving away, it is characterized as overidentification. There are five subtypes:

1. *Dependency:* client-therapist symbiosis or overinvolvement in the patient's personal life.

2. *Enmeshment:* role boundary problems, dual relationships, and possible sexual acting out.

3. *Overidealization or overidentification:* preoccupation, STSD, disequilibrium, being overwhelmed akin to the patient, and engaging in the "me too" identification.

4. *Rescuer or healer:* engaging in rescue fantasies, narcissistic focus in therapy, and grandiosity.

5. *Overemphasis on traumatic event:* excessive advocacy, having a trauma-only focus in treatment, and no exploration of Axis II pathology.

The Issue of Therapist Neutrality

This issue of expected therapist neutrality is extremely important in PTSD. In a classic Freudian sense, the therapist should be the blank screen. We know, both intuitively and through experience, that this is a virtually impossible stance to maintain. Both clinician and patient are human beings involved in addressing the power of trauma, with subsequent and expected human reactions. Sandra Bloom (1995) states the an inevitable consequence of being a trauma clinician is becoming a public health clinician (p. 263) because of what she identifies as an epidemic of violence and violence-related trauma and PTSD in our contemporary world. She states, "the personal is political" (p. 264) and

> the problems of our patients are not entirely their own. Even if they are now "sick," their sicknesses spring from their injuries. They have been unable to protect themselves from the infection of violence, and no one else was effective at providing the necessary protection. (p. 264)

Bloom (1995) proposes that part of the clinician self-care repertoire may necessarily be an attempt to address the causes of trauma on a societal, political, and activist level. She criticizes the sole focus of professionals on what might be considered an after-the-fact approach to trauma, stating in essence that eradication is as therapeutic as catharsis, for example. This is both a noble and daunting call. The eradication of trauma from violence requires the eradication of violence itself. Bloom powerfully states.

> If you are not a victim or a perpetrator, you are a bystander. . . . It is of vital interest to note that among many acts of perpetration which have been studied, it is the behavior of the bystanders that determines how far the perpetrators will go in carrying out their behavior. (p. 270)

Empathic Attunement

How do we avoid Type I and Type II countertransference reactions? Wilson and Thomas suggest using the model of *empathic attunement* as a means to connect and support a patient by utilizing the therapist's countertransference reactions in a positive manner. Empathic attunement is defined as "The psychobiological capacity to experience, understand, and communicate knowledge of the internal psychological state of being of another person" (p. 20). From the perspective of PTSD as an allostatic dysfunction (see Chapter 7 for more on allostasis), empathic attunement can help in restoring positive allostasis in several important ways. Issues of hyperarousal and disequilibrium can be addressed through the stabilization of response thresholds. Psychobiological reactivity is brought under more modulated and stable affective control. Empathic attunement can help increase a client's ability to self-monitor accurately, and through increased feedback based on accurate interaction, a client can learn to more accurately process his or her experiences, relationships, and threats. Attunement can provide a stable and predictable continuity to the patient's experience, which is often disrupted and sometimes is manifested in dissociative states. Finally, stress responses can be more easily habituated to, and ultimately there can be a return to homeostatic balance.

Summary

The professional treating PTSD must respect the important role he or she plays in shaping the healing process of clients and patients. The clinician's reactions can help or impair the process. Because the treatment of PTSD so often involves facing horrific situations and hearing about horrible events, it can elicit a number of responses from professionals, ranging from simple avoidance to the development of STSD. A respect for the power of working with trauma victims is the starting point for learning how to maximize one's ability to work effectively with PTSD sufferers.

Quick Review

- Sound clinical practice begins with adopting an ethical stance and set of principles.

- Clinicians need to be mindful of the risks that working with certain populations necessarily entails.

- Working with PTSD involves the potential risk of developing symptoms and a disorder in and of itself, similar to PTSD, in the form of compassion fatigue or STSD.

- Preventive factors for STSD include personal balance, support, and training.

- Treatment of STSD may involve acknowledging altered schemas, seeking consultation, and even seeking treatment for oneself.

- Countertransference with trauma victims can exist in at least two forms, the avoidant Type I or the overidentified Type II. Empathic attunement is a possible antidote for the development of negative countertransference.

References

Bloom, S. L. (1995). The germ theory of trauma: The impossibility of ethical neutrality. In B. H. Stamm (Ed.), *Secondary traumatic stress: Self-care issues for clinicians, researchers, and educators* (pp. 257–276). Baltimore: Sidran Press.

Chrestman, K. R. (1995). Secondary exposure to trauma and self-reported distress among therapists. In B. H. Stamm (Ed.), *Secondary traumatic stress: Self-care issues for clinicians, researchers, and educators* (pp. 29–36). Baltimore: Sidran Press.

Danieli, Y (1985). The treatment and prevention of long-term effects and intergenerational transmission of victimization: A lesson from Holocaust survivors and their children. In C. R. Figley (Ed.), *Trauma and its wake: The study and treatment of Post-Traumatic Stress Disorder* (pp. 295–313). New York: Brunner/ Mazel.

Dutton, M. A., & Rubinstein, F. L. (1995). Working with people with PTSD: Research implications. In C. R. Figley (Ed.), *Compassion fatigue: Coping with secondary traumatic stress disorder in those who treat the traumatized* (pp. 82–100). Philadelphia: Brunner/Mazel.

Figley, C. R. (Ed.). (1995). *Compassion fatigue: Coping with secondary traumatic stress disorder in those who treat the traumatized.* Philadelphia: Brunner/Mazel.

Herman, J. L. (1992). *Trauma and recovery.* New York: Basic Books Inc.

Miller, L. (1998). Our own medicine: Traumatized psychotherapists and the stresses of doing therapy. *Psychotherapy: Theory, Research, Practice, Training, 35,* 137–146.

Pearlman, L. A., & Saakvitne, K. W. (1995). Treating therapists with vicarious traumatization and secondary traumatic stress disorders. In C. R. Figley (Ed.), *Compassion fatigue: Coping with secondary traumatic stress disorder in those who treat the traumatized* (pp. 150–177). Philadelphia: Brunner/Mazel.

Plante, T. G. (1999). Ten strategies for psychology trainees and practicing psychologists interested in avoiding ethical and legal perils. *Psychotherapy: Theory, Research, Practice, Training, 36,* 398–403.

Shay, J. (1995). No escape from philosophy in trauma treatment and research. In B. H. Stamm (Ed.), *Secondary traumatic stress: Self-care issues for clinicians, researchers, and educators* (pp. 247–256). Baltimore: Sidran Press.

Stamm, B. H. (Ed.). (1995). *Secondary traumatic stress: Self-care issues for clinicians, researchers, and educators.* Baltimore: Sidran Press.

Szasz, T. S. (1974). *The myth of mental illness: Foundations of a theory of personal conduct* (Rev. ed.). Oxford, England: Harper & Row.

van der Kolk, B. A., & McFarlane, A. C. (1996). The black hole of trauma. In B. A. van der Kolk, A. C. McFarlane, & L. Weisaeth (Eds.), *Traumatic stress: The effects of overwhelming experience on mind, body, and society* (pp. 3–23). New York: Guilford.

Williams, M. B., & Sommer, J. F., Jr. (1995). Self-care and the vulnerable therapist. In B. H. Stamm (Ed.), *Secondary traumatic stress: Self-care issues for clinicians, researchers, and educators* (pp. 230–246). Baltimore: Sidran Press.

Wilson, J. P., & Lindy, J. D. (Eds). (1994). *Countertransference in the treatment of PTSD.* New York: Guilford.

Wilson, J. P., & Thomas, R. B. (2004). *Empathy in the treatment of trauma and PTSD.* New York: Brunner-Routledge.

Yassen, J. (1995). Preventing secondary traumatic stress disorder. In C. R. Figley (Ed.), *Compassion fatigue: Coping with secondary traumatic stress disorder in those who treat the traumatized* (pp. 178–208). Philadelphia: Brunner/Mazel.

CHAPTER 20

Posttraumatic Stress Disorder in Children, Adolescents, and Families

There are a number of critical issues that make a discussion of PTSD in children, adolescents, and families worthy of being placed in a special section of a book on PTSD. Perhaps the most important of these are the issues of change, dynamism, and fluidity. Children in development are constantly changing. Two-year-olds' clothing changes with the days, for example, and adolescents live in one of the most dynamic times of their lives, with relationships, goals, aspirations, and motivations in constant, but not necessarily chaotic, flux. The complexity of families sometimes looks like disorder, but underneath the surface of often tumultuous flows are deep and sophisticated currents, holding families together in networks of emotions, behaviors, and complex cognitions. The goal of this chapter is to try and understand how PTSD manifests, differentially impacts, and should be approached for both study and treatment in these constantly moving persons and systems.

Posttraumatic Stress Disorder in Children and Adolescents

Children are considered a high-risk population for PTSD, with research showing higher prevalence rates than with adults (9.2 percent compared to 8 percent) and a higher chance of developing the disorder after exposure to traumatic stress (Gabbay, Oatis, Silva, & Hirsch, 2004). Part of these differences is attributed to the serious health problem of child maltreatment or child physical and sexual abuse, with exposure to maltreatment being associated with eventual development of PTSD in 20 to 60 percent of victims.

The types of traumatic stressors children and adolescents are exposed to are different from adult traumas in many ways, although considerable overlap exists as well. Children are exposed with more frequency to such different stressors as severe burns, physical abuse, sexual abuse, sexual assault, witnessing domestic violence, and kidnapping. For children, trauma also seems inordinately associated with loss, such as the sudden death of a loved one or parent.

Posttraumatic Stress Disorder in children cannot be adequately addressed without an understanding of child development. But this would be a book in and of itself. It is important to keep in the mind the immense changes in all of the various psychological, biological, and social aspects of the developing child. Having some of the more comprehensive models and more specific but highly important theories in mind when addressing PTSD is crucial, including, the work of Jean Piaget, Erik Erikson, D. J. Siegel, Daniel Stern, John Bowlby, Mary Ainsworth, and countless others.

Impact and Manifestation

Children represent a particularly vulnerable population for many reasons. To begin with, their capacity for independent functioning is more limited. They are more dependent by nature, and their very existence and psychological development is constantly changing and growing. Perturbations in a changing system can often have more profound effects than in a stable system. Ironically, however, such a system is also ripe with the potential for growth and positive adaptation as well.

Posttraumatic Stress Disorder is both the same and different for this complex system we call *children.* Children can experience the same symptoms identified in the *DSM-IV-TR* as adults, but as a consequence of developmental issues, such as language development and behavioral and interpersonal sophistication, there can be variation and alternative expressions as well. Scheeringa and Gaensbauer (2000) propose that the *DSM* criteria have significant shortcomings when applied to very young children. The *DSM* criteria are very dependent on verbal sophistication and are seen as not sensitive to issues of developmental level. The Zero to Three, National Center for Infants, Toddlers, and Families developed the *Diagnostic Classification of Mental Health and Developmental Disorders of Infancy*

Clinician Alert

The issue of the appropriateness of the *DSM* criteria is an important one, but it need not be too bothersome when it comes to practice in my opinion. The procedures of using the *DSM* include room for clinical judgment and responsibly considering diagnoses that do not quite fit each patient. If a diagnosis does not fit exactly, we shouldn't let textbook practice override good, sound clinical judgment. If a child has PTSD, I will give the diagnosis, even if the criteria do not fit exactly. This is where knowledge of how trauma manifests itself differently in children is extremely important.

---

and Early Childhood (*DC: 0–3*), with alternative criteria from the *DSM-IV-TR*. These alternative criteria require only one symptom from each symptom cluster (reexperiencing, arousal, and avoidance), with the addition of two new symptom categories, a fear cluster, and an aggression cluster. These alternative criteria require four symptoms to the *DSM-IV-TR*'s six required symptoms.

On that point, Stien and Kendall (2003) and other researchers propose the following differences in the ways that children experience and manifest PTSD:

- Somatization, such as headaches or stomachaches
- More intense normal fears, such as fear of being alone or fear of monsters
- Hyperactivity
- Aggressive behavior and delinquency
- Temper tantrums
- Pessimism
- Magical thinking
- Reexperiencing in the form of dreams in which the child is killed and so on
- Immature behavior and regression (e.g., in toileting or language)
- School problems, such as truancy
- Revenge seeking

Children with PTSD may be unable to express themselves in a way that would lead to the easy identification and diagnosis of PTSD. Oftentimes, the actual symptoms of the disorder may not be readily apparent, with perhaps the exception of nightmares, but rather a general pattern of behavioral disruption and dysfunction in school, home, and socialization will be apparent. Children may become withdrawn, and their schoolwork may suffer. They may be engaged in more conflict than typical.

The impact of a traumatic stressor will be a function of the developmental stage and level a child is at. Trauma can both disrupt normal development and lead to ongoing abnormal development thereafter. Preschool children, for example, will display more regressive behaviors such as bed-wetting, talking less, dependence, and separation anxiety, while older children might display somatic symptoms, cognitive distortions, and learning problems. Adolescent experience is similar to adults but may result in more acting out or self-destructive behavior, such as sexual promiscuity, life-threatening reenactments, or aggression.

The impact on subsequent development may manifest itself in altered personality and relationship dynamics. Children may have difficulty forming trusting bonds or a sense of autonomy and independence.

Three key aspects of psychological development that are central to PTSD in children are the development of the self, brain development, and social and interpersonal development. As we have seen in previous chapters, trauma is often understood in changes in these three areas. Cognitively we may develop an altered view of ourselves as inept or incapable, our bodies and brains may be on perpetual high-alert status, and people may be sources of mistrust. Stien and Kendall (2003) state, for example, that the effects of trauma on children can often be so profound because they are still developing their sense of self. Further, self-complexity has been identified as a resilience factor in coping with extreme stress, and, certainly, children typically have less complex selves than their adult counterparts. (For more on resilience, see Chapter 22.)

Scheeringa and Gaensbauer (2000), in discussing PTSD in our youngest victims, infants and toddlers, outline six psychological "capacities that seem to be relevant to produce PTSD symptomatology" (p. 371):

1. Perceptual abilities are necessary for the awareness of the traumatic.

2. Memory is necessary for storage of the event.

3. Affective expression provides a mode of symptom communication, including distress, wariness, fear, irritation, anger, sadness, and startle.

4. Behavioral expression also provides a mode for symptom expression, including purposeful arm movement, multistep coordinated means-end behavior, walking, and imaginative play.

5. Verbal expression, again, provides a mode for symptom expression.

6. Socioemotional relationship factors include social smiling, enhanced eye contact, expanding periods of engagement, cognitive capacity for intersubjectivity, and attachment formation.

The Work of Lenore Terr

Psychiatrist Lenore Terr has provided a very extensive, insightful, and compassionate analysis of PTSD in children. Her work has outlined in detail how PTSD can be different for this population. As was previously mentioned, traumatized children may be too young to verbalize their experience or to report their symptoms. This ushers in the question, what is the youngest age at which PSTD can affect a child? Can an infant have PTSD, for example? Terr (1990) cites that a victim below the mental age of 28 to 36 months will typically not remember a trauma in words; they simply lack the psychological capacity for storing trauma memories in this manner. However, they do retain it in other, very profound ways. Terr tells us that traumatic memories in children, even those younger than 28 months, are stored in behaviors such as play, fear reactions, and even dreams. Terr (1991) proposes that trauma in children is characterized by four phenomena: repeatedly perceived memories; repetitive behaviors; trauma-specific fears; and changed attitudes about people, aspects of life, and the future.

Traumatized children will "repeatedly 'see' what happened to them" (Terr, 1990, p. 138). Terr cites several situations in which these visualizations can be triggered: by visiting the locale of the event; when someone else mentions the event; when someone connected to the trauma comes to mind; and the when smells, the atmosphere, or the season remind the child of being there. Children's visualizations are viewed as different from adult-style flashbacks. They do not typically interrupt ongoing thought in an intrusive manner but instead function more like daydreams, passive episodes of visualization that occur when the mind is in idle (Terr, 1990).

Terr (1990) proposes three forms of behavioral repetition or working through phenomena in childhood trauma: dreams, play, and reenactment. The dreams of traumatized children are repetitive in theme, if not in content. Terr identifies four types of repeated or repetitive dreams: exact repetitions, modified repetitions, deeply disguised dreams, and terror dreams the child does not remember having when he or she wakes up. Exact repetitions are replays and represent blow by blow the exact event or a feature of it. The dreamer does not always recognize these dreams as replays. Modified repetitions involve the incorporation of newer life material into the replay dreams. Terr (1990) reminds us, however, that "the central horror of a post-traumatic dream, no matter how elaborate it becomes, stays the same" (p. 212). Deeply disguised dreams are replays in the service of wish gratification and become altered in a way that makes them difficult to connect to the original trauma. Terr (1990) gives the example of Leslie Grigson, a victim of the infamous Chowchilla kidnapping, and her repetitive dream of eating ice cream at Disneyland. Leslie connected this dream to the fact that because of the kidnapping, "We didn't get to eat ice cream at Disneyland" (p. 213). Finally, terror dreams are not remembered upon waking up, but their existence is inferred from a child's fear of going to sleep, or of sleeping alone, fears of the dark, sleep interruptions, sleep talk, and occasional sleepwalking. They sometimes have a bad feeling regarding having dreamed.

In *traumatic play*, the event is acted out in what is called *two-dimensional play* that is monotonous and involves themes of helplessness, unpredictability, terror, or death (Stien & Kendall, 2003; Terr, 1981). Terr calls this traumatic play in which children "compulsively replaying elements of the original trauma in a vain attempt to process their experience" (Stien & Kendall, 2003, p. 77). Terr (1990) states that traumatic play is literally dark and repetitive.

Behavioral reenactments differ from traumatic play. These behaviors involve everyday behavior and routine and are not acted out in discrete episodes of play necessarily. According to Terr (1990), they "take far more action" (p. 265). She makes the powerful claim that traumatic reenactments can lead to long-standing changes in personality. Sexualized behavior and sexual acting out in sexually abused children is cited as an example of this (Stien & Kendall, 2003). Terr (1990) also identifies the phenomenon of *psycho-physiological reenactments* in which under subsequent stress, children reexperience the same sensations or bodily experiences they had during the original trauma. She identifies *self-anesthesia* in which children go numb or to describe children who are constantly overexcited or overstimulated, mutism, paralysis, and nighttime feelings of pressure on one's chest. Terr discusses single-episode behavioral reenactments that can be very dramatic and intense. For example, a patient, when recalling being involuntarily hospitalized and losing her children to social services, reenacted the event and acted out violently for fear of losing her children all over again. Terr (1990) cites many forms of artistic expression as forms of reenactment.

Trauma-specific fears are rather self-explanatory. If an adolescent was hit by a car while riding his bicycle, he may fear cars coming down the street as he rides his bike on the sidewalk, for instance. Terr (1990) also states, however, that traumatized children have strong panic and avoidant reactions to mundane things that a lot of children are less severely afraid of, such as the dark, strangers, being alone, being outside, or even food.

The change in attitudes about people, life, and the future can be profound in traumatized children. These children might talk as if they were much older than their chronological age about dying and have what is called a *sense of foreshortened future*. They talk about not living long or not living beyond a certain age. They act as if another trauma is inevitable. Trust in others can be significantly damaged, particularly in people who resemble a perpetrator.

Finally, Terr (1995) identifies two types of PTSD in children: Type I, which is the consequence of a single event, and Type II, which is the consequence of repeated or multiple traumas. Stien and Kendall (2003) equate these to the more common terms of *common PTSD*, referring to *Type I*, and *complex PTSD*, referring to *Type II*. Each type has specific characteristics worth mentioning.

Type I trauma is considered by Terr to be more common than Type II. Victims will have "full memories of the event with rather clear recollection. They also engage in what Terr calls *omens*, retrospective explanations for what happened and how they could have or should have maybe done something different. This type of thinking often reflects attempts at cognitive mastery. Finally, Type I traumas are characterized by perceptual distortions and misperceptions in which there might be visual hallucinations or significant distortions in time.

Type II traumas are characterized by some very profound and disturbing responses, sometimes in the service of defense or coping. There can be denial and psychic numbing in which children deny the event and may say they feel as if they are dead, and they may even forget large portions of their lives. Type II trauma may also engender dissociative phenomena such as depersonalization and spontaneous self-hypnosis, which is considered a form of mental escape. An extreme form of a dissociative phenomenon is Dissociative Identity Disorder, previously known as Multiple Personality Disorder. Finally, very intense rage is not uncommon with Type II trauma. Episodes of angry reenactment may occur, and children may even engage in self-injurious behavior or suicidal behavior. Type II trauma is virtually synonymous with Herman (1993) and other researchers' concept of *disorders of extreme stress not otherwise specified* (DESNOS) to account for symptoms and difficulties following trauma that do not quite meet criteria for PTSD, such as somatization, personality disturbances, chaotic relationships, harm-seeking behavior, and revictimization. Finally, Jenkins and Bell (1997, p. 17) list numerous "trauma-related disorders other than PTSD in children and adolescents": brief reactive psychosis, Dissociative Fugue, Conduct Disorder, attachment disorders in infancy, Panic Disorder, Dream Anxiety Disorder, and Conversion Disorder, to name just a few.

Biological Issues

In my study of infant, toddler, and child neuropsychology, there is but only one constant—change. Trying to map psychological processes to a growing brain is both quantitatively and qualitatively different than adult neuropsychology. Understanding neuropsychological functioning is a fairly reductionist enterprise but a complex one, now try to imagine how complex the clinical phenomenon of PTSD, with its neurological, neuropsychological, and various other processes, must be for children.

We know that traumatic stress changes the brain. How does it change the changing or growing brain? Psychological science and the various disciplines involved in mental health have largely accepted the concept that experience alters brain functioning and development. As Stien and Kendall (2003) state, the "quality, quantity, and timing of infant stimulation has enduring effects on brain development" (p. 7). They go on to state that traumatic stress produces, "chaotic biochemical changes that interfere with the maturation of the brain's coping systems, leading to problems with emotional regulation, relationships, and identity formation" (p. 7), and "abuse [and trauma more generally] impedes brain maturation and interferes in the normal hierarchical development and integration of brain systems" (p. 10).

Stien and Kendall (2003) characterize trauma's effects on the brain as disrupting the integrated activity of various brain systems and functions. The brain grows in "fits and starts," if you will, periods of relatively faster or slower brain development with some periods of relative stagnation and periods of rapid neuronal and synaptic expansion. The developing brain's plasticity can be positive with respect to trauma in that the potential for recovery is higher, but, in turn, negative sequelae can linger in more long-term manifestations.

Work by researchers at the Center for the Study of Childhood Trauma (Perry, 1994) has outlined the role of catecholamine dysfunction in children with PTSD. Catecholamines have been found to play a critical role in neural development. Alterations in catecholamines early on in brain development from exposure to traumatic stressors during critical brain-development periods, particularly periods involved in the development of stress-related brain areas, could lead to alterations in neuronal differentiation and organization and ultimately result in a neuronal dysregulation syndrome. Studies with such changes in mind have shown catecholamine-related hyperreactive sympathetic nervous system activity in PTSD children, abnormal resting heart-heart and baseline or resting tachycardia, and dysfunction in the locus coeruleus.

Similar to adults, alterations in the functioning of the hypothalamic-pituitary-adrenal axis (HPA-axis) have been found in children as well (Kowalik, 2004). This may result in sensitized fear reactions, for example. (For more on the HPA axis, see Chapter 6.) There have also been findings of reduced hippocampus volume, decreased overall brain volume, and increased glucocorticoids in PTSD children (Kowalik, 2004).

Parental, Family, and Practical Issues

Many developmental theorists and PTSD researchers have come to focus on the power of *attachment* in influencing both normal development and a child's capacity for coping with distress and stress. Attachment can be used as an over-arching model for conceptualizing the impact of trauma on children within a social context. Secure attachment is the essential antithesis of trauma in many respects. John Bowlby (1988) and Mary Ainsworth (1979) talk about attachment in terms of a child's internal representation of a secure base in which the primary attachment figure is someone who represents safety and security from which an exploration of the world can be launched. Trauma challenges this sense of a secure base, and, therefore, it is not a leap to consider the importance of attachment in childhood PTSD.

The development of emotional and self-regulation in children is also important in understanding childhood trauma. Parents help children regulate their emotions in an interactive manner in which they help children identify their emotional states through acknowledgment and labeling and then help them cope by maintaining a separate emotional stance and coping response. If this process is somehow disrupted, the possibility for poor adjustment to stress is perhaps more likely. Research has shown that young children's posttrauma behavior following a natural disaster, for example, is less a function of the disaster itself and more a function of and response to the mother's behavior. Certainly, children are dependent on their families and the adults in their lives for safety and security. Schwarz and Perry (1994) refer to a child-parent relationship that contributes to the production of PTSD as a "symptomatic child-parent system" that may serve to perpetuate maladaptive coping and facilitate the existence of ongoing trauma stimuli and behavioral reactions and coping patterns. They state, "Components of such a system may synergistically trigger each other and escalate arousal, reexperiencing, and avoidance symptoms in vicious cycles."

This traumatized system can interfere with the process D. W. Winnicott (2002) refers to as *good-enough-mothering* in which a child learns to internalize secure caregiver representations around which to organize one's personality. Schwarz and Perry (1994) also state:

> Exquisitely sensitive to caretaker's emotional states and behavior more than to cognitive-mediated assessment of danger, infants may respond with symptomatic disturbances of global functioning, excessive crying, eating, sleeping, psychophysiological lability, overstimulated states, or apathy and failure to thrive.

Schwarz and Perry (1994) also propose something called *the symptom accumulation with development process* in which developmental tasks and stages add their particular flavor to the symptom picture. Toddlers may express trauma in terms of the contemporaneous developmental tasks of rapprochement and separation-individuation, while adolescents' symptoms may manifest in acting out and boundary testing behavior such as delinquency or sexual promiscuity.

There is sometimes the unfortunate event in families in which parents or other family members act in ways that worsen symptoms. They may deny or minimize a traumatized child's experience or level of distress. This is sometimes the case with sexual abuse. Parents may engage in denial or avoidance, leading to feelings of rejection, being discounted, insignificance, and of being ultimately unsafe. Siblings may repeat a trauma with intense episodes of conflict, physical aggression, or bullying. Parents may coddle or overindulge a child, impairing his or her sense of independence. Parents who live in violent areas, for example, may place restrictions on their children's movements, activities, and social connections. Parents may be too overwhelmed in their own right to adequately respond to their children's most basic needs, let alone their child's posttraumatic experiences. Cited as a particularly harmful situation by Greenwald (2000) are situations in which parents lose control and yell excessively, discipline in a physically harsh and angry manner, or engage in unreasonable or inconsistent punishment. This leads to further feelings of being in an unsafe environment that is unpredictable.

Finally, there is the issue of safety. When working with children who are traumatized, particularly victims of violence, the continued and ongoing safety of their environment must be assessed. A child's safety is a clinical, ethical, and legal priority. Further, working with children always carries with it the potential for mandatory reporting of child abuse or maltreatment.

Long-Term Consequences of Trauma in General

As has been discussed, a child's developmental trajectory can be forever altered by trauma. This can ultimately result in long-term or long-standing changes in numerous areas of biopsychosocial functioning. Perry and Azad (1999) report a number of long-term sequelae from childhood trauma, including Eating Disorders; suicidal behavior; alcoholism; gastrointestinal problems; gynecological problems; somatic problems, including headaches and chronic fatigue; and, of course, PTSD.

Children, Violence, and Trauma

Social critics, researchers, the media, and concerned citizens all seem to agree that the violence toward, among, and around children is at epidemic proportions. Murder is one of the top causes of death in both children and adolescents. Although one might be tempted to attribute the seeming commonness of youth violence to simply more media exposure, the statistics just don't bear this out. We live in more violent times. This is a fact, and children are extremely vulnerable. It follows logically then that where there is violence, traumatic experiences and subsequent PTSD are not far behind. There are at least two types of exposure to violence for children, direct (e.g., assault or abuse) and indirect (e.g., witnessing, living in a violent environment or home, or hearing about other victims).

Abuse and Interpersonal Violence
No discussion of trauma in children would be complete without discussing the effects of physical abuse, sexual abuse, and maltreatment with respect to PTSD. Many professionals and public policy makers consider these phenomena to be of epidemic proportions. Research has shown that exposure to physical maltreatment and abuse can lead to PTSD and other comorbid problems such as poor impulse control, rage, detachment, estrangement, and other enduring personality changes. Sexually abused children are also at risk for PTSD.

Complex PTSD and Maltreatment
As was previously mentioned, Lenore Terr's concept of Type II refers to PTSD following repeated traumas and their cumulative effects. Stien and Kendall (2003) equate this to *complex trauma*, which refers to the effects of chronic and repeated trauma, and, according to these authors, there are seven core symptoms of complex PTSD in children:

1. Problems with emotion and arousal regulation.
2. Alterations in consciousness and memory.
3. Damage to self-concept and identity.
4. Disruptions in cognitive capacities.
5. Hyperactivity and attention problems.
6. Relationship problems.
7. Alterations in systems of belief.

The concept of complex PTSD is part of a seemingly growing movement within both research and clinical practice, but primarily within clinical practice, that the effects of trauma cannot be adequately captured by the traditional concept of PTSD in all individuals, particularly not in children.

Witnessing and Exposure to Violence in the Home and Community
Stien and Kendall (2003) consider children that are exposed to domestic violence to be one of the most unrecognized populations with chronic PTSD. There is also a 30 to 50 percent overlap between domestic violence and child abuse (Elders, 1999; Stien & Kendall, 2003). Children who witness homicide have been found to develop PTSD, and numerous studies surveying both exposure rates to violence and PTSD symptomotology in preschoolers, elementary school children, and adolescents have shown a connection (Fitzpatrick & Boldizar, 1993;

Professional Alert

Does childhood Physical Abuse or Sexual Abuse always lead to PTSD? The quick answer to the question is no. Many people exposed to any traumatic stressor will not develop PTSD for that matter, be it abuse or a natural disaster. Rates of PTSD resulting from physical abuse range from 40 percent to 50 percent, depending on the study one reads. Lubit (2005) puts the figure at about 42 percent for meeting diagnostic criteria for PTSD. As is the case for sexual abuse as well, although full criteria for PTSD are not met in many cases, many posttraumatic symptoms can be found as well as numerous comorbid conditions such as behavior problems and aggression. Regarding rates of PTSD in cases of sexual abuse, Donaldson and Gardner (1985) report that 36 percent of adult survivors of sexual abuse may have PTSD. The picture is slightly more complicated, however, as Saunders et al. (1992) found that 66 percent of child victims of sexual penetration developed PTSD in their lifetime. The take-away point is that there is a possibility for PTSD to develop in both of these populations and should always be considered worthy of clinical attention.

Horowitz, Weine, & Jenkel, 1995; Martinez & Richters, 1993). Essentially, it is important to keep in mind that children exposed to violence, either directly or witnessing it, are potentially at risk for PTSD.

Assessment

Clinicians have at their disposal several psychometric instruments for objectively assessing PTSD in children and adolescents. These instruments can be used in the initial diagnosis and identification of PTSD and related symptoms and difficulties and to assess treatment progress. Five specific instruments are identified by Greenwald (2000). The Impact of Event scale is an empirically respectable instrument for use with children. It can be used to assess a child's reaction to a recent traumatic event. The Trauma Symptom Checklist for Children is considered a preferred instrument with good psychometric properties. There is also the Los Angeles Symptom Checklist–Adolescent, which is considered a good instrument. The trauma symptoms checklist and the LA symptoms checklist are not specific to PTSD, instead measuring a wider range of posttraumatic phenomena. They do, however, have PTSD subscales. Finally, The Child Report of Post-Traumatic Symptoms and the Parent Report of Post-Traumatic Symptoms are considered very promising instruments but have less adolescent research support.

Although objective instruments are preferred for psychometric and empirical reasons, sometimes a clinician must rely on less objective measures, going to his or her projective test toolbox or relying on less formal methods. This may be the case because a child is untestable; or there are other inhibiting factors, such as parental minimization of trauma's role in their child's difficulties; or there is parental denial. Less formal methods always play an important role in clinical work. One informal method that has shown to be helpful with children is to analyze the content and process of their play. Attention should be paid to elements of reenactment and repetition. In abuse cases, elements of developmentally inappropriate content should catch one's attention.

Treatment

Cohen, Berliner, and March (2000a, b) provide a solid review of the empirical literature of treatment techniques for children and adolescents with PTSD. Their concise summary and discussion is welcomed, as the literature for treatment of child PTSD is very large and very complex, particularly if one considers the dense and complicated psychoanalytic and psychodynamic literature. Ultimately, their review shows that the class of cognitive-behavioral therapies is first-line treatment that have empirical support. These treatments include exposure, cognitive restructuring, anxiety management, and a psychoeducation component. Psychodynamic psychotherapy, art therapy, or group therapy are supported by anecdotal evidence but cannot be considered first-line treatments. There is a lack of research support for psychopharmacological treatment of children with PTSD. However, some clinical and anecdotal data suggest that the SSRIs and clonidine are promising medications.

These authors also make some specific recommendations for specific populations. For physically abused children, these authors recommend beginning with individual therapy and eventually expanding into exposure and rehearsal with parental involvement. Regarding parental involvement in general, they suggest that parental involvement is critical as parents can provide needed support, monitoring, and behavioral management. Keep in mind that parents may need treatment for themselves as well, if not for PTSD then perhaps for secondary traumatic stress disorder, compassion fatigue, or burnout (for more on STSD, compassion fatigue, or burnout in families, see the following section and Chapter 19). Finally, group therapy is recommended for groups of children, particularly for school-related traumatic events in which children have experienced trauma in common or as a group.

Treating children, of course, involves a level of expertise and a knowledge base that adult-oriented clinicians may not always possess, including knowledge of developmental theory and its role in trauma. In choosing a treatment approach, Kathleen Nader (2001) makes the following helpful observations:

1. For preschoolers, the focus is often on play with accompanying clinician verbalization of sequences and reactions.

2. For younger, school-aged children, play and drawing can be combined with cognitive review and clinician-child discussion.

3. For adolescents, discussion is the focus.

She identifies a key element in child treatments as engaging in the continual review of the traumatic event, reprocessing memory material, restoring a sense of competence and safety, and increasing the sense of control. Special adjunctive techniques may have to be utilized when comorbid conditions or complications occur, such as dissociation.

Finally, something should be said about play therapy, as it is one of the more well-known forms of childhood therapy for many disorders. The focus is on symptom reduction and assisting development through verbalization in play and, oftentimes, interpretation of the play and verbalizations by a clinician (Nader, 2001; Terr, 1983; Webb, 1991). Toys, dolls, figures, and replicas are often used for recreation or reenactment.

E. R. Parson (1994) proposed the unique concept of *urban violence traumatic stress syndrome* (UVTS) and an accompanying treatment, *posttraumatic child therapy* (PTCT) to address it. At the core of the theory is the idea that ethnicity, culture, and race interact in inner-city children, resulting in UVTS manifesting in five dimensions: damaged sense of self and confused self-identities, attachment disruptions, cognitive stress-responses, emotional stress-responses, and a moral stress response and distortion of ethnocultural values. PTCT consists of four phases: (1) pretherapy in which goals and a focus are established, (2) stabilization, (3) return to scene in which focusing is on reprocessing, and (4) completion and integration of self.

Posttraumatic Stress Disorder in Families

The Traumatized Family

One of the most important contexts in which PTSD occurs is within the family. Individuals with PTSD have characteristic patterns of interaction with family members that play a very powerful role in symptom expression and recovery. Also, multiple family members can be traumatized simultaneously, creating a PTSD family of sorts. There are also the profound effects that living within a family with someone who suffers from PTSD can have on the other family members and the family system and dynamics as a whole.

Studying trauma within families is part of what Charles Figley calls *systemic traumatology*, the study of groups, institutions, and other human systems exhibiting stress reactions that are a direct result of a traumatic event or series of events. Figley (1989) conceptualizes a traumatized family as a family that is "struggling to recover from, to cope with, an injury or wound to their [family] system" (p. 5). This type of traumatized family suffers from systemic traumatic stress. He also defines a subset of traumatized families as consisting of families in which at least one member is suffering from PTSD and the others experience STSD, compassion fatigue, or burnout as a result of being traumatized from exposure to the actual traumatized member or members of the family. He goes on to define a *family trauma* as an event in which there is a general sense that the family is in some kind of danger or a major upheaval that involves all or one of its members.

Donald Catherall (1998) identifies numerous areas of dysfunction and pathology in traumatized families. To begin with, a family or one of its members experiences a traumatic event, which is followed by dysfunctional coping and a breakdown in the family's collective mourning process. This is followed by dysfunction in the following domains:

- *Disruptions in the family's connection and caretaking.* This consists of issues of emotional disconnection and inaccessibility among members, children's needs not being met, children feeling isolated, children feeling insecure, parentification of the children and placing them in the caretaker role, and an altered sense of self.

- *Distortions in the family's consensual reality.* This consists of distortions in world view, isolation and maladaptive beliefs and attitudes, family myths about the event, emotional and relational constriction, dysfunctional rules, and decreased problem solving.

- *Familywide traumatic symptoms.* This consists of replications of themes, reenactments, and projections; identifications with undifferentiated family members; continuing safety concerns and preoccupations; anxiety, distrust, and insecurity; survivor missions; suppression of aspects of self; symptomatic members; and stress on family as a whole.

How do traumatized families form or develop? Figley (1998) provides the *trauma transmission model* to explain how traumatized families form. In essence, traumatized families develop as members act out of concern or empathy for one another and engage in answering what Figley calls the *five victim questions* for the victim: What happened? Why did it happen? Why did I act as I did then? Why have I acted as I have since? If it happens again, will I be able to cope? Figley states:

> supporters try to answer these questions for the victim in order to change his or her behavior accordingly. Yet, in the process of generating new information, the system member experiences emotions that are strikingly similar to the victim's. This includes visual images (e.g. flashbacks), sleeping problems, depression, and other symptoms that are a direct result of visualizing the victim's traumatic experiences, exposure to the symptoms of the victim, or both. (pp. 20–21)

He characterizes this process as being swept up in the victim's experience and emotion.

Not all families who have a PTSD sufferer within them are traumatized families per se. These families struggle in some similar ways as traumatized families but in other ways as well. There is often a reciprocal or mutual-influence effect between the sufferer and the rest of the family members. The difficulties that can arise can also be amplified if they go unconnected to or are not identified as being related to trauma.

Harkness and Zador (2001) discuss numerous ways in which PTSD can affect family functioning. The individual sufferer's symptoms get played out within the relationships and dynamics of the family. Reexperiencing symptoms interfere with the sufferer's ability to pay attention, concentrate, and be present within the family or when among family. Avoidance symptoms may manifest as emotional detachment and interaction difficulties. Hypervigilance may result in significant trust issues. There may be difficulties in either forming or maintaining attachment due to unresolved grief or fear of another loss. Feelings of demoralization, self-hate, and shame might lead to self-pity and thoughts such as "Why would anyone want to be with me?"

Aggression and poor modulation of anger can lead to outbursts, rages, hostility, and even domestic violence or child physical abuse. Sometimes, a sufferer might fear his or her violent tendencies or lack of control and isolate him or herself from the rest of the family in order to protect them. Feelings and perceptions of danger might lead to overreactions to perceived slights, feelings of humiliation, and add to a general sense of emotional mistrust. Sometimes the feelings of shame, self-hate, or demoralization can get projected onto the family and its various members, leading to severe defensiveness, paranoia, and sometimes aggression.

Harkness and Zador (2001) point out that *a* central, if not *the* central struggle, of PTSD in families is the emotional inaccessibility of the identified victim or sufferer. This unavailability can sometimes result in boundary problems between the victim and the children in a family. There can be intense emotional detachment and periods of negative self-focus and preoccupation. In an effort to protect him- or herself from overstimulation, a sufferer might "space out" or tune out those around him or her. This sometimes manifests in excessive movie watching, reading, or plain physical absence. Strong feelings of emotional estrangement and emptiness can develop in such as system. Family members may fill the absence of the missing sufferer with a sense of guilt and responsibility. Family life may be patterned around not overwhelming or overstimulating the sufferer. There is also the issue of the very real functional loss of a working and contributing family member as the sufferer may cease to be a functioning family member (Harkness & Zador, 2001). The other family members end up overcompensating, which can lead to burnout or being overburdened. Family members and the sufferer can get stuck in a mutual pattern of invalidation in which the family members want the sufferer to "get over it" as they feel that their day-to-day lives and current circumstances cease to be important to the sufferer because he or she is living in the past. In turn, the sufferer feels as if he or she is isolated and is misunderstood. Harkness and Zador (2001) identify this pattern as a critical issue for healing within the family. Posttraumatic Stress Disorder families must develop the ability to live with the paradox of remembering and accepting, and moving on.

Treatment of the Traumatized Family

Figley (1989) proposes the *empowerment approach* for the treatment of traumatized families. As one can tell from the name, the main objective is to empower the family to help themselves and engage in functional coping and the healing process. Figley's model consists of five treatment phases:

> *Phase One: Building commitment to the therapeutic objectives.* Agreed-upon objectives are established and committed to.

> *Phase Two: Framing the problem.* By telling the trauma story, the issues, struggles, and dysfunctions are laid out.

> *Phase Three: Reframing the problem.* The family works to develop a new way to tell or retell their ongoing story in more tolerable and adaptable ways.

> *Phase Four: Developing a healing theory.* This consists of propositions that help explain the current situation, the need for help, and the need to predict the future.

> *Phase Five: Closure and preparedness.* Finally, families assess their progress with appreciation and faithfully acknowledge their preparedness for the future.

Harkness and Zador (2001) propose that there are three essential components of treatment for the traumatized family. They are psychoeducation, disclosure of traumatic material, and addressing the dialectical nature of living with PTSD. The psychoeducation component, by means of various techniques such as videos or books, seeks to educate the family members about the sufferer's symptoms affect functioning, his or her perception of the world, and relationships. The isolation and communication difficulties within traumatized families are addressed through the disclosure component. Reenactment is hopefully diminished as the traumatic material is shared and coprocessed amongst the family. Finally, the paradox of balancing acceptance and acknowledgment with forward progress must be developed and the family system learns how to contain the trauma while it is processed.

Transgenerational Trauma

Can the trauma of one generation lead to trauma for the next? Research and clinical work have shown that in survivors of mass trauma, such as the Holocaust, Japanese internment during World War II, and the children of Vietnam veterans, there can be a *transgenerational* transmission of sorts of PTSD symptomotology. Children of traumatized parents or other significant relatives can experience the same symptoms as these people without direct exposure. In addition to PTSD, they may also have other clinical problems such as depression or substance abuse. Children at risk have very close relationships with the sufferers and are exposed to symptoms of rage, depression, guilt, loss of impulse control, nightmares, and flashbacks. They may take on the role of rescuer within the family as well. They may be seen as symbols of those lost, such as dead relatives, friends, or combat buddies (Steinberg, 1998). This may be reflected in the naming of a child after someone deceased. Interestingly, this population is also more at risk for developing PTSD in their own right as adults.

Summary

Posttraumatic Stress Disorder in children and families is complicated in numerous ways that PTSD in individual adults is not. Issues of developmental milestones and complex family interactions and dynamics can change the way the disorder manifests itself and how it is treated. Respect and knowledge for these issues are vital tools in addressing trauma effectively in these populations.

Quick Summary

- Children and adolescents are considered at-risk populations for PTSD because of issues of dependence, limited resources, and developmental vulnerability.

- Although they may present with traditional PTSD, the disorder may also look very different in children and adolescents, including symptoms of acting out, somatization, and various forms of specific reenactment.

- The family environment and parenting issues are powerful influences on childhood PTSD.

- The general class of cognitive-behavioral treatment is considered an empirically tested, first-line treatment for children and adolescents with PTSD.

- Children exposed to violence, particularly Physical and Sexual Abuse, are at higher risk for PTSD.

- Traumatized families can consist of families with one or more member with PTSD or subsequent members with STSD or Compassion Fatigue or burnout.

- Traumatized families struggle with the manifestation of the individual sufferer's symptoms within the family dynamics.

- Issues of isolation, communication, acceptance, and moving on are central themes in traumatized families.

- Treating traumatized families involves empowering them to move toward self-healing and improving the systemic acknowledgment and processing of traumatic material.

- Posttraumatic Stress Disorder is considered to sometimes be transmitted across generations, with children of PTSD sufferers developing symptoms of their own.

References

Ainsworth, M. S. (1979). Infant-mother attachment. *American Psychologist, 34*, 932–937.
Bowlby, J. (1988). *A secure base: Parent-child attachment and healthy human development.* New York: Basic Books.

Catherall, D. R. (1998). Treating traumatized families. In C. R. Figley (Ed.), *Burnout in families: The systemic costs of caring* (pp. 187–215). Boca Raton, FL: CRC Press.

Cohen, J. A., Berliner, L., & March, J. S. (2000a). Treatment of children and adolescents. In E. B. Foa, T. M. Keane, & M. J. Friedman (Eds.), *Effective treatments for PTSD: Practice guidelines from the International Society for Traumatic Stress Studies* (pp. 106–138). New York: Guilford.

Cohen, J. A., Berliner, L., & March, J. S. (2000b). Treatment of children and adolescents. In E. B. Foa, T. M. Keane, & M. J. Friedman (Eds.), *Effective treatments for PTSD: Practice guidelines from the International Society for Traumatic Stress Studies* (pp. 330–332). New York: Guilford.

Davidson, J. R. T., & Foa, E. B. (Eds.). (1993) *Posttraumatic Stress Disorder:* DSM-IV *and beyond.* Arlington, VA: American Psychiatric Publishing.

Donaldson, M. A, & Gardner, R. (1985). Diagnosis and treatment of traumatic stress among women after childhood incest. In C. R. Figley (Ed.), *Trauma and its wake: The study and treatment of Post-Traumatic Stress Disorder.* New York: Bruner/Mazel.

Elders, J. (1999, January). *The call to action.* A plenary presented at the San Diego Conference on Responding to Maltreatment, San Diego, CA.

Figley, C. R. (1989). *Helping traumatized families.* San Francisco: Jossey-Bass.

Figley, C. R. (1998). Burnout as systemic traumatic stress: A model for helping traumatized family members. In Charles R. Figley (Ed.), *Burnout in families: The systemic costs of caring* (pp. 15–28). Boca Raton, FL: CRC Press.

Fitzpatrick, K. M., & Boldizar, J. P. (1993). The prevalence and consequences of exposure to violence among African-American youth. *Journal of the American Academy of Child & Adolescent Psychiatry, 32,* 424–430.

Gabbay, V., Oatis, M. D., Silva, R. R., & Hirsch, G. S. (2004). Epidemiological aspects of PTSD in children and adolescents. In R. R. Silva (Eds.), *Posttraumatic Stress Disorders in children and adolescents: Handbook* (pp. 1–17). New York: W. W. Norton.

Greenwald, R. (2000). The trauma orientation and child therapy. In K. N. Dwivedi (Ed.), *Post-Traumatic Stress Disorder in children and adolescents* (pp. 7–24). Philadelphia: Whurr.

Harkness, L., & Zador, N. (2001). Treatment of PTSD in families and couples. In J. P. Wilson, M. J. Friedman, & J. D. Lindy (Eds.), *Treating psychological trauma and PTSD* (pp. 335–353). New York: Guilford.

Herman, J. L. (1993). Sequelae of prolonged and repeated trauma: Evidence for a complex posttraumatic syndrome (DESNOS). In J. R. T. Davidson & E. B. Foa (Eds.), *Posttraumatic stress disorder:* DSM-IV *and beyond* (pp. 213–228). Washington, DC: American Psychiatric Press.

Horowitz, K., Weine, S., & Jekel, J. (1995). PTSD symptoms in urban adolescent girls: Compounded community trauma. *Journal of the American Academy of Child and Adolescent Psychiatry, 34*(10), 1353–1361.

Jenkins, E. J., & Bell, C. C. (1997). Exposure and response to community violence among children and adolescents. In J. D. Osofsky (Ed.), *Children in a violent society* (pp. 9–31). New York: Guilford.

Kowalik, S. C. (2004). Neurobiology of PTSD in children and adolescents. In R. R. Silva (Ed.), *Posttraumatic Stress Disorders in children and adolescents: Handbook* (pp. 83–122). New York: W. W. Norton.

Lubit, R. (2005). Posttraumatic Stress Disorder in children. Retrieved September 2005 from http://www.emedicine.com.

Martinez, P., & Richters, J. E. (1993). The NIMH Community Violence Project: II. Children's distress symptoms associated with violence exposure. *Psychiatry: Interpersonal and Biological Processes, 56,* 22–35.

Nader, K. (2001). Treatment methods for childhood trauma. In J. P. Wilson, M. J. Friedman, & J. D. Lindy (Eds.), *Treating psychological trauma and PTSD* (pp. 278–334). New York: Guilford.

Parson, E. R. (1994). Inner city children of trauma: Urban violence traumatic stress response syndrome (U-VTS) and therapists' responses. In J. P. Wilson & J. D. Lindy (Ed.), *Countertransference in the treatment of PTSD* (pp. 151–178). New York: Guilford.

Perry, B. D. (1994). Neurobiological sequelae of childhood trauma: PTSD in children. In M. M. Murburg (Ed.), *Catecholamine function in Posttraumatic Stress Disorder: Emerging concepts* (pp. 233–255). Washington, DC: American Psychiatric Association.

Perry, B. D., & Azad, I. (1999). Post-Traumatic Stress Disorders in children and adolescents. *Current Opinion in Pediatrics, 11,* 121–132.

Saunders, B. E., Villeponteaux, L. A., Lipovsky, J. A., Kilpatrick, D. G., et al. (1992). Child sexual assault as a risk factor for mental disorders among women: A community survey. *Journal of Interpersonal Violence, 7,* 189–204.

Scheeringa, M. S., & Gaensbauer, T. J. (2000). Posttraumatic Stress Disorder. In C. H. Zeanah, Jr. (Ed.), *Handbook of infant mental health* (2nd ed., pp. 369–381). New York: Guilford.

Schwarz, E. D., & Perry, B. D. (1994). The post-traumatic response in children and adolescents. [Electronic version]. *Psychiatric Clinics of North America, 17,* 311–326.

Steinberg, A. (1998). Understanding the secondary traumatic stress of children. In C. R. Figley (Ed.), *Burnout in families: The systemic costs of caring* (pp. 29–46). Boca Raton, FL: CRC Press.

Stien, P., & Kendall, J. (2003). *Psychological trauma and the developing brain: Neurologically based interventions for troubled children.* Binghamton, NY: Haworth Maltreatment and Trauma Press.

Terr, L. C. (1981). Psychic trauma in children: Observations following the Chowchilla school-bus kidnapping. *American Journal of Psychiatry, 138,* 14–19.

Terr, L. C. (1983). Chowchilla revisited: The effects of psychic trauma four years after a school-bus kidnapping. *American Journal of Psychiatry, 140,* 1543–1550.

Terr, L. (1990). *Too scared to cry: Psychic trauma in childhood.* New York: Harper & Row.

Terr, L. C. (1991). Childhood traumas: An outline and overview. *American Journal of Psychiatry, 148,* 10–20.

Terr, L. C. (1995). Childhood traumas: An outline and overview. In G. S. Everly, Jr. & J. M. Lating (Eds.), *Psychotraumatology: Key papers and core concepts in post-traumatic stress* (pp. 301–320). New York: Plenum Press.

Webb, N. B. (1991). Play therapy crisis intervention with children. In N. B. Webb (Ed.), *Play therapy with children in crisis: A casebook for practitioners* (pp. 26–42). New York: Guilford.

Winnicott, D. W. (2002). *Winnicott on the child.* Cambridge, MA: Perseus.

Zero to Three, National Center for Infants, Toddlers, and Families. (1994). *Diagnostic classification: 0–3: Diagnostic classification of mental health and developmental disorders of infancy and early childhood.* Washington, DC: Zero to Three, National Center for Infants, Toddlers, and Families.

CHAPTER 21

War, Terrorism, Torture, and Posttraumatic Stress Disorder

The sheer power and intensity of the *war experience* is undeniable. Whether you are a pacifist, a *just war* supporter, or an outright supporter of aggressive warfare, war and similar human-to-human violent acts can be considered among the most horrific experiences in human existence. The horrors of war are documented throughout history and intimately captured in countless works of art and literature, including Homer's *The Iliad* and Stephen Crane's *The Red Badge of Courage*. Films such as *The Deer Hunter, Casualties of War, The Pawnbroker*, and *The Killing Fields* are intense and powerful depictions of the horrors of war in general and the trauma of war specifically. In this chapter, we take time to reflect on the trauma of war and two other often-related forms of human violence, terrorism and torture, as uniquely powerful birthplaces for PTSD. Their unique status among the countless stressors that can lead to PTSD is based in part on their ability to produce so many victims, the seeming inevitability of their stimulation of trauma, and the complex web in which victims and perpetrators find themselves caught.

War and Combat

At any given time, no matter what historical period and no matter what year in which you gather statistics, there are hundreds of armed conflicts and wars being waged. Conflict on a mass scale is massive in its effects. Moreover, the modern world has found more and more efficient ways to kill more and more people in war. Technology has played a huge role. I have heard that the twentieth century has seen the death of nearly 100 million people in relation to wars in one form or another. Rightfully, the horrors of war can lead to PTSD. In turn, however, those who make it their business to wage war work hard to eliminate or reduce the natural repulsion to killing that many human beings have. This can lead to its own complications. Those of the political left or pacifist persuasion might view war as a mental health issue in and of itself. Regardless of one's political views, however, war undoubtedly has significant effects on the mental health of those it touches.

The history of war-related and combat-related trauma is rich in detail about the profound effects of its participants and victims. The famous ancient Greek stories by Sophocles about the warrior Ajax depict his powerful post-battle breakdown as a hopeless breakdown. David Marlowe (2001) states, "The overwhelming psychological power of combat to alter behavior and to overwhelm 'normalcy' was recognized by the ancient world, . . . " (p. 9).

The modern era has seen a progression of the concepts used to describe and view war and combat trauma from shell shock in World War I to PTSD following Vietnam. Vietnam is considered to have produced a very high number of posttraumatic reactions compared to its actual casualties and deaths and in comparison to other wars of similar magnitude. Although the formal diagnosis of PTSD did not come into play until well after the Vietnam War, vets were returning home and reporting a wide range of symptoms that mapped directly onto the diagnosis, such as anxiety, depression, nightmares, sleep problems, flashbacks, and physiological reactivity (Keane, 1998). The National Vietnam Veterans Readjustment Study in 1990 found that 31 percent of vets had a lifetime prevalence of PTSD, with 15 percent of male Vietnam War veterans meeting criteria at the current time. The Centers for Disease Control Vietnam Experience Study found 15 percent for lifetime prevalence in this population, with 2 percent prevalence for the previous month. There is research support for the notion that Vietnam War veterans suffer from higher rates of PTSD when compared to numerous groups and even in studies with rigorous statistical control for confounding variables, such as race, education level, and premorbid psychiatric illness. Vietnam veterans with PTSD report much higher rates of related social difficulties than non-PTSD Vietnam veterans, such as higher rates of homelessness, violence, aggression, crime, and anger and hostility.

Flack, Litz, and Keane (1998) outline the following trauma-relevant factors of the Vietnam veteran's experience:

- Participation in killing of enemy soldiers
- Frequent exposure to the threat of death
- Risk of death from civilians, including children
- Witnessing maiming and slaughter of fellow soldiers
- Witnessing acts of violence against civilians
- Participation in atrocities against civilians
- Witnessing of atrocities against civilians and a failure to prevent them

In the more recent Persian Gulf War (the first war with Iraq), estimates show that 19 percent of soldiers met criteria for PTSD (Sutkcr, Uddo, Brailey, & Allain, 1993). Marlowe (2001) conducted a survey of Gulf War veterans and their evaluation of their exposure to traumatic stressors that generated "quite a bit of stress" or "extreme stress." Table 21.1 is an adaptation of a table in his work.

Fairbank, Friedman, and Southwick (2001) report the prevalence rate of PTSD in veterans varies as a function of the nature of the exposure and characteristics of the participants themselves. They remind us that the experience of war and combat is highly idiosyncratic, but research has shown some consistent findings for postwar adjustment in PTSD sufferers. For men who served in combat, there is an increased risk for developing Antisocial Personality Disorder; Major Depressive Disorder; Dysthymic Disorder; Obsessive-Compulsive Disorder; Alcohol Dependence; more somatic problems; and higher rates of risky health practices, such as smoking, unemployment, and marriage problems. Women who served in the military in combat theaters are also subject to higher rates of depression and Dysthymic Disorder.

In Chapter 8 we discussed disorders of extreme stress not otherwise specified (DESNOS), and in Chapter 20 we discussed complex PTSD to characterize the condition of posttraumatic symptoms and phenomena in situations of enduring and chronic traumatic stress. Disorders of extreme stress not otherwise specified are characterized by extreme affect dysregulation (e.g., rage, suicidality, unmodulated sexual activity), pathological dissociation, somatization, and altered beliefs about self and relationships (Ford, 1999). Disorders of extreme stress not otherwise specified and PTSD are not necessarily the same disorder with shared variance being reported in studies that measure both in select

TABLE 21.1

Soldier Exposure to Traumatic Stressors

34.5%	Witnessed a buddy wounded in action
43.5%	Witnessed a buddy killed in action
21.7%	Wounded or injured
22.4%	Had a leader wounded or killed in action
23.8%	Had a confirmed enemy kill
23.1%	Saw an enemy soldier killed or wounded
31.7%	Was attacked by enemy tanks
35.8%	Was attacked by enemy artillery

populations. Ford measured rates of both DESNOS and PTSD in a sample of military veterans seeking inpatient PTSD treatment and found that 31 percent met criteria for both, 29 percent had PTSD only, 26 percent had DESNOS only, and 13 percent did not meet criteria for either disorder.

Posttraumatic Stress Disorder and Peacekeeping

Starting around the early 1990s, the United States found itself involved in what have been called *peacekeeping missions,* sometimes in conjunction with the United Nations. These military actions have many things in common with what is typically considered a war or traditional combat but may also have features that make the development and experience of PTSD following these actions unique. There appears to be a trend for involvement in more and more of these types of actions as opposed to traditional wars or combat, and, as such, analyzing the similarities and differences between PTSD in a traditional war context versus the peacekeeping context seems worthwhile.

In two studies, both published in 1997, Brett Litz and his colleagues (Litz et al., 1997a, b) examined PTSD in veterans of the infamous peacekeeping mission in Somalia from 1992 to 1994 dubbed *Operation Restore Hope* or *Operation Continue Hope.* Litz et al. propose that a soldier on a peacekeeping mission has a unique set of responsibilities, including monitoring, protecting civilians and noncombatants, ensuring access to humanitarian aid, and helping to build infrastructure. Their combat-related action is typically related to maintaining order and peace but nonetheless involves dangerous missions and constant threat. The first study by Litz and colleagues found that 8 percent of Somalia veterans met criteria for PTSD. What is unique is that in addition to exposure to war-zone stressors, perceived negative aspects of the peacekeeping mission itself were associated with PTSD severity: "Soldiers who were distressed by the unique role demands of peacekeeping and peace enforcement were more at risk for PTSD" (Litz et al., 1997a, p. 1002). In the second 1997 study, Litz and colleagues made similar findings with some added complexity. Posttraumatic Stress Disorder was associated with traditional combat exposure, negative aspects of the peacekeeping experience, and pressure to uphold restraint. Restraint itself was not associated with PTSD as the pressure to do so was. Negative aspects of the peacekeeping experience include situations that engendered a sense of personal discomfort, aggravation, or distress that "might have lead to a sense of being disheartened but did not pose an eminent threat to life for military personnel. . . " (Litz et al., 1997a, p. 1004)

Society and Its Soldiers

It is certainly no secret that the military personnel who served during the Vietnam War returned to a very complex, confusing, and even hostile cultural and social environment back home in the United States. People were conflicted by the war from the beginning and even to the present day. Should we have been there? Should we have fought the war? How could we have won? Did the government support the troops? These questions arise out of a context that some have argued contributes heavily to the experience of PTSD in Vietnam veterans.

Whether it is Vietnam or some other war, the social and cultural construction of the war, including media coverage, plays a huge role in determining what gets classified as *legitimate* suffering. Despite its scientific merit, on some level PTSD is a cultural construct, albeit a scientifically supported one with some universal appeal across cultures. What a war means and what it means to be at war and a soldier are critical issues in military personnel's psychological assessment, acceptance, and adjustment to being at war. Soldiers ask themselves, Why am I fighting? Why am I being asked to kill these people? Soldier's families ask similar questions and additional ones as well such as, Why did my son die? When a soldier develops PTSD, he or she might ask, Was it worth it? Was this the price I had to pay? They might question the sincerity of the society they return to. They may question its desire to support and help them heal. Soldiers may develop deep feelings of resentment, feeling as if they were asked to put their lives on the line and to kill without anyone wanting to know the details about it or to hear about what it was like. Do the job; spare the details.

War is an ugly human phenomenon, and most people don't want to face it if they do not have to. But this attitude can have powerful effects on the experience of trauma and even on whether PTSD develops or is recognized. The social view of a war and its participants can affect how the difficulties of those who return are viewed. Vets returning home from Vietnam were referred to as *baby killers* by some in the antiwar movement. Marlowe (2001) cites how the media and society as a whole often portrayed this same group negatively:

> [They are] plundering junkies who would unleash an era of crime and violence upon American society such as had never been seen before. He [the returning vet] was also characterized, as we have seen, as a seething mass of psychiatric disabilities. Employers were often suspicious of him and fellow students often rejected him and treated him with great hostility. The stress of this kind of homecoming on the vulnerable cannot be overestimated.

Israel and its citizens are no strangers to war and strife. Witztum and Kotler (2000) discuss the cultural and societal appraisal of trauma and the "perception of the combat stress reaction" in Israeli society. They propose that these appraisals and perceptions change over time, depending on the political, ideological, and social factors of the day. In their view, the very concept of combat trauma has been essentially incompatible with Israeli cultural identity and that Israeli society did not have time for such a concept as it fought for national and cultural survival. The very experience of trauma and its experience of vulnerability to hopelessness is the antithesis of the image that Israelis had of themselves as a strong, safe, mastery-oriented, assertive, heroic, and resilient people. Witzum and Kotler (2000) state:

> Against this background, one can understand how, for the first 30 years of Israel's existence, CSC [combat stress reaction] and PTSD were "forgotten," denied by military authorities, by society, and even by mental health systems. The state of matters was defined at that time by a former surgeon general, Brigadier General, Dr. M. Kordova: "We do not have this problem and we cannot afford this 'American luxury.'" (p. 106)

Prisoners of War (POWs)

Not all war-related trauma involves death necessarily. Prisoners of war have been found to have high rates of PTSD. Estimates as high as 30 to 70 percent for POWs of World War II and 15 percent for Vietnam veterans have been proposed (Eberly & Engdahl, 1991; Kulka et al., 1990). The conditions POWs are exposed to are often severe and include captivity, fear, terror, pain, suffering, shame, humiliation, beatings, untreated medical problems, being deprived of food and shelter, forced relocation, excessive work regimes, and witnessing executions (Engdahl & Fairbank, 2001). Levels of comorbid conditions are also high, including depression and even neurological impairment.

Farber, Harlow, and West (1957) explored the tactics used by captors and identified three main components: (1) debility brought on by starvation, fatigue, infliction of pain, and failure to provide medical care; (2) dread induced through anticipatory anxiety, uncertainty of death, pain, and threat of nonrelease; and (3) dependency on captors for virtually everything. These authors remind us that understanding the specifics of the survivor's captivity and the survivor's attempts to cope with the efforts at isolation, and their demeanment are critical aspects for intervention. The power dynamics that develop between captor and captive are strong determinants of how a therapeutic relationship will develop and play out.

Engdahl and Fairbank (2001) state that many former POWs have never received and may never receive needed mental health care. They state that this is perhaps due, in no small measure, to the captivity experience itself including the existence of a POW's mind-set of passivity, resignation, or guilt. Still other POWs might feel resentful of their experience and feel that the government and society abandoned them.

Perpetrator-Induced PTSD in Combat

Kill or be killed. This is the undeniable reality of war. In his book *On Killing: The Psychological Cost of Learning to Kill in War and Society*, military psychologist Dave Grossman (1996) states, "Looking another human being in the eye, making an independent decision to kill him, and watching as he dies due to your action combine to form the single most basic, important, primal, and potentially traumatic occurrence of war" (p. 31).

Green (1990) cites that causing death or severe harm is among the categories of stressors that can lead to PTSD. Rachel MacNair (2002) introduces the concept of *perpetration-induced traumatic stress* (PITS) and defines it as PTSD symptomatology resulting from situations in which the sufferer is the causal agent. MacNair states, "Killing . . . [is a] . . . Stressor" (p. 13). Studies have shown that participation in atrocities represents a unique and additive risk for PTSD (Breslau & Davis, 1987; Strayer & Ellenhorn, 1975) and that PTSD is more severe in perpetrators with PTSD compared to nonperpetrators with PTSD (MacNair, 2002). Perpetrators in MacNair's analysis had higher levels of violent outbursts and strong associations with hypervigilance, alienation, and survivor guilt.

Treatment of War and Combat PTSD

Creamer and Forbes (2004) provide a review of treatment for PTSD in veterans. Treatment for vets is unique in several keys way. To begin with, research indicates that overall, treatment is less beneficial for vets; they come to treatment much longer after the initial trauma and have a more complex presentation, higher levels of comorbidity, and higher levels of social and occupational dysfunction. Those vets with PTSD currently serving in the military present another complex group, and treatment suggestions include focusing on increasing coping and resilience factors and preventing relapse. Vets may also have a tendency to focus on somatic complaints.

Treatment participation may be an initial obstacle of some severity with vets due to a number of factors. Some clinicians cite the role that military training itself plays in teaching soldiers to ignore their emotions and to be less emotionally expressive. The exception, of course, is anger. Treatment that focuses on arousal management may be difficult, as some believe that military training often involves pairing stress with anger as a way to manage fear. This may interfere with counterconditioning in treatment. Anger has been found to interfere with treatment, and, according to Foa, Riggs, Massie, and Yarczower (1995), anger interferes with the ability to access fear and appropriately process it. Research has shown that vets with PTSD often have very high levels of anger.

Because of the complexity of combat-related PTSD, Creamer and Forbes (2004) recommend that treatment be more modest in its goals and should sometimes even take on a more rehabilitation-type focus, with the primary goals being improving relationships, social functioning, and occupational functioning and stability. Cognitive-behavioral therapy and its various components have been shown effective for combat-related PTSD. A psychoeducation component is suggested in order to help the vet focus on overcoming self-views of being weak—believing that his or her training was sufficient and that his or her development of PTSD is a failure. Creamer and Forbes also suggest that a crucial component to treatment is the use of prolonged exposure techniques and suggest that cognitive therapy and restructuring techniques, although not fully supported by research, may be particularly suited for vets. They suggest that issues central in cognitive therapy such as distortions in views of self, world, and others are very common issues for soldiers as they are "brought sharply into question" (p. 392) when entering the bizarre and intense world of war. Exposure to death and suffering on such as scale and involvement in or witnessing of killing or atrocities may be particularly shattering to a soldier's sense of self. Further, if the soldier's social support for the war is lacking, the protective factor of believing that one is on the good side or fighting for truth and justice might not be there. This can lead to confusions and distortions with regard to one's social standing and social view of oneself.

A treatments for vet-particular issues is Creamer and Forbes's (2004) imagery rehearsal therapy (Krakow, Kellner, Pathak, & Lambert, 1995) as it is a specific technique for treating the treatment resistant symptoms of posttraumatic nightmares is recommended, and some research supports this. Nightmares are often lingering symptoms that resist amelioration even after treatment has been completed and other symptoms have been successfully addressed or reduced. Soldiers may often have a very intense and deep sense of guilt and shame. Kubany's cognitive therapy for trauma-related guilt is cited as a promising technique as well (Kubany, 1994, 1997; Kubany & Watson, 2003).

Finally, Creamer and Forbes (2004) indicate that little empirical evidence supports prolonged inpatient treatment for 3 to 6 months, which is often used in the Veterans Administration hospitals. Group therapy is another popular technique that has very little empirical support with the exception of CBT-oriented group therapy. Traditional rap groups have shown marginal effects on symptoms in research, but clinicians with years of experience with vets still consider this type of group as potentially beneficial.

Terrorism, Trauma, and PTSD

The goal of terrorism is PTSD, both individually and on a mass scale. The term *terrorism* can be made to mean a great many things, depending on the person, group, or government doing the defining. Some have said, "One person's terrorist is another person's freedom fighter." But rather than go down any dangerous political roads, we'll use the United Nation's (1993) definition:

> Any other acts intended to cause death or serious bodily injury to a civilian, or to any other person not taking an active part in the hostilities in a situation of armed conflict, when the purpose of such act, by its nature or context, is to intimidate a population, or to compel a government or an international organization to do or abstain from doing any act.

Although some experts would not include the civilian qualifier in their definition, I think that it is important to do so because violent acts against military personnel fall under the heading of *acts of war* or *combat*. If *terrorism* was more narrowly defined as the use of violence to induce fear, virtually all acts of war or combat could be considered terrorism. The definition of *terrorism* is controversial as Brandon Hamber (2004) states, "Calling someone a 'terrorist' poses as a one-word explanation as to why her/his voice should be silenced. Clearly, as a descriptive label 'terrorism' and how we use it is deeply linked with debates about the legitimate use of violence by the state and combatants" (p. 191). From my perspective, states and governments can be terrorists as well. Now that the controversy pot has been thoroughly stirred, let's talk about the trauma of terrorism.

Laurence Miller (2002) proposes:

> Essentially, terrorism is the "perfect" traumatic stressor, because it combines the elements of malevolent intent, actual or threatened extreme harm, and unending fear of the future. Indeed, the very purpose of terrorism fully meets the Criterion A of the *Diagnostic and Statistical Manual of Mental Disorders*. . . diagnostic classification of posttraumatic stress disorder. (p. 284)

The point is to create fear, the hallmark of PTSD. Terrorism is psychological warfare. The very nature of trauma and how it manifests is used as a blueprint of sorts for the use of terrorism. It's as if terrorists have a thorough understanding of posttraumatic reactions. For example, at least one goal of a terrorist attack is to utilize the spreading of mass fear to eventually lead to pressure being put upon the target power group. Ganor (2004) proposes that the often natural reaction to personalize a traumatic event, such as "I was only there last week!" is utilized by the perpetrators as a means to spread fear. He states:

> By such "personalizing" of terrorist attacks, the effect on the target population is made to extend beyond the immediate victims to include people who were not even in the area at the time of the attack.... Members of the target population come to believe that only by a coincidence were they, or someone dear to them, saved from harm, and that such as coincidence cannot be counted upon next time. (p. 41)

On September 11, 2001, millions of Americans and people around the world watched the collapsing of the World Trade Center towers in real time. Did this have an effect? This is, in fact, witnessing the attack after all. Proximity is an issue. The closer someone is to the event, the higher his or her chances are of experiencing trauma. Ahern, Galea, Resnick, and Vlahov (2004) found that anywhere between 7.3 percent to 15 percent of those people directly affected by the attack and who watched the towers collapse exhibited symptoms "probable of PTSD" (p. 109). There was no association for those who watched these same images but were not directly affected. These researchers did find, however, that there was an association (ranging from 2.8 percent to 6.6 percent) between watching a totality of images, including watching the planes hit the tower, bodies falling, people jumping, the towers collapsing, and rescue workers' and survivors' reactions afterward, and probable PTSD.

Exposure to death and the presence of dead bodies and human remains is considered a risk factor for the development of more severe PTSD reactions

(Miller, 2002). Proximity to bodies and the wounded and dying are considered particular risks, and often include thoughts such as "That could have been me" (Miller, 2002).

Pyszczynski, Solomon, and Greenberg (2003) have attempted to utilize a theory known as *terror management theory* to explain the traumatic impact of terrorist attacks. They state, "The terrorist attacks. . . disrupt our normal means of managing our natural terror and, in doing so, threatened to undermine the psychological equanimity necessary for people to function effectively on a daily basis" (p. 9).

According to terror management theory, in order for all us to maintain control over our very natural but overwhelming fear of death, we must feel we are important beings with roots in reality. According to terror management theory, American reactions to the terrorist attacks included denial, distraction (e.g., using drugs or shopping), fortification against future attack, looking for meaning behind the event, patriotism, nationalism, suppressing dissent, increased bigotry, calling for tolerance, increased altruism, and an increased need for heroes and heroic representations in popular culture.

Worldwide, statistics reveal that 20 percent to 40 percent of people directly targeted by a terrorist attack meet criteria for PTSD (Curran et al., 1990; McFarlane & de Girolamo, 1996; Weisaeth, 1993). Two months after the 9/11 attacks, Galea et al. (2002) found that 7.5 percent of adults living in Manhattan south of 110th Street were probable cases of PTSD. Several other studies have collected data over different time frames, ranging from several weeks to a year after 9/11, with rates of PTSD ranging from 7 to 15 percent of those directly affected.

Finally, Miller (2002) makes the following suggestions for intervention and treatment after a terrorist attack. On-scene crisis intervention and psychological first aid are a must. There must also be practical activities with powerful psychological value such as body identification and mass physical casualty care. Individual and family therapy are appropriate interventions for long-term issues. Various community, national, and international responses are also vitally important, including victim advocacy, training for involved and affected professionals, public awareness and education campaigns, and what Miller states as justice, "true justice may be a prerequisite for true healing" (p. 294).

Torture, State Terror, and Violent Political Repression

In 1948, the United Nations developed and adopted the Universal Declaration of Human Rights as an instrument to acknowledge the rights of all human beings on the planet and to provide a set of principles to guide social and governmental conduct. It is perhaps ironic, however, that in the same century that such a declaration was developed, the degree and enormity of human suffering at the hands of other human beings was unprecedented. Certainly, the peoples of the twentieth century did not invent human-induced suffering, but the particular forms of systematic violence in the form of torture, state terror, and political repression were on a scale never seen before and hopefully will never be seen again. The premise of this section is that trauma that results from these particular forms of violence and assault is unique in numerous ways.

Torture

In 1993, the United Nations' World Conference on Human Rights in the Vienna Declaration stated:

> The World Conference on Human Rights emphasizes that one of the most atrocious violations against human dignity is the act of torture, the result of which destroys the dignity and impairs the capability of victims to continue their lives and activities. (United Nations General Assembly-Secretariat, 1993)

The mental health consequences of such "atrocious" acts of violence include a wide range of posttraumatic reactions. Peter Suedfeld (1990) defines *torture* as "the deliberate infliction of severe pain or discomfort" (p. 1). Baker (1992) estimates that somewhere between 700,000 to 4.9 million of the world's 14 million refugees have had at least one torture experience. Torture victims have higher lifetime and current PTSD rates compared to controls (Basoglu et al., 1994).

Research has shown that the perceived severity of a torture incident is more highly correlated with the development of PTSD than is the frequency of torture episodes (Basoglu & Paker, 1995). Melamed, Melamed, and Bouhoutsos (1990) identify the following conditions that lead to such distress in torture:

1. *Intensity.* The more intense it is, the worse the experience.

2. *Unpredictability.* The very point of much torture is to decrease the victim's sense of control except for doing what the perpetrator wants.

3. *Lack of control.* Learned helplessness and numbing may develop as ways to gain control, even in an illusory sense.

4. *Guilt and shame.* These conditions occur over being caught or giving in.

Melamed et al. (1990) state, "If the state becomes chronic, and if the victim believes that the cause of the event is in the nature of humanity, then the symptoms will be more pervasive and exhibited in many situations in which one's self-esteem is questioned" (p. 16).

Treatment of Torture Victims

Jaranson et al. (2001) discuss some important aspects of treatment of PTSD in torture survivors. They draw a distinction between treatment from a medical-psychological perspective and from a sociopolitical perspective. Treatment from a medical-psychological perspective should include validation, facilitation of reprocessing, and encouragement of active engagement in living. From a sociopolitical perspective, treatment should include issues of reintegration into the social and political process and documenting the facts of the torture. From a generic treatment perspective, treatment of torture survivors should always promote a sense of safety.

Varvin and Hauff (1998) discuss treatment from a psychoanalytic perspective. From this viewpoint, torture trauma is intrinsically tied to the relationship between victim and perpetrator. The victim is reduced to a state of regressed dependence. Subsequently, object relations issues are activated, such as attachment, separation, and individuation. The victim is placed in a position of extreme helplessness as if a child but is also under the protection of the perpetrator. The torturer exploits these psychodynamics.

Cognitive-behavioral therapy and its various techniques have also been used with torture survivors with some degree of success although no sound empirical studies have been done (Basoglu, 1998). Regardless of the treatment modality, however, the issue of informed consent and the voluntary nature of treatment are critical issues that constitute treatment issues in and of themselves. Standard CBT techniques have been used, including exposure and cognitive reframing. Basoglu (1998) makes the important point that specific cognitive reframes relevant to torture victims may be useful. For example, when a survivor blames him- or herself, the reframe might be, "It is the torturers who should be blamed for having committed such atrocities," or "Torture is deliberately designed to undermine one's self-respect and dignity. Therefore, blaming myself for what happened is an admission of the torturer's victory."

State Terror and Violent Political Repression

Perhaps an understanding of the concepts of *state terror* and *violent political repression* are in the eye of the beholder, but I think that in today's world, the view that human beings have the right to democratic forms of government or self-determination of government are widely, if not universally, held. However, this is not a polemic on democracy but rather a discussion of violence committed by national governments or their proxies on the people they govern when not at war with said population (Wikipedia Encyclopedia, 2005)

Ignacio Martín-Baró, Jesuit priest, psychologist, and founder of Liberation Psychology, was intimately connected to the trauma of war in El Salvador. He was murdered by a death squad in 1989. In his essay *War and Mental Health*, he reminds us that the casualties of war include civilians as well as soldiers and that the unavoidable core of war is violence. Also, civilians have to often face displacement, fleeing their homes to oftentimes live in horrible conditions.

He states, "Above all, the violence. This is the most immediate fact, the most wounding. . . " (p. 112).

From his perspective, war is about the destruction of the enemy. This focus on destruction makes war the prototypical PTSD stressor. In reference to the civil war in El Salvador, he states, "The spectacle of rapes or tortures, of assassinations or mass executions, of bombings and the leveling of entire villages is traumatizing almost by definition" (p. 117).

Martín-Baró draws our attention to the social devastation of war and its destruction of normal, healthy social ties. This, in turn, plays out in the psychological dynamics of those who suffer from PTSD as they struggle with their sense of self in relation to others, particularly if those relations produced the trauma. For Martín-Baró, the trauma of war is psychosocial and always results not only in traumatized individuals but also in traumatized systems and whole societies.

Pilar Hernández (2002) proposes a combined approach of political analysis and clinical practice as a way to understand the trauma of political repression, which is referred to as *political trauma*. Narrative psychology is cited as providing a useful contribution to this analysis. From the narrative psychology perspective, violence damages our sense of having a continuous self-image across time and space within an orderly world. This creates confusion and a sense of disintegration. We try to make sense of this violence-induced disruption by creating a narrative or story. These stories are influenced by and either facilitated or thwarted by the dominant cultural stories and are developed in a dynamic between victims and perpetrators. When perpetrator versions of the story predominate, healing is blocked, and treatment should be about giving as loud a voice to the victims as possible. Who determines what is real is crucial for the exposure of trauma and violence (Sluzki, 1993).

Martín-Baró promoted what he called "concientizacion" (Hernandez, 2002, p. 17) or a raising of consciousness as a way to treat political trauma. Healing is achieved through teaching, reflection, and action that remodels victims' lives and puts the telling of the story back into their hands (Hernández, 2002). Trauma is healed by developing new social identities and eventual social movements.

Hernández (2002) suggests, "Practitioners who work with victims of state-sponsored violence should aim to destabilize denial and official stories" (p. 18). Victims in these settings conceptualize their trauma in sociopolitical terms, sometimes seeing their wounds as necessary sacrifices and not as a disorder. In this sense, PTSD as a *DSM-IV-TR* category might not fit (Hernández, 2002). The ongoing nature of the traumatic stressors in political trauma is also problematic to some extent because, in essence, many of the victims may suffer from a chronic form of Acute Stress Disorder with comorbid PTSD for specific events. Some professionals also take issue with the concept of disorder, instead viewing victim reactions as normal and expected consequences of living in a disturbed society (Hernández, 2002).

Two powerful examples of state terror and repression come from South America. Becker and Diaz (1998) characterize the terror of Pinochet's rule in Chile as a form of state-trauma that "surpasses the capacities of psychic structure and therefore cannot be integrated" (p. 438).

Tactics of imprisonment, death, and disappearing people were common practices. Chileans lived in constant uncertainty of disappearance or death. The Argentine dictatorship between 1976 and 1983 is another good example of state terror. An estimated 30,000 people disappeared. Imprisonment, killings, torture, and the kidnapping of children and changing their identities were common practice.

Massive Trauma and Genocide

In the modern era, humanity's power to kill or injure a massive amount of people at once or over a period of time is immense. Unfortunately, this is not a theory or hypothesis; it has been proven in dozens and dozens of episodes throughout the modern era, including the nineteenth and twentieth centuries. The effects of such massive killing have led to an equally devastating form of massive trauma that not only affects the immediate victims and survivors but also their children and sometimes their children's children. In this section, we will cover some of these infamous events and eras. I would like to say that the examples discussed here are not considered worse or more worthy than ones not listed. Nor are they privileged in any way other than having more information about them available. Not listing any particular example should not be taken as a minimization of the experience of those who went through it. Sadly, an entire book could be devoted to these forms of suffering. For the sake of respect, here is a list of similar events and other massively traumatized people that are not covered here: slavery, Palestinians, Rwandans, Soviets, Sudanese, Nigerians, Ugandans, Guatemalans, Iranians, Iraqis, Bosnians, the Kurds, South Africans, Australian Aborigines, and Japanese-American interment camp survivors.

Armenia

In the early 1900s, the Turkish government killed an estimated 1.5 million Armenians. Some observers compare this event to the Jewish Holocaust in ways other than the sheer number of victims. Kupelian, Kalayjian, and Kassabian (1998) propose that Armenians, like Jews, were selected as victims simply by virtue of their birth; this event was massive, and the personal nature of the hatred was similar to the Holocaust. Survivor symptoms include anxiety, depression, compulsive associations to trauma material, guilt, nightmares, irritability, anhedonia, feelings of emptiness, and fear of loving (Boyajian & Grigorian, 1987). An added insult and complication to this horrendous event was the essential ignoring of and silence about the event by the outside world. Intergenerational effects have been seen in follow-up research and are considered related to the children's and grandchildren's "symbolic relationship to the parent's traumatic experience and/or to the impact of parents' 'pathogenic behaviors'" (Kupelian, 1998, p. 203).

Hiroshima and Nagasaki

Although we all live in the nuclear era with the possibility of world-destruction through nuclear war and nuclear war is never completely out of our consciousness, only one group of people have actually experienced a nuclear attack. The Japanese citizens of Hiroshima and Nagasaki, as well as the people in the surrounding towns and countryside, have experienced first hand the destructive power of nuclear weapons. Survivors of the atomic bombings are referred as the *Hibakusha* in Japanese. According to Mikihachiro Tatara (1998), these events were particularly powerful because they were massive, instantaneous, and affected an entire community for generations. Tatara brings up the interesting point that the traumatic effects of Hiroshima and Nagasaki are sometimes minimized because we still live in an era in which nuclear weapons are favored as a means of self-defense and that these bombings were seen as necessary to defeat the "evil" regime of Imperial Japan. The long-lasting effects of the bombings include economic and social effects in addition to psychological and physical consequences. Because of the physical disabilities that survivors have suffered with over the years, low employment rates and financial problems have been pervasive. There are also current and ongoing fears of the effects of radiation on the offspring of those who are married to a relative of a *Hibakusha*. Survivors may have ongoing traumatic reactions to the physical symptoms they have, even if these physical symptoms are unrelated to the bombing.

The Holocaust
The atrocities of the Holocaust were massive and total, with physical destruction, psychological damage, psychosocial damage, and cultural damage. Before the formal diagnosis of PTSD came along, professionals working with the survivors of the Holocaust developed the concept of *concentration camp syndrome* to capture the complexity of suffering. The symptoms of this syndrome include some PTSD symptoms but also several others, such as increased fatigability, bitterness, vertigo, vegetative lability, headaches, and feelings of insufficiency. Of concentration camp survivors, rates of PTSD measured tens of years later have found that rates are higher in those who were in an extermination camp as opposed to a work camp (Kuch & Cox, 1992). Kuch and Cox (1992) assessed PTSD in 124 survivors and found that 46.8 percent met *DSM-III* criteria for PTSD. This is a very powerful statistic when you consider that this data was collected 50 to 55 years after the traumatic event!

Cambodia
During a 4-year reign in the 1970s, the Khmer Rouge, under the leadership of Pol Pot, killed an estimated 1 to 3 million Cambodian citizens out of a total population of 7 million. Clinicians and researchers that have followed the effects of these events and have referred to the trauma of survivors as a "severe form of posttraumatic stress disorder" (Kinzie, Boehnlein, & Sack, 1998, p. 212). Because close family ties play a significant role in Cambodian society, the transmission of PTSD amongst family members was and is common. Some of the more profound effects have been poor parental care of children, particularly in refugee and immigrant populations in which high male death rates have lead to a very high percentage of single-parent homes and a diminished authority role for the surviving mother. There are often reversals of roles between immigrant parents (e.g. to the U.S.) and better-acculturated children. There are strong and intense feelings and motivations to keep the family together at all costs. Even positive

family events such as marriage may activate intense fears and memories of loss and exacerbate symptoms. In one study of Cambodian refugee high school students in the United States, 50 percent were found to meet criteria for PTSD (Kinzie et al., 1998). Other studies have shown that 10 years after leaving Cambodia in 1979, 50 percent of men, 30 percent of women, and 20 to 30 percent of adolescents met criteria for PTSD.

Native Americans

Duran, Duran, Brave Heart, and Yellow Horse-Davis (1998) discuss the concept of *soul wound* as the particular form of massive trauma manifest in the Native American or American Indian population as a consequence of colonial and European conquest and domination. The term *Native American Holocaust* is sometimes used to refer to the massive killings, forced relocations, and deliberate exposures to disease of Native American peoples. This form of trauma is sometimes referred to as *historical trauma* and is considered cumulative and intergenerational. Intergenerational effects similar to those of Holocaust victims have been found in the Lakota people, including "persecutory fantasies, and [beliefs] of the world as dangerous; the fantasy of the return of the old way of life, analogous to compensatory fantasies; apprehension, shame, withdrawal, grandiosity in daydreams, and anxiety about aggressive impulses" (Duran et al., 1998, p. 342). As with the descendents of slavery in the United States, there is also the complicating issue of Native Americans continuing to live among and with the perpetrators of their trauma, the United States Government and its people.

Summary

The potential for violence to lead to trauma and PTSD is undeniable. What is remarkable, however, is that despite the worldview shattering power of human-on-human violence, most victims do not develop PTSD. War, terrorism, torture, and political repression are virtually fixed historical themes. Unfortunately, as long as this fact remains and regardless of how few people develop PTSD in response to these events, wherever you find violence, you'll find trauma and a powerful need to address its victims and help them begin to heal.

Quick Review

- The National Vietnam Veterans Readjustment Study in 1990 found that 31 percent of vets had a lifetime prevalence of PTSD, with 15 percent of male Vietnam theater veterans meeting criteria at the current time. The Centers for Disease Control Vietnam Experience Study found 15 percent for lifetime prevalence in this population, with 2 percent prevalence for the previous month.

- In the Persian Gulf War (the first war with Iraq) estimates of 19 percent of soldiers met criteria for PTSD (Sutker et al., 1993).

- The role a soldier is serving (e.g., a peacekeeping mission) and the social and cultural milieu he or she returns to after combat are powerful factors in shaping the development and course of traumatic stress and PTSD.

- Soldiers, particularly combat veterans of Vietnam, have been less responsive to treatment than survivors of other forms of traumatic stress.

- Terrorist attacks are capable of producing high rates of PTSD in part because of their unpredictability. In essence, the very goal of terrorism is a form of mass PTSD.

- Torture has been shown to produce PTSD, with complicating factors of cultural issues and interpersonal mistrust playing a role in treatment.

- Sometimes, states and governments are perpetrators of their own form of terrorism and violent repression that have a unique impact on victims with respect to social identity and the importance of truth and recognition.

- Mass trauma that leads to PTSD has occurred throughout history in, sadly, dozens of examples, including the Holocaust, Cambodia, and Rwanda.

References

Ahern, J., Galea, S., Resnick, H., & Vlahov, D. (2004). Television images and probable Posttraumatic Stress Disorder after September 11: The role of background characteristics, event exposures, and perievent panic. *Journal of Nervous and Mental Disease, 192,* 217–226.

Baker, R. (1992). Psychosocial consequences for tortured refugees seeking asylum and refugee status in Europe. In M. Basoglu (Ed.), *Torture and its consequences: Current treatment approaches* (pp. 83–106). New York: Cambridge University Press.

Basoglu, M. (1998). Behavioral and cognitive treatment of survivors of torture. In J. M. Jaranson & M. K. Popkin (Eds.), *Caring for victims of torture* (pp. 131–148). Washington, DC: American Psychiatric Association.

Basoglu, M., & Paker, M. (1995). Severity of trauma as predictor of long-term psychological status in survivors of torture. *Journal of Anxiety Disorders, 9,* 339–353.

Basoglu, M., Paker, M., Paker, O., Özmen, E., et al. (1994). Psychological effects of torture: A comparison of tortured with nontortured political activists in Turkey. *American Journal of Psychiatry, 151,* 76–81.

Becker, D., & Diaz, M. (1998). The social process and the transgenerational transmission of trauma in Chile. In Y. Danieli (Ed.), *International handbook of multigenerational legacies of trauma* (pp. 435–445). New York: Plenum Press.

Boyajian, L., & Grigorian, H. (1987). Psychosocial sequelae of the Armenian genocide. In R. G. Hovannisian (Eds.), *The Armenian genocide in perspective* (pp. 177–185). Somerset, NJ: Transaction Books.

Breslau, N., & Davis, G. C. (1987). Posttraumatic Stress Disorder: The etiologic specificity of wartime stressors. *American Journal of Psychiatry, 144,* 578–583.

Creamer, M., & Forbes, D. (2004). Treatment of Posttraumatic Stress Disorder in military and veteran populations. *Psychotherapy: Theory, Research, Practice, Training, 41,* 388–398.

Curran, P. S., Bell, P., Murray, A., Loughrey, G., et al. (1990). Psychological consequences of the Enniskillen bombing. *British Journal of Psychiatry, 156,* 479–482.

de Girolamo, G., & McFarlane, A. C. (1996). The epidemiology of PTSD: A comprehensive review of the international literature. In A. J. Marsella, M. J. Friedman, E. T. Gerrity, & R. M. Scurfield (Eds.), *Ethnocultural aspects of Posttraumatic Stress Disorder: Issues, research, and clinical applications* (pp. 33–85). Washington, DC: American Psychological Association.

Duran, E., Duran, B., Brave-Heart, M. Y. H., & Yellow Horse-Davis, S. (1998). Healing the American Indian soul wound. In Y. Danieli (Ed.), *International handbook of multigenerational legacies of trauma* (pp. 341–354). New York: Plenum Press.

Eberly, R. E., & Engdahl, B. E. (1991). Prevalence of somatic and psychiatric disorders among former prisoners of war. *Hospital & Community Psychiatry, 42,* 807–813.

Engdahl, B., & Fairbank, J. A. (2001). Former prisoners of war: Highlights of empirical research. In E. T. Gerrity, T. M. Keane, & F. Tuma (Eds.), *The mental health consequences of torture* (pp. 133–142). Dordrecht, Netherlands: Kluwer Academic.

Fairbank, J. A., Friedman, M. J., & Southwick, S. (2001). Veterans of armed conflicts. In E. T. Gerrity, T. M. Keane, & F. Tuma (Eds.), *The mental health consequences of torture* (pp. 121–131). Dordrecht, Netherlands: Kluwer Academic.

Farber, I. E., Harlow, H. F., & West, L. J. (1957). Brainwashing, conditioning, and DDD (debility, dependency, and dread). *Sociometry, 20,* 271–285.

Flack, W. F., Jr., Litz, B. T., & Keane, T. M. (1998). Cognitive-behavioral treatment of war-zone-related Posttraumatic Stress Disorder: A flexible, hierarchical approach. In V. M. Follette, J. I. Ruzek, & F. R. Abueg (Eds.), *Cognitive-behavioral therapies for trauma* (pp. 77–99). New York: Guilford.

Foa, E. B., Riggs, D. S., Massie, E. D., & Yarczower, M. (1995). The impact of fear activation and anger on the efficacy of exposure treatment for Posttraumatic Stress Disorder. *Behavior Therapy, 26,* 487–499.

Ford, J. D. (1999). Disorders of extreme stress following war-zone military trauma: Associated features of Posttraumatic Stress Disorder or comorbid but distinct syndromes? *Journal of Consulting and Clinical Psychology, 67,* 3–12.

Ganor, B. (2004). Terrorism as a strategy of psychological warfare. *Journal of Aggression, Maltreatment & Trauma, 9,* 33–43.

Galea, S., Ahern, J., Resnick, H., Kilpatrick, D., Bucuvalas, M., Gold, J., et al. (2002). Psychological sequelae of the September 11 terrorist attacks in New York City. *New England Journal of Medicine, 346,* 982–987.

Green, B. L. (1990). Defining trauma: Terminology and generic stressor dimensions. *Journal of Applied Social Psychology, 20,* 1632–1642.

Grossman, D. (1996). *On killing: The psychological cost of learning to kill in war and society.* New York: Little, Brown and Co.

Hamber, B. (2004). Voice: "So what is it like now that your country is run by a terrorist?" *Journal of Aggression, Maltreatment & Trauma, 9,* 189–191.

Hernández, P. (2002). Trauma in war and political persecution: Expanding the concept. *American Journal of Orthopsychiatry, 72,* 16–25.

Jaranson, J. M., Kinzie, J. D., Friedman, M., Ortiz, S. D., Friedman, M. J., Southwick, S., et al. (2001). Assessment, diagnosis, and intervention. In E. T. Gerrity, T. M. Keane, & F. Tuma (Eds.), *The mental health consequences of torture* (pp. 249–275). Dordrecht, Netherlands: Kluwer Academic.

Keane, T. M. (1998). Psychological effects of military combat. In B. P. Dohrenwend, (Ed.), *Adversity, stress, and psychopathology* (pp. 52–65). New York: Oxford University Press.

Kinzie, J. D., Boehnlein, J., & Sack, W. H. (1998). The effects of massive trauma on Cambodian parents and children. In Y. Danieli (Ed.), *International handbook of multigenerational legacies of trauma* (pp. 211–221). New York: Plenum Press.

Krakow, B., Kellner, R., Pathak, D., & Lambert, L. (1995). Imagery rehearsal treatment for chronic nightmares. *Behaviour Research and Therapy, 33*, 837–843.

Kubany, E. S. (1994). A cognitive model of guilt typology in combat-related PTSD. *Journal of Traumatic Stress, 7,* 3–19.

Kubany, E. S. (1997). Application of cognitive therapy for trauma-related guilt (CT-TRG) with a Vietnam veteran troubled by multiple sources of guilt. *Cognitive and Behavioral Practice, 4,* 213–244.

Kubany, E. S., & Watson, S. B. (2003). Guilt: Elaboration of a multidimensional model. *Psychological Record, 53,* 51–90.

Kuch, K., & Cox, B. J. (1992). Symptoms of PTSD in 124 survivors of the Holocaust. *American Journal of Psychiatry, 149,* 337–340.

Kulka, R., et al. (1990). *Trauma and the Vietnam War generation: Report of findings from the National Vietnam Veterans Readjustment Study.* New York: Brunner/Mazel.

Kupelian, D., Kalayjian, A. S., & Kassabian, A. (1998). The Turkish genocide of the Armenians: Continuing effects on survivors and their families eight decades after massive trauma. In Y. Danieli (Ed.), *International handbook of multigenerational legacies of trauma* (pp. 191–210). New York: Plenum Press.

Litz, B. T., Gray, M. J., & Bolton, E. E. (2003). Posttraumatic Stress Disorder following peacekeeping operations. In T. W. Britt & A. B. Adler (Eds.), *The psychology of the peacekeeper: Lessons from the field* (pp. 243–258). Westport, CT: Praeger.

Litz, B. T., King, L. A., King, D. W., Orsillo, S. M., & Friedman, M. J. (1997a). Warriors as peacekeepers: Features of the Somalia experience and PTSD. *Journal of Consulting and Clinical Psychology, 65,* 1001–1010.

Litz, B. T., Orsillo, S. M., Friedman, M., Ehlich, P., et al (1997b). Posttraumatic stress disorder associated with peacekeeping duty in Somalia for U.S. military personnel. *American Journal of Psychiatry, 154,* 178–184.

MacNair, R. M. (2002). *Perpetration-induced traumatic stress: The psychological consequences of killing.* Westport, CT: Praeger.

MarLowe, D. H. (2001). *Psychological and psychosocial consequences of combat and deployment with special emphasis on the Gulf War.* Report prepared for the Office of the Secretary of Defense. Santa Monica, CA: National Defense Research Institute-RAND.

Martín-Baró, I., Aron, A., & Corne, S. (Eds.). (1994). *Writings for a liberation psychology.* Cambridge, MA: Harvard University Press.

McFarlane, A. C., & de Girolamo, G. (1996). The nature of traumatic stressors and the epidemiology of posttraumatic reactions. In Bessel A. van der Kolk, Alexander C. McFarlane, & Lars Weisaeth (Eds.), *Traumatic stress: The effects of overwhelming experience on mind, body, and society* (pp. 129–154). New York: Guilford.

Melamed, B. G., Melamed, J. L., & Bouhoutsos, J. C. (1990). Psychological consequences of torture: A need to formulate new strategies for research. In P. Suedfeld (Ed.), *Psychology and torture* (pp. 13–30). Washington, DC: Hemisphere.

Miller, L. (2002). Psychological interventions for terroristic trauma: Symptoms, syndromes, and treatment strategies. *Psychotherapy: Theory, Research, Practice, Training, 39,* 283–296.

Pyszczynski, T., Solomon, S., & Greenberg, J. (2003). Terror management theory: An evolutionary existential account of human behavior. In T. Pyszczynski, S. Solomon & J. Greenberg (Eds.), *In the wake of 9/11: The psychology of terror* (pp. 11–35). Washington, DC: American Psychological Association.

Sluzki, C. E. (1993). Toward a model of family and political victimization: Implications for treatment and recovery. *Psychiatry: Interpersonal and Biological Processes, 56,* 178–187.

Strayer, R., & Ellenhorn, L. (1975). Vietnam veterans: A study exploring adjustment patterns and attitudes. *Journal of Social Issues, 31,* 81–93.

Suedfeld, P. (1990). Torture: A brief overview. In P. Suedfeld (Ed.), *Psychology and Torture* (pp. 1–12). Washington, DC: Hemisphere Publishing.

Sutker, P. B., Uddo, M., Brailey, K., & Allain, A. N. (1993). War-zone trauma and stress-related symptoms in Operation Desert Shield/Storm (ODS) returnees. *Journal of Social Issues, 49,* 33–50.

Tatara, M. (1998). The second generation of Hibakusha, atomic bomb survivors: A psychologist's view. In Y. Danieli (Ed.), *International handbook of multigenerational legacies of trauma* (pp. 141–146). New York: Plenum Press.

United Nations General Assembly-Secretariat. (1993). *Vienna declaration and programme of action.* World Conference on Human Rights. Vienna, Austria: United Nations.

Varvin, S., & Hauff, E. (1998). Psychoanalytically oriented psychotherapy with torture survivors. In J. M. Jaranson & M. K. Popkin (Eds.), *Caring for victims of torture* (pp. 117–129). Washington, DC: American Psychiatric Association.

Weisæth, L. (1993). Disasters: Psychological and psychiatric aspects. In L. Goldberger & S. Breznitz (Eds.), *Handbook of stress: Theoretical and clinical aspects* (2nd ed., pp. 591–616). New York: Free Press.

Witztum, E., & Kotler, M. (2000). Historical and cultural construction of PTSD in Israel. In A. Y. Shalev, R. Yehuda, & A. C. McFarlane (Eds.), *International handbook of human response to trauma* (pp. 103–114). Dordrecht, Netherlands: Kluwer Academic.

CHAPTER 22

Resilience, Recovery, and Hope

When I was training in my graduate department's psychology clinic, a supervisor and professor of mine told me something that I wasn't sure I wanted to hear as a young upstart psychologist and therapist: "You may never know the impact you have on a client or patient." At the time, I thought I knew what those words meant, but I'm not sure I did, and I'm not so sure I even know what he really meant even today. What I think he meant was that there will be many patients that you'll seem to help but the extent to which you may not be able to truly understand. You might appear to relieve symptoms, and they glean a new spiritual sense of life, for example. There are also patients that you may seem to help, only to watch them deteriorate later. You might be thinking, "How could you not know? How could you be so off sometimes?" My answer to that question is perhaps a cop out but is, perhaps, as valid an answer as I can come up with. Human beings are complex.

Such complexity is epitomized in our reactions to almost dying or serious injury. Some of us will stand tall like the proverbial oak in the windstorm, while others might shrink from the danger and freeze from fear. Still others may manage to find a way through, somehow making it out alive, with some residual traumatic stress but no real sign of psychopathology. The pathways that lead away from trauma are as diverse as there are people on the planet. In our complexity, however, we sometimes find a sense of order from chaos, stability from instability, and hope amidst darkness. Whether trauma merely touches us or slams us face first into the reality of death, we often seem to manage, to get through, or to grow beyond it. My professor's statement bothers me less today than the day I first heard it, in part because I have known and witnessed my impact on patients, for better or for worse, and in part because I have seen the complexity of human beings give birth to hope, a sense of well-being, and even a vitality toward the future in the face of horrible trauma and suffering. I'll never forget the day I ran into a patient of mine on the street a couple of days after we had a breakthrough session in treating his PTSD. He picked me up (being much larger than I was), hugged me while holding me off the ground, and while crying said, "Thank you, Dr. Cash, thank you." To my old professor, I would say, I knew how much I helped this man, at least for that moment.

This book has been about trauma, its causes, its cures, and its complications. In many ways it has been about suffering. So I thought we could end with a vision of hope in discussing just how people get through those terrible experiences that they just can't seem to get past. This chapter is about strength, courage, and perseverance.

Positive Psychology and Human Strengths

In 2000, the flagship journal of the American Psychological Association, *American Psychologist,* introduced many psychologists for the first time to a relatively new movement in psychology, *positive psychology.* According to Martin Seligman, positive psychology focuses on (among other things of course), "human strengths that act as buffers against mental illness: courage, future-mindedness, optimism, interpersonal skill, faith, work ethic, hope, honesty, perseverance, the capacity for flow and insight. . . " (p. 7). As was already mentioned, some people go through a trauma seemingly unscathed, and still others seem somehow transformed by trauma, having gained some deep growing experience from having gone through trauma. A universal of trauma appears to be change. It could be negative change in the form of psychopathology, or it could be positive change in the form of transformation. But one thing is for sure, change happens with trauma. The study of resilience, recovery, and hope after trauma is an answer to Seligman's and Csikszentmihalyi's (2000) call for a more positive psychology, a psychology of human strengths.

When thinking about my own struggles and traumatic experiences, I think I can say without revealing too much that I have often wondered how I was going to get through something, how I was going to keep on going, and how I was going to survive. My thoughts would turn to people who seemed to represent strength, those I consider survivors. To some, the term *survivor* in a minimalist sense may simply mean someone who managed to survive without too much wear and tear and residual suffering. But from a positive psychology perspective, a survivor is someone who not only makes it but also represents an example of how to do it for other people. These are the people that people say things about like, "He's strong," or "She can get us through this." Is there a survivor personality? I don't think that research has borne this out, but research has certainly given us a list of characteristics and psychological variables that are associated with being one such person.

Before we go on, I want to make something very clear. I don't wish to paint a picture that certain people fail at trauma while others succeed. This is far too simplistic, inaccurate, and perhaps judgmental. In fact, as James Maddux (2002) states, "adaptive and maladaptive psychological phenomena differ not in kind but in degree and [that] continuity exists between normal and abnormal and between adaptive and maladaptive" (p. 19). We are all succeeding and failing all at once and at the same time, all together. It varies by perspective, and, of course, the trauma survivor's perspective is of primary importance. Now let's turn to some of those positive psychological principles.

Resilience

George Bonanno (2004) defines *resilience* "to loss and trauma" as "the ability in adults in otherwise normal circumstances who are exposed to an isolated and potentially highly disruptive event, such as the death of a close relation or a violent or life threatening situation, to maintain relatively stable, health levels of psychological and physical functioning" (p. 20). Masten and Reed (2002) define *resilience* as a "class of phenomena characterized by patterns of positive adaptation in the context of significant adversity or risk" (p. 75). Resilient individuals possess and exhibit protective factors, such as personality features or characteristic coping patterns. This is not to say that resilient individuals do not have difficulties in the face of traumatic stress, but it is typically of a shorter duration and less intense overall.

Bonanno (2004) cites multiple pathways to resilience, including hardiness, self-enhancement, repressive coping, and positive emotion and laughter. Hardiness is a personality trait with three dimensions that buffer extreme stress: commitment to finding meaning in life, a belief that one can influence one's surroundings, and the belief that one can learn and grow from both positive and negative life experiences. According to Bonanno (2004), hardy individuals appraise potentially stressful situations as less threatening, are more confident, use more adaptive coping, and use more social support. Self-enhancement involves having an overly positive and even somewhat unrealistic view of oneself in the face of trauma. This includes inflated levels of self-esteem and even narcissism. Repressive coping is a mechanism that allows us to avoid unpleasant thoughts, emotions, and memories. This coping response is more dissociative in that these individuals report being less distressed consciously but have higher levels of autonomic arousal. Finally, positive emotion and laughter can help reduce levels of negative emotion and help maintain a sense of social connectedness and support.

Masten and Reed (2002) make the important point that resilience is not a unidimensional construct that exists inside an individual only. It can be perceived as an outcome for individuals that is produced by the dynamic interaction of various environmental forces and individual characteristics. In discussing resilient children, they cite the following internal characteristics: good cognitive abilities, such as problem solving; positive self-perceptions; and a good sense of humor. Family characteristics include close relationships with care giving adults, organized home environments, and socioeconomic advantages. They cite community characteristics such as good emergency social services and good public health and health care. In keeping with the work of Judith Herman, trauma is seen within a social-ecological context, with resilience as a consequence of factors beyond any one individual and its enhancement seen within the context of group or community responsibility. As with trauma, resilience does not happen in a vacuum.

Stanton, Parsa, and Austenfeld (2002) talk about the importance of "coping with adversity through actively processing and expressing emotions" (p. 149) in which emotional expression, recognition, understanding, and communication are utilized in a focused, not ruminative, manner. Research has shown that coping through processing and expressing emotions can be very beneficial. Foa and Kozak (1986) promote the power of coping by approaching and processing emotions, which may facilitate habituation to a stressor and its associated emotions.

Optimism is a personality trait that involves a tendency to see positive outcomes as more likely as opposed to negative outcomes. Carver and Scheier (2002) state, "optimists experience less distress than pessimists when dealing with difficulties in their lives" (p. 235). Positive expectations of the future can result in continued effort and forward movement, even in the face of adversity. Optimists utilize a number of adaptive psychological skills, including problem-centered coping, emotion-focused coping, acceptance of reality, having a plan, and trying to learn from bad situations. These are, however, some warnings when it comes to optimism. Too much or overreliance on it may result in failing to prepare for future threat and an overestimate of one's ability to cope, leading to inaction, for example (Schwarzer, 1994; Tennen & Affleck, 1987).

Snyder, Rand, and Sigmon (2002) talk about the power of hope theory in successful coping. Hope theory holds that thinking and believing in a manner such as "I can find my way to my goals and be motivated to use those pathways" is a powerful tool for coping. Individuals who are high in such a characteristic "produce more strategies for dealing with stressors and express a greater likelihood of using those strategies" (p. 265). They are also less likely to use avoidance as a coping mechanism and are more likely to find benefits in stressors, also a useful coping mechanism in and of itself.

Some professionals propose that both cognitive complexity and self-complexity are protective factors. People who are high in these traits or characteristics are able to generate and pursue alternatives and "flexible means to achieve them" (Tennen & Affleck, 1998, p. 71). *Self-complexity* is defined as having a greater number of discrete roles or identities used to organize self-schemas. This is seen as a buffer because there are less global effects on how we mentally represent ourselves. It is important to be able to view yourself from many different perspectives, particularly if one of those views has been damaged or disrupted by the traumatic event.

Positive coping can also occur through artistic expression. I would argue that some literature that deals with ghosts and hauntings, for example, are creative attempts at resolving trauma. Creativity can lead to adaptive solutions. In fact, *creativity* has been defined as the ability to produce creative products that are original and adaptive (Simonton, 2002). Adaptation to trauma might just be a creative act in and of itself.

Biological Issues in Resilience and Recovery from Positive Psychology

Dienstbier and Zillig (2002) discuss the importance of a psychobiological concept called *toughness*. The basic idea of toughness is that repeated episodes of challenge or threat followed by periods of recovery lead to physiological changes in neurochemical and physiological processes that lead to improved adaptability in response to future challenges. The authors refer to these processes as part of a *neuroendocrine training process* in which changes in the central nervous system "enhance the capacity for various tissues in the CNS to generate monoamines, especially noradrenaline and serotonin, and enhance the capacity of the body to generate noradrenaline and adrenaline" (p. 517). These increased capacities lead to resistance to depletion during subsequent stress and under the strain of longer periods of stress. These changes lead to a "syndrome of positive changes in personality and performance" (p. 518) such as a greater capacity for arousal and energy when required, optimistic appraisals, providence of resources for focused action, and lower baseline levels of arousal.

Recovery

How does someone begin to heal from PTSD? How do we get from the shattering of our assumptions of a safe world we can effectively manage and cope with to the state Wilson, Friedman, and Lindy (2001) identify as a:

> restoration of a meaningful sense of self-sameness and self-continuity. . . which encompasses their view of themselves as persons having worth, dignity, wholeness, purpose, and an essential feeling of vitality (p. 12)

and as

> the extraordinary changes that occur when those afflicted by trauma emerge with a human radiance, energy, and dignity that is the total antithesis of illness, despair, suffering, and fragmentation of personality. Healthy and resilient survivors of trauma are persons who have found pathways to reverse or attenuate the destructiveness of psychic burdens which affect their health. They have freedom of consciousness to create active minds and bodies. They are also potential guides, healers, and teachers. (p. 13)

As was discussed by Bonanno (2004), *resilience* and *recovery* are two different processes. Some may even define *recovery* as simply returning to the baseline level of functioning prior to a trauma. However, in the context of this chapter, recovery takes on a wider meaning to encompass the phenomenon sometimes referred to as *posttraumatic growth* (Tedeschi & Calhoun, 1995). People are in fact able to grow psychologically, interpersonally, and even spiritually in response to trauma. Let's now turn to a discussion of this transformative process.

Calhoun and Tedeschi (2001) state, "the struggle with major losses in life can be a source of enhanced meaning in life and the impetus for positive change" (p. 157). They define *posttraumatic growth* as "positive change that the individual experiences as a result of the struggle" (p. 158). This is not just a wishful-thinking philosophy; it has been empirically observed and recorded (Silver, Boon, & Stones, 1983; Calhoun & Tedeschi, 1989–1990). Growth is characterized by changes in three critical areas, changes in the sense of self, changes in relationships, and changes in one's philosophy of life.

Changes in one's sense of self are characterized as paradoxical because the sense of increased vulnerability coexists alongside a sense of increased strength and capability. This sense of confidence might develop as we are essentially forced to deal with situations of struggle. After all, when trauma hits, it is not as if we have a choice. Also, simply because we go on and keep living, we might see ourselves as stronger.

Our relationships might benefit from increased connectedness, deeper empathy, and the ability to connect emotionally. With posttraumatic growth there is an increased ability to express emotions and engage in self-disclosure, increasing the potential for intimacy, something Tedeschi (1999) calls *empathy training*.

Finally, changes in our philosophy of life can result from the process of working through the shattered assumptions. We engage in this process as a way to make sense of what happened to us. Deeper meanings of a spiritual and metaphysical nature are explored.

What are some of the factors that can lead to posttraumatic growth (PTG)? PTG is more likely to occur if a trauma is very disruptive and of a major scale. Small-scale traumas are not likely to bring about such life transforming change. Some personality traits and psychological factors are associated with the likelihood of PTG, such as extraversion, openness to one's own subjective experiences, complex belief systems, and a higher sense of personal control. The process of PTG involves constructive cognitive processing to find meaning and the noticing of changes in oneself, including recognizing the blocking of goals and alterations in the meaning of the world and of life. Calhoun and Tedeschi (2001) state, "For posttraumatic growth to occur, something has to replace the goals and beliefs from which a survivor of trauma and loss has necessarily disengaged" (p. 165). Something lost has to be regained. Deliberate processing, instead of out of control rumination, ultimately results in a "revised life narrative that divides things into the 'old me' and the 'new me' or 'my life before' and 'my life since'" (p. 165). The trauma itself spurs the growth of a new identity, simultaneously breaking you apart, but allowing for renewal after the trauma. This position has been classically represented in literature time and time again and perhaps most famously in the legend or myth of the Phoenix.

Updegraff and Taylor (2000) discuss the potential positive effects of a traumatic or extremely stressful life experience. They cite that as many as half of all people who experience a trauma report some sort of positive outcome. Taylor (1983) developed the cognitive adaptation theory to account for this process in which he posits that victims and survivors actively work to restore their psychological equilibrium. Trauma's challenge leads to motivated action to enhance self-esteem, meaning, and mastery by thinking in self-enhancing ways. Positive reinterpretation and reflective focus are mental tools that help restore one's view of him- or herself in the world.

Donald Meichenbaum developed stress inoculation training (for more on stress inoculation training, see Chapter 12) to help us be prepared for future stress. The stress inoculation training theory is a model to help account for posttraumatic growth. In essence, the model states that prior experience with moderate-level stressors may inoculate us against the damaging effects of more intense subsequent events. This is kind of like a "What doesn't kill us only makes us stronger" model. Although this may sound cliché, there is research support for Meichenbaum's model.

Recovery from trauma is characterized in many different ways, as relearning (Attig, 2001), as narrative reconstruction (Sewell & Williams, 2001) and, of course, as growth (Tedeschi & Calhoun, 1995), and as positive change. In addition to the models of Taylor and Meichenbaum, there are several other models of positive change after trauma.

Nerken's model (1993) focuses on a concept called the *reflective self,* which pertains to meaning making and appraisals of performance, particularly in reference to our attachments and relationships. With loss, the reflective self is damaged, and growth occurs with the enhancement of the reflective self's change in the possibility of prospects. That is, change is the consequence of hoping for new versions or forms of the reflective self, with new attachments and new relationships.

Mahoney and Patterson (1992) propose that change begins with disequilibrium, resulting in either a return to the pretrauma status quo or a total restructuring. This restructuring leads to a new psychological and behavioral system that integrates change with forward movement. Trauma is framed as change with the potential for moving us forward. Change is inevitable with trauma, and, with this reframe of change as something positive, it is as if we have no choice but to just move on, if you will.

Schaefer and Moos (1992) developed the life-crises and personal growth model, which integrates both individual factors with contextual or environmental factors for growth. Growth is not just an individual process; it occurs within a context, of course. The importance of their model is this contribution of seeing both individual and environmental factors as important. Growth should not be seen as something wholly inside the individual as if we live in a vacuum as the lone wolves of trauma. There are critical components of our environment and ecological contexts, and how we interact with these is critical. Schaefer and Moos identify three of these components or factors: (1) features of the event, (2) features of the environment, and (3) features of the community.

Features of the event can play a specific role in growth. For example, growth after trauma from physical illness is more likely if there is a very severe threat initially with very successful initial treatment. In disasters, there is more immediate distress, but if there is a good initial mobilizing of resources, there are better long-term outcomes. Hurricane Katrina in 2005 is a good example of when poor initial mobilization of resources can lead to increased levels of distress. Conversely, when an entire community is affected, there can be a diffusion of responsibility effect of sorts, with less help being offered by individuals and to individuals because bystanders assume someone is taking care of things.

Environmental factors that are critical to growth include the availability of social support, a positive family environment, and other social resources. Research has found that the worse an event, the more support is available. The larger the social group one belongs to, the more support one will receive. Other environmental factors include stable and cohesive family structures, high levels of marital intimacy, low levels of social conflict, and an optimistic family outlook. For divorced families, important and helpful factors include a quality parent-child relationship, stability across families, stability in each home, mutual affection, support in both homes, firm limits, and clear boundaries between generations Finally, community factors include the existence of social services, emergency services, self-help groups, and mutual aid organizations.

Sandra Bloom (1998) discusses the concept of the "social transformation of trauma" (p. 179). She states, "the natural human response to danger is to gather together, to seek out the safety of human companionship" (p. 179).

Collective trauma can generate group cohesion and identity, for example. Sociologists have even argued that this is a primary function of conflict, war, and battle between groups, to facilitate group identity formation and cohesiveness. After all, who else would you fight alongside other than your brother or sister? Bloom (1998) outlines seven categories by which trauma is transformed socially:

1. *Transformation through education and prevention.* This involves such groups as Mothers against Drunk Driving (MADD), Doctors without Borders, and the Green Cross.

2. *Transformation through mutual self-help.* This includes community groups and social groups such as Alcoholics Anonymous.

3. *Transformation through rescuing.* Rescuing people from trauma can have a powerful effect on one's sense of control and commitment to positive action.

4. *Transformation through witnessing and seeking justice.* This process is reflected in such events as the formation of the Nuremberg Trials, the Geneva Conventions, and the Truth and Reconciliation Commission of South Africa.

5. *Transformation through political action.* This involves attempts at reform, progressive political change, and the struggle for political change that ultimately will serve to prevent the formation of government institutions that produced trauma and atrocity in the first place.

6. *Transformation through humor.* Laughter and comedic expression can be a powerful healing force.

7. *Transformation through artistic expression.* Artists have long engaged in the expression of trauma and atrocity in cathartic, informative, and challenging ways.

Miller and C'de Baca (1994) introduced quantum change theory to account for therapeutic change in general, but it is applicable to posttraumatic recovery. To these authors, the important factors for change are a desire to be helped, motivation to change, personal distress, and the establishing of personal goals. Quantum change is sudden and unexpected and can be spurred by small perturbations in our psychological systems. There are four mechanisms that may lead to such quantum change, according to Miller and C'de Baca: self-regulation involving conscious and effortful behavioral control, a perceptual shift yielding a new worldview, value conflict and eventual changes in values, and transcendence that sometimes involves reorienting oneself to a greater or higher force or power—something external.

Finally, Tedeschi and Calhoun (1995) provide us with a very comprehensive model of positive change and growth. They propose a task-oriented model in which an individual progresses and grows by achieving specific tasks along the way, building in succession. They group all the various tasks into three general categories: tasks of manageability, tasks of comprehensibility, and tasks of meaningfulness. Survivors strive to make their experience manageable, comprehensible, and meaningful.

They may engage in ruminative thought, sometimes positively referred to as *working through* in which there is an alternating process of going from denial and avoidance of traumatic material to acknowledging it. (For more on working through, see the section about Mardi Horowitz in Chapter 13.) Rumination is seen as inevitable but something to overcome. It is reduced when "the person comes to terms with the trauma. . . as the person is able to manage it, understand it, and find it meaningful" (Tedeschi & Calhoun, 1995, p. 60). Rumination includes thinking about the negative implications of the event or events and a feeling that one needs to talk about it and "troubleshooting the frustration of attempts to achieve important goals" (Tedeschi & Calhoun, 1995, pp. 60–61). This process can be observed in survivors' pressing to talk about what happened to them. Unfortunately, it can linger almost indefinitely and never lead to posttraumatic growth for some individuals.

To make the crisis manageable, the survivor utilizes a number of tactics. There are attempts to reverse the crisis, to undo it. There are attempts to improve upon initial crises and disruptions, attempts at control through appraisal, and engaging in self-blame for a sense of control. After these attempts and tactics have been attempted, the survivor arrives at a state of adjustment in which he or she can realistically appraise what can be changed and what cannot be changed as a consequence of the trauma.

Finally, to make the crisis comprehensible, life is seen as something that does have ultimate meaning; views of self, the world, and others undergo schematic transformation, and there may even be a new existential or metaphysical sensibility emerging.

Tedeschi and Calhoun (1995) also introduce us to seven principles of growth after a trauma:

1. *"Growth occurs when schemas are changed by traumatic events"* (p. 78). Trauma interrupts the process of constructing schemas that explain and predict events. New schemas develop in response to this new information, such as "I almost died!" One's beliefs in his or her invulnerability are challenged, "Why did this happen to me?"

2. *"Certain assumptions are more resistant to disconfirmation by any events and therefore reduce possibilities for schema change and growth"* (p. 81). These beliefs serve to buffer us against initial emotional distress but do not contribute to growth because they don't allow for schema change.

3. *"The reconstrual after trauma must include some positive evaluation for growth to occur"* (p. 82). Growth must include positive evaluations of oneself, even if those evaluations involve taking pride in knowing that one cannot change, alter, or effectively cope with everything. Changes in the way the self and world are viewed can involve negative self-negative world ("The world is bad and I'm a victim."), negative self-positive world ("I just can't seem to take advantage of what is offered me."), or positive self-negative world ("I'm a survivor in a dangerous world!")

4. *"Different types of events are likely to produce different types of growth"* (p. 83). If an event is seen as due to the actions of oneself, growth can occur when changes in self-schemas occur and so on for attributions to the external environment and others as well.

5. *"Personality characteristics are related to possibility for growth"* (p. 84). One's ability to see the growth in oneself is connected to certain personality characteristics such as optimism, self-efficacy, internal locus of control, and hardiness.

6. *"Growth occurs when the trauma assumes a central place in the life story"* (p. 85). The trauma serves as a turning point or reference point in which people refer to events prior to or after the event. Positive change from the trauma is framed as only possible because of the trauma itself.

7. *"Wisdom is a product of growth"* (p. 86). There is an appreciation of paradox, increased tolerance, acceptance, and knowledge of what is changeable and what is not.

Ultimately, growth after trauma comes from the process of knowing that one is changed as a consequence of a traumatic event. This change is viewed, not in a passive light, but as something one has control of, and that direction is found within. Ironically, growth from trauma seems to avoid avoidance and forgetting. Instead, growth engenders the necessity of acceptance and embraces the reality of mortality.

Hope

Sometimes it seems that the everyday and mundane complexity of our lives is enough to cope with. Then tragedy strikes! As if life wasn't difficult enough, we can easily find ourselves faced with the ultimate issues of death and survival. In the oft-comfortable surroundings of modern life, we can take the struggle for life and death for granted through our illusions of security, predictability, and order. But in an instant, these can all be shattered. We find ourselves gripped by fear, tormented by the pain of loss or its potential, grappling for understanding, and searching for a foothold on an earth that is spinning wildly out of control. It doesn't make sense, probably because death doesn't. We've spent generations trying to figure death out, confronting it, dancing around it, and even romanticizing it.

The hope that comes from the threat of death is an affirmation of life. Life can make a lot of sense in the face of death. Our postmodern, postindustrial, and techno-fabulous lives so often seem empty and void of meaning. The ironic rescuer of death and trauma need not be invited or provoked in order for us to overcome our contemporary ailments of the soul. Trauma and its reminder of our mortality are constants, inevitable happenings that strangely organize the complexity of our lives. But before this turns into an advertisement for the worship of pain and death, let me be clear that it is not death that we should seek, for it seeks us regardless. It is hope. Just as PTSD and trauma are forms of relentlessly permanent memories, hope cannot be about purging ourselves of reminders. For regardless of how hard we try, trauma is inscribed in our bodies, minds, relationships, and cultures in ways that defy forgetting. Hope is not about forgetting. It is the literal light at the end of the tunnel. It is a ship on the horizon. It is landfall from the crow's nest. It is a radio message from mission control in Houston to Apollo 13. It is your newborn son opening his eyes after being unconscious for 5 days. It is that sense of coherence, of clarity, and of reassurance on a grand scale that *everything will be alright!* This sense of reassurance is and will always be a hypothesis begging for disconfirmation, but it nonetheless allows for our temporary triumph of life over death.

Summary

Resilience in the aftermath of trauma is facilitated by personal characteristics and environmental factors alike. Recovery is different from resilience and represents a situation in which one can return to baseline levels of functioning or transform and grow. Ultimately, the reality of trauma can leave us feeling as if we stand at the precipice or on a horizon. Whether an individual is looking toward a horizon of dawn or of dusk depends upon myriad factors. Ultimately, one message is clear; hope is optional, but change is mandatory.

Quick Review

- Positive psychology's emphasis on human strength and health without a focus on pathology provides a framework for understanding positive response to trauma.

- Bonanno (2004) defines *resilience* as "the ability in adults in otherwise normal circumstances who are exposed to an isolated and potentially highly disruptive event. . . to maintain relatively stable, health levels of psychological and physical functioning" (p. 20).

- Resilience is facilitated by such characteristics as hardiness, self-enhancement, repressive coping, positive emotion, optimism, self-complexity, cognitive complexity, and laughter.

- Toughness involves the process in which with repeated episodes of challenge or threat followed by periods of recovery leads, physiological changes in neurochemical and physiological processes occur that lead to improved adaptability in response to future challenges.

- Recovery from trauma is represented in more general models of change and by more specific models of change, such as Tedeschi and Calhoun's model of posttraumatic growth (PTG).

- Sandra Bloom (1998) reminds us that transformation from trauma can go well beyond our individual selves to include the power of groups and community.

References

Attig, T. (2001). Relearning the world: Making and finding meanings. In R. A. Neimeyer (Ed.), *Meaning reconstruction, and the experience of loss* (pp. 33–53). Washington, DC: American Psychological Association.

Bloom, S. L. (1998). By the crowd they have been broken, by the crowd they shall be healed: The social transformation of trauma. In R. G. Tedeschi, C. L. Park, & L. G. Calhoun (Eds.), *Posttraumatic growth: Positive changes in the aftermath of crisis* (pp. 179–213). Mahwah, NJ: Erlbaum.

Bonanno, G. A. (2004). Loss, trauma, and human resilience: Have we underestimated the human capacity to thrive after extremely aversive events? *American Psychologist, 59,* 20–28.

Calhoun, L. G., & Tedeschi, R. G. (1998). Posttraumatic growth: Future directions. In R. Tedeschi, C. L Park, & L. Calhoun (Eds.), *Posttraumatic growth: Positive changes in the aftermath of crisis* (pp. 65–98). Mahwah, NJ: Erlbaum.

Calhoun, L. G., & Tedeschi, R. G. (2001). Posttraumatic growth: The positive lessons of loss. In Robert A. Neimeyer (Ed.), *Meaning reconstruction and the experience of loss* (pp. 157–172). Washington, DC: American Psychological Association.

Carver, C. S., & Scheier, M. F. (2002). Optimism. In C. R. Snyder & S. J. Lopez (Eds.), *Handbook of positive psychology* (pp. 231–243). New York: Oxford University Press.

Dienstbier, R. A., & Zillig, L. M. P. (2002). Toughness. In C. R. Snyder & S. J. Lopez (Eds.), *Handbook of positive psychology* (pp. 515–527). New York: Oxford University Press.

Foa, E. B., & Kozak, M. J. (1986). Emotional processing of fear: Exposure to corrective information. *Psychological Bulletin, 99,* 20–35.

Maddux, J. E. (2002). Stopping the "Madness": Positive psychology and the deconstruction of the illness ideology and the *DSM.* In C. R. Snyder & Shane J. Lopez (Eds.), *Handbook of positive psychology* (pp. 13–25). New York: Oxford University Press.

Mahoney, M. J., & Patterson, K. M. (1992). Changing theories of change: Recent developments in counseling. In S. D. Brown & R. W. Lent (Eds.), *Handbook of counseling psychology* (2nd ed., pp. 665–689). Oxford, England: Wiley.

Masten, A. S., & Reed, M. J. (2002). Resilience in development. In C. R. Snyder & S. J. Lopez (Eds.), *Handbook of positive psychology* (pp. 74–88). New York: Oxford University Press.

Meichenbaum, D. (1977). *Cognitive-Behavioral Modification: An integrative approach.* New York: Plenum Press.

Miller, W. R., & C'de Baca, J. (1994). Quantum change: Toward a psychology of transformation. In T. F. Heatherton & J. L. Weinberger (Eds.), *Can personality change?* (pp. 253–280). Washington, DC: American Psychological Association.

Nerken, I. R. (1993). Grief and the reflective self: Toward a clearer model of loss resolution and growth. *Death Studies, 17,* 1–26.

Schaefer, J. A., & Moos, R. H. (1992). Life crises and personal growth. In B. N. Carpenter (Ed.), *Personal coping: Theory, research, and application* (pp. 149–170). Westport, CT: Praeger.

Schwarzer, R. (1994). Optimism, vulnerability, and self-beliefs as health-related cognitions: A systematic overview. *Psychology & Health, 9,* 161–180.

Seligman, M. E. P., & Csikszentmihalyi, M. (2000). Positive psychology: An introduction. *American Psychologist, 55,* 5–14.

Sewell, K. W., & Williams, A. M. (2001). Construing stress: A constructivist therapeutic approach to posttraumatic stress reactions. In R. A. Neimeyer (Ed.), *Meaning reconstruction and the experience of loss* (pp. 293–310). Washington, DC: American Psychological Association.

Silver, R. L., Boon, C., & Stones, M. H. (1983). Searching for meaning in misfortune: Making sense of incest. *Journal of Social Issues, 39,* 81–101.

Simonton, D. K. (2002). Creativity. In C. R. Snyder & Shane J. Lopez (Eds.), *Handbook of positive psychology* (pp. 189–201). New York: Oxford University Press.

Snyder, C. R., Rand, K. L., & Sigmon, D. R. (2002). Hope theory: A member of the positive psychology family. In C. R. Snyder & S. J. Lopez (Eds.), *Handbook of positive psychology* (pp. 257–276). New York: Oxford University Press.

Stanton, A. L., Parsa, A., & Austenfeld, J. L. (2002). The adaptive potential of coping through emotional approach. In C. R. Snyder & S. J. Lopez (Eds.), *Handbook of positive psychology* (pp. 148–158). New York: Oxford University Press.

Taylor, S. E. (1983). Adjustment to threatening events: A theory of cognitive adaptation. *American Psychologist, 38,* 1161–1173.

Tedeschi, R. G. (1999). Violence transformed: Posttraumatic growth in survivors and their societies. *Aggression and Violent Behavior, 4,* 319–341.

Tedeschi, R. G., & Calhoun, L. G. (1995). *Trauma and transformation: Growing in the aftermath of suffering.* Thousand Oaks, CA: Sage.

Tennen, H., & Affleck, G. (1998). Personality and transformation in the face of adversity. In R. Tedeschi, C. L Park, & L. Calhoun (Eds.), *Posttraumatic growth: Positive changes in the aftermath of crisis* (pp. 65–98). Mahwah, NJ: Erlbaum.

Updegraff, J. A., & Taylor, S. E. (2000). From vulnerability to growth: Positive and negative effects of stressful life events. In J. H. Harvey & E. D. Miller (Eds.), *Loss and trauma: General and close relationship perspectives* (pp. 3–28). New York: Brunner-Routledge.

Wilson, J. P., Friedman, M. J., & Lindy, J. D. (2001). Treatment goals for PTSD. In J. P. Wilson, M. J. Friedman, & J. D. Lindy (Eds.), *Treating psychological trauma and PTSD* (pp. 3–27). New York: Guilford.

Appendixes

Professional Resources

Professional Organizations

Academy of Traumatology
Phone: 850-656-7158
www.traumatologyacademy.org

Anxiety Disorders Association of America
Phone: 240-485-1001
www.adaa.org

The International Society for Traumatic Stress Studies
Phone: 847-480-9028
www.istss.org

National Center for PTSD
Phone: 802-296-6300
www.ncptsd.va.gov

The Sidran Institute
Phone: 410-337-0747
www.sidran.org

Web Sites

Academy of Cognitive Therapy
www.academyofct.org

The American Academy of Experts in Traumatic Stress
www.aaets.org

American Foundation for Suicide Prevention
www.afsp.org

American Medical Association
www.ama-assn.org

American Psychiatric Association
www.psych.org

American Psychological Association
www.apa.org

Association for the Advancement of Behavior Therapy
www.aabt.org

Association of Behavioral Sciences and Medical Education
www.absame.org

Association of Family Practice Physician Assistants
www.afppa.org

European Society for Traumatic Stress Studies
www.estss.org

The Gift from Within
www.giftfromwithin.org

International Trauma Studies Program
www.itspnyc.org

Mental Health InfoSource
www.mhsource.com

Mood and Anxiety Disorders Program at NIMH
  (National Institutes of Mental Health)

http://intramural.nimh.nih.gov/

National Council for Community Behavioral Health Care

www.nccbh.org

National Council on Patient Information and Education

www.talkaboutrx.org

National Mental Health Association

www.nmha.org

National Mental Health Information Center

www.mentalhealth.org

National Women's Health Resource Center

www.healthywomen.org

Partnership for Prescription Assistance

www.pparx.org

PTSD Alliance

www.ptsdalliance.org

Treatment Guidelines

American Academy of Child and Adolescent Psychiatry–Treatment
  Guidelines for PTSD

www.aacp.org

American Psychiatric Association

www.psych.org

Behavenet.com

www.behavenet.com

The VA/DoD (Veteran's Administration/Department of Defense)
  PTSD Practice Guidelines

www.oqp.med.va.gov/cpg/PTSD/PTSD_Base.htm

Patient Resources

Professional Organizations

Academy of Traumatology
Phone: 850-656-7158
www.traumatologyacademy.org

Anxiety Disorders Association of America
Phone: 240-485-1001
www.adaa.org

The International Society for Traumatic Stress Studies
Phone: 847-480-9028
www.istss.org

National Center for PTSD
Phone: 802-296-6300
www.ncptsd.va.gov

The Sidran Institute
Phone: 410-337-0747
www.sidran.org

Self-Help Resources

The Gift from Within
Phone: 207-236-2818
www.giftfromwithin.org

The National Alliance for the Mentally Ill (NAMI)
Phone: 703-524-7600
www.nami.org

Other Web Sites

American Medical Association
www.ama-assn.org

American Psychiatric Association
www.psych.org

American Psychological Association
www.apa.org

Center for Anxiety and Stress Treatment
www.stressrelease.com

Find the Light Support Group
www.findthelight.org

Green Cross Foundation
www.greencross.org

International Victimology Web Site
http://www.victimology.nl/

Mental Health InfoSource
www.mhsource.com

National Mental Health Association
www.nmha.org

National Women's Health Resource Center
www.healthywomen.org

Psychological Self-Help
www.mentalhelp.net

PTSD Alliance
www.ptsdalliance.org

PTSD Support Services
www.ptsdsupport.net

VetFriends.com
www.vetfriends.com

Worrywisekids.org
www.worrywisekids.org

Books

Achilles in Vietnam: Combat Trauma and the Undoing of Character, by Jonathan Shay (1994)

Coping with Trauma: A Guide to Self-Understanding, by Jon G. Allen (1995)

I Can't Get Over It: A Handbook for Trauma Survivors, by Aphrodite Matsakis (1992)

Recovering from the War: A Women's Guide to Helping Your Vietnam Vet, Your Family, and Yourself, by Patience Mason (1990)

Soul Murder: The Effects of Childhood Abuse and Deprivation, by Leonard Shengold (1989)

Trauma and Recovery, by Judith Herman (1992)

Trauma and the Vietnam War Generation, by Richard Kulka et al. (1990)

Movies

All Quiet on the Western Front (1930)
Casualties of War (1989)

Death and the Maiden (1999)

The Deer Hunter (1979)

Distant Thunder (1988)

Fearless (1993)

Hanoi Hilton (1987)

Jackknife (1989)

The Killing Fields (1984)

K-PAX (2001)

Missing (1983)

The Ninth Configuration (1980)

Nuts (1987)

The Pawnbroker (1964)

The Prince of Tides (1991)

Stand by Me (1986)

Sum of Existence (2004)

Sybil (1976)

The Three Faces of Eve (1957)

INDEX